Palgrave Studies in European Union Politics

Edited by: **Michelle Egan**, American University USA, **Neill Nugent**, Visiting Professor, College of Europe, Bruges and Honorary Professor, University of Salford, UK, and **William Paterson OBE**, University of Aston, UK.

Editorial Board: **Christopher Hill**, Cambridge, UK, **Simon Hix**, London School of Economics, UK, **Mark Pollack**, Temple University, USA, **Kalypso Nicolaïdis**, Oxford UK, **Morten Egeberg**, University of Oslo, Norway, **Amy Verdun**, University of Victoria, Canada, **Claudio M. Radaelli**, University of Exeter, UK, **Frank Schimmelfennig**, Swiss Federal Institute of Technology, Switzerland.

Following on the sustained success of the acclaimed *European Union Series,* which essentially publishes research-based textbooks, *Palgrave Studies in European Union Politics* publishes cutting edge research-driven monographs.

The remit of the series is broadly defined, both in terms of subject and academic discipline. All topics of significance concerning the nature and operation of the European Union potentially fall within the scope of the series. The series is multidisciplinary to reflect the growing importance of the EU as a political, economic and social phenomenon.

Titles include:

Jens Blom-Hansen
THE EU COMITOLOGY SYSTEM IN THEORY AND PRACTICE
Keeping an Eye on the Commission?

Oriol Costa and Knud Erik Jørgensen (*editors*)
THE INFLUENCE OF INTERNATIONAL INSTITUTIONS ON THE EU
When Multilateralism Hits Brussels

Falk Daviter
POLICY FRAMING IN THE EUROPEAN UNION

Renaud Dehousse (*editor*)
THE 'COMMUNITY METHOD'
Obstinate or Obsolete?

Kenneth Dyson and Angelos Sepos (*editors*)
WHICH EUROPE?
The Politics of Differentiated Integration

Michelle Egan, Neill Nugent, and William E. Paterson (*editors*)
RESEARCH AGENDAS IN EU STUDIES
Stalking the Elephant

Theofanis Exadaktylos and Claudio M. Radaelli (*editors*)
RESEARCH DESIGN IN EUROPEAN STUDIES
Establishing Causality in Europeanization

David J. Galbreath and Joanne McEvoy
THE EUROPEAN MINORITY RIGHTS REGIME
Towards a Theory of Regime Effectiveness

Jack Hayward and Rüdiger Wurzel (*editors*)
EUROPEAN DISUNION
Between Sovereignty and Solidarity

Wolfram Kaiser, Brigitte Leucht, and Michael Gehler
TRANSNATIONAL NETWORKS IN REGIONAL INTEGRATION
Governing Europe 1945–83

Robert Kissack
PURSUING EFFECTIVE MULTILATERALISM
The European Union, International Organizations and the Politics of Decision Making

Xymena Kurowska and Fabian Breuer (editors)
EXPLAINING THE EU's COMMON SECURITY AND DEFENCE POLICY
Theory in Action

Karl-Oskar Lindgren and Thomas Persson
PARTICIPATORY GOVERNANCE IN THE EU
Enhancing or Endangering Democracy and Efficiency?

Daniel Naurin and Helen Wallace (editors)
UNVEILING THE COUNCIL OF THE EUROPEAN UNION
Games Governments Play in Brussels

Dimitris Papadimitriou and Paul Copeland (editors)
THE EU's LISBON STRATEGY
Evaluating Success, Understanding Failure

Emmanuelle Schon-Quinlivan
REFORMING THE EUROPEAN COMMISSION

Roger Scully and Richard Wyn Jones (editors)
EUROPE, REGIONS AND EUROPEAN REGIONALISM

Mitchell P. Smith (editor)
EUROPE AND NATIONAL ECONOMIC TRANSFORMATION
The EU After the Lisbon Decade

Asle Toje
AFTER THE POST-COLD WAR
The European Union as a Small Power

Richard G. Whitman and Stefan Wolff (editors)
THE EUROPEAN NEIGHBOURHOOD POLICY IN PERSPECTIVE
Context, Implementation and Impact

Richard G. Whitman (editor)
NORMATIVE POWER EUROPE
Empirical and Theoretical Perspectives

Sarah Wolff
THE MEDITERRANEAN DIMENSION OF THE EUROPEAN UNION'S INTERNAL
SECURITY

Jan Wouters, Hans Bruyninckx, Sudeshna Basu and Simon Schunz (editors)
THE EUROPEAN UNION AND MULTILATERAL GOVERNANCE
Assessing EU Participation in United Nations Human Rights and
Environmental Fora

Palgrave Studies in European Union Politics
Series Standing Order ISBN 978-1-4039-9511-7 (hardback)
ISBN 978-1-4039-9512-4 (paperback)

You can receive future titles in this series as they are published by placing a standing order. Please contact your bookseller or, in case of difficulty, write to us at the address below with your name and address, the title of the series and one of the ISBNs quoted above.

Customer Services Department, Macmillan Distribution Ltd, Houndmills, Basingstoke, Hampshire RG21 6XS,UK.

European Disunion

Between Sovereignty and Solidarity

Edited by

Jack Hayward
*Research Professor of Politics, Department of Politics and
International Relations, University of Hull, UK*

and

Rüdiger Wurzel
*Reader and Jean Monnet Chair in European Union Studies,
Department of Politics and International Relations,
University of Hull, UK*

First published 2012 by
PALGRAVE MACMILLAN

Palgrave Macmillan in the UK is an imprint of Macmillan Publishers Limited, registered in England, company number 785998, of Houndmills, Basingstoke, Hampshire RG21 6XS.

Palgrave Macmillan in the US is a division of St Martin's Press LLC, 175 Fifth Avenue, New York, NY 10010.

Palgrave Macmillan is the global academic imprint of the above companies and has companies and representatives throughout the world.

Palgrave® and Macmillan® are registered trademarks in the United States, the United Kingdom, Europe and other countries

ISBN: 978–0–230–36773–9

This book is printed on paper suitable for recycling and made from fully managed and sustained forest sources. Logging, pulping and manufacturing processes are expected to conform to the environmental regulations of the country of origin.

A catalogue record for this book is available from the British Library.

A catalog record for this book is available from the Library of Congress.

10 9 8 7 6 5 4 3 2 1
21 20 19 18 17 16 15 14 13 12

Printed and bound in Great Britain by
CPI Antony Rowe, Chippenham and Eastbourne

Contents

List of Tables and Figures   viii

Notes on Contributors   ix

List of Abbreviations   xii

Introduction   1
Jack Hayward and Rüdiger K.W. Wurzel

1. Union without Consensus   5
   Jack Hayward

Part I   Enfeebled Democratic Legitimacy

2. The Difficult Emergence of a European People   17
   Michael Bruter

3. A Nascent Transnational Civil Society   32
   Elizabeth Monaghan

4. An Obdurately National Party Politics   48
   Robert Ladrech

Part II   Institutional Deadlock: A Surfeit of Would-be Leaders

5. National Governments, the European Council and
   Councils of Ministers: A Plurality of Sovereignties. Member
   State Sovereigns without an EU Sovereign   65
   Jack Hayward

6. The European Commission Bureaucracy: Handling
   Sovereignty through the Back and Front Doors   82
   Edward C. Page

7. The Empowerment of Parliaments in EU Integration:
   Victims or Victors?   99
   Maja Kluger Rasmussen

8. National Courts and European Union Courts   115
    Patrick Birkinshaw

9. Defending the Euro: Unity and Disunity among
    Europe's Central Bankers   131
    David Howarth

10. Territorial Flexibility   146
    Michael Keating

Part III   Policy Divergences and Convergences

11. Foreign and Defence Policy: The Sovereignty
    Obsession and The Quest for Elusive Solidarity   165
    Anand Menon

12. Economic and Monetary Disunion?   181
    Kenneth Dyson

13. Social and Labour Market Policy: The (Re-)Emergence of
    Competitive Tension   200
    Nick Parsons

14. From Environmental Disunion towards
    Environmental Union?   215
    Rüdiger K.W. Wurzel

Part IV   Adjusting to the Receding Sovereignty
of Member States

15. A Contested Franco-German Duumvirate   235
    William Paterson

16. Opt-Out: Britain's Unsplendid Isolation   252
    Philip Norton

17. The Nordic Countries: The Causes and Consequences
    of Variable Geometry   267
    Nick Sitter

18. Southern Europe and the 'Trade Off': Architects
    of European Disunion?   283
    Martin J. Bull

19. The Central and East European Countries:
    From Weak Latecomers to Good Citizens of the Union   298
    Vesselin Dimitrov

Conclusion: European Disunion: Between Solidarity
and Sovereignty   314
Rüdiger K.W. Wurzel and Jack Hayward

Index   329

Tables and Figures

Tables

2.1   Comparative trust in the European Commission and
      national governments   25
2.2   Comparative trust in the European Parliament and
      national parliaments   26
17.1 Major decisions on European integration: yes/no
      ratio in referendums   269
17.2 Nordic parliamentary (and some ex-parliamentary)
      parties   271
17.3 European integration   277

Figure

17.1 Pro-EU opinion 1993–2011: share of Danish, Swedish
      and Finnish voters who regard EU membership a
      'good thing', and Norwegian voters who favour
      EU membership   270

Contributors

Patrick Birkinshaw is Professor of Public Law and Director of the Institute of European Public Law at Hull University. His many publications include *European Public Law* (2003) and *Freedom of Information; the Law, the Practice and the Ideal* (2010, 4th ed.). He has been editor since 1995 of the journal *European Public Law*.

Michael Bruter is Reader in Political Science at the London School of Economics and currently directs a large-scale European project in electoral psychology. His books include *Mapping Extreme Right Ideology* (2011) and *The Future of Our Democracies* (2009) both with Sarah Harrison, as well as *Citizens of Europe* (2005).

Martin Bull is Professor of Politics at the University of Salford and Academic Director of the European Consortium of Political Research. His publications include *Forty Years of European Political Science* (special issue of *European Political Science,* Supplement 2010, edited with J. Briggs, L. de Sousa and J. Moses), *Italy – A Contested Polity* (2009, edited with M. Rhodes), and *Italian Politics: Adjustment under Duress* (2005, with J. Newell).

Vesselin Dimitrov is Reader in the Department of Government, at the London School of Economics and Political Science. His publications include *Governing after Communism: Institutions and Policymaking* (2006, with K. H. Goetz and H. Wollmann), 'EMU and Fiscal Policy' in K. Dyson (ed.) *Enlarging the Euro Area: External Empowerment and Domestic Transformation in East Central Europe* (2006), and *The National Coordination of EU Policy in the New Member States* (Special Issue of *Public Administration,* forthcoming, edited with H. Kassim).

Kenneth Dyson is a Fellow of the British Academy, a Fellow of the Learned Society of Wales, and Research Professor in European Political Studies at Cardiff University. His most recent books are the two-volume *European Economic Governance and Policies* (2010, with Lucia Quaglia) and the edited volumes *Euro at 10* (2008), *Central Banks in the Age of the Euro* (2009, with Martin Marcussen) and *Which Europe? The Politics of Differentiated Integration* (2010, with Angelos Sepos).

Jack Hayward is Fellow of the British Academy, Emeritus Professor of Politics, Oxford University and Research Professor of Politics, Hull University. His other edited publications include *Elitism, Populism and European Politics* (1996) and *Leaderless Europe* (2008).

David Howarth is Senior Lecturer and Jean Monnet Chair in European Political Economy at the University of Edinburgh. He is the author or co-author of three books and several journal articles on economic and monetary union. He has recently co-edited *The Political Economy of Europe's Incomplete Single Market* (2011) and *Market-Based Banking and the Financial Crisis* (forthcoming).

Michael Keating is Professor of Politics at the University of Aberdeen. His recent books include *The Independence of Scotland* (2009) and *Political Autonomy and Divided Societies* (2012, edited with Alain Gagnon).

Robert Ladrech is Professor of European Politics, Keele University. His most recent book is *Europeanization and National Politics* (2010). His has published articles in journals such as *West European Politics, European Journal of Political Research* and *Party Politics*. His most recent research is focused on the party politics of climate change.

Philip Norton (Lord Norton of Louth) is Professor of Government, and Director of the Centre for Legislative Studies, at the University of Hull. He is the author or editor of 29 books. His recent publications include *A Century of Constitutional Reform* (2011, editor), *Politics UK* (2010, 7th ed., co-author), and *The British Polity* (2010, 5th ed.).

Anand Menon is Professor of West European Politics at the University of Birmingham. His recent works include *The Oxford Handbook of the European Union* (forthcoming, co-edited with E. Jones and S. Weatherill) and *Europe: The State of the Union* (2008).

Elizabeth Monaghan is Lecturer in Politics in the Department of Politics and International Studies at the University of Hull. She works on issues of democracy and legitimacy in the European Union and is the author of 'Public Debate in the European Union' (with L. Hoffmann), *Politics*, 31 (3) (2011), and various chapters on civil society in Europe.

Edward C. Page is Sidney and Beatrice Webb Professor of Public Policy at the London School of Economics and Political Science. His recent books include *Policy Bureaucracy* (2005) and *Governing by Numbers* (2001). He is currently completing a comparative study of bureaucracies titled 'Policies without Politicians'.

Nick Parsons is Reader in French in the School of European Studies, Cardiff University. He has written extensively on French and European employment relations and social policy, including *French Industrial Relations in the New World Economy* (2005) and *Economic Globalisation and Employment Policy* (2004, edited with Yuan Zhigan).

Nick Sitter is Professor of Political Economy at BI Norwegian Business School and Professor of Public Policy at Central European University. His books include *Europe's Nascent State: Public Policy in the European Union* (2006, co-edited with Johan From) and *Understanding Public Management* (2008, co-authored with Kjell A. Eliassen).

William Paterson is Honorary Professor for German and European Politics at the Aston Centre for Europe at Aston University. He retired as Director of the Institute for German Studies at the University of Birmingham in 2008. His many publications centre on European and German politics. He has received lifetime achievement awards from the International Association for the Study of German Politics (2004), the University Association for Contemporary European Studies (2007) and the Political Studies Association (2011).

Maja Kluger Rasmussen is a doctoral candidate in the Department of Government at the London School of Economics and Political Science, and is conducting research on lobbying in the European Parliament.

Rüdiger K.W. Wurzel is Reader and Jean Monnet Chair in European Union Studies at the University of Hull where he is Director of the Centre for European Union Studies (CEUS). His books include *The European Union as a Leader in International Environmental Politics* (2011, edited with J. Connelly) and *Environmental Policy-making in Britain, Germany and the European Union* (2002).

Abbreviations

ALDE	European Alliance of Liberals and Radicals
BRICS	Brazil, Russia, India, China and South Africa
BVerfG	German Constitutional Court (Bundesverfassungsgericht)
CAP	Common Agricultural Policy
CATNIP	cheapest available technology not involving prosecution
CC	Conseil Constitutionnel (French Constitutional Court)
C d'E	Conseil d'Etat
CFI	Court of First Instance
CFR	Charter of Fundamental Rights
CFSP	Common Foreign and Security Policy
CHR	Court of Human Rights
CJEU	Court of Justice of the European Union
CoR	Committee of Regions
COREPER	Comité des Représentants Permanents (Committee of Permanent Representatives)
COSAC	Conférence des organes specialisés aux affaires européenes (Conference of Community and European Affairs Committees)
CoR	Committee of the Regions
CSDP	Common Security and Defence Policy
DG	Directorate-General (for the European Commission)
EAC	European Affairs Committee (national parliaments)
EAP	Environmental Action Programme
EC	European Community
ECB	European Central Bank
ECHR	European Court of Human Rights
ECJ	European Court of Justice
Ecofin	Economic and Finance Minister Council
ECSC	European Coal and Steel Community
EDA	European Defence Agency
EEA	European Economic Area
EEC	European Economic Community
EEB	European Environmental Bureau
EEG	European Employment Guidelines
EES	European Employment Strategy
EFSF	European Financial Stability Facility

EFTA	European Free Trade Area
EIB	European Investment Bank
EMI	European Monetary Institute
EMU	Economic and Monetary Union
EP	European Parliament
EPP	European People's Party
ERDF	European Regional Development Fund
ERM	Exchange Rate Mechanism
ESC	Economic and Social Committee
ESCB	European System of Central Banks
ESDC	European Security and Defence College
ESDI	European Security and Defence Identity
ESDP	European Security and Defence Policy
ESM	European Stability Mechanism
ESRB	European System Risk Board
ETS	emissions trading scheme
ETUC	European Trade Union Confederation
EU	European Union
Euratom	European Atomic Energy Treaty
FoE	Friends of the Earth
GDP	gross domestic product
IGC	Intergovernmental Conference
JHA	Justice and Home Affairs
NATO	North Atlantic Treaty Organization
NCBs	National Central Banks
NGO	non-governmental organization
NSRF	National Strategic Reference Framework
OCE	Optimum Currency Area
OECD	Organization for Economic Cooperation and Development
OMB	Office of Management and Budget
OMC	open method of coordination
OSCE	Organization for Security and Cooperation in Europe
PES	Party of European Socialists
PSC	Political and Security Committee
QMV	qualified majority voting
RegLeg	regions with legislative power
S&D	Group of the Progressive Alliance of Socialists & Democrats in the European Parliament
SEA	Single European Act
SEM	Single European Market
SGP	Stability and Growth Pact

SIs	statutory instruments
SNE	seconded national expert
TFEU	Treaty on the Functioning of the European Union
UK	United Kingdom
UN	United Nations
UNCED	United Nations Conference on Environment and Development
UNFCCC	United Nations Framework Convention on Climate Change
WTO	World Trade Organization

Introduction

Jack Hayward and Rüdiger K.W. Wurzel

This edited volume is the third in a series from the Centre for European Union Studies (CEUS) in the Department of Politics and International Studies at the University of Hull. The first, *Leaderless Europe*, edited by Jack Hayward, appeared in 2008 before the onset of the financial crisis that further exposed the institutional weaknesses previously analysed in an historical perspective. It demonstrated their deep seated nature. The second, *The European Union as a Leader in International Climate Change Politics,* edited by Rüdiger Wurzel and James Connelly, published in 2011, presented a more dynamic and positive view of EU leadership in environmental policy. *European Disunion* returns to the EU incapacity, pinpointed particularly by the eurozone crisis, to act expeditiously and decisively. It places these failings in the broader context of a pervasive tension between the democratic demands of national sovereignty and the functional imperatives of solidarity in dealing with collective predicaments. The draft papers presented at a workshop in Hull on 30 September/1 October 2011 were revised to produce a more cohesive and updated volume in a fast evolving context.

The persisting focus of investigation is how much distrustful divergence the European Union can contain without degenerating into ineffectiveness and fragmentation. Managing receding member state autonomy without sacrificing democratic legitimacy or losing impetus necessitates overcoming mutual recrimination in the resolution of crises that threaten to surge beyond control. We identify the complex and intractable character of the difficulties that the decision makers should confront if the promised 'ever closer union' is not to become a precipitate retreat from incremental integration.

The Euro crisis catapulted the EU into its most serious political crisis since its inception, leaving it simultaneously torn between opposing demands for more sovereignty and solidarity. Both sovereignty and solidarity are contested but interacting political concepts. Sovereignty has traditionally been associated with states' legal and territorial independence. However, European integration and increased international interdependence have posed serious challenges to the monopoly of (member) states' capacity to manage spatial economies under the constraints of globalisation and a single European market that allows for the free movement of people, goods, services and capital. Although solidarity can mean different things to different actors it nevertheless constitutes an important political concept. While some of the economically more prosperous member states have insisted on greater sovereignty in order to be able to practice a higher degree of domestic solidarity, the economically weaker member states have traditionally supported a higher degree of European integration in exchange for greater solidarity from the EU, notably through structural funds.

While European political elites reluctantly recognised the failure of traditional humdrum crisis response mechanisms when confronted with a swiftly deepening economic and political crisis, the European integration project threatened to turn from European Union mode and into European disunion in the face of demands for greater sovereignty and solidarity. The permissive consensus between governing political elites and the member states' publics on European integration issues was being tested beyond breaking point by speculators in the global financial markets and anti-European populist and right-wing extremist parties which were keen to see the break-up of the Euro and the unravelling of the European integration project.

European disunion is a controversial concept which covers a wide analytical spectrum that ranges from relatively minor dissent about European integration (weak disunion) to the reversal of integration (strong disunion). In its weakest form, European disunion includes relatively minor disagreements which can be papered over with vague compromises enshrined in complex package deals. In its strongest form, European disunion implies fundamental dissent that leads to the exit of one or several of its member states or even the complete break-up of the EU. There are many different 'shades of disunion' in between its weakest and strongest forms. Differentiated integration can overcome disunion. However, differentiated integration does not necessarily bring about greater union. It may also trigger disunion. There comes a point when an overly differentiated union ceases to be a union because it either disintegrates gradually or breaks up suddenly.

Structure of the book

The chapters in this edited volume analyse the tensions between opposing demands for more sovereignty and solidarity which were greatly exacerbated by the euro crisis. Part I puts forward a critical analysis of the EU's enfeebled democratic legitimacy following upon a union without consensus (Chapter 1 by Hayward), the difficult emergence of a European people (Chapter 2 by Bruter), the nascent transnational European civil society (Chapter 3 by Monaghan) and the obdurately national party politics within European parties and party groupings (Chapter 4 by Ladrech).

Part II offers a critical assessment of the interplay between repeated deadlock and piecemeal integration which has been created by EU institutional would-be leaders. It analyses five major EU institutional actors while also paying attention to the increasing importance of regional actors and territorial politics. The chapters accordingly focus on the European Council and Councils of Ministers as well as the tensions between union and disunion that have been created by national governments within these two central EU institutions (Chapter 5 by Hayward), the EU Commission (Chapter 6 by Page), the European Parliament and national parliaments (Chapter 7 by Rasmussen), the European Court of Justice and national judiciaries (Chapter 8 by Birkinshaw) and the European Central Bank (Chapter 9 by Howarth). Part II concludes with a chapter on territorial and regional politics (Chapter 10 by Keating).

Part III shifts the analytical focus to five significant EU policy sectors which are of central importance for explaining the rising tensions between further European integration and increased European disunion. Foreign and defence policy (Chapter 11 by Menon), economic and monetary policy (Chapter 12 by Dyson), social and labour market policy (Chapter 13 by Parsons) and environmental policy (Chapter 14 by Wurzel) are all analysed in this part.

Part IV offers a critical assessment of the how particular member states or groups of member states adjust their decreased national steering capacity to receding sovereignty. Assessed are the Franco-German Duumvirate (Chapter 15 by Paterson), opt out Britain (Chapter 16 by Norton), the Nordic Countries (Chapter 17 by Sitter), the Southern European states (Chapter 18 by Bull) and the Central and Eastern European states (Chapter 19 by Dimitrov). Finally the conclusion

(Chapter 20 by Wurzel and Hayward) offers a critical summary assessment of the main empirical findings and analytical conclusion put forward in the preceding chapters.

The chapters which follow all address, from the perspective of the main actors and/or policy sectors on which they focus, the three key themes of disunion, sovereignty and solidarity.

1
Union without Consensus

Jack Hayward

It has been pertinently observed that theories of integration should comprehend the possibility of disintegration, just as a process of enlargement should also include the possibility of contraction (Schmitter 2004: 71). Yet in the case of European Union (EU) integration and enlargement, the prevailing teleological presumption of progress towards an 'ever closer union', albeit with spurts and pauses, has precluded serious consideration of either disunion or contraction. Consequently, a predominant conceptual inclination has resulted analytically in a systematic distortion of a complex process. While there have been occasional allusions in passing to the fact that confederal unions of states have historically led either to federal unity or disintegration, its implications for the EU have not been appreciated. Yet the hybrid EU has incorporated both surviving constituents of its initial federalising impetus as well as subsequent divergences of a more inter-state nature, as member governments have increasingly asserted their particular interests, according priority to what divides rather than what unites. Lacking a shared enemy or purpose, the EU's institutions have increasing difficulty in sharing authority between its member states.

In considering the tensions between the generally polarising demands of sovereign territoriality and the integrating incentives of solidaristic functionality, Schmitter warned of the danger of institutional and policy collisions resulting in improvised elite compromises, in pursuit of an unidentified political objective, lacking popular legitimacy. In a context in which 'varying and overlapping scales of territorial aggregation would interact with varying and overlapping domains of functional competence', what he called a 'condominio' might emerge from a 'scenario of divergent interests, distracted actors, improvised measures and compromised solutions...as the least threatening outcome'

(Schmitter 1996: 33, 31; cf. 29–30). While his outlandish appellation has not commended itself to other EU scholars, it does identify a particular type of hybrid entity that has defied satisfactory categorisation. The increasing variety and dispersed ways in which shared and overlapping activities are incrementally improvised is consistent with the absence of any single policy style; of any overall hegemonic member state in terms of both problem-solving capacity and resources; reliance upon multi-committee detailed compromises devised by national and EU officials that are a triumph of opacity over transparency; a discrediting 'implementation deficit' resulting from the national state delays and failures to transpose EU directives, combine to threaten 'utter incoherence' (Schmitter 1996: 35–6). That Brussels, the non-exclusive location of many of the EU's institutions and activities, is the capital of a federal state, Belgium, which is itself in the slow motion process of disintegration, is not a reassuring augury, although it may be able to stabilise as a confederation.

Rather than adopting Schmitter's neologism, it is more useful to adapt for the EU a traditional term and follow Daniel Elazar and Giandomenico Majone in what the former dubbed a 'reinvention of confederation' and the latter 'the successful prototype of post-modern confederation' (Elazar 1998: 112; Majone 2005: v, 221). Elazar argued that 'The need to establish proper relationships while at the same time preserving... national integrities makes confederal solutions not always ideal, but often the most practical. The European Union has shown the way', 'breaking new ground all the time' (Elazar 1998: 204–5, 214). Majone even more bluntly asserted that 'the federalist project was doomed from the start' because there was no European people to sustain such an ambition (Majone 2005: 219). Instead, the European Community and then European Union proceeded by special piecemeal agreements, avoiding grandiose schemes. The Constitutional Treaty rejected in 2005, which was largely rescued by the subsequent 2007 Lisbon Treaty, made the EU's confederal character formally explicit by providing for the right of a member state to secede (proposed by ex-president Giscard d'Estaing, president of the Constitutional Convention) with a procedure for 'voluntary withdrawal' by notification to the European Council (Majone 2005: 215–16; Lisbon Treaty, 13 December 2007, art. 49A, 46–7). However, Greenland, then part of Denmark, had already exited in a 1982 referendum. The eurozone has faced the problem of optimistically not providing for exit if solidarity is insufficient to sustain membership in financial crisis.

In his retrospective assessment of *The EU at Fifty*, Majone (2009) maintained that even more than its implicit operational principles of giving priority to integration over democracy and the strategy of *fait accompli* through interstate bargaining to serve national purposes, it has been the open-ended commitment to ever closer union, presupposing the 'irrelevance of ultimate ends', that has – in conjunction with 'suboptimal performance' in dealing with everyday problems – caused a groundswell of public disenchantment (Majone 2009: 2, 10; cf. 170). The expectations aroused by integration as an infinitely progressive process were dashed with the impact of financial crisis, rising unemployment, energy prices, transnational crime and immigration. The massive enlargement of the EU in 2004 furthermore posed the danger of a 'Union too heterogeneous to support a common framework in a growing number of policy areas' (Majone 2009: 212). It increased optouts, exemptions and derogations for some countries to secure compromise agreements to avoid deadlock, resulting in confusion and loss of cohesion. When in 1996 I asked the rhetorical question: 'Has European Unification by Stealth a Future?' because the EU's elites were losing touch with their peoples, the signs were already clear that EU policies were no longer so remote from public concerns that people would be willing to ignore increasing integration costs while its benefits were shrinking (Hayward 1996: 252–6). Circumventing referendums when they are avoidable is eloquent testimony to the mutual distrust of the leaders and the led.

Negotiating the EU quagmire

The ambitions and capacities of member states for coordinating the complexity of EU policies are so diverse that they compound the inherent problems posed by the continuous interaction between nation-state and EU institutions. Vincent Wright was not intimidated by the task of tracing pathways through the quagmire and he still makes a reliable guide on this hazardous venture. First, there is the structural ambivalence of EU decision-making that leads to a blurring of identities and responsibilities between political and administrative actors in the context of a confusion of powers. Second, the heterogeneity arising from enlargements, already alluded to, has a destabilising and retarding effect on EU decision-making. Third, the expansion in the scope, diversity and politically controversial nature of the EU agenda through package deals, side payments and interdependence increase complexity and uncertainty. Fourth, the interplay in fluid and overlapping bargaining of Commission, Council of Ministers and national officials in hundreds of micro-level expert committees and working groups in Brussels endeavour to prepare decisions for their administrative and political masters. Fifth, coalition building is difficult because of multiple bilateral negotiations, complicated by cross-cutting and intranational cleavages. Sixth, national official and unofficial networks often do not have EU counterparts, which weakens coordination. Seventh, the administrative EU directorate–national lead ministry mismatch hampers coordination of policy preparation and implementation, especially as the latter is the responsibility of the member states. Eighth, cultural and multi-lingual communication problems and legalistic versus more informal norms render coordination (Wright 1996; Peters and Wright 2001: 156–61; cf. 2000: 40) more likely to confuse than to clarify problem-solving (Wright and Hayward 2000: 40).

More fundamentally than these specific inbuilt immobilising factors is what Anand Menon has called 'the logic of leaderlessness' (Menon 2008: 131). It inclines the EU to indecision and evasion, failures and paralysis when its consensus facilitating procedures either work too well or break down. Because compromise bargains are made covertly by the confidential exchange of concessions after often prolonged negotiation, the resulting lack of transparency exacerbates the delegitimising effect of such indirect democratic decision-making as can be said to exist. The shamefully misleading *post facto* presentation of the facts accomplished by formal ratification of informal elite understandings and mutual concessions to resolve conflicts that were incapable of settlement in isolation, has often worked on more routine issues. However, resort to non-democratic institutions with an independent influence on major outcomes such as the European Commission, the European Central Bank and the European Court of Justice (ECJ) has been necessary to overcome the lack of democratic consensus. The limited if increased role of the European Parliament has been a partial corrective but the failure to institutionalise legitimate, accountable and clearly identifiable executive leadership is the fundamental problem.

Even after the Lisbon Treaty, the EU has relied upon a six-monthly rotating presidency of the fictional Council of Ministers (which in fact works as a number of specialised sectoral councils, a pluralism that belies its spurious unitary appelation) and a permanent president of the European Council, both of which have reflected the predominantly confederal nature of the EU. The former allows each member state to take its turn in coordinating EU affairs, the provisional presidencies not being chosen for their personal qualities or action programme but by rotation (Schout 2008). The lack of both has been painfully evident, especially from some of the smaller, post-2004 member states. The

European Council has been the increasingly important arena in which such collective leadership as has been possible has taken place, inhibited by the rule of unanimity between sovereign states. It was the recognition that these fora for collective decision were prone to muddling through inefficiency rather than providing inspiring heroic leadership even in times of crises that led to attempts by first the Constitutional Convention and then the Lisbon Treaty to achieve an effective EU in the increasing absence of consensus.

While acknowledging that structural deadlock is 'the normal case in European policy-making' because the diverse EU was 'intentionally constructed without a clear centre of political leadership', Adrienne Héritier paradoxically argues that it is precisely because of this that the EU has overcome the consequences of its leaderless propensity (Héritier, 1999: 16, 23). Systematic recourse to the creative use of 'subterfuge by stealth' in support of issue linkage package deals has enabled the EU to surmount deceit, dissensus and deadlock, despite the fact that the only thing on which all member states agree is reluctance to relinquish sovereignty (Héritier 1999: 97–8). She bluntly concedes that 'European institutions have been designed in such a way as to safeguard differences, and constructed so as to make them inherently ambiguous. Their rules are open to interpretation, their power is fragmented and decision-making processes lock diverse actors into joint processes. As a consequence the decisional processes are obstacle-ridden, cumbersome and, to say the least, prone to stalemate...subterfuge being the only way to keep policy-making going' (Héritier 1999: 97). However, because of the divergence between ambiguous talk and action, inconsistencies between 'decisions' and their non-implementation are concealed (Héritier 1999: 18–19).

While such 'strategies of deceit' (Héritier 1999: 96) may have worked unobtrusively as long as EU activities did not impinge controversially on the everyday lives of the European peoples, complexity and opacity have been decreasing deterrents to popular pressure on national governments and the EU. As a result, 'creative' policy initiatives that side-step through improvisation the immobilising institutions are much less likely to be successful, so making a virtue of the vices of remoteness and fragmentation, as Héritier does, implausible. This is especially true at times when output legitimacy is at a low ebb and distrust extends not only to the politicians and officials who are suspected of misrepresenting sections of the public by making bargaining concessions but to the organisations that are dedicated to defending their interests in Brussels. This results in retreat to national sovereignty at the expense of EU solidarity and the European social model (Ross and Borgmann-Prebil 2010: chapter 1).

While the European Parliament's increased role is a largely forlorn attempt to counteract these democratic forces of deadlock, other attempts to avoid stalemate are in decline. Leaving matters to market forces, to the brokering skills of the Commission or to litigation before the Luxembourg European Court of Justice as ways of sidestepping the member states are all in retreat as ways of acting without political consensus. Markets have become discredited in terms of efficacy and equity, the Commission because of its technocratic lack of legitimacy and the judiciary owing to a suspicion of creeping constitutionalisation without popular consent. Subterfuge and recourse to unaccountable economic, bureaucratic and judicial institutions have become ineffective substitutes for uneuropeanised traditional national political processes. To ignore this is to neglect the deleterious consequences of elites losing touch with their peoples, reflected both in declining mainstream support and increasing populist extremisms of Right (particularly) and Left. Symptomatic of this disjunction was that over half the EU citizens had not heard of the Constitutional Convention's deliberations that duly went down to referendum defeats in France and the Netherlands in 2005. This was the price of governmental double-talk, with nationalistic posturing about 'winning' in Brussels for domestic audiences inconsistent with concessions there that would be perceived as 'losses' at home. Member state sovereignty and European solidarity are institutionally out of step. So, the EU has been unable to fulfil the ambition of the Maastricht Treaty (para 3, clause 2), which proclaimed that the EU's 'task shall be to organise, in a manner demonstrating consistency and solidarity, relations between the Member States and between their peoples'. Europeanisation of capital markets has outpaced both national and EU solidarities inhibiting 'democratic solidarity among strangers' (Brunkhorst 2005: 170; cf. 6–7).

Another sanguine analysis of what she calls the EU's 'dynamic confusion of powers' is offered by Vivien Schmidt, who rejects the confederal model in favour of regarding the EU as a 'quasi-federal system' with 'two-level sovereignty' (Schmidt 2006: 53, 47, 20). She accepts that confederalism applies to the negotiation of European treaties; that national ministers compose the European Council and Councils of Ministers; that national officials staff the Comité des représentants permanents (COREPER) and working parties; the EU Commissioners and judges of the European Court of Justice are appointed by national

governments; the European Parliament is chosen by national electorates largely on national issues; while the transposition and enforcement
of EU directives and regulations are national responsibilities (Schmidt
2006: 52). She sidesteps the question of who if anyone is 'in charge'
(Schmidt 2006: 53–4). Instead she concentrates on the worthwhile
task of contrasting the ways major member states have conceived and
adapted to the EU.

France self-deceptively continued to present 'European integration as
an extension of national sovereignty through the country's leadership
in Europe...as if France still led Europe, despite the fact that France has
followed much more than led since the early 1990s' (Schmidt 2006:
37–8; cf. 176). A more plausible contender for leadership thereafter,
Germany treated the EU as 'an add-on to German federalism while using
it to enhance national identity' (Schmidt 2006: 93; cf. 88–92). However,
its increasing reluctance to be the open-ended paymaster of integration was compounded by the German Constitutional Court's resistance
to conceding power to an insufficiently democratic EU. Britain minimised Europeanisation by the defensive brinksmanship of negotiating
protocol opt-outs but has had a better compliance record than most.
Preferring self-regulation by business and deregulated markets and
promoting enlargement to widen at the expense of deepening integration, it regards the latter as a threat, not an extension, to national sovereignty. Italy was the keenest federalist, regarding the EU as 'saving Italy
from itself': generally accepting 'everything, overlooking the incompatibilities, unwilling to choose between the alternatives' and poor at
implementing EU directives (Schmidt 2006: 95–6; cf. 94–8, 147–54).
Later chapters will explore more fully these and other examples of
national diversity in member states seeking to turn EU membership to
their maximum advantage while minimising their commitment when
it does not do so in negotiating the quagmire.

Interdependence without solidarity

The EU suffers from the tension between conflicting types of interdependence. From its origins and still at its core, the EU is a common internal
market linked with world markets that constrain state sovereignty.
It integrates within the EU but also exposes it to international forces
beyond its reach but controlled by self-interested, profit-seeking actors
that owe loyalty to no country. This EU remains essentially a common
product, labour and money market, without the collective capacity and
cohesion to develop – despite French urging – an 'economic government' or a defensive protectionism against dumping to preserve the

welfare states created in the post-war years of plenty (Hayward 2012). Even when confronted by a profound and pervasive financial crisis, the political and banking elites in its common currency eurozone show a suicidal preference to hang separately rather than hanging together. They cling to the semblance of countervailing power that their ill-informed citizens treasure rather than the potentiality of power conferred by collective action. Interdependence without solidarity points towards a lowest common denominator union, although the Lisbon Treaty on the Functioning of the European Union (article 188R) has a 'solidarity clause' if a member state is the victim of a terrorist attack or natural disaster (Lisbon Treaty: 115; cf. 116; Myrdal and Rhinard 2010). Market interdependence triumphs over institutional interdependence, as the events of 2011 demonstrated with cruel clarity.

The perception of EU disunity is even greater than the reality because national governments arrange to shift the blame, whenever possible, for unpopular policies to which they have more or less willingly given their consent. Their citizens are induced to believe that an alien super-state, divorced from its member state constituents, has imposed decisions for which elected governments are not responsible or accountable, thereby discrediting the EU. Meanwhile, national governments readily claim the credit for popular policies or 'winning' opt-outs in the national interest dictated often by short-term partisan interests. Inertia in enforcing or transposing EU rules to placate sectional interests or clienteles distort their application, resulting in ineffectiveness and/or unfairness.

The EU was the post-Second World War offspring of European weakness. The continent that had for centuries dominated the world has accelerated its relative decline, demographically, economically, politically and militarily. Its EU members are too dispersed and disunited to exert maximum bargaining power with a fading US superpower and its challenger China, with others like India and Brazil flexing their muscles. Despite expanding in extent, the EU has weakened in autonomy, cohesion and decision-making capacity. The 2007 Lisbon Treaty was meant to be a response to the insistent demand for an institutional reinforcement of the EU. What it supplied was a weak and increasingly fragmented leadership, as explored more fully in chapter 5.

It is unusual for those with power to give it up voluntarily. A few may do so for the common good but when it happens, it is under the pressure of circumstances that cannot be controlled. As the ideal of European integration has faded, even among the elites, it is only under the remorseless pressure of circumstances that the endeavour of national governments to retain as much of their power as possible will be overcome by a more integrated Union. Meanwhile, it lurches from consensus through compromise to dissensus through disunion. So the hypothesis explored is that the EU is exacerbating its adversarial rather than its consensual characteristics, as it alternates between sovereignty and solidarity to avoid splitting into two or more Europes.

Bibliography

Brunkhorst, H. (2005) *Solidarity. From Civic Friendship to a Global Legal Community* (Cambridge, MA: MIT Press).

Elazar, D. (1998) *Constitutionalizing Globalization. The Postmodern Revival of Confederal Arrangements* (Lanham: Rowman and Littlefield).

Hayward, J. (1996) 'Conclusion. Has European Unification a Future' in J. Hayward (ed.), *Elitism, Populism and European Politics* (Oxford: Clarendon Press).

Hayward, J. (2012) 'From Citizen Solidarity to Self-Serving Inequality: Social Solidarity, Market Economy and Welfare Statecraft' in J. Connelly and J. Hayward (eds), *The Withering of the Welfare State. Regression* (Basingstoke: Palgrave Macmillan).

Héritier A. (1999) *Policy-Making and Diversity in Europe. Escaping Deadlock* (Cambridge: Cambridge University Press).

Lisbon Treaty (2007) Stationary Office, CM7294, London.

Majone, G. (2005) *Dilemmas of European Integration. The Ambiguities and Pitfalls of Integration by Stealth* (Oxford: Oxford University Press).

Majone, G. (2009) *Europe as the Would-be-World Power. The EU at Fifty* (Cambridge: Cambridge University Press).

Menon, A. (2008) 'Security Policy and the Logic of Leaderlessness' in J. Hayward (ed.), *Leaderlesss Europe* (Oxford: Oxford University Press).

Myrdal, S. and Rhinard, M. (2010) *The European Union's Solidarity Clause: Empty Letter or Effective Tool?* (Stockholm: Swedish Institute of International Affairs).

Peters, B. G. and Wright, V. (2001) 'The National Co-ordination of European Policy-making: Negotiating the Quagmire', in J. Richardson (ed.) *European Union. Power and Policy-making*, 2nd edn, (London: Routledge).

Ross, M. and Y. Borgmann-Prebil (eds) *Promoting Solidarity in the European Union* (Oxford: Oxford University Press).

Schout, A. (2008) 'Beyond the Rotating Presidency' in J. Hayward (ed.), *Leaderless Europe* (Oxford: Oxford University Press).

Schmidt, V. (2006) *Democracy in Europe. The European Union and National Polities* (Oxford: Oxford University Press).

Schmitter, P. (1996) 'Some alternative futures for the European polity and their implications for European Public Policy' in Yves Mény *et al.* (eds), *Adjusting to Europe* (London: Routledge).

Schmitter, P. (2004) 'Neo-Neofunctionalism' in A. Wiener and T. Diez (eds) *European Integration Theory*, (Oxford: Oxford University Press).

Wright, V. (1996) 'The National Coordination of European Policy-making. Negotiating the Quagmire' in J. Richardson (ed.) *European Union Power and Policy-making* (London: Routledge)..

Wright, V. and J. Hayward (2000) 'Governing from the Centre: Policy Coordination in Six European Core Executives' in R.A.W. Rhodes (ed.) *Transforming British Government*, Vol. 2 (Basingstoke: Macmillan).

Part I
Enfeebled Democratic Legitimacy

2
The Difficult Emergence of a European People

Michael Bruter

No demos?

When academics and journalists alike think of the 'failures' of European integration, one of the most usual arguments to be heard is that 60 years of European integration have yet failed to create a widely felt sense of European identity. This 'non-identity' thesis takes a more formal meaning in academic research, whereby scholars complain that there is no such thing as a 'European demos' (for example, Gabel and Anderson 2001; Scharpf 1999). For too long, the notion that there is no such thing as a European demos has been accepted as a given despite remarkably little conceptual precision and empirical evidence.

The supporters of the absence of demos argument usually dismiss it around three main ideas. They first claim that citizens of Europe do not feel European 'but' French, German or British instead and they are, in fact further and further away from Europe as evidenced by the success of Eurosceptic ideas in many European Union (EU) countries. They then accuse European Parliament elections of being a failure based on a turnout perceived as low and ever-declining. Finally, they suggest that democratic movements are not synchronic across Europe but instead completely country-specific. In this chapter, we question all three aspects of this argument, and provide elements that suggest that most either correspond to a very partial view of the European reality or even rely on wholly mistaken or outdated perceptions.

Understanding the extent to which a mass European identity has emerged, and whether this identification movement is centrifugal across member states or, on the contrary, places national polities on diverging identity trajectories represents important stakes, developed by Hayward (see Chapter 1 in this volume), in terms of the hiatus between sovereignty and solidarity as proposed ways forward for the EU. Firstly, the theme of divergence is essentially exploited by those who assert that the political unification of the EU is not matched by an emerging identity but instead a threat to the sovereignty not only of states but also of people. Secondly, the theme of an underlying identity is used by those who require Europeans to engage significant economic and social sacrifices in the name of solidarity. At a time when the increasing politicisation of Europe transforms the very nature of citizen identities (Harrison and Bruter 2012), whether the salvation of Europe must stem from a return to more safeguarded national sovereignty or an increase in the instutionalisation of European political solidarity will therefore continue to determine the terms of the political debates which are exposed to citizens as the fundamental choices that will define the available routes for European integration in coming years.

Paradoxes of identity

Remember May 2005? Within a week, French and Dutch citizens voted against the ratification of the treaty which was supposed to 'establish a Constitution for the European Union'. The interpretations of the press (and particularly the British press) were remarkably severe: there was a divorce between Europe and its citizens, Europeans wanted less Europe, not more, people simply did not feel Europeans. The reactions of politicians – including Eurocrats – followed the same logic; President Barroso suggested that citizens wanted a more 'technical' Europe that would deal with the economy and not with politics. We should get rid of the symbols of the EU because citizens did not identify with the EU. Such interpretations of the democratic earthquake of the spring of 2005 did not seem to rely on much serious empirical assessment of European identity, while the more serious analysis existing so far (for example, Hooghe and Marks 2006) is much more cautious in its interpretation of the referenda results.

When we look at the existing political science literature, a first body of work routinely claims that there is no such thing as a European identity and that it has never emerged (see full discussion in Bruter 2005). Direct references to a lack of identity, however, are increasingly rare in contemporary academic research, and a more preponderant claim does not revolve around identity per se but suggests, instead, that typical levels of scepticism towards European integration are not lower today than they were 10 years ago (McLaren 2007; Herrmann et al. 2004). Authors back this claim by reference to Eurobarometer results, which confirm that overall, in Europe, the proportion of citizens who find that European integration is benefiting their country is lower today within the EU than it was in the late 1980s.

What is more, throughout Europe, some Eurosceptic parties, be they from the extreme right, the extreme left, or supposedly cross-ideology manage to secure significant proportions of the vote in European and national elections on a largely Eurosceptic political platform (Harrison and Bruter, 2011). They include the likes of UK Independent Party (UKIP) in the UK, the National Front in France, True Finns in Finland and Jobbik in Hungary on the right, as well as the Linke in Germany and the Greek and Portuguese Communist parties on the left, but also the June Movement in Denmark or the List Dedecker in Belgium, which claim to sit outside of traditional left right cleavages.

On the basis of these two empirical elements, a significant proportion of the academic literature posits that a European identity has failed to arise and that instead of European integration creating European citizens, it may have reached its limits and only managed to alienate them. Interestingly enough, however, none of the empirical literature that directly tackles the question of European identity per se (as opposed to perceived benefits of integration or within certain limits support for integration) concludes that identity is lacking. McLaren's (2007) evaluations support these findings. Risse (2010) does not discount the possibility that European identity may be progressing steadily, which is more assertively suggested by Bruter (2005, 2009).

However, it is Bruter (2011) and Bruter and Harrison (2011) who provide blunt empirical evidence that European identity is in fact rather high. Let us delve further into these results, which have been produced by. *Feeling European,* a study conducted by Bruter with the support of Harrison between 2009 and 2011.[1] It consisted of approximately 250 politicians interviews as well as a three-wave panel study survey conducted in all 27 member states of the EU (for the first wave) during the 2009 European Parliament elections and with a total of over 30,000 respondents in that first wave. A second wave was conducted in eight countries in 2010, and a third only in the UK in 2012.

Firstly, according to this mass survey, on a 10-point scale, the level of self-perceived general European identity of the average EU citizen is 7.09. Even in Europe's most Eurosceptic countries, a majority of citizens feel European. For instance, in the UK, 55.2 per cent of Britons and 68 per cent of Northern Irish have an identity score of 5 out of 10 or above. Using our data, we can create statistical instruments that enable us to evaluate the evolution of European identity over time. This way we can show that the level of European identity is constantly progressing in a unified way across the EU at the very time support for European integration is stagnating and perceived benefits of European integration altogether declining.

Our findings show that there are essentially two separate dimensions of European identity that are very distinct – a civic dimension (whereby individuals politically 'feel' like citizens of the EU) and a cultural dimension (which means that individuals feel part of a European human and cultural community). While cultural identity highlights a certain success of European integration, when it comes to making Europeans feel closer together, it has little 'institutional' value. By contrast, civic identity can work as a 'reservoir of good will' that leads citizens to tolerate policy decisions they find far from perfect. On the whole, a majority of citizens tend to feel more 'civically' than 'culturally' European (the average 'civic' score is 7.15 on a scale of 0–10, while the average 'cultural' score is 6.05). However, this situation hides some important differences across EU member states. Indeed, while obviously inter-related, these two dimensions are clearly distinct and their respective advancement varies from country to country. To simplify, in general terms, European identity tends to be higher in Western Europe and cultural identity in Central and Eastern Europe.

Social and demographic factors also have a strong impact on citizens' likeliness to feel European (Herrmann et al. 2004). For instance, the UK has the largest proportion of citizens who do not feel European at all, but also one of the largest proportions of people feeling very European across the whole EU. There are proportionally more people very strongly European in Northern Ireland than in Belgium, France or Germany. Of course, this begs the question of what sort of social and demographic characteristics are most highly related to the level of European identity of citizens. A survey of the impact of major social and demographic variables proves very telling.

For instance, education is strongly correlated with European identity but wealth is not. Younger citizens feel significantly more 'civically' European than older ones but cultural identity is not related to age. Similarly, while centre-left voters are more 'civically' European than centre-right ones, and more supportive of EU citizenship rights, cultural identity is not strongly related to ideological preferences. Finally, women tend to feel more European than men in general terms and in terms of support for EU citizenship rights, but men have higher levels of civic identity than their female counterparts. Even more paradoxical, the impact of gender on European identity is not the case across all countries. For instance, women tend to feel more European than men in Austria, Germany or the UK, but it is exactly the opposite in France, Spain, or the Czech Republic.

However, European identity is not simply a fatality that stems from social or demographic differences. Instead, our findings show that it can be actively encouraged by politics. The European experience of citizens is thus one of the best predictors of their level of European identity. As increasing proportions of younger (and less young) Europeans get a chance to travel, speak foreign languages, or live or study in other European countries, this can only result in interesting transformations of the meaning of European identity. Travelling, speaking languages, living in another European nation or indeed having some family doing so means that citizens get more and more chances to 'experience' European integration in their daily life. This direct experience of the EU proves to have a major impact on citizens' identity.

In the context of the study of European identity, one of the greatest current paradoxes is that while public attitudes towards various specific aspects of European policy point to a certain 'disunion' across the EU, the evolution of European identity clearly goes in the direction of a 'union' of European people. Indeed, by comparative standards, there are remarkably few systematic cross-national differences between the various European member states in the evolution of European identity levels. Indeed, while a few years ago, Central European countries and some Northern European countries tended to have a predominantly strong cultural European identity but a weak civic identity (Bruter 2005); the differences between 'civic' and 'cultural' European member states has clearly faded with civic identity becoming predominant across most of the European scene.

The paradox of European Parliament elections?

Based on the findings of the 'Feeling European' study, we can thus confirm that the intuition of much of the identity specific literature that a European identity is in fact developing is effectively supported empirically. How can we reconcile these findings with the more pessimistic theories of Euroscepticism and citizens involvement mentioned earlier in this chapter? Is the emerging European identity a mere 'feeling' without any practical political consequences? Is it a 'consolation prize' for a EU that would see citizens feel 'implicitly' and uselessly European while they would increasingly reject European integration as a political process and act in an increasingly a-European way in their everyday life? Indeed, one of the seemingly strongest argument of the supporters of the identity failure thesis is that turnout in European Parliament elections has seemingly continuously decreased between the first elections in 1979 and 2009. Is the situation so straightforward?

In June 2009, Europeans voted in the seventh direct European Parliament elections. As widely suggested, on this occasion, the average turnout across the whole of the EU reached a record low previously set five years earlier in June 2004. Journalists and politicians alike deduced that the democratic crisis of the EU must therefore be symmetrically reaching an all-time high, and hastened to conclude that Europeans are not interested in the EU, that they do not trust their European institutions, and that by and large, they simply do not feel European. The starting point of this argument was rather dubious in the first place. When comparing turnout in the 25 member states that voted in both 2004 and 2009, turnout was by and large stable, and similarly, while the overall European turnout seemed to have dramatically declined between the 1999 election and that in 2004, when comparing the 15 'old' member states which alone voted on both occasions, turnout had in fact increased (Déloye and Bruter 2007; van der Brug and van der Eijk 2007).

In the context of studying the relationship between the emergence of a mass European identity and its political implications, this hasty interpretation of an apparently 'obvious' public opinion measure (whereby one conveniently ignores that completely different countries are voting in the three elections being compared) has a major symbolic purpose. Journalists largely explain their lack of coverage of European news by the fact that EU citizens would not be interested in them. Conversely, politicians explain the mainly domestic focus of their European Parliament campaigns by the suggestion that voters would be more interested in them than in European issues, despite the fact that European Election Studies show time and again that a dominant and increasing proportion of voters would like to hear more about Europe (van der Eijk and Franklin 1996) and that the French 2005 referendum on an EU Constitution saw – literally – several million citizens effectively reading the incredibly obscure and fairly long document and buying books detailing and interpreting its most minute details.

Similarly, the overall decline in turnout in European Parliament elections since the 1970s seems in no way sharper or more worrying than the parallel participation decline in the context of national level elections in the same countries (see an analysis of factors in Franklin, 2001). In this sense, in terms of European elections as well, the centrifugal 'union' theory of convergence seems far more supported than the more classic 'disunion' hypothesis. There is absolutely no empirical support for the suggestion that pro-European countries would vote more than those who feel less European, the 'second order model' seems to be partly verified in a similar way across all member states, and everywhere as well, parties which campaign on Europe (whether negatively or positively) get an electoral bonus while parties which campaign on national themes get a symmetric malus.

There is therefore a triangle of legitimacy crisis associating citizens, the media and the European project, whereby the media are claiming not to be in a position to force citizens to get interested in something which they do not like (Bain and Holland 2007) let alone influence them, while citizens are claiming that they are poorly and inadequately informed about the EU. At the heart of this paradoxical triangle, however, the question of the emergence of a European demos now seems to beg even more sharply for some understanding of the nature of how legitimate citizens perceive the European institutional architecture to be. Indeed, if citizens feel more European than many believe, and if European Parliament elections are not the massive democratic failure that journalists often describe, how can we decipher the sustained criticisms of the EU, which, as we mentioned earlier, many authors have equated with persistent Euroscepticism?

Paradoxes of popular legitimacy

Indeed, as we have seen, the bulk of popular elite interpretations – from the mass media to many political parties and through to EU institutions themselves – is that Euroscepticism is paradoxically on the rise. It has led to a recent string of 'no votes' in referenda on EU questions, that turnout in European Parliament elections keeps declining and betrays a disaffection of citizens for a EU, which is, consequently, supposed to face a widespread and dangerous crisis of legitimacy. In fact, a significant number of quality academic publications accept this interpretation (Cederman 2001).

While not questioning the fact that European integration is indeed facing a crisis of legitimacy in the sense that there is a mismatch between public preferences in terms of European integration and what is actually proposed to them by their elites, the assumption that this must mean a rise in anti-EU sentiment and a lack of European identity of citizens is less than obvious. In fact, surprisingly, there are as many signs pointing to a rise in general support for the European project and civic engagement as there are signs of dissatisfaction with specific aspects of integration.

Let us consider a concrete example. Seen from a certain perspective, the argument of the victory of the 'no' in a number of referenda on questions relating to the EU is in fact rather weak. The most emblematic of these 'no's', that of the French population in May 2005 occurred at a time when support for European integration was at its peak. Similarly, for the first time in the history of French referenda on EU questions, the dominant argument of the 'no' camp, regardless of its (lack of) credibility, was based not on a rejection of integration – or a claim for slower integration – but instead, on a claim for faster and more generalised integration that would be increasingly social and political.

Finally, the question of popular legitimacy is hard to disconnect from the question of institutional trust. There again, the evolution of public opinion when it comes to trust in EU institution since the early 1980s is highly symptomatic. Twenty-five years ago, there was no EU country where EU institutions were globally more trusted than their national equivalent. By the mid-2000s, however, almost all of the 'old' member states and a large majority of the new ones trust the European Commission more than their national government, and the European Parliament more than their national one (Tables 2.1 and 2.2). The only exceptions tend to be Sweden and, to a lesser extent, Denmark (Parliament only) and Finland (where the scores for national Parliament and the European Commission are tied). For the protagonists of widespread Euroscepticism, this is a shocking truth. Who would think that in 13 of the 15 old member states, including the United Kingdom, the European Commission is in fact significantly more trusted than the national government? And how can we reconcile these findings with suspicion of declining popular legitimacy and never emerging identity?

Clearly, in terms of changing legitimacy, evidence seems to point towards a fairly monolithic trend across the member states, where a near unanimity between European citizens exists to progressively confer greater perceived legitimacy on European Union institutions than on their national counterparts.

The argument of this chapter is therefore that it is exceedingly simplistic to start from the assumption that Europeans 'don't care' about the EU and don't feel European, and that it is because of this presumed lack of interest or indeed supposed lack of European identity that powerless media would not be in a position to participate in the strengthening of a European public sphere. We will therefore use findings from a long-term panel study experiment on the impact of

Table 2.1 Comparative trust in the European Commission and national government

Country	European Commission	National Government	Difference
Poland	49	7	+42
Italy	63	26	+37
Slovakia	54	17	+37
Belgium	63	34	+29
Hungary	58	31	+27
Slovenia	52	27	+25
France	52	29	+23
Ireland	61	39	+22
Portugal	56	34	+22
Germany	39	23	+16
Netherlands	54	39	+15
Lithuania	45	31	+14
Spain	53	42	+11
Czech Republic	35	25	+10
Greece	63	55	+ 8
Austria	47	39	+ 8
United Kingdom	26	19	+7
Luxembourg	66	61	+ 5
Latvia	32	28	+4
Denmark	47	44	+ 3
Malta	50	49	+1
Sweden	48	48	0
Finland	59	59	0
Estonia	44	45	–1
Cyprus	49	75	–26

Figures in the first two columns correspond to the proportion of citizens who tend to trust the institution. Figures in column 3 correspond to the trust advantage (+) or disadvantage (–) of the European Commission when compared to the national government.

Source: Compiled by the author from Eurobarometer 61 data, Tables 4.1b and 8.4.

news on European identity to show that the media, far from simply 'following' citizens' news demand do participate in shaping their identity over time.

Demos or no demos? Making sense of paradoxes

Our suggestion here is that European identity is in fact growing, and growing in a unified way across the member states of the EU, but that precisely because an increasing number of EU citizens feel European, they now judge the various policies and institutional reforms of the

Table 2.2 Comparative trust in the European Parliament and national parliaments

Country	European Parliament	National Parliament	Difference
Poland	53	8	+45
Slovakia	59	19	+40
Italy	68	32	+36
Hungary	64	29	+35
Slovenia	59	25	+34
Lithuania	52	19	+33
Belgium	64	38	+26
Czech Republic	44	18	+26
Ireland	64	40	+24
France	57	35	+22
Germany	51	29	+22
Portugal	58	37	+21
Spain	62	42	+20
Latvia	40	20	+20
Netherlands	57	43	+14
Estonia	49	35	+14
Luxembourg	67	56	+11
Malta	55	47	+8
Greece	70	63	+7
United Kingdom	30	25	+5
Finland	61	58	+3
Austria	43	41	+2
Sweden	55	58	−3
Denmark	55	63	−8
Cyprus	55	74	−19

Figures in the first two columns correspond to the proportion of citizens who tend to trust the institution. Figures in column 3 correspond to the trust advantage (+) or disadvantage (–) of the European Commission when compared to the national government.

Source: Compiled by the author from Eurobarometer 61 data, Tables 4.1b and 8.4.

EU 'from the inside', as citizens, and thus on their own merits, rather than in terms of integration. Thus, we would not be witnessing a lack of European identity and rise in Euroscepticism, but an increasing European identity and switch from an 'outside' Euroscepticism that targets the principles of integration to an 'inside' Euroscepticism that takes the principle of durable, continuing integration for granted but targets specific policies and reforms (compare the analyses of Hooghe and Marks, 2007; Harrison and Bruter, 2012). This would partly explain the paradoxical evolution in European opinion. What is more, the fact that citizens who do feel increasingly European do, in fact, criticise relatively similar aspects of European integration across member states. Ideological preferences would not be a sign of a lack of demos but instead an emerging one. It also suggests that while the conditions of European solidarity dictated by national and European leaders may be criticised by many citizens, there is no majority support for a return to national sovereignty as a panacea to European problems across the European Union.

Indeed, once we have acknowledged that feeling European is completely different from assessing various EU policies, institutions, or even the perceived benefits or principle of European integration in general, the interpretation we can derive from the various identity, attitudinal, and behavioural elements which we have briefly discussed in this chapter become quite different from the simplistic journalistic models that we referred to at the beginning of the chapter.

Empirically, using statistical instruments and recreating time series data, we can see that increasingly, a large proportion of citizens feel European without having the impression that European integration is beneficial to themselves or to their countries. These citizens tend to support European integration despite not perceiving it as beneficial, precisely because they identify with 'Europe' as a political and human community. At a time when the limits of European identity have been tested by the need for the EU to prove its solidarity with near-bankrupt Greece, this finding is essential. Indeed, it may well explain why citizens from the rest of the Eurozone were not rebelling against the gesture of financial solidarity that some countries that face economic difficulties have shown towards each other, nor against the very prominent dominance of the Franco-German duumvirate (see Chapter 15 by Paterson), which national leaders seem to question far more vibrantly than their citizens.

Another proof of this paradoxical consequence of identity is that the more citizens criticise some EU policies, the more they support a strengthening of EU citizenship. Our findings show that there is overwhelming support for all current aspects of EU citizenship, and equally high demand for a furthering of EU citizens rights, even when they mean that we would grant more rights to (European) 'foreigners' on our soil. When it comes to the assessment of current rights associated with EU citizenship, 89 per cent of citizens approve the rights for all Europeans to live anywhere they want in the European Union, 85.6 per cent are happy for foreign EU citizens to vote in local elections in their country and 87.8 per cent are happy with the borderless environment created by the Schengen agreements.

Similarly, when it comes to possible future extensions of EU citizenship rights, 88.6 per cent of citizens would recommend that new treaties be adopted by EU-wide referenda such as those held in federal systems, and 84.4 per cent would support a direct election of the EU president by citizens, a measure largely refused by heads of states and governments because it is considered far too federalist. Majorities of citizens across the member states would also support a controversial right of EU citizens to vote in general elections in their country.

Last but certainly not least paradox in our findings, even the people who feel least European tend to think that their children and grandchildren will feel far more European than them. In fact, at a time when many academics and citizens alike do not hesitate to claim that the EU is facing on of its worst democratic crises and could even be 'endangered', well over 90 per cent of Europeans remain persuaded that their children and grandchildren will feel more European than them, and even in countries such as the UK, this proportion is above 80 per cent. All in all, it is as though European integration was still seen as a process, a pioneering adventure which had left part of the current generations on the side but would not fail to gain the hearts and minds of their descendents.

These results, as the other elements that we have mentioned (and many of our other similar findings) also seem to contradict 'common knowledge' about European identity. Indeed, while we have established that on the whole, citizens feel far more European on average than many would expect, and feel increasingly European where many claimed that identification with Europe was on the decline, it would be wrong to assume that such a growing European identity necessarily means that heads of states and governments have a 'blank cheque' to do whatever they want with European integration. On the contrary, when interpreting our findings one should bear in mind that citizens' cynicism and dissatisfaction is not EU-specific but related to the way we 'do' politics in general. In fact, what our findings suggest is that in many ways, the growing level of European identity of citizens may largely be responsible for what many have seen as a surge in Eurosceptic attitudes. Indeed, as citizens feel more and more European, as they appropriate the EU as their political system, they are also less and less willing to accept its institutional and policy shortcomings. In particular, the quasi-unanimous demand for greater mechanisms of direct democracy (pan-European referenda, direct election of the EU president) suggests that citizens are simply no longer ready to tolerate the best efforts of heads of states and governments to keep the EU institutional system far less democratic than it should be. In a context of increasing cynicism of citizens towards their politicians and their elites in general, European citizens are simply no longer willing to accept that their politicians know what is best for them. While they feel largely and increasingly European, they are also telling us that they have the right to see the EU develop into a better, more democratic, more transparent and more engaging political system than what it is and what national institutions are.

This may be the nature of an emerging European demos. In some ways, the demos debate sometimes seems fuelled by semantics. Strictly speaking, demos is a simple translation for 'people', and it is perhaps not a coincidence that the 'lack of demos' argument largely started in Germany and France where this same 'people' is conceived as a singular as opposed to the English plural. The suggestion that diversity and heterogeneity are incompatible with an emerging demos is harder to sustain by the year. While Europeans are diverse, it is increasingly true that all European nations are divided by deep fractures which resemble each other across countries, and, perhaps, objectively unify those who benefit from progress and those who are left out of it across countries.

Political convergence is even more striking. Political scientists long mused over the fact that the extreme right seemed to be such a strong phenomenon in some countries while it was nearly absent in others. Nowadays, differences in scores do not nearly follow the same geographical lines (Harrison and Bruter 2011) and countries that had long seemed immune to the extreme right phenomenon, such as the UK, Hungary, Sweden or Finland, have seen sharp increases in the scores of extremist parties. Similarly, could we possibly ignore that in an unprecedented way, the political heart of many EU countries had seemed to synchronically move to the left in the late 1990s when left-wing parties won major elections in Germany, France, the UK, Italy, Belgium, the Netherlands, etc., while it has equally clearly shifted back to the right in the early 2010s (with Germany, France, the UK, Italy, Belgium, Portugal, and many others this time being governed by the right).

Increasingly parallel political cycles, superimposed political divisions, strengthening identity and very similar forms of 'inside' criticism of what the EU does seem, if anything, to provide the basis for a vibrant emerging European demos and to an unexpected extent support a solidarity discourse which adverse economic conditions would have led many public opinion specialists to predict to be an impossibility. Perhaps, however, this demos, exceedingly critical of its national leaders and European elites alike, is simply not the one current partisan elites would have chosen if they had been asked.

Note

1. It was supported by the ESRC. Reference RES-062-23-1838.

Bibliography

Bain, J. and M. Holland (eds) (2007) *European Union Identity: Perceptions from Europe and Asia* (Baden-Baden: Nomos).

Brug, van der W. and C. van der Eijk (eds) (2007) *European Elections and Domestic Politics* (Notre Dame: University of Notre Dame Press).

Bruter, M. (2011) 'Europolity? Seven paradoxes about European identity' *Salzburg Papers in European Integration,* no 03–11.

Bruter, M. (2009) 'Time Bomb – News, Media, and European Identity', *Comparative Political Studies,* 42:12, 1498–1536.

Bruter, M. (2005) *Citizens of Europe? The Emergence of a Mass European Identity* (Basingstoke: Palgrave).

Bruter, M. and S. Harrison (2011) *Feeling European: A Report on European Identity and Attitudes to EU Citizenship in the 27 Member States* (London: ECREP).

Bruter, M. and S. Harrison (2009) *The Future of our Democracies?* (Basingstoke: Palgrave Macmillan).

Cederman, H. (2001) 'Nationalism and Bounded Integration: What it Would Take to Construct a European Demos.' *European Journal of International Relations,* 7:2, 139–174.

Déloye, Y. and M. Bruter (eds) (2007) *Encyclopaedia of European Elections* (Basingstoke: Palgrave).

Eijk, van der C. and M. Franklin (1996) *Choosing Europe* (Ann Arbor: Michigan University Press).

Franklin, M. (2001) 'How Structural Factors Cause Turnout Variations at European Parliament Elections', *European Union Politics,* 2:3, 309–328.

Gabel, M. and C. Anderson (2001) 'Exploring the European Demos (or Lack Thereof): the Structure of Citizen Attitudes and the European Political Space'. *CEUS Papers Series,* Bremen, no. 2001/4.

Harrison, S. and M. Bruter, M. (2012) 'Media and Identity – the Paradox of Legitimacy and the Making of European Citizens' in T. Risse and M. Van de Steeg (eds) *European Public Sphere – Bringing Politics Back in* (Cambridge : Cambridge University Press).

Harrison, S. and M. Bruter (2011) *Mapping Extreme Right Ideology* (Basingstoke: Palgrave Macmillan).

Herrmann, R., T. Risse and M. Brewer (eds) (2004) *Transnational Identities* (Boulder, CO: Rowman & Littlefield).

Hooghe, L. and G. Marks (2006) 'Europe's Blues: Theoretical Soul-Searching After the Rejection of a European Constitution', *PS: Politics and Political Science* 39 (April), 247–250.

Hooghe, L. and G. Marks (2007) 'Sources of Euroscepticism' *Acta Politica*, 42 (2–3): 119–127.

McLaren, L. (2007) 'Explaining Mass Level Euroscepticism: Identity, Interest, and Institutional Distrust.' *Acta Politica*, 4:2/3, 233–251.

Risse, T. (2010) *A Community of Europeans? Transnational Identities and Public Spheres*, Ithaca, NY: Cornell University Press.

Scharpf, F.J.W. (1999) *Governing in Europe. Effective and Democratic?* (Oxford: Oxford University Press).

3
A Nascent Transnational Civil Society

Elizabeth Monaghan

The idea that civil society could help to strengthen the European Union's (EU) enfeebled democratic legitimacy emerged and become widespread in the context of concerns about a 'democratic deficit' and a 'legitimacy crisis' from which the EU was said to suffer. This reflects a broader renaissance of the civil society idea in political theory since the 1980s, and a tendency of governments and governing institutions across the world to cite it 'as a solution to social, economic and political dilemmas by politicians...from left, right and all perspectives in between' (Edwards 2009: 2). The near universal appeal of the civil society idea and its celebration as providing the solution to all manner of democratic problems reflects its inherently multi-faceted nature. Although we may refer to the 'concept' of civil society, it is more accurate to think of it as a set of different ideas that have emerged and developed in parallel over several hundred years (Taylor 1995). In connection with the EU, Finke (2007) has written how two scholars who refer to civil society do not necessarily mean the same thing, and that this is even more the case when journalists, politicians and public officials allude to it. The range of views on what civil society is and how it works is the first dimension of potential disunion.

A second potential dimension of disunion is that in the context of an expanded role for civil society in EU governance, there has not been linear, uni-directional progress towards the goal of strengthened democratic legitimacy. The structures and processes of representative democracy are weak. The EU lacks many of the conditions found at the national level that underpin democracy on the representative model, including a sense of a Europe-wide political community bound by feelings of solidarity. On the one hand, there is an acknowledgement in the scholarly debate that it is possible for the EU to be democratic and yet for this not to look like national democracy. On the other, what would 'count' as democracy at the EU level is disputed. In what follows, potential disunion is analysed under three themes: different institutional approaches to civil society; the diversity of European civil society; and different ideas and empirical manifestations of civil society's democratic contribution.

The EU institutions and civil society: democratic legitimacy and solidarity

The idea of civil society emerged and became widely held in the context of the broader global 'rediscovery' of civil society from the late 1980s onwards. As such, it might be tempting to understand the turn towards civil society in the EU in terms of 'an idea whose time had come'. This, however, does not fully capture the involvement of the EU institutions in promoting the role of civil society organisations in EU politics. In the post-Maastricht period and intensifying in the 2000s, the role of civil society was linked to strengthening democratic legitimacy and helping to bring EU institutions and citizens closer together. There has been some convergence between the institutions exhibited by the establishment of the Joint Transparency Register of Organisations that seek to influence the European Parliament and the Commission. Despite this, in broad terms there has been a lack of unity concerning the exact mechanisms at work and specifically whether the contribution is to input legitimacy or output legitimacy, or both.

Of the four main institutions, the Commission has been at the forefront of promoting a role for civil society. A 2000 discussion paper, entitled 'The Commission and Non-Governmental Organisations: Building a Stronger Partnership' outlined its rationale for co-operation based on five quite different considerations[1]. The fifth, 'Contributing to European Integration', outlined how non-governmental organisations (NGOs) contributed to the formation of a European public opinion as a feature of a 'true European political entity' (European Commission 2000: 5). As such, the assumption was that such organisations, as a 'significant component of civil society' (European Commission 2000: 4) could help to foster feelings of solidarity amongst Europeans. The 2001 Governance White Paper developed these ideas and incorporated them into a broader discussion of EU democracy and the legitimacy of the institutions and decision-making processes. 'Generating a sense of belonging to Europe' and mobilising public support (European Commission 2001: 11–12) were discussed as objectives of reforming governance. Civil society was an addressee of the white paper, the Commission having been enlightened as to the 'legitimacy capital' of civil society during the Convention that drafted the Charter of Fundamental Rights, which involved the consultation of civil society organisations in hearings (Smismans 2003: 480). The extensive use of the term 'civil society' throughout the Governance White Paper was notable. Although it was not the first document to adopt such language it did much to popularise the term and in doing so conveyed a certain normative desirability given that 'civil society' and 'non-governmental organisations' implied 'democratically superior vehicles' to 'interest groups', which could be viewed as 'democratically damaged goods' (Van Deth and Maloney 2008: 13). Indeed, the white paper defined civil society solely in terms of the organisations that populated it,[2] organisations of the type that the Commission had existing consultative relationships with prior to the White Paper, and which might have been described as 'interest groups' in an earlier era, highlighting the continuity between the civil society agenda and earlier systems of interest group consultation.

The White Paper on Governance received a fairly frosty reception, in part because of its treatment of civil society (Armstrong 2002) and the conflation of 'citizens' and 'civil society organisations' (Magnette 2003). Nevertheless, the idea of civil society continued to permeate subsequent Commission initiatives aimed at democratic reform. Plan D ('for Democracy, Dialogue and Debate'), which was its response to the 'period of reflection' called for by the European Council following the rejection of the Constitutional Treaty in French and Dutch referendums in 2005, involved funding projects run by civil society organisations to promote debate with citizens on the future of Europe (European Commission 2005). This overlapped with a new Communication Policy, led (as was Plan D) by Margot Wallström, then Vice President of the Commission with responsibility for Institutional Relations and Communication Strategy. The Communication White Paper, like that of the Governance White Paper, returned to the idea of 'partnerships' with civil society organisations for communicating about Europe with citizens (European Commission 2006). Support for the idea of civil society as agents for sparking debates and communicating with, and facilitating the participation of citizens was a characteristic of Wallström's approach. However, with the commencement of the mandate for a new Commission after 2010 and the slight re-organisation of responsibilities, the emphasis of the relationship between the Commission and civil society shifted. Rather than presenting civil society organisations as agents of European solidarity, linking society with the institutions, the focus has moved back to a narrower one of consultation and dialogue (European Commission 2011).

The idea of civil society has proven to be so irresistible to the Commission for two main reasons relating to its original *raison d'etre* and role under the treaties. Firstly, it is, by national standards, at least a relatively small bureaucracy but is required to prepare legislative proposals across a wide range of areas. Lacking the requisite in-house technical expertise, and bearing in mind the parallel need to prepare proposals that will not be rejected by the Council and European Parliament (see Chapter 6), it has always relied on external sources of expertise. Secondly, as an unelected body, it has been the target of criticism for lacking democratic legitimacy. It has always justified itself on the basis that being 'above' national interests it is best placed to understand the collective European interest – very much in terms of output-oriented legitimacy. However, guaranteeing superior outcomes has become increasingly difficult, and as the EU has developed policy competences which see it having a greater impact in people's everyday lives, the pressures for input legitimacy increased. Invoking civil society has allowed the Commission to tackle both of these problems since the groups targeted by the Commission were seen as possessing the informational resources as well as being able to act as 'effective representative vehicles' that could generate policy outcomes that closely matched citizens' preferences (Van Deth and Maloney 2008: 6). These motivations explain the logic of the Commission's so-called constituency mobilisation strategy observed by Mazey (1995) and others whereby it recognised early on that a transnational system of interest representation would be one that supported and demanded transnational action in a given policy area, allowing it to expand its own policy and executive role. It could also make the Commission's job easier by helping to inform and implement policy. It could justify EU action and in particular the Commission's role by signalling that the preferences articulated and aggregated by these organisations were legitimate due to their basis in and congruence with those found in European societies.

The European Parliament has a rather different relationship with the outside world to the Commission, which accounts for and is reflected by its relationship with civil society, and its institutional perspective on the contribution of the latter to strengthening the democratic legitimacy of the EU. The Parliament's status as the only directly elected institution in the EU means that it faces a certain tension between defending a system of representative democracy, which has serious weaknesses, and embracing participatory democracy measures which might challenge its legitimacy, in turn the basis of its expanding powers. These tensions were apparent in the Parliament's response to the Commission's Governance White Paper, and specifically the proposals for better consultation including the establishment of part-nership agreements with certain organisations (European Parliament 2001: para 11). This was indicative of a lack of agreement amongst the institutions on the proper relationship between the EU and civil society (Greenwood 2007a: 4). Nevertheless, the European Parliament has not been completely closed and hostile to outside influences. After the Commission, it is generally viewed as the second most important institutional venue by groups (Richardson 2007: 239), a situation inten-sified as its decision-making powers of have increased. The Parliament's image as a positive force for certain environmental and consumer inter-ests strengthen its relationships with particular parts of civil society. Nevertheless, the basis of these relationships has tended to differ from the Commission's. As Bouwen (2004: 476) has argued, the Parliament favoured developing relationships with civil society as a means of gath-ering information – in some cases technical expertise, but more impor-tantly, what he refers to as the 'European encompassing interest', i.e. the needs and preferences of a specific sector. As such, the relationship between the Parliament and civil society can be understood largely in terms of output legitimacy. There is little indication that civil society actors are viewed as agents of solidarity by parliamentarians, and civil society is not generally viewed as the solution to the EU's democratic legitimacy problems. Rather, it is viewed as a necessary source of infor-mation but one which has to be managed in order to secure democratic legitimacy, as the involvement of the Parliament in the creation of the Joint Transparency Register testifies.

By the time the Commission and Parliament had launched the Register in June 2011, the culmination of several years of discussion between the two institutions, the Council of the European Union had indicated only that it was 'ready to consider having a role in the Register' (Council of the European Union 2011). This non-committal approach reflected the Council's portrayal of itself as an institution where lobbying did not take place, and its insistence that 'all contact with NGOs is handled by the European Commission' (Friends of the Earth, cited in Greenwood 2007a: 28). The European Council, for its part, has largely confined its position on the role of civil society in the EU to rhetoric. The Declaration on the Future of the Union called for a deeper and wider debate on the future of Europe, involving all interested parties, and naming civil society directly (European Council 2001a). This was followed up by the Laeken Declaration, which in convening the constitutional Convention outlined a role for civil society in ensuring that the process of treaty reform would be closer to the people (European Council 2001b). However, when it came to implementing this idea it was harder than anticipated and organisations that took part in the Convention process expressed disappointment that civil society 'involvement' amounted to little more than a website.[3] Beyond declaratory statements implying a role for civil society in making the EU more democratic, the European Council has, of course, made more concrete commitments to the role of civil society organisations in acting as a counterweight to business interests by agreeing to successive budget lines in Commission budgets resulting in the channelling of €2 billion annually through NGOs (Kallas 2005). Furthermore, the symbolic importance of the creation of a 'participatory norm' as a feature of EU governance cannot be dismissed (Saurugger 2010).

A disunited European civil society?

The idea of civil society refers in part to a normative or utopian project (Zimmer and Freise 2008) whereby society can structure itself and coordinate its actions through free associations that are not under the tutelage of state power but which nevertheless may determine or influence the course of state policy (Taylor 1995). As such, civil society implies an arena in which certain actors engage in activities of self-organisation (Young 2000: 160). The EU institutions, led by the Commission as we have seen, have consistently favoured a descriptive interpretation of the idea which focuses on the actors. 'Civil society' is used as a synonym for a wide range of organisations that populate the space between EU or state institutions and the market. Empirically, there is not much to distinguish civil society organisations from interest groups, emphasising again that the term 'civil society' is used in the EU as a normatively superior label for 'interest groups', but also that the 'discovery' of civil society in the EU is not as new as the neologism might imply. At the same time, the two are not different things: systems of interest representation are one empirical manifestation of the civil society idea; but they are not constitutive of the idea in its entirety. There are consequences for the extent to which civil society acts as a surrogate source of democratic legitimacy. Edwards (2009) warned of problems in equating the structural elements of the idea with the normative elements of the idea, and assuming that the existence of the structures of civil society will automatically convey the normative democratic benefits of the idea.

The dominance of a descriptive interpretation of the civil society idea at the EU level is no accident. Rather, it is due in large part to the role of EU political institutions in group formation and maintenance, which, Greenwood (2007b: 342) argues, are some of the most striking elements of the civil society picture in the EU. Some of the earliest studies of interest intermediation identified an indirect influence of the Commission on group formation. Kirchner (1980: 96–97), for example, found that many of the groupings established at Community level were in response to the formation of a new centre of decision-making and as a result of advantages expected from Community action. A more direct role of the Commission in shaping the formation of EU level groups was identified by Sidjanski who observed that not only did groups form at around the same time as the European Economic Community's (EEC) own institutions, some formed as it became clear that the institutions' regulatory powers could significantly affect different interests in society (1970: 402). Moreover, the Commission's early preference for engaging with only EU level groups was important in the formation of umbrella- and federation-type groups (1970: 411). Some of the most prominent of and these organisations include Union of Industrial and Employers' Confederation of Europe (UNICE) and The European Trade Union Confederation (ETUC), representing the social partners – employers and trade unions respectively; the European Environmental Bureau (EEB) in the environment policy area; BEUC, the European Consumer Organisation. One of the largest confederated organisations (in terms of members) is the Civil Society Contact Group, which formed to co-ordinate responses to the Convention on the Future of the EU in 2002, and which has since developed a more permanent existence (EU Civil Society Contact Group 2011). The designation of European 'action years' has also resulted in the mobilisation of European level alliances around various worthy issues,[4] which are then charged with co-ordinating activities around the year and in turn generate demands for subsequent Commission action.[5]

The role of the EU institutions in contributing to the maintenance of a European civil society is perhaps most visible in the funding relationships that exist between them and groups representing a range of societal interests. Many civil society organisations that are active in Brussels are financially dependent upon the Union budget, often for a large part of their overall income. The European Youth Forum in 2005 estimated that around 80 per cent of their funding came from the EU,[6] and the Social Platform said it could be up to 90 per cent, with the director estimating that a similar proportion of his time was spent securing funding.[7] At least in the area of social policy these proportions are not atypical (Geyer 2001). There are, however, exceptions. In the area of environmental policy, Greenpeace has consistently refused to accept state – or in this case EU – funding and its non-membership of the EEB is due to this (Wurzel and Connelly 2011: 217). The issue of funding goes to the heart of questions about the separation between civil society and the state, with some arguing that state funding fundamentally compromises the independence of organisations and leads to their being co-opted by the state. On the other hand is the argument that only state funding can guarantee the independence of civil society organisations since without it they would be forced to seek funding from other, perhaps nefarious, sources and that in order to ensure a level playing field, the state ought to provide funding for diffuse interests such as consumers, people with disabilities, the socially excluded and so on as a way of mitigating the more powerful position of big business. The EU is not alone in providing funding for NGOs since many democratic states do the same, as do other transnational institutions including the World Bank and UN. Nevertheless, its unique legitimacy challenges account for criticisms that it is problematic when the organisations funded by the EU budget – drawn up by the Commission – promote messages congenial to the Commission (*The Economist* 2004).

One might expect a high degree of unity to characterise European civil society as a consequence of this fairly extensive involvement on the part of the institutions in its formation and maintenance. Yet the empirical picture seems to be of considerable diversity and variation. There is the issue of sheer size: although the adoption by the institutions of a definition which frames civil society largely in terms of umbrella organisations in Brussels, the number and variety of these organisations is significant. In a speech launching the European Transparency Initiative in 2005, Commissioner Siim Kallas, stated that 'at the moment there are about 15,000 lobbyists established in Brussels while around 2600 interest groups have a permanent office in Brussels' (Kallas 2005). This figure has been disputed by public affairs professionals (*Euractiv* 2008) and Berkhout and Lowery (2008) point out the difficulties of coming up with an accurate figure due to the possibility of double-counting economic interests and under-counting national interests and those who may use intermediaries. Nevertheless, Coen and Richardson (2009: 6) have suggested that the overall figure includes some 300 firms and 843 trade associations, 429 citizen interest bodies, 198 regions, 103 think tanks, 115 law firms and 153 public affairs companies. What this disaggregation also highlights is the range of organisations and the infinite variety of the interests that they represent. As a snapshot of the EU civil society landscape, it may not be a perfect pluralist picture but it offers a reminder that, as economic interests are joined by citizen or public interests, disunion is not necessarily undesirable.

In addition to considerable variety and fragmentation, disunion on the second dimension – in terms of a lack of progress towards strengthened democratic legitimacy – is also apparent and can be traced to the characteristics of the organisations involved. Armstrong illustrated this succinctly in a critique of the Commission's Governance White Paper, which 'instead of embracing a multi-form, multi-dimensional and multi-level conception of civil society ... offered is a strictly transnational relationship between transnational structures of governance and a transnationalised organised civil society which may suffer from the same sorts of legitimacy problems as transnational governance itself' (2002: 103). The European-level groups, favoured over national groups by the Commission in particular, tend not to admit individuals as members. Their members are national groups, and there is little direct engagement between the office in Brussels and individual members in the states. Illustrative of the lack of such 'downward' linkages is that public appeal campaigning tactics, which can be an important element of group activities in many democratic systems, are minimised by groups in Brussels. Greenwood (2003) cites the example of Greenpeace, a traditionally activist organisation, which has a policy office rather than a campaigning office in Brussels and whose activities are more on the side of 'building alliances and making private compromises with other policy players' (Greenwood 2003: 53). In addition to the structural weakness of the organisations in this respect, and in line with the oligarchical tendencies of organisation, the behaviour of actors within the organisations is also important. Group leaders, Saurugger (2007: 348) observed, had become increasingly professionalised, seeking to represent their constituents in an efficient way, in response to perceptions of greater access that this would afford. And rather than supply-side pressure from members for more participation Warleigh (2001) found evidence that chequebook participation is the preferred method of involvement, and that individual members in the member states were not interested in getting more involved in the activities of NGOs.

Debates on civil society and the EU's enfeebled democratic legitimacy

Disunion – in terms of a lack of agreement – certainly characterises assessments of the relationship between civil society and the EU's democratic legitimacy. Greenwood (2007b) described the various perspectives on this relationship as ranging on a spectrum from 'optimistic' to 'hostile'. Optimistic accounts included those which considered civil society organisations to play a significant role in bringing interests found within European society to the attention of the EU institutions; arguments that all citizens could benefit from the activism of NGOs in Brussels (Magnette 2003); and that groups can act as a kind of unofficial opposition in the absence of a clear government–opposition dynamic in the Parliament and Council. Hostile accounts have argued that it is the federated, and therefore elite, nature of some of the most influential groups in Brussels that exacerbates rather than ameliorates the distance between citizens and the EU (Warleigh 2001); and that informal governance networks of which they are often part blur lines of accountability and increase the opacity of the decision-making process. Intervening in these assessments of the relationship between civil society and democratic legitimacy is the 'type' of legitimacy being discussed, with a range of perspectives on whether civil society organisations contribute to input as well as output legitimacy, and if not whether output-oriented arguments are a sufficient basis for legitimacy.

A further faultline runs through the discussion on the relationship between civil society and democratic legitimacy in the EU, relating not to the type of legitimacy but the type of democracy. The so-called standard version of the democratic deficit, codified by Weiler et al. (1995), holds that the inability of the Parliament to fully hold the executive to account or initiate legislation, the lack of serious and programmatic political parties, the second order nature of elections, means that democratic control lost at the national level is not fully compensated for at the EU level. However, this view is based on a rather idealised picture of parliamentary democracy, which arguably not even national systems can measure up to entirely (Coultrap 1999). In the meantime, the academic debate on the democratic deficit has progressed: there is a sense that democracy at the EU level cannot and ought to not resemble national democratic structures and therefore an opportunity has opened up for a consideration of additional or alternative normative benchmarks. Empirically, various elements of the role and characteristics of civil society organisations can be found to correspond to different models of democracy.

The role of civil society organisations in contributing to the EU democracy outside formal representative structures has most often been framed in terms of participatory democracy. Many of the opportunities for participation in EU politics (the exceptions being voting in elections and referendums) have tended to favour organised rather than individual citizens (Nentwich 1998). The same could be said for the provisions of Article 11 of the Lisbon Treaty, which enshrines the principle of participatory democracy, alongside that of representative democracy, as a fundamental part of the Union's democratic life. Two of Article 11's four points are addressed directly to 'representative associations' and 'civil society'[8]. Another refers to consultation which is the dominant framework for relations between the Commission and civil society organisations. The fourth – the so-called citizen's initiative – is addressed to citizens but civil society organisations were heavily involved in consultations leading to the development of the regulation, and of the signature collection campaigns that had been launched either prior to or following the establishment of a legal basis, most were co-ordinated by civil society organisations.

Participatory models encourage a focus on the actual observable involvement of civil society organisations in EU political process, but the nature of their democratic contribution can be viewed in terms of the basis of, or meaning behind their involvement. The weaknesses of representative democracy at the EU level poses the question of whether it would be more reasonable for citizens to be involved in EU politics through associations instead of, or as well as through elected representatives. Indeed, the creation of the Economic and Social Committee, which as Armstrong (2002) points out, originates out of the consultative committee established under Article 18 of the European Coal and Steel Community, is an implicit acknowledgement of the need for some form of associational element to EU democracy. For early twentieth century pluralists such as G.D.H. Cole, the limits of representative structures in capturing the true nature of society was evident given that 'it is simply not true that the social relations of which a man is most directly and constantly aware are ... his relations with the state' (1920: 4). Smismans (2003: 486–487) has argued that this logic permeates both the European Economic and Social Committee's (ESC) and the Commission's ideas of the role of organisations in EU democracy.

A further interpretation of the relationship between civil society and EU democracy arises out of the argument that studies of EU politics have taken a 'deliberative turn' in recent years (Neyer 2006). The EU, it has been argued, lends itself to democratisation through deliberation because of its non-hierarchical, decentralised, multi-national and transnational character, and because of the existence of multiple and varied actors and interests (Curtin 2003). As Eriksen explains, emphasising the particular role of civil society in deliberation 'in the discourse approach it is the flow of free communication between the associational network of civil society and the parliamentary complex that constitutes and ensures popular sovereignty, not the formal aggregative procedures that the liberals place their trust in' (2000: 20–21). Whether civil society can strengthen the EU's democratic legitimacy in deliberative terms is itself a matter for discussion. In part, this may be due to the absence of viable opportunity structures for this kind of activity. Also, the 'informal' nature of politics (at least as perceived from the perspective of representative democracy) under a deliberative model is challenging from an accountability perspective, and for some, the way in which deliberation is actually manifested in EU politics is likely to prove too radical or counter-intuitive, as Greenwood notes: 'none other than comitology, that notorious system of inter-bureaucratic negotiation-diplomacy that even parliamentarians wish to abolish in the interest if democracy, is supposed to bring an element of democratically-legitimated politics into the Community' (Kohler-Koch, in Greenwood 2007b: 354).

What this brief reflection illustrates is the chronic 'disunion' on the question of whether and how civil society might enhance democratic legitimacy in the EU. Although it is possible to highlight empirical examples of the democratising effects of civil society organisations according to different models, they are of course based on values and therefore as 'blueprints' for reform progress is limited due to the differences in their descriptive and normative functions. Enacting the democratising reforms required by one model would mean making institutional changes that another model would consider 'undemocratic'. As Katz (2001: 74) pointed out, 'there appears to be disagreement over the proper meaning of democracy, and therefore not simply over what reforms would most improve democracy but indeed over whether particular reforms would make the Union more or less appropriately democratic'. In this context, Héritier (2003) has called for a 'composite democracy' whereby different parts of the EU's authority are subject to different legitimating criteria. What this implies is that the fundamental disunion that is inherent to that in the EU means that a single 'big idea' for legitimating it is unlikely to be found.

Conclusion

Despite some unity around the idea that civil society could enhance democracy in the EU, the hoped-for enhanced democratic legitimacy and increased solidarity between European societies has not transpired because of disagreements over what civil society is and what it does; and over what democracy means or ought to mean at the EU level. But the picture is not entirely bleak. Some incremental progress has been made: there is a treaty base for the consultation of societal interests; the civil society idea has contributed to the debate on whether democratic legitimacy in the EU may be found outside parliamentary structures; organisations provide a source of criticism of and opposition to the institutions even when they receive funding from the EU institutions. Furthermore, and following Held (2006), it may not be possible to resolve which model of democracy is most desirable or appropriate for the EU level, but in looking at the role and characteristics of European civil society, one can hope to illuminate why certain positions are more attractive than others. Finally, disunion proves challenging to the EU's enfeebled democratic legitimacy, but it may not be a wholly bad thing. 'Disunion' could be seen as a natural feature of a pluralist system of civil society organisations, highlighting that for the Union as a whole, it may be unavoidable but may also be desirable. Given the innate social and cultural diversity of Europe, a telos on European integration, and the absence of disunion, could be viewed as reductive, simplistic or not sufficiently sophisticated, and could even be harmful to those whose interests it does not represent.

Notes

1. These were 'fostering participatory democracy', 'representing the views of specific groups of citizens to the European institutions', contributing to policy making', 'contributing to project management', and 'contributing to European integration'.
2. 'Civil society includes the following: trade unions and employers' organisations ('social partners'); non-governmental organisations; professional associations; charities; grassroots organisations; organisations that involve citizens in local and municipal life with a particular contribution from churches and religious communities' (European Commission, 2001: 14). It referred to a more precise definition provided by the Economic and Social Committee in its 1999 'ESC Opinion on the role and contribution of civil society organisations in the building of Europe' (European Economic and Social Committee, 1999), which in addition to identifying civil society actors also discussed certain ideas which were components of the civil society concept. One such component was 'Solidarity': 'civil society is

underpinned by a "culture of solidarity"', which manifests itself in a willingness to place limits on one's own interests and take on obligations as the prerequisite for acting in the common interest' (1999: 32).
3. Interview with civil society organisation, 11 January 2005, Brussels.
4. 2011 being the European Year of Volunteering, 2012 of Active Ageing and Solidarity between the Generations, 2013 being the year of citizens.
5. Interview, AEDH, 16 November 2011, Brussels.
6. Interview, 11 January 2005, Brussels.
7. Interview, 17 February 2005, Brussels.
8. Parts one and two of Article 11 hold that 'The institutions shall, by appropriate means, give citizens and representative associations the opportunity to make known and publicly exchange their views in all areas of Union action' and that 'The institutions shall maintain an open, transparent and regular dialogue with representative associations and civil society" respectively (European Council, 2007).

Bibliography

Armstrong, K. (2002) 'Rediscovering Civil Society: The European Union and the White Paper on Governance', *European Law Journal*, 8(1) 102–132.

Berkhout, J. and Lowery, D. (2008) 'Counting Organised Interests in the European Union: A Comparison of Data Sources', *Journal of Public Policy*, 15(4) 489–513.

Bouwen, P. (2004) 'The Logic of Access to the European Parliament: Business Lobbying in the Committee on Economic and Monetary Affairs', *Journal of Common Market Studies*, 42 (3) 473–495.

Coen, D. and Richardson, J. (2009) 'Learning to Lobby the European Union: 20 years of Change', in D. Coen and J. Richardson, (eds) *Lobbying in the European Union: Institutions, Actors and Issues* (Oxford: Oxford University Press), pp. 3–15.

Cole, G.D.H. (1920) *Social Theory* (London: Metheun).

Coultrap, J. (1999) 'From Parliamentarism to Pluralism: Models of Democracy and the European Union's Democratic Deficit', *Journal of Theoretical Politics* 11, 107–135.

Council of the European Union (2011) Council Statement on the 'Transparency Register'. Brussels, 23 June 2001.

Curtin, D. (2003) 'Private Interest Representation or Civil Society Deliberation? A Contemporary Dilemma for European Union Governance', *Social and Legal Studies*, 21 (1) 55–75.

Edwards, M. (2009) *Civil Society: Theory and Practice* (Cambridge: Polity).

Eriksen, E. (2000) 'Deliberative Supranationalism in the EU', in E. Eriksen and J. Fossum (eds), *Democracy in the European Union. Integration through Deliberation* (London: Routledge), pp. 42–64.

Euractiv (2008) 'EU Lobbyists Scramble Over Their Exact Numbers', available at: http://www.euractiv.com/pa/eu-lobbyists-scramble-exact-numbers/article-173152, 10 June, 2008. Last accessed 30 November 2011.

European Commission (2000) *The Commission and NGOs: Building a Stronger Partnership*, Brussels, 18 January 2000.

European Commission (2001) *European Governance: A White Paper,* Brussels, 25 July 2001.

European Commission (2005) *The Commission's Contribution to the Period of Reflection and Beyond: Plan D for Democracy, Dialogue and Debate,* Brussels, 13 October 2005.

European Commission (2006) *White Paper on a European Communication Policy,* Brussels, 1 February 2006.

European Commission (2011) *The European Commission and Civil Society,* http: //ec.europa.eu/civil_society/apgen_En.htm, last accessed 24 November 2011.

European Council (2001a) *The Treaty of Nice amending the Treaty on European Union, the Treaties Establishing the European Communities and Certain Related Acts. Final Act and Declarations,* Nice, 26 February 2001.

European Council (2001b) *Laeken Declaration on the Future of the European Union,* Brussels, 15 December 2001.

European Council (2007) *The Treaty of Lisbon amending the Treaty on European Union and the Treaty Establishing the European Community,* Lisbon, 13 December 2007.

European Economic and Social Committee (1999) *The Role and Contribution of Civil Society Organisations in the Building of Europe,* ESC Opinion. Brussels, 22 September 1999.

European Parliament (2001) *Committee on Constitutional Affairs. Final Report on the Commission White Paper on European Governance,* Brussels, 15 November 2001.

EU Civil Society Contact Group (2011) 'About Us' – 'History', http://www.act4europe.org/code/en/about.asp?Page=261&menuPage=261, accessed 25 November 2011.

Finke, B. (2007) 'Civil Society Participation in EU Governance', *Living Reviews in European Governance,* 2 (2) cited 30 November 2011, http://europeangovernance.livingreviews.org/Articles/lreg-2007-2/.

Geyer, R. (2001) 'Can EU Social NGOs Co-operate to Promote EU Social Policy?', *Journal of Social Policy,* 30 (3) 477–493.

Greenwood, J. (2003) 'The World of EU NGOs and Interest Representation' in *NGOs, Democratisation and the Regulatory State* (London: European Policy Forum).

Greenwood, J. (2007a) *Interest Representation in the European Union* (Basingstoke: Palgrave Macmillan).

Greenwood, J. (2007b) 'Review Article: Organized Civil Society and Democratic Legitimacy in the European Union', *British Journal of Political Science,* 37, 333–357.

Held, D. (2006) *Models of Democracy* (Cambridge: Polity).

Héritier, A. (2003) 'Composite Democracy in Europe. The Role of Transparency and Access to Information', *Journal of European Public Policy,* 6, 814–833.

Kallas, S. (2005) 'The Need for a European Transparency Initiative', Speech to the European Foundation for Management. Nottingham, 5 March 2005.

Katz, R. (2001) 'Models of Democracy: Elite attitudes and the democratic deficit in the European Union', *European Union Politics,* 2 (1) 55–79.

Kirchner, E. (1980) 'International Trade Union Collaboration and the Prospect for European Industrial Relations', *West European Politics,* 3 (1) 124–137.

Magnette, P. (2003) 'European Governance and Civic Participation: Beyond Elite Citizenship?', *Political Studies,* 51 (1) 144–160.

Mazey, S. (1995) 'The Development of EU Equality Policies: Bureaucratic Expansion on Behalf of Women?' *Public Administration,* 73 (4) 591–610.

Nentwich, M. (1998) 'Opportunity Structures for Citizens' Participation: the Case of the European Union', in A. Weale and M. Nentwich (eds) *Political Theory and the European Union,* (London: Routledge).

Neyer, J. (2006) 'The Deliberative Turn in Integration Theory', *Journal of European Public Policy,* 13 (5) 779–791.

Richardson, J. (2007) 'Organized Interests in the European Union' in K. E. Jorgensen, M. Pollack and B. Rosamond (eds) *Handbook of European Union Politics* (London: Sage), pp. 231–246.

Saurugger, S. (2007) 'Democratic "Misfit"? Conceptions of Civil Society Participation in France and the European Union', *Political Studies,* 55 (2) 384–404.

Saurugger, S. (2010) 'The Social Construction of the Participatory Turn: the Emergence of a Norm in the European Union', *European Journal of Political Research,* 49, 471–495.

Sidjanski, D. (1970) 'Pressure Groups and the European Economic Community', in C. Cosgrove and K. Twitchett (eds) *The New International Actors* (London: Macmillan), pp. 222–236.

Smismans, S. (2003) 'European Civil Society: Shaped by Discourses and Institutional Interests', *European Law Journal,* 9 (4) 482–504.

Taylor, C. (1995) *Philosophical Arguments* (Cambridge MA: Harvard University Press).

The Economist (2004) 'A Rigged Dialogue with Society', Charlemagne, 21 October 2004.

Van Deth, J. and Maloney, W. (2008) 'Introduction: from bottom-up and top-down towards multi-level governance in Europe', in W. Maloney and J. Van Deth (eds) *Civil Society and Governance in Europe* (Cheltenham: Edward Elgar), pp. 3–18.

Warleigh, A. (2001) 'Europeanizing Civil Society: NGOs as Agents of Political Socialisation', *Journal of Common Market Studies,* 39 (4) 619–639.

Weiler, J. H. H. with Haltern, U. R. and Mayer, F. C. (1995) 'European Democracy and its Critique', *West European Politics,* 18 (3) 4–39.

Wurzel, R. and Connelly, J (2011) 'Environmental NGOs. Taking a Lead?', in R. Wurzel and J. Connelly (eds) *The European Union as a Leader in International Climate Change Politics* (London, Routledge).

Young, I.M. (2000) *Inclusion and Democracy* (Oxford: Oxford University Press).

Zimmer, A. and Freise, M. (2008) 'Bringing Society Back In: Civil Society, Social Capital and the Third Sector', in W. Maloney and J. Van Deth (eds) *Civil Society and Governance in Europe* (Cheltenham: Edward Elgar), pp. 19–42.

4
An Obdurately National Party Politics

Robert Ladrech

Despite early neo-functionalist expectations of a transfer of loyalties to a supranational level in which the nascent parliamentary groups of the European Coal and Steel Community (ECSC) Common Assembly could represent proto-European parties (Haas 1958; Lindberg 1963), party politics remains overwhelmingly encased within national contexts. As for evidence of the Europeanisation of national party politics, paraphrasing Smith (1989) regarding change in western European party systems, there has been 'peripheral' change with the 'core' remaining intact. Following the Europeanisation theme, there is no argument that the European Union (EU), especially since the Single European Act (SEA) in the late 1980s, has had an impact on the domestic institutions and policies of its member states (Bulmer and Lequesne 2005); what is more surprising is the degree to which this interwoven relationship between the EU and member states is *not* reflected in the competitive politics of member states nor in the organisational structure of the parties themselves.

To be clear, there do exist transnational party federations representing four party families: the European Green Party, the Party of European Socialists (PES), the European Alliance of Liberals and Radicals (ALDE) and the European People's Party (EPP), the latter originally representative of Christian democratic parties but today including some liberal and conservative parties; it is their general *irrelevance* to national party politics that is the issue when considering the continuing unchallenged primacy of national party politics. This is not to deny that these transnational party federations, especially the three representing the major national parties from the centre-left through to the centre-right, have not had some influence, and in the case of post-Communist Party institutionalisation, their role was quite tangible (Pridham 2001); it is simply that their level of activity – the transnational and the supra-national – does not impinge on the national dimension of party politics. In other words, although one can make the argument of a partisan dimension at the European level, including the internal politics of the European Parliament (EP), the neo-functional magic of 'spill-over' into the domestic level of party politics has not transpired.

How do we explain this obdurately national character of party politics? Furthermore, what does the disjuncture between EU policy competence (and even leadership in some areas) and the national focus of party politics mean for EU legitimacy? In this chapter, it is argued that national party leaderships – and this includes party leaders as prime ministers – have maintained the primacy of national party politics due to the uncertainty that having a more direct link with EU level political dynamics might generate for the domestic competitive position of national parties. In so doing, as the EU has expanded its policy mandates since the Maastricht Treaty in 1992, the politicisation of the EU has not been integrated within national politics – except at the margins of the party systems by euro-sceptic parties – and this has in turn undermined the legitimacy of the European project itself. Not only has there not been a 'spill-over' of political loyalties to the supra-national level, instead pressure for re-nationalising EU policies, growing euro-scepticism as well as a de-politicisation of national politics (Mair 2007a) appears to be the unintended consequence of this state of affairs. Finally, if we accept that at least until the Maastricht Treaty ratification that a 'permissive consensus' (Lindberg and Scheingold 1970) existed, thereby allowing key decisions to be made by political elites without taking into account their domestic reception (and ratification), and that since this time the consensus has by and large dissipated without some new form of legitimate decision-making filling the void, then the present condition injects huge uncertainty into inter-governmental bargaining itself when the need for an historic deal is necessary to continue the integration process. The rhetoric of national politicians, both centre-left as well as centre-right, has begun to display more nationalist or defensive posturing, adding weight to the 'sovereignty' aspect of the EU at the expense of 'solidarity'.

Why the persistence of national party politics?

Hix and Lord (1997) listed the key criteria for 'party democracy' and applied this to the EU. In most of the five criteria, the answer explaining why this had yet to become instrumental at the European level rested with the role of national parties, whether it ranged from the view by national party leaderships of the second-order nature of EP elections to the resistance to more organisational cohesion for transnational parties. As Hix and Lord recognised, EP party groups and transnational party federations have developed to the extent they have by consent of national parties, but their impact remains marginal to national politics. The first question to answer, however, is why the limited development at the European level was allowed, together with the development of some modest positions within the national party organisation. The second question is why, since the 1980s, have national party leaderships continued to resist a more substantial adaptation to the influence of the EU, if after all, the 'EU confronts domestic political parties with a new structure of threats and opportunities' (Hix and Lord 1997: 5).

Political participation at the European level: why engage?

Transnational party federations' initial formation was instigated by the decision to hold direct elections for the EP in 1979. All of the major parties in the EC fielded candidates for this election (whether they belonged to one of the three party federations or not, e.g. British Conservatives or French Gaullists). One argument as to why national parties bothered to invest time and resources is that the opportunity of contesting an election stimulated the party goal of winning votes (Carter et al. 2007). In other words, following the thesis by Müller and Strøm (1999) that parties are motivated by the goals of votes, office and or policy, Carter et al. suggest the fact that direct elections to the EP would be held explains national party 'adaptation'. The problem with this thesis is that in the national context, winning votes leads to an even greater goal, whether it is forming government directly or as a coalition partner, or at least, through size of parliamentary representation, affecting policy development. In the end, though, the bottom line is that elections to a parliament determine the make-up of government. As was obviously the case in 1979 (and formally so still today, though the Lisbon Treaty has elevated the significance of EP election results), elections to the EP do not determine a European government, or the composition of the Commission to be exact. An EP election in a single member state does not determine the size of an EP parliamentary group, as this is dependent on all other member state elections. Direct election of the EP is a very weak rationale for parties, especially mainstream parties, to become involved simply as a result of their primary goal of winning votes.

What then may explain this behaviour? Two reasons can be advanced. One, as the decision to allow direct elections to the EP was a result of an inter-governmental bargain from an EC summit (Dinan 1999), participation in elections was therefore a state-sanctioned action. Despite the opposition or at least ambivalence of some member states to a more legitimate EP (e.g. France and the UK), it was not agitation on the part of supporters for more democratic and legitimate supranational decision-making by an elected EP that won the day; once the decision was reached in the European Council, mainstream parties were politically (not legally) mandated to participate. The argument of a motivation by the vote maximisation goal is further undermined by the decidedly modest efforts by mainstream parties to actually win votes, as the continuing second-order election status of EP elections demonstrates (Schmitt 2005).

A second argument explaining why mainstream national parties took part en masse in EP elections, and continue to do so despite the weak rewards, is that they cannot afford *not* to do so. This argument invokes the work of Panebianco (1988) into party organisational change, especially on the interaction of party goals and party environments. Adapting the EU to the party change thesis as an environment from which a stimulus to a party may emerge, it is clear that regardless of the power of the EP from 1979 onwards, the external environment – the EU – was now intruding into competitive party politics in general, and from the perspective of national party leaderships, with unknown consequences. Uncertainty, unpredictability or growing complexity in a party's environment can stimulate a response according to Panebianco: 'Unpredictability pushes the organization towards internal specialization, i.e. to the multiplication of specialized roles dealing with different aspects of the environment, in the hope of dominating it' (1988: 205). Providing party representatives to the EP, and further, creating a few specialised roles within the national party organisation such as a European secretary as well as statutory changes obliging the party's EP delegation leader to sit, *ex officio*, on the national party's executive committee, are all examples of national parties making just enough of an effort to establish a presence and an 'organizational relay' (Panebianco 1988) in case the EP were to develop substantial influence or a truly European party system were to arise, both intruding and thereby complicating domestic affairs. This perspective is further strengthened by the fact that all of these personnel have been essentially 'ring-fenced' from the operation of the national party, internally as well as in domestic politics (Raunio 2000). Therefore, the national party response to direct election of Members of European Parliament (MEPs) was defensive in nature, providing personnel because not to do so had unknown consequences. It is this limited adaptation or Europeanisation by national parties (Ladrech, 2007a, 2007b) that partially explains the reluctance of national party leaderships to integrate EU policy-making into domestic politics, despite the exponential growth of EU policy influence since the mid-1980s.

Europeanisation and national party politics constraints on adaptation

The development of the EU's policy competence since the SEA has had direct and indirect impacts on national parties. Examples of direct impact include 'the emergence of new anti-European parties, or anti-European sentiments within existing political parties' (Mair, 2007b: 157). Examples of an indirect impact are those that affect the national state, especially policy-making, and consequently the ramifications of these changes may influence national parties, especially mainstream parties. Mair includes 'hollowing out of national party competition, constraints on domestic decision making, devaluation of national electoral competition' (2007b: 157). These indirect pressures underpin the party Europeanisation thesis (Ladrech 2002), that is, it represents the environmental stimulus which may pressure party leaderships to adapt aspects of party organisation, programme, party competition strategy, etc. Mair's definition of indirect impact centres on the changed nature of national policy-making, such that key decisions are shared between national and EU actors, but more importantly it is national executives rather than national parliaments that are involved. In this respect, parties find themselves removed to a certain degree from the policy-making process, with the EU level acting as a platform for other national interests to be integrated into the inter-governmental and supranational process. For some, de-parliamentarisation is a result (O'Brennan and Raunio 2007), which itself further aggravates the democratic deficit within the national political system. Mair's definition also claims an indirect impact on competitive party politics, as increasing areas of policy are transferred or shared with Brussels they are no longer legitimate for purely partisan contestation; this is the so-called hollowing out of party competition. Diminishing choice in policy areas can also appear as an emasculation of the national state, a perception that fuels euro-sceptic nationalist sentiments. All of these examples of pressure on national party leaderships could lead to some significant change; on the one hand in the way that national party politics is practiced, with the EU dimension integrated in a more constructive manner. On the other hand, it could result in a more balanced integration of the EU dimension such that European level partisan politics gains a profile that diminishes the primacy of national politics, at least to the extent it has been practiced until the present (Bartolini 2005).

The fact that neither of these hypothesised changes or adaptations has occurred, despite the growing constraint on national political leaders to fulfil their EU level commitments, undermines not just EU but national legitimacy as well. What can explain this impasse? Three levels of analysis are involved in answering this question, which will be tackled in turn. Briefly, the literature on party change alluded to above concerning party goals is invoked to explain internal party constraints; second, national level factors including the role of the media and the nature of executive–legislative relations; and third, the unique nature of 'politics' such as it is practiced within the EU policy- and decision-making process. All three dimensions combine to produce a situation in which national party politics continues to be practiced as if the EU had no bearing at all in national politics and elections, as if the distinction between domestic politics and foreign policy (i.e. involvement with the EU on the part of national government actors) was one of complete separation, rather than one of interdependence (see Chapter 11 by Menon).

Party organisational factors

Party leaderships' perceptions regarding the uncertainty of European integration outcomes is a powerful factor in preserving the *status quo* in any discussion about the integration of EU dynamics into domestic politics. More specifically, we can return to the party goals thesis outlined by Müller and Strøm (1999), namely votes, office and policy, and add party cohesion, especially when considering a potentially divisive issue such as European integration (Steenbergen and Scott 2004). In their theory of party change, Harmel and Janda (1994) suggest that an external stimulus may impact a party's primary goal, and thereby trigger a change or adaptation. If we confine our argument to the period of the 1990s to the present, that is, a period of a much more enhanced post-SEA European Union in terms of policy competence, how might the EU impact the four party goals listed? Vote maximisation as a primary goal with regard to the EU would suggest that either a strongly pro- or anti-EU position may be attractive in terms of party competition. Salience theory (Budge et al. 2001) refines this perspective by bringing into the picture the position of the rival party or parties. In the case of a divisive issue such as the EU, if the other major party in a two-party system refuses to be drawn into a debate over the issue, any anticipated competitive edge is absent. The British Conservative Party campaign in 2001 under then party leader Hague to 'save the pound' is an example of just such an experience (see Chapter 16 by Norton). As for office-seeking, in a multi-party system where attaining office will usually require a coalition partner, a pronounced anti-EU position, when other prospective parties are pro-EU, may damage coalition potential. The goal of policy-seeking is least likely to be impacted by the EU as a single party in a single member state cannot realistically promise to change EU policy; this last point pertains more to mainstream parties than parties on the left or right margins of the party system, for whom resistance to EU policy, for example immigration policy, is part of their partisan identity. Finally, with regard to party cohesion, party leaderships have an incentive to avoid the EU as an issue if it is internally divisive, as a divided party sends mixed cues to its voters (Gabel and Shreve 2007), thus undermining the goal of vote maximisation.

As far as the analysis based on party change and party goals is concerned, mainstream political parties have no incentive to openly engage with the EU. Political parties are conservative organisations, and only change with great reluctance and again only when their primary goals are threatened. The direct and indirect impacts listed by Mair (2007b) may be evaluated in terms of their 'threat' level. As for direct impacts, the emergence of euro-sceptic parties, as opposed to euro-sceptic attitudes, has not been enough to upset most patterns of party competition, whether in older or newer member states. They have by and large gained a foothold in only a small minority of member states, and usually not enough to exercise any substantial influence. This state of affairs is present in post-communist party systems as well as in older member states, where the patterns of party-EU relations appear similar, i.e. the limited nature of Europeanisation (Lewis and Mansfeldova 2006; Haughton 2011). More prevalent is the incorporation of euro-sceptic positions by populist right-wing parties on issues such as immigration, and by populist left-wing parties on issues of economic liberalisation (Hooghe and Marks 2009). Even so, these parties exercise influence only in small minority of member states, Austria and Denmark, from the right-wing during the first decade of the 2000s the exception proving the rule. Euro-sceptic attitudes within mainstream parties follows the pattern just mentioned, but is managed by party leaderships as a party cohesion matter and is only inflamed during extraordinary moments, such as a treaty referendum. Regarding indirect impacts, such as the 'hollowing out' of party competition, the removal of areas of policy competition affects mainstream parties alike, and there is certainly no incentive in lamenting the fact of a shrinking basis with which to distinguish one's party from rivals. The narrowing of national government policy maneuvrability in those areas transferred to or shared with the EU is the great unspoken fact of national politics. Again, what emerges from this discussion is that the 'threat level' from the EU onto domestic politics is low from the perspective of party leaderships for whom any substantial change from 'politics as usual' holds uncertain outcomes.

National system factors

If internal party organisational factors militate against any substantial change with regard to the influence of the EU in domestic politics, there are also systemic factors embedded at the national level that contribute to the status quo. One key factor in terms of influencing attitudes towards the EU is the media, both print and electronic. Research investigating the effect of how news about the EU is framed and its consequent impact on attitudes demonstrates a clear link. In general, studies show a negative framing of the EU in the news and public attitudes, especially during EP election campaigns (De Vreese et al. 2006). Finally, apart from when the EU is reported in the news as a conflict – e.g. during EU budget negotiations – it is usually allotted minimum attention during EP election campaigns. The sum of these remarks demonstrates that the national media play an important part in publicising (or not) the EU to national electorates, and it is therefore not too surprising that most voters have a low opinion of the EU and very little knowledge of its role in the policies that affect them.

We have already discussed the lack of incentives at the individual national party level to engage with the EU because it represents a Pandora's box of political uncertainties. In keeping with the thesis of national party leadership control over how the EU is managed in national politics, another factor is the nature of national executive–legislative relations. On the one hand, national executives have an incentive to restrict the scope of outside involvement in inter-governmental bargaining in the Council of Ministers and the European Council for efficiency reasons. By virtue of their privileged position interacting at the supranational level in the Council and through their representatives to the COREPER, national executives have an advantage in terms of information and bargaining strategies. Having to share decision-making with their respective parliaments is a decidedly sub-optimal position from their perspective, and the literature is clear regarding the relatively weak position of national parliaments (or their EU affairs committee) vis-à-vis the national executive in EU policy-making. This represents the heart of the de-parliamentarisation thesis (O'Brennan and Raunio 2007).

National executives are, of course, party politicians, yet significant mobilisation within their parties to re-balance this relationship is absent. Further, within national parliaments, the EU is treated mostly within the logic of government–opposition dynamics (Holzhacker 2007). Most national parliamentary EU affairs committees, apart from Denmark and a couple of other member states, are weak in comparison to policy-oriented standing committees. In other words, there is an absence of political attention given to the EU between the executive and the legislature and within most national legislatures. There are informal methods that have arisen in member states within relatively strong legislatures (e.g. Germany) such that parliamentary leaders are informed of government positions in EU matters, but again this relationship arises from the nature of executive–legislative relations in general, not because of the perceived importance of EU policy-making per se. We see, consequently, two powerful national structural impediments to the integration of the EU into domestic politics, the lack of consistent reporting of EU decision-making in the news and national political-institutional factors that make knowledge of the EU a highly specialised – and uncontested – fact.

EU system factors

In 2006, Bartolini and Hix debated the merits of politicising the EU in national politics. Hix argued that transnational political parties should be strengthened to the extent that elections to the EP could be viewed as a classic contest between left and right, thus making the politics of EU policy-making more understandable to national electorates. The democratic deficit of the EU would be reduced, Hix argued, by the fact that EP elections run on this basis would increase turnout, and secondly, national parties would now have to communicate their positions on EU policy in a clear and open manner. Bartolini, however, argued that awakening the 'sleeping giant' of public opinion (van der Eijk and Franklin 2007) regarding the EU had unforeseen consequences, not just for national parties and their patterns of competition but also for the EU itself, as public opinion might in fact support *anti-EU* parties to a great extent. He was also doubtful as to the efficacy of depending on transnational parties to construct a European-level party system as well as whether EU policies were sufficient in number to align themselves into a left versus right pattern. What this debate highlighted, for purposes of this discussion, is the problem of translating the politics at the European level into a format that concisely integrates various policies into a binary competition, as historically the left–right cleavage has been able to do.

This difference in the contestable content of EU policy issues on a left–right basis is not the sole problem of integrating the EU level of politics into the national framework. Institutionally, the inter-governmental dimension of EU politics, represented in the Council of Ministers as well as in European Council summits, also occludes decision-making from all but EU experts. Although the players in inter-governmental bargaining are, by and large, party politicians, their mandate at this level of politics is national rather than partisan, especially on sensitive issues. The left–right contest in the EP is itself altered on issues requiring a qualified majority, and historically this has been supplied by a qualified majority (PES plus EPP). Transforming the EU into a majoritarian and parliamentary system, which in principle would indeed allow national electorates to translate EU politics into a more familiar pattern, has the potential to de-stabilise and thereby de-legitimise the EU (Dehousse 1995). This is because national interests represented in the inter-governmental mode of policy- and decision-making would be subject to a majority arising from EP elections. Noting the pattern of national government incumbent losses at EP elections – the mid-term election phenomenon, one can easily imagine a centre-left EP and Commission versus a centre-right Council; although this can occur at present, it is not an insurmountable political obstacle to member state governments as it could be under a more Westminster-style of EU government. The potential for constitutional crises arising from such a situation is tangible.

Three different, but interrelated, political and structural impediments therefore explain the nature of the party-political status quo as it relates to the EU and national party politics. Further substantiating this argument is the *lack* of divergence between post-communist parties in Central and Eastern Europe and those in the older EU member states, suggesting that the rules and logic of contemporary party systems remain immune from substantial intervention from EU considerations. In many post-communist states, when the goal of joining the EU was seemingly paramount during the 1990s until accession in 2004, the main parties of government in fact colluded to push legislation through their parliaments without debate, so as to expedite the accession process (see Chapter 19 by Dimitrov).

The opening reference to Smith (1989) was concerned with the lay of the western European party system landscape after the upheavals from the late 1960s through to the early 1980s, where new issues, challenger parties, declining turnout, etc., had characterised national party politics.

The underlying question he answered was based on the Lipset and Rokkan (1967) thesis of 'frozen' party systems, thus his comment that the 'core' remained intact referred to the primacy of mainstream national parties as well as the left–right, or class, cleavage. Again, applying his verdict to the relationship between national party politics and the EU, it would seem that after the direct elections to the EP in 1979 and the limited organisational enhancement of transnational party federations by the early 1990s, the relationship can also be characterised as 'frozen'. Although the EU has, under the Maastricht and subsequent treaties, expanded the scope of its policy competence, and the EP the scope of its institutional influence through co-decision and its widened application through to the Lisbon Treaty, national party politics carries on as before, with only the odd hiccup of a politicised EU intruding into domestic politics at the time of a referendum. What are the consequences then, of this obdurately national party politics for the democratic legitimacy of the EU, if not the European integration process itself?

Democratic legitimacy, the EU and national politics

Political systems, especially those for which at least a modicum of popular legitimacy is crucial to their maintenance, have seldom been engineered from scratch without such support. Even the contested establishment of the federal system of the United States toward the end of the eighteenth century required at least the popular election of the president to help legitimate the new institutions. The European integration project's founders made the fateful choice, perhaps inevitable, that economic integration would precede political integration. Stumbling blocks along its development have included an inter-governmental (or more accurately, French) backlash, i.e. the empty chair crisis and the subsequent Luxembourg Compromise (see Chapter 5 by Hayward). Forward leaps such as the SEA were based on a collective sense of threat emanating from without – economic dominance by the United States and Japan; and perhaps another leap forward is imminent, this time in economic governance, but again due to a collective sense of threat from without – financial markets operating in a near-unregulated international capital market. At each leap forward, proposals were made to add a dose of popular or at least representative legitimacy to the enhanced institutions of the EU, usually emanating from the EP and allied member state governments such as Germany. The Commission has evolved into another supranational actor seeking a stronger basis for EU legitimacy, especially as it is the EU institution which has most to lose in any legitimacy crisis of the European project. The Commission strategy to facilitate a 'European Public Sphere' is part of its contribution to what it acknowledges is a potential legitimacy crisis. What we can say regarding the persistence of unreconstructed national and European political arenas is that an increasingly unhealthy symbiosis is emerging, with issues of legitimacy circulating between the two, though for reasons elaborated above, any action to address the relationship depends on national political leaders.

A symbiosis suggests that two different organisms (here organisations) exist in a close, mutual and dependent relationship. The Europeanisation literature has attempted to investigate how the growing interdependence of the two political systems – the EU and national – has transformed parts of the member states themselves. What is also becoming clear to many political analysts is that a number of negative symptoms have emerged from this symbiotic relationship for the member states, such as de-politicisation and de-parliamentarisation, which impact national legitimacy. So the 'frozen' if not obdurate nature of national party politics has implications for the EU's democratic legitimacy as well as its own. Negative media reporting, occasional remarks by national politicians that 'Brussels made me do it' with regard to unpopular policy implementation, sniping by euro-sceptic parties and the lack of a discourse justifying EU membership (Schmidt, 2010), all combine to produce, as Hayward describes in the Chapter 1, a situation in which 'the peoples are becomingly increasingly eurosceptical, less inclined to vote for the European Parliament and more inclined to abstain or reject proposals in referendums when these are conceded or required' (Hayward 2012). The rhetoric of national leaders has itself evolved to exhibit a more (soft) nationalist tone, increasing the 'sovereignty' emphasis in the EU at the expense of 'solidarity'. Where political parties had provided a linkage between the governed and the government in the national context, their ability to do so in a national-EU context, however this would be constructed, is constrained by party leaderships' fear of the loss of national sovereignty. Where an environmental stimulus could conceivably trigger an adaptational response, in the case of national party politics and the EU, stalemate characterises the present predicament.

Conclusion

In the 1970s and 1980s, party politicians, mostly from liberal and Christian democratic parties in Western Europe, consistently made the case that a federal European union was the *finalité politique* for the European integration project. They supported direct elections and expanded powers for the EP, and a role for transnational party federations as linkages between the peoples of Europe and EU institutions. Although one might still hear the phrase, in relation to one of the EU's more significant problems, including the 2011 eurozone crisis (see Chapters 12 and 18 by Dyson and Bull, respectively), that the solution 'is not less Europe but more Europe', the days when the European integration process generated an image of a juggernaut are over. Even within the transnational EPP, once the standard bearer for Euro-federalism, the nationalist positioning has relegated 'closer European union' to a mere footnote in their manifesto for EP elections. Perhaps today's national political leaders are of a generation that lacks the life experiences that shaped the commitment to European unity by its founders through to the likes of Kohl and Mitterrand.

Hix and Lord opened their book *Political Parties in the European Union* stating that 'EU politicians are party politicians', and it is certainly the case that party politics is present in various formats within the EU and member states. Whereas the early supporters of federal union saw parties as positive instruments for their goal, today, national party politics, in its resistance to fundamental change, now represents a barrier to that goal. In late 2011, when the very existence of the eurozone, and by implication the EU itself, was being tested, the distinction between the EU's tendency to balance 'sovereignty' with 'solidarity' was brought into stark relief. However, as predicted by the logic of national party immunity from EU intrusions, the response by most national politicians, especially government incumbents, was to seek defensive national mechanisms and thereby devaluing 'solidarity' to a greater extent than has been the case for decades (see Chapter 13 by Parsons). Though in different circumstances, both the British and German governments maintained an approach to the crisis led by national considerations, thus highlighting that any 'more union' will emphasise the inter-governmental sovereignty approach to the political identity of the EU.

Bibliography

Bartolini, S. (2005) *Restructuring Europe: Centre Formation, System Building, and Political Structuring between the Nation State and the European Union* (Oxford: Oxford University Press).

Bartolini, S. and S. Hix (2006) Notre Europe, Paris, Policy Paper no. 19, 'The Right or Wrong Sort of Medicine for the EU?

Budge, I., H.-D. Klingemann, A. Volkens, J. Bara and E. Tanenbaum, with R.C. Fording, D. J. Hearl, H. M. Kim, M. McDonald and S. Mendez (2001) *Mapping Policy Preferences, Estimates for Parties, Electors, and Governments, 1945–1998* (Oxford: Oxford University Press).

Bulmer, S. and C. Lequesne (2005) *The European Union and the Member States* (Oxford: Oxford University Press).

Carter, E., K.R. Luther and T. Poguntke (2007) 'European Integration and Internal Party Dynamics' in T. Poguntke, N. Aylott, E. Carter, R. Ladrech and K. R. Luther (eds) *Europeanization and National Political Parties: Adaptation and Power* (Abingdon: Routledge), pp. 1–27.

Dehousse, R. (1995) 'Constitutional Reform in the European Community: Are There Alternatives to the Majoritariam Avenue?', *West European Politics* 18 (3): 118–136.

Dinan, D. (1999) *Ever Closer Union: An Introduction to European Integration* (Basingstoke: Macmillan).

Eijk, C. van der and M. Franklin (2007) 'The Sleeping Giant: Potential for Political Mobilization of Disaffection with European Integration', in W. van der Brug and C. van der Eijk (eds) *European Elections & Domestic Politics: Lessons from the Past and Scenarios for the Future* (Notre Dame, IN: University of Notre Dame Press), pp. 189–208.

Gabel, M. and K. Scheve (2007) 'Mixed Messages: Party Dissent and Mass Opinion on European Integration', *European Union Politics* 8 (1): 37–59.

Haas, E. (1958) *The Uniting of Europe* (Stanford: Stanford University Press).

Harmel, R. and K. Janda (1994) 'An Integrated Theory of Party Goals and Party Change', *Journal of Theoretical Politics* 6 (3): 259–287.

Haughton, T. (2011) *Party Politics in Central and Eastern Europe: Does EU Membership Matter?* (Abingdon: Routledge).

Hayward, J. (2012) 'Introduction. Union Without Consensus', this volume.

Hix, S. and C. Lord (1997) *Political Parties in the European Union* (London: Macmillan).

Holzhacker, R. (2007) 'Parliamentary Scrutiny', in P. Graziano and M.P. Vink (eds) *Europeanization: New Research Agendas* (Basingstoke: Palgrave), pp. 141–153.

Hooghe, L. and G. Marks (2009) 'A Postfunctionalist Theory of European Integration: From Permissive Consensus to Constraining Dissensus' *British Journal of Political Science* 39 (1): 1–23.

Ladrech, R. (2002) 'Europeanization and Political Parties: Towards a Framework for Analysis' *Party Politics* 8 (4): 389–403.

Ladrech, R. (2007a) 'Europeanization and National Party Organization: Limited but Appropriate Adaptation?', in T. Poguntke, N. Aylott, E. Carter, R. Ladrech and K. R. Luther (eds) *The Europeanization of National Political Parties: Power and Organizational Adaptation* (Abingdon: Routledge), pp. 211–229.

Ladrech, R. (2007b) 'National Political Parties and European Governance', *West European Politics* 30 (5): 945–960.

Lewis, P. and Z. Mansfeldova (eds) (2006) *The European Union and Party Politics in Central and Eastern Europe* (Basingstoke: Palgrave).

Lindberg, L. (1963) *The Political Dynamics of European Economic Integration* (Stanford: Stanford University Press).

Lindberg, L. and S. Scheingold (1970) *Europe's Would-Be Polity: Patterns of Change in the European Community* (Englewood Cliffs, NJ: Prentice Hall).

Lipset, S.M. and S. Rokkan (1967) *Party Systems and Voter Alignments: Cross-National Perspectives* (New York: Free Press).

Mair, P. (2007a) 'Political Opposition and the European Union' *Government and Opposition* 42 (1): 1–17.

Mair, P. (2007b) 'Political Parties and Party Systems', in P. Graziano and M. Vink (eds) *Europeanization: New Research Agendas* (Basingstoke: Palgrave), pp. 154–166.

Müller, W. and K. Strøm (1999) *Policy, Office, or Votes? How Political Parties in Western Europe Make Hard Decisions* (Cambridge: Cambridge University Press).

O'Brennan, J. and T. Raunio (2007) *National Parliaments within the Enlarged European Union: from 'Victims' of Integration to Competitive Actors?* (Abingdon: Routledge).

Panebianco, A. (1988) *Political Parties: Organization & Power* (Cambridge: Cambridge University Press).

Pridham, G. (2001) 'Patterns of Europeanization and Transnational Party Cooperation: Party Development in Central and Eastern Europe', in Paul Lewis (ed) *Party Development and Democratic Change in Post-Communist Europe* (London: Cass), pp. 179–198.

Raunio, T. (2000) 'Losing Independence or Finally Gaining Recognition? Contacts between MEPs and National Parties', *Party Politics* 6 (2): 211–223.

Schmidt, V. (2010) 'The European Union in Search of Identity and Legitimacy: Is More Politics the Answer?', Working Paper No. 5, Institute for European Integration Studies, Austrian Academy of Sciences, Vienna.

Schmitt, H. (2005) 'The European Parliament Election of 2004: Still Second-Order?' *West European Politics* 28 (3): 650–679.

Smith, G. (1989) 'Core Persistence: System Change and the People's Party' *West European Politics* 12 (4): 161–182.

Steenbergen, M. and Scott, D. (2004) 'Contesting Europe? The Salience of European integration as a Party Issue', in G. Marks and M. Steenbergen (eds) *European Integration and Political Conflict* (Cambridge: Cambridge University Press), pp.165–192.

Vresse, C. de, S. Banducci, H. Semetko and H. Boomgaarden (2006) 'The News Coverage of the 2004 European Parliamentary Election Campaign in 25 Countries' *European Union Politics* 7 (4): 477–504.

Part II

Institutional Deadlock: A Surfeit of Would-be Leaders

5
National Governments, the European Council and Councils of Ministers: A Plurality of Sovereignties. Member State Sovereigns without an EU Sovereign

Jack Hayward

The contested but inescapable concept of sovereignty is our starting point in an investigation of power struggles at the summit of the European Union (EU). Uneasy references to pooled, shared and split sovereignty collide with sovereignty's connotation of the purported unity and indivisibility of a supreme coercive power. At the interface between law and politics, sovereignty is the focus of an 'ongoing dialectic' between them in a polycentric EU whose variable boundaries are non-exclusive territorially and where sovereignty is functionally limited (Walker 2003: 20; cf. 22–4). The results are 'constitutional collisions' between 'sovereignty-encroaching claims' in a context of 'contingency, ambiguity and disagreement' with, 'profoundly unforeseeable and unintended consequences' (Walker 2003: 26, 28). It is a constitutional discourse that dares not speak its name for fear that would formalise explicitly on open-ended process of 'shifting alliances and competitions between different geopolitical strategies and different substantive policy aspirations' of the member states (Walker 2003: 27; cf. 30).

From a legal standpoint, member states transfer particular sovereign powers to the EU but not their sovereignty. 'Once the delineation of competences and the lines of actual political authority and control have become so blurred that powers over most policy spheres are complexly shared by both the EU and the Member States, the notion of functionally limited sovereignty becomes more difficult to comprehend' (de Búrca 2003: 458–9; cf. 456). The tension between extending interstate solidarity within the EU and preserving as much as possible of the sovereignty of member states was present from the start but has been exacerbated by the sovereign debt crisis of 2011. The German Constitutional Court has been especially resolute in insisting on a national parliamentary sovereignty veto over the handover of power to the EU.

Has the concept of sovereignty been devalued into redundancy as has often been asserted? Despite being disaggregated by what Neil Walker has called 'the remorseless dynamic of fragmentation' (Walker 2003: 27), it retains a residual but significant utility because it continues to play a legally normative and politically substantive role without an adequate substitute. Once one concedes that power is pluralistic and even fragmented in multi-centred EU, the fact that it is both a habitual part of constitutional terminology and influences the way in which power distribution is described in controversial arguments over its contingent location means that sovereignty remains an indispensible component of the explanatory framework of EU power struggles (W. Wallace 1999: 507; cf. 503–21).

As argued in Chapter 1 and as the constitutional authority Joseph Weiler has put it, 'From the political, but not legal point of view the Community is in fact a confederation' (Weiler 1999: 83; cf. 270–1). Because of the EU's neo-confederal practice, political scientists prefer to focus upon the exercise of specific powers rather than becoming embroiled in problematic normative and legalistic arguments about the precise location of an overarching sovereignty. This avoids procrustean efforts to torment empirical complexity into a simplistic semblance of unity by accommodating an interrelated diversity that is closer to EU reality. As also mentioned in Chapter 1, the right to secession reflects the fact that member state sovereignty persists, Michael Keating reminding us that the EU is 'based precisely on the existence of state sovereignty' and derives its 'authority from it' (Keating 2003: 199; cf. 197). So, despite his judgement that 'The normative claims of sovereignty have always rested on a certain mystification of the state', he calls for a 'reformulated conception of sovereignty' that accepts new sovereignty claims that seek 'recognition as legitimate actors in complex systems of authority' (Keating 2003: 204, 207 and Chapter 9 by Keating).

The EU is not only at the interface between law and politics. In the context of an unintegrated transnational interdependence, the sovereignty issue links the internal and external state autonomy and power especially of larger EU members with imperial pasts like state nations Britain and France. Far from being obsolescent, Stanley Hoffmann pointed out in 1966 that states remain the EU's constituent units. The transfer of powers has been 'limited, conditional, dependent and reversible' (Hoffmann 1995: 101; cf. 71–2). So, 'The factors that make the federal model irrelevant to diverse and divided nations also make all forms of union short of federalism precarious' (Hoffmann 1995: 102). (This pertinent judgement also clearly applies to neo-confederalism.) Monnet's reliance on the 'self-propelling power of the unifying process', dependent upon indefinitely postponing specification of the ultimate purpose of incremental integration, was decisively challenged in 1965 by de Gaulle who dispelled the suprantionalists' evasive ambiguities. He demonstrated that a Europe of nation-states could never be sufficiently cohesive to act effectively by bluntly stressing the conflicts of national interest between them. Why this led to a 'cumulative retreat from integration' is explained by Hoffmann. 'Ambiguity lures and lulls the national consciousness into integration so long as the benefits are high, the costs are low, the losses high, the hopes dashed or deferred' (Hoffmann 1995: 84; cf. 81–3, 94, 97).

As the pessimistic alternative has prevailed, the reliance upon monetary integration exposed the EU's institutional reality of weak authority, limited power and declining public support that threatens it with unsustainability. Once Germany struggled to absorb the massive cost of reunification in the 1990s, it was increasingly reluctant to become the open-ended paymaster of a single currency transfer union in which the free-riding Club Med countries especially could rely on it to save them from the consequences of their systematic laxity at best and their endemic clientelism, corruption and fraud at worst. Solidarity with East Germany exhausted the goodwill of German taxpayers for pan-European solidarity. The French fear of being subservient to what in practice was a Deutschmark zone led to desperate attempts to institute a collective European 'economic government' alongside the European Central Bank, both to assert control over freeriding states who wanted the benefits of monetary integration without paying the fiscal costs and to protect their own position. Later chapters will deal with these issues. They exemplify the recurrent test to which European integration is exposed: fleeing forwards, splitting into a two or multi-tier EU, with possible repatriation of powers.

To conclude this preliminary discussion of why intergovernmentalism has emerged as an ever more intrusive presence, sovereignty has assumed the unattractive form of unsociable sovereign debtor states at the mercy of the financial markets and dependent mainly upon the bailouts of sovereign creditor states like Germany, albeit masquerading as a collective Eurozone rescue to prevent sovereign defaults. However, just as in a confederation there is an ultimate exit option, so in the Eurozone financial circumstances rather than political choice may lead to voluntary or enforced withdrawal.

At the conspicuous risk of provoking conceptual controversy by coining an appellation that nevertheless seems appropriate to the EU predicament, it may be worth proposing one. The foundational presupposition of the EU is pragmatic sovereignty. It implies that member states have selectively been willing to concede some of their autonomous powers, provided that they retain the veto of unanimity to defend the indispensable core of their separate status, judged by them to be necessary in matters of overriding national interest. If unwilling to compromise, they can opt out of specific Treaty provisions or ultimately secede, although no state has yet done so. The Lisbon Treaty has made explicit what was previously implicit.

However unlikely resort to this exit option may be, awareness that it exists has an undoubted if unspoken presence when prolonged negotiations prepare the way for either ultimate summit agreement or deadlock in the European Council. It is nevertheless worth emphasising that pragmatic sovereignty as the EU's foundational presupposition should only be adopted provided sovereignty is understood as relative autonomy rather than as an absolute or static conception. This brings it closer to a less formal, more flexible and dynamic notion of expansive or restrictive state powers. More precisely, to avoid the traditional monist connotations of sovereignty, it might be preferable to use the less draconian designation of pragmatic autonomy. This allows us to accommodate the mutual concessions made frequently in the EU to minimise the issues on which national governments intransigently collide.

Overcoming institutional immobilism: heroic statecraft and humdrum coordination of conflicting interests

To appreciate the fundamental motivation for the 1974 creation of the European Council, which marked a decisive reorientation of the governance of the European Communities through 'a strengthening of the confederal elements in the Community system and a decline of supranationalism' (Werts 1992: 74), it is necessary to recall the abortive Gaullist attempts in 1953 and again in the 1961 Fouchet

Plan to establish such a body. The initiative was always taken by Frenchmen, whether it was the supranationalist Monnet or the inter-governmentalist de Gaulle. However, it was the heroic statesman rather than the mastermind manipulator (appointed by de Gaulle as French Planning Commissioner in 1945) who was to impart an insufficiently acknowledged imprint to the evolution of a Europe of nation-states. Rather than his initial intention of wrecking the *apatride* European Community Treaty institutions or his 1965 'empty chair' paralysing boycott asserting the necessity of nation-state unanimity, it was through Giscard d'Estaing's 1974 initiative that de Gaulle's purpose of bypassing the federalist 'Community method' of the founding fathers was achieved. Thereafter, when the member states, led by a Franco-German axis, were able to agree, they could modify the working of the Treaties despite the reservations of the Commission, the European Parliament and even the European Court of Justice (ECJ), guardian of the Treaties.

In June 1952, 22 years before the establishment of the European Council, in opposition to the proposed supranational European Defence Community, de Gaulle called for a confederation, elaborating in a November 1953 press conference his advocacy of 'an associa-tion of nations in a confederation of states' (Sutton 2007: 70). Michel Debré suggested in 1953 that, unlike the technocratic Coal and Steel Community, there should be a council of heads of government to control a European Political Union. Appointed first Fifth Republic Prime Minister by de Gaulle, on 15 January 1959 Debré proposed 'regular consultations among Heads of State or Government from the Member States, outside the framework of the Community' (Werts 1992: 4–6; cf. 18–20, 70–1). In May 1960, de Gaulle envisaged 'organised cooper-ation' between states leading to an 'imposing confederation' (Sutton 2007: 91; cf. 94) but in deference to Chancellor Adenauer's preference in the context of Franco-German proposals that emerged as the Fouchet Plan in 1961, the former term was preferred to the latter. The revised Gaullist project of a 'Union of States' headed by a council of heads of state or government was blocked by the supranationalist Netherlands and Belgium, so de Gaulle fell back to Franco-German bilateral coopera-tion and a proposed book of his writings and speeches on *L'Europe des nations* was shelved (Sutton 2007: 95–9, 114; Werts 1992: 22–7). The essentials of the Fouchet Plan were revived a decade later.

The death of de Gaulle meant that the project passed into other hands. It has been insufficiently acknowledged that with his adroit capacity to exploit an opportunity, in 1972–3 Monnet prepared the way for the future European Council by advocating a process of authoritative political decision in place of inconclusive discussions. He did so with the support of Chancellor Brandt, Prime Minister Heath and President Pompidou, although they were unwilling to call it a 'Provisional European Government'. However, in early 1974 all three had left office and fortuitously in May Helmut Schmidt became German Chancellor and Giscard d'Estaing French President almost simultaneously. With Harold Wilson embroiled in the forthcoming 1975 referendum on UK membership, it was left to the friendly two former Finance Ministers, communicating in English, to make the running, with Monnet's discreet encouragement.

Nevertheless, the rejection of Monnet's 'Provisional European Government' was not simply a matter of terminology. When he wrote in his memoirs that the heads of government should create 'a more complete and profound union – whether federal or confederal I cannot say,' he still hoped that spillover would inexorably lead in a federalist direction (Monnet 1976: 599; cf. 591–605). The opposite proved to be the case, as the European Council increasingly encroached upon the roles of the Council of Ministers and Commission, leading the European Union to veer in a confederal direction.

As the Secretary General of the Commission for the previous decade observed in 1985 that 'the Community system is gradually degenerating into intergovernmental negotiations must be fully recognised. The concentration on unanimity and the constant intervention of the European Council are to a great extent responsible for the degeneration' (Noël 1985: 149). Political leaders acted primarily and predictably to serve their *distinct* national interests, although cooperating and compromising pragmatically when they could as necessitated by the interdependence between interests that were generally *inseparable.* De Gaulle's nationalist conception may have had the last word, albeit without his abrasive assertiveness but also without his decisiveness. Although the European Union was predominantly led by the Franco-German duumvirate he had institutionalised outside its structures, from the 1990s a reunified Germany was increasingly to replace France as the senior partner (see Chapter 15 by Paterson).

Announcing its name at the start of the press conference after the 1974 launch meeting, Giscard marked the shift from ad hoc improvisation to institutionalisation with the dubious assertion: 'summits are over, long live the European Council' (Werts 1992: 77; cf. 319–25). However, in promoting both the intergovernmental European Council and the Western Economic Summits with the United States, President

Giscard d'Estaing was applying the logic of *hyper personalisation* of decision-making on the model of the Fifth French Republic. Heads of government (or of state in the French case) were better able collectively to lead, resolve disputes and deal with the crises that lower level ministers and officials were unable to provide. Summiteering thereafter became the order of the day, not only within the EU but internationally in various configurations, as the ultimate recourse when all else had failed. The political elevation of a problem raised expectations that maximised the pressure to find a solution. The result might be outright failure, partial success through compromise or the achievement of a fully satisfactory consensus. Whatever the outcome, it was the supreme test of statecraft as practiced at the summit of political power (Putnam and Bayne 1987: 25–35, 41).

Brief European Council meetings lasting some 24 hours spread over two days required careful preparation by the national officials in Brussels as well as by a multiplicity of informal bilateral contacts. This applied even more to meetings of the specialised Councils of Ministers to resolve the less controversial issues, whose agendas were themselves simplified by several hundred working groups securing agreement on about 70 per cent of problems, with the Committee of Permanent Representatives and their deputies resolving about 20 per cent, leaving the ministers to deal with the remaining 10 per cent (H. Wallace et al. 2005: 58; cf. 57–9). Rather than catchall references to a singular 'Council of Ministers' which misleadingly attributes to the ultra complex policy process of EU decision a greater cohesion and expedition than it has in practice, it is better to acknowledge that it is a 'legal fiction' for sectionalised councils lacking the coordinating oversight of the European Council (Wessels 1991: 134) and explore its implications. It is the European Council, with its informal agenda and flexible procedure that is the decisive arena for dealing with the most controversial and/or the most important EU predicaments, although not confined to them.

The EU political executive developed by incremental, informal and improvised changes punctuated by treaties between pragmatically sovereign states whose leaders periodically try to practice heroic statecraft out of necessity rather than deliberate volition. These are exceptions to the routine of humdrum coordination to overcome a propensity to institutional immobilism. The European Council in particular acts from two complementary motives: principle and expediency. As a matter of principle, as sovereign state protagonists, the European Council is concerned to keep control in the hands of governments normatively and electorally accountable to their national publics rather than in those of the supranational and non-democratic Commission, European Central Bank (ECB), ECJ and even the elected European Parliament, remote from the voters. As a matter of expediency, with the broadening of the EU's membership and range of activities, it was necessary to improve the organisation, policy preparation and coordination, as well as monitoring implementation of the decisions made when they proceeded beyond indecision.

The EU co-decision triangle recalls the ingenuous Sieyès 1799 constitution that instituted a complicated system of checks and balances whose consequential deadlock prepared the way for the Napoleonic dictatorship. Although the EU is immune to such a threat, while the Commission has the initiating legislative power but not of decision, the Councils of Ministers and the European Parliament decide without initiating. This is less prone to paralysis than Sieyès' three chamber legislature in which the Council of State alone proposed legislation, with members in the *Tribunat* able to speak but not vote, while the Senators could vote but not speak. In a context of mutual distrust that is not conducive to consensus, reliance upon an honest broker, rotating presidency jointly of the European Council and the Councils of Ministers proved inadequate to the task of providing expeditious transformative leadership going beyond short-term compromises (Schout 2008). The post-Lisbon Treaty establishment of an elected President of the European Council, who in 2011 had added to his functions presiding over the Eurozone, has complicated not clarified the EU's governance.

When the abortive constitutional reform leading to the Lisbon Treaty of December 2007 that retrieved the stabilising of the European Council presidency was being discussed, Philippe Schmitter warned that 'The EU is already the most complex polity ever created by human artifice and it is going to become even more so ...' (Schmitter 2004: 69). This was because of the EU's multi-level and polycentric governance, regulated by incremental treaties between mutually distrustful states not sharing an identity or politico-administrative culture. It was becoming increasingly diverse in economic and political capability, as well as in size with enlargement, leaving most action to sectoralised interaction between privileged elite insiders, especially the complex of Brussels and national officials, lobbied by business organisations, with an independent ECB controlling its fragile financial affairs (Schmitter 2004: 48–52).

In 1974 when the European Council was established, the Commission feared it would be tempted 'to choose the low road of inter-governmental cooperation when we should be taking the high road of integration' (Eighth General Report 1974, quoted in Werts 1992: 142). Its anxiety was well founded. Nearly 20 years later, 'Instead of the original system in which the Commission proposes and the Council (of Ministers) disposes, there is now a European Council which sometimes acts as a surrogate for other institutions' (Werts 1992: 146). Encouraged by Margaret Thatcher, the European Council went from strength to strength, although it only resolved the vexed question of the UK's financial contribution in 1984 after 16 acrimonious European Councils thanks to President Mitterrand's dexterity (Werts 1992: 276–7). Unlike the Commission, the European Parliament welcomed this development, having as early as 1972 championed a single decision-making centre taking binding decisions. While wishing to preserve its independence by not being represented in the European Council (unlike the Commission President) it asked to be regularly informed and consulted, not by-passed, rather than joining in the chorus bewailing the EU's 'democratic deficit' (Werts 1992: 155–8). Was the European Council in a position to assume such an authoritative role?

Although it has implausibly been claimed that a 'club spirit' pervades all levels of the Councils of Ministers from top to bottom (Westlake 1995: 111) the European Council was generally agreed to have a British elite style club atmosphere. Its meetings are characterised by informal bilateral exchanges over lunch and dinner or relaxed general 'fireside chats'. This congenial environment is more conducive to compromise rather than the formal EU processes exemplified by institutionally intransigent, turf defending national officials. Nevertheless, David Spence has argued that even the latter are usually more concerned with 'joint problem-solving' rather than winning or losing particular negotiations who 'usually see themselves as rivals and partners', he goes on to claim: 'The essential point is that the club reaches compromise in the Council because the framework of overall commitment to the EU presumes and requires it. The promise of Council negotiation is that wise agreement will meet the legitimate interests of all sides as far as possible' (Spence 1995: 375). Much turns on the weight attached to rivalry rather than partnership; the 'inexorable' 'premise' of 'wise' agreed outcomes is presumed to prevail over 'sporadic acute conflicts' (Spence 1995: 376). While compromises are presented as victories to their respective national presses, the negotiators are usually willing to settle for 'sub-optimal outcomes in strictly national terms' (Spence 1995: 377) while sometimes expressing written reserves in the minutes to placate domestic constituencies. Because each negotiation involves spin-offs for others, package deals and side payments offered are an essential part of the process but these are made not by officials but in the Councils of Ministers and in the European Council (Spence 1995: 379–86). However, since the post-2004 enlargement, there is less of a club atmosphere (Hayes-Renshaw and Wallace 2006).

Dealing with member state policy coordination, Spence also discusses the process of lobbying of and by national governments that precede the search for a compromise. He describes this desired outcome as often the 'euphemism for a policy reached after a hard battle, with some Member States outvoted and others successful in setting the EU agenda along the lines of their own national priorities' (Spence 1995: 354). While on each issue there is a lead ministry to coordinate the national position, it is at the Comité des représentants permanents (COREPER) level of permanent representatives in Brussels that the ultimate negotiations take place before unresolved matters are handed on to the appropriate Council of Ministers and, if necessary, to the European Council. While Britain and France have effective overall coordinating bodies, other member states (notably Germany) are less capable of adopting a coherent negotiating posture (Hayward and Wright 2002: 136–45 on the French SGCI). Spence distinguishes four objectives of administrative coordination at the national level: the anticipation of opportunities to promote national interests; devising damage limitation and trade-offs as part of negotiating strategy; monitoring implementation by lead ministries; subordinating interministerial disputes and particular ministerial views to the overall national interest. Coordination also includes advising ministers on negotiating tactics, coalition building and margins for manoeuvre, fall-back positions and avoiding the reputational and actual harm of isolation except on issues that are ultimately non-negotiable (Spence 1995: 368–9, 382–8; cf 357).

Rather than undifferentiated descriptions of Council processes in the context of conflict and coalition-building, there are enlightening analyses of the extent to which transactions are qualitatively characterised by genuine deliberation on the merits as against strategic bargaining. The emerging consensus is that deliberation is more likely in the lengthy pre-negotiations by officials and in making humdrum decisions in secrecy but diminish with transparency and politicisation. By the time an issue reaches a Council of Ministers or the European Council, strategic bargaining predominates, so that deliberation on the merits 'arguing seems to be most common when it matters least, i.e. the political stakes are low' (Naurin 2010: 50; cf. 31–44; Niemann 2008: 141–2). Consensus is exaggerated by recording only overt conflicts, hence the importance of 'insulated deliberation' in masking the extent of international disunity, with the best arguments if necessary having to give way before the strongest arguments of power politics (Lewis 2008: 171; cf. 166, 172–5).

The glaring lack of democratic accountability of the European Council and the Councils of Ministers either to the EP or to national parliaments has been blamed upon the 1966 de Gaulle-provoked Luxembourg compromise, which induced member states to 'paper over significant differences…by means of informal, *ad hoc* agreements between elites' (Heisenberg 2005: 68). The consensus culture of avoiding explicit divisive voting and *fait accompli* accountability when decisions have already been taken is conflated with differences on issues and between countries when issues are put to the vote. Heisenberg finds that large member states – especially Germany – with strong preferences are more likely to record their opposition by voting against or abstaining and that dissensus is most explicit 'when money and agricultural subsidies are at stake' (Heisenberg 2005: 77). She points out serious defects in the urge towards consensus. It not only leads to inefficient decision-making by deferring disagreed matters but to inadequate democratic accountability, with decisions 'shrouded in secrecy to avoid nationalist characterisation of the voting' (Heisenberg 2005: 83; cf. 82–4). The ability to hold someone identifiable accountable is crucial to representative democracy, so EU's diffuse collectivisation of responsibility, when combined with confidentiality, leaves the member state mass publics with frustrated feelings of being duped and deceived, owing to their powerlessness to punish those to blame when things go wrong (More generally, Curtin et al. 2010).

Member state government behavioural contrasts

In identifying how countries translate their initial bargaining positions through coalition-building into voting behaviour in the Councils of Ministers, what emerges are two overlapping dimensions: a North–South split and between net-contributors and net-recipients from the EU budget. This resolves itself into Northern net-contributors (Scandinavia, Netherlands and UK) versus Southern net-recipients (Club-Med and France). Germany is located in pivotal position between North, South and the enlarged East, with France and Germany inclined to move from differing initial positions to problem-solving cooperation. This is important because voting studies do not reveal that 'two big states opposing the same proposal will usually be able to gather enough votes to stop it …' (Naurin and Lindahl 2008: 67; cf. 64–77; Zimmer et al. 2005: 403–22). However, whereas in the

Councils of Ministers, preferences are determined mainly by specific national interest and regulatory cultures, in the European Council more fundamental concerns over the implications for EU integration figure prominently (Zimmer et al. 2005: 44).

National actors seek to retrieve in implementation what they conceded at decision, in divergent ways and with significant national differences. They do so when faced by a regulatory complexity motivated by mutual distrust through 'delay in the enactment of directives, lax interpretation, intentional or tolerated fraud, the corrupting of the original goals, ill will on the part of the judicial authorities, or even outright refusal to enforce the policy' (Mény et al. 1996: 7). 'Low politics' can unobtrusively often trump 'high politics'.

The differential effectiveness of EU directives between member states depends upon four factors. First, coordination and steering capacity, which is especially low in Spain, Greece, Ireland and Portugal. Second, inspectorate resources are modest in Greece, Ireland and Portugal. Third, administrative sanctions are weak, notably in France because of congestion in the courts. Fourth is the lack of information, with Greece again the main culprit. The general comparative assessment of the inertial effect of poor enforcement is that Greece, Ireland, Italy and Portugal are 'neglecting their duty to ensure not only legal transposition, but also a reasonable level of practical compliance' (Faulkner et al. 2005: 275; cf. 270–6). It is not by chance that these are also the countries that suffered the greatest loss of credibility and credit worthiness in the eurozone sovereign debt crisis of 2011.

The threat of financial sanctions by the ECJ under the infringement procedure clearly has an effect on national implementation but there are three inductively ascertainable types of response. Particularly in the compliance cultures of Scandinavia, law observance overrides domestic concerns, politically and administratively. In Germany, Austria, the UK, Netherlands, Belgium and Spain, national cost–benefit political considerations predominate over both hard and soft EU law. Finally, other countries are guilty of inertia and neglect unless compelled to act. Whereas Greece and Portugal are inert both in transposition and enforcement, Italy and Ireland are good at transposition but not when faced by a regulatory complexity motivated by mutual distrust through enforcement, while – partly due to national arrogance – France is sluggish in transposition but not eventually in enforcement (Faulkner et al. 2005: 324–6; cf. 228). The problem of overcoming institutional immobilism is less a matter of heroic statecraft than of a capacity for humdrum coordination and administrative determination. They are present variably in EU member states, with stark, conspicuous contrasts that contribute towards desolidarising resentment and distrust. Some national governments are thus identifiably guilty of public injustices to rival the private injustices of markets.

The Lisbon Treaty: institutional inertia and the stabilisation of authority

In his study of *Political Order in Changing Societies*, Huntington argued that while political institutionalisation facilitated achievement, he acknowledged that 'the organisation may be a victim of its past successes and be unable to adjust to the new challenge' (Huntington 1968: 13). He went on to explain why. 'Institutionalisation makes the organisation more than simply an instrument to achieve certain purposes. Instead its leaders and members come to value it for its own sake and it develops a life of its own quite apart from the specific functions it may perform at any given time. The organisation triumphs over its function' (Huntington 1968: 15 and more generally Hayward 1975). Overinstitutionalisation, opacity and excessive complexity mean that the Union is poorly rooted in the affections of EU citizens. They stifle those changes that are not sprung upon unsuspecting member peoples. The 2007 Lisbon Treaty was an attempt to overcome the institutional sclerosis from which the EU has suffered, following the failure to secure the adoption of a constitution. By electing the President of the European Council, has it succeeded in institutionalising an authorative *deus ex machina* capable of overcoming the EU's chronic ailment?

Both the proposed Constitution and the Lisbon Treaty's wish institutionally to strengthen the European Council were partly motivated by the increasing incoherence in the first decade of the twenty-first century of the massively enlarged EU after 2004. Resolving conflicts of interest within and presenting a common front outward, coordination of fragmented policies and imparting impetus by overcoming the propensity to inertia and immobilism were the challenges to be met. The proposed answer was a tentative stabilisation of the EU political executive to achieve efficiency of outcomes while retaining collective control by the heads of national governments. This makes it difficult for power or even undisputed authority to be exerted by office holders like the European Council presidency, still less the High Representative for External Relations, who have the implausible appearance rather than convincing reality of personalised leadership. The aspiration that they will impart consistency and coherence to a process dedicated to muddling through under the pressure of unpredictable events is an illusory indulgence in 'visionary' rhetoric, coupled with an invitation to delusions of spurious grandeur. To avoid these dangers, the initial appointments to these offices were deliberately selected for their unsuitability to aspire to such pretensions.

While some still hanker after a federal EU government towards which the consolidation of the European Council's power has been a cautious shuffle, the confusion of roles and functions persists. When faced with choices both on institutional or policy matters, the latter-day EU leaders show their ineptitude in remaining addicted to half-hearted compromise instead of clearcut choices. Thus they were unwilling to call the High Representative a Minister of Foreign Affairs, still less designate a Finance Minister (proposed in 2011 by an exasperated Jean-Claude Trichet, outgoing ECB President) because this would have precisely and explicitly carried the connotation of an 'EU government'. When faced with the 2011 euro crisis, the eurozone ministers, notably the German paymaster to fund the defaulting sovereign state debts, would only agree on postponed half-measures that the markets judged to be too late too little. The member states were conspicuously failing their political stress tests.

The euro crisis of 2011 was the EU's moment of truth regarding its institutional and political incapacity to resolve a collective macro-problem by divergent micro-interests. Despite Europhobic 'superstate' accusations, the EU has been excessively weak by comparison to federal or centralised states. The uncircumspect headlong pursuit of currency integration under the aegis of an independent, powerful and unaccountable ECB was undertaken without any corresponding political authority. The member states have been unwilling to surrender their semblance of financial and fiscal sovereignty, on the perception of whose exercise and outcomes national electorates base the confidence they give or withdraw from their political leaders. The monetary crisis and the reluctance to correct its structural failings or even its conjunctional consequences lay in wait for imprudent institutional architects who hoped for the best and contented themselves with another package deal, consideration of whose implications were imprudently postponed.

While it may be too facile to personalise the blame for what are in large measure structural, systemic failures or regret the 1970s Giscard-Schmidt tandem, the national appointments to the Eurogroup, the ECOFIN Council of Finance Ministers, the European Council and the

European Commission have hesitated and prevaricated, allowing volatile market forces and arbitrary stress tests by the European Banking Authority and self-validating credit notation agencies to impose their verdicts on sovereign debtors at the risk of precipating a prolonged economic recession. National imperatives reasserted themselves when the EU governments looked to Germany to foot the bill. However, the German government is accountable to its parliament and electorate, not to the EU in general or the Eurozone states in particular. The post-First World War slogan that a defeated 'Germany will pay' reparations is not acceptable as a response to the laxity and lapses of its EU 'partners' locked in a contagious solidarity. Avoiding a German Europe without a sufficiently European Germany poses a conundrum for which the Lisbon Treaty had no answer.

The lamentable way in which Germany, which had imposed the Stability and Growth Pact, disembowelled its offspring in 2003, showed that 'whatever sovereignty large countries are willing to cede...they will take it back – legally or less legally if necessary' (Alesina and Perroti 2004, cited by Menon 2008: 236). Anand Menon goes on to comment: 'There is nothing worse for the Union than member states signing up for initiatives they subsequently realise are too important to be dealt with in Brussels' (Menon 2008: 237). The appointment of a Prime Minister of Belgium, Herman Van Rompuy, to serve for a 2.5-year term, renewable once as European Council President coexisting with the rotating Presidency of the Councils of Minister, may be a tribute to his skill in briefly holding together a fragile government in a country that subsequently survived for over a year with only an interim government but an honest broker cannot provide a backbone for a broken back institutional system.

The EU has no common external enemy of the kind once identified with Soviet Russia. So it is content to find its adversaries within a dissensual European disunion. The EU summit policy process too often takes the following conjunctive form: 'I discuss, you discuss, we discuss...and they pragmatically prevaricate and postpone whenever possible'. The representatives of the member states scuttle pretentiously between meetings, seldom taking the actions necessary to implement such commitments as are made. Ineffective confederal improvisation is no substitute for resolute assertion of state power in the merciless skin game with market speculators that dominates daily life in the contemporary world. The 2011 spectacular collision between the desperate need of some debt-ridden member states for the financial solidarity of others provoked the bitter resentment at the counterpart humiliating intrusive discipline that made a mockery of the sovereignty of the Greek and Italian governments. The resignation of their prime ministers for this and other reasons demonstrates that solidarity with strings exposes the hollowness of a spendthrift sovereignty.

Bibliography

Búrca, G. de (2003) 'Sovereignty and the Supremacy Doctrine of the European Court of Justice' in N. Walker (ed.) *Sovereignty in Transition* (Oxford: Hart).

Curtin, D. et al. (2010) 'Accountability and European Governance', special issue *West European Politics* xxxiii/5, 930–1164.

Faulkner, G. et al. (2005) *Complying with Europe. EU Harmonisation and Soft Law in Member States* (Cambridge: Cambridge University Press).

Hayes-Renshaw, F. and H. Wallace (2006) *The Council of Ministers*, 2nd ed. (Basingstoke: Palgrave Macmillan).

Hayward, J. (1975) *Political Inertia* (Hull: University of Hull).

Hayward, J. and V. Wright (2002) *Governing from the Centre. Core Executive Coordination in France* (Oxford: Oxford University Press).

Heisenberg, D. (2005) 'The Institution of "Consensus" in the European Union: Formal versus Informal Decision-Making in the Council', *European Journal of Political Research*, xxxxiv, 65–90.

Hoffmann, S. (1995) *The European Sisyphus. Essays on Europe, 1964–1994* (Boulder, CO: Westview Press).

Huntington, S.P. (1968) *Political Order in Changing Societies* (New Haven, CT: Yale University Press).

Keating, M. 'Sovereignty and Plurinational Democracy: Problems in Political Science', Chapter 8 in Walker (ed) *Sovereignty in Transition* (Oxford: Hart).

Lewis, J. (2008) 'Strategic Bargaining, Norms and Deliberation' in D. Naurin and H. Wallace (eds) *Unveiling the Council of the European Union* (Basingstoke: Palgrave Macmillan).

Menon, A. (2008) *Europe. The State of the Union* (London: Atlantic Books)

Mény, Y. et al. (eds) (1996) *Adjusting to Europe* (London: Routledge).

Monnet, J. (1976) *Mémoires* (Paris: Fayard).

Naurin, D. (2010) 'Most Common When Least Important: Deliberation in the European Council of Ministers', *British Journal of Political Science*, XL/1, 31–50.

Naurin, D. and R. Lindhal (2008) 'East-North-South: Coalition-Building in the Council before and after Enlargement', in D. Naurin and R. Lindhal (eds) *Unveiling the Council of the European Union* (Basingstoke: Palgrave Macmillan).

Niemann, A. (2008) 'Deliberation and Bargaining' in D. Naurin and H. Wallace (eds) *Unveiling the Council of the European Union* (Basingstoke: Palgrave Macmillan).

Noël, E. (1985) 'The European Community: What Kind of a Future?' *Government and Opposition*, 20, 2, 147–56.

Putnam, R.D. and N. Bayne (1987) *Hanging Together. Cooperation and Conflict in the Seven Power Summits* (London: Sage).

Schmitter, P. (2004) 'Neo-Neofunctionalism' in A. Wiener and T. Diez (eds) *European Integration Theory* (Oxford: Oxford University Press).

Schout, A. (2008) 'Beyond the Rotating Presidency', in J. Hayward (ed.) *Leaderless Europe* (Oxford: Oxford University Press).

Spence, D. (1995) 'Negotiations, Coalitions and Resolution of Interstate Conflicts' in M. Westlake (ed.) *The Council of the European Union* (London: Cartermill).

Sutton, M. (2007) *France and the Construction of Europe, 1944–2007. The Geopolitical Imperative* (Oxford: Berghahn Books).

Walker, N. (2003) 'Late Sovereignty in the European Union' in Walker (ed.) *Sovereignty in Transition* (Oxford: Hart).

Wallace, H. et al. (eds) (2005) *Policy-Making in the European Union,* 5th ed. (Oxford: Oxford University Press).

Wallace, W. (1999) 'The Sharing of Sovereignty: the European Paradox', *Political Studies,* xxxxvii/3, 503–521.

Weiler, J.H.H. (1999) *The Constitution of Europe* (Cambridge: Cambridge University Press).

Werts, J. (1992) *The European Council* (Amsterdam: North-Holland).

Wessels, W. (1991) 'The EC Council: The Community's Decision-making Centre', in R. O. Keohane and S. Hoffmann (eds) *The New European Community. Decision-making and Institutional Change* (Boulder, CO: Westview Press).

Westlake, M. (1995) *The Council of the European Union* (London: Cartermill).

Zimmer, C. et al. (2005) 'The Contested Council: Conflict Dimensions of an Intergovernmental EU Institution', *Political Studies,* L111/2, 403–422.

6

The European Commission Bureaucracy: Handling Sovereignty through the Back and Front Doors

Edward C. Page

An unexpected success story

The bureaucracy of the European Union is an unlikely success story; it has managed to develop a level of activism and an ability to shape policies in member states that appears improbable in the light of its composition, mode of operation and constitutional limitations. The bureaucratic setup of European integration was conceived by Monnet as essentially based on sovereignty – an impermanent core European administration drawing in officials from member states developing frameworks for common policies that member state bureaucracies apply and implement (see Hooghe 2005: 37ff). While a more permanent and routinised form of European bureaucracy actually emerged from the Treaty of Rome, it was hardly one based on a centralisation of authority. Moreover, the fragmentation of authority in the European Union (EU) as a whole might at first glance appear to be exacerbated by basic features of the design of the Commission (see Kassim 2003). It is a non-executant bureaucracy reliant on member states for the execution of policies and on member states and others for its technical expertise. Its main power is the power to propose and its recommendations can be turned down or substantially modified by inter-institutional bargaining between the Commission, Council and member states in the shadow of the authority of the European Court of Justice (see Héritier and Lehmkuhl 2011). It is a multi-national bureaucracy in which the principle of merit promotion is at least tempered if not undermined by the principle of securing fair shares among plum jobs for all its member states. The working processes of the Commission appear to be riddled with opportunities for member states to shape what it does.

Yet in many respects the broad administrative setup of the European Union, with its relatively small European core relying on national bureaucracies to apply and implement European policy objectives, has produced a degree of activism and penetration into the policy-making processes of its member states than one might reasonably have expected. The implementation literature in political science suggests that it is extraordinarily difficult for a single lawmaker to attempt to shape the details of a wide range of environmental, agricultural and competition policies (among others) in 30[1] highly diverse politico-administrative systems (see, for example, Hill and Hupe 2002). More pessimistic students of public policy would say that the number of 'clearance points' associated with such a setup creates a probability of effective implementation very close to zero (Pressman and Wildavsky 1984). Variable though national implementation records may be (Falkner et al. 2005), it would be extraordinarily difficult to argue that EU legislative initiatives do not shape the policies and practices of member states broadly in the manner envisaged in the directives, regulations and decisions issued in the name of EU institutions.

Despite the fact that it has a multinational bureaucracy constrained by several often competing sources of authority, and even without taking account of the limited range of its functional responsibilities, the level of legislative activity is not dissimilar to that of a member state. It is notoriously difficult to measure quantities of legislation cross nationally (Miller 2010), yet French levels of law production in 2010 (around 21,542 pieces of secondary and 134 pieces of primary legislation, is greater than the 1,638 regulations and decisions and 166 directives produced by all EU institutions in the same year. It is clearly on this measure more productive than the German (on average producing 125 *Rechtsverordnungen* (regulations) and 150 pieces of primary legislation at federal level each year and the UK producing 2,971 statutory instruments (SIs) in UK and 41 Acts of Parliament in 2010. If one considers the immense difficulties that arise from inter-institutional bargaining within the EU, partially shaped and augmented by the basic tensions between European and intergovernmental modes of operation and the instability that accompanies the fragmentation of authority between and within the Commission, the Council and the Parliament, one could well argue that the Commission is the organisation that gives the European Union the appearance of an activist state, reforming practices in member states so that they conform with broad principles it has developed in the policy areas where it has asserted its legislative pre-eminence.

How has it managed to achieve this? This chapter begins by exploring how, despite the apparent intrusion of principles of organisation based on sovereignty offering member states the chance to shape the work of the Commission, the available evidence shows a much weaker impact of sovereignty principles in practice. Although the internal operation of the Commission might be less concerned with handling member state initiatives and vetoes than often supposed, the Commission still has to devise and legitimise its proposals in a wider institutional environment where authority is fragmented and the principle of sovereignty remains powerful. The chapter goes on to set out how the Commission appears to achieve a high level of legislative activism in such an environment and the implications of this method for the notion of 'solidarity' as understood in this volume.

Sovereignty by the back door?

The Commission is faced with a range of structural and constitutional constraints that might seem to disadvantage the Commission from acting as an efficient executor of state-like powers. Perhaps the most obvious is that it is a multi-national bureaucracy. Running a bureaucracy with officials from vastly different administrative traditions with different native tongues evokes the image of the Tower of Babel. The idea that the Commission is a collection of individuals with separate languages, networks and ways of doing business, and that this affects the ability of the Commission to develop policy, has little to substantiate it. Evidence on the interpersonal practices of communication and national identification suggest that the cosmopolitanism of EU officials renders nationality as largely irrelevant to the dealings among Commission officials (Suvarierol 2008, 2011). Moreover, the evidence that multinationality and the need to make sure that the requirement that each member state is 'represented' in the ranks of the bureaucracy has had a profound impact on the abilities or suitability of officials in key positions in the Commission is not at present strong. There have been significant steps to reduce the importance of nationality in recruitment and promotion since the Kinnock reforms, but nationality continues to play an important part in both. While there have been some spectacularly inept incumbents of top jobs in the Commission, ineptness is not a noticeable feature of the EU any more than it is of member state bureaucracies. Moreover, the emphasis on background as a basis for recruitment and promotion is also found in many member states that seek greater gender, ethnic and regional balances among middle and senior officials without raising significant questions about the effect on the 'quality' of administration.

A more plausible impact of multinationality on the operation of the Commission is that it can lead to a fragmentation within the Commission as the variety of direct links between the European Commission and member states allows member states directly, but less obviously than through the Council and the permanent representations, to shape policy in its interests. One possibility might be that EU officials consciously or unconsciously 'represent' the national interests of their home states. Yet evidence of this is extremely weak and the most convincing survey analysis points to strong supranational orientations among Commission officials (Hooghe 2002). Nevertheless, three other institutions connected to the Commission offer the possibility of entrenching sovereignty in the work of the Commission: the position of Commissioner, extensive use of seconded national experts in the Commission and the supervisory role of the comitology committees.

Commissioners

Although supposed neither to 'seek nor take instructions from any Government...' Commissioners are often suspected of serving as representatives of the nation-states that sent them. Here the available systematic evidence, limited though it is, shows clearly that the nationality of Commissioners has some impact on matters of controversy. Thomson's (2008) study looked at how close the Commission's position on 70 key issues was to the position of the member state from which the responsible Commissioner came. For those proposals to be considered under qualified majority voting (QMV), where one would expect Commissioners' room for manoeuvre to be greater as they are not trying to find a position unanimously acceptable, Commission positions are significantly closer to those of the home state of the relevant Commissioner. Wonka (2008: 1159) similarly finds, on the basis of two case studies that 'how...Commissioners position themselves in internal Commission decision-making is itself a product of their national political ties and the intra- and inter-institutional political situation that they face'. Egeberg's (2006) debriefing of several 'key informants' who had observed College of Commissioner meetings who tended to point out that the 'country role' of Commissioners can be detected in Commission deliberations.

While the evidence certainly suggests that nationality has an impact on Commissioner positions, it has to be added that this impact is not huge. Egeberg (2006: 11) gives it a relatively low value and concludes the 'College can probably not be portrayed as being permeated by national interests'. Thomson (2008: 182) makes a simple direct comparison of how close the Commission position is to that of the home state from which the Commissioner responsible for the proposal comes: 'the results do not suggest that the nationality of responsible commissioners has such an overall effect'. Even with QMV, it must be added that the effects Thomson detects, significant though they are, are not great – the Commission position on an issue is around 13 per cent closer to the position of a member state whose Commissioner is responsible for the proposal than it is to the position of other member states. Wonka's analysis points to circumstances where Commissioners did not behave in a manner consistent with national positions as well as to those where they did. Moreover, if one takes the view that individual Commissioner preferences and their impacts on eventual policy outcomes are heavily diluted and constrained by the institutional environment in which they operate (a point recognised by Wonka, Egeberg and Thomson) the significance of the nationality of Commissioners as a means for sovereign member state interests to break into Commission decision-making by relying on their Commissioner to put forward their views, detectable though it certainly is, diminishes.

Seconded national officials

The terms used to describe seconded national experts (SNEs), who are paid by member states but work in the Commission as Commission officials for the period of their secondment (up to four years), are even more suggestive of a subversion of the solidary aspirations of the Commission bureaucracy by the sovereign ambitions of member states: 'Trojan horses' for member states, 'sleepers' ('*sous marins*') serving their home state at the same time as the Commission (Bellier 2007). Thus officials might be effectively either single or double agents working partly in the interests of their home state (see also Kassim 2003).

The evidence certainly does not point to SNEs as a force for sovereignty pole in the development of European administration. Trondal's (2007) research, limited though it may be due to its small sample size, concludes that the evidence does not support 'the suspicion early voiced by Coombes (1970) that SNEs are highly conscious of their national background' and the fear that '"the secondment system would tend to produce an unmanageable cacophony" of officials loyal to the national civil service'. Rather his analysis of role perceptions emphasises institutional socialisation and adaptation to the life in the Commission as a far stronger basis for action than any instruction, direct or indirect, from the member state (see also Trondal 2006). Geuijen et al. (2009: 126) reach a broadly similar conclusion based on their work on Dutch SNEs. They argue that while they may bring a distinctly national approach to decision making, '[t]his... should not be interpreted as a direct national influence. Firstly, the Commission welcomes the experience, networks and input of the SNEs because the success of policy proposals depends on the member states themselves. SNEs also stress how loyal they are to the Commission during their secondment. Secondly, the influence is exercised fairly indirectly through the SNE's own thought processes which they characterise as having been shaped by their national background and upbringing' rather than conscious representation of a member state negotiating position.

Comitology committees

Similarly the members of the diverse comitology committees, usually composed of officials from member state bureaucracies might be expected, because of their appointment by member states, to 'enable the Council to control Commission implementation activities and decisions' (Schäfer 2006: 50). A formal modelling of comitology reaches the opposite conclusion: 'comitology committees move outcomes closer to the Commission's (more integrationist) preferences, and away from the Council's. Thus we show that the committees are an instrument of greater, rather than less, integration in the EU' (Ballmann et al. 2002: 571). That they reach this conclusion without looking at a single comitology decision might lead one to wonder how one would classify as integrationist or not some of the types of detailed technical issues that, as far as we know, make up the bulk of comitology agendas. The most important of such regulations, such as those covering fishing quotas, are about the details of how such schemes are to be regulated, who wins and loses from their application. The less controversial cover issues such as what antibiotics should be allowed to be administered to horses that might end up for human consumption. In such cases it is not obvious what the 'integrationist' preference is. Moreover, the discretion of the Commission and committees too in developing regulations is often very limited by the terms of the directives and other legislation under which delegated powers are exercised.

Wessels' (1998: 277) analysis of comitology shows that members of comitology committees do not necessarily become 'Trojan horses of the EC in their national capitals' in part since they create bureaucratic networks that 'are seemingly particularly successful in keeping their political masters out of the game. Even where voting actually took place, few issues were shifted to the Council for final arbitration. The complexity of their form and function is an obvious attempt to keep other actors out.... Some features of the interaction style also support certain functionalist expectations of a smooth technocratic problem-solving *"Zweckverband"'* (Wessels 1998: 227). Trondal (2009: 239) offers the interesting possibility that participation in comitology committees rather undermines member state participation in the EU since typically those who participate in such bodies are civil servants from the lower echelons about whose work senior officials and politicians are not always well informed and participation leads to a 'de-hierarchization of decision-making behaviour' where civil servants have 'few contacts with the [national] politico-administrative leadership'.

Dealing with sovereignty by the front door

A somewhat less disputed and more profound challenge to the activism of the Commission is found in the fragmentation of authority within the executive of the EU. The authority to legislate in systems of party government where legislative majorities generally support executive leadership is clearly absent in the European Union. Not only does the Commission as executive not control the legislature, the executive and the legislatures are themselves divided as Council serves both executive (setting priorities for policy development) and legislative functions. In a nutshell, where a policy proposal has the support of the political leadership of ministries in national bureaucracies, it is usual to expect that the proposal has a very good chance of getting through the legislative process required to put it into effect. The Commission is an exception to this since most things of any significance it proposes require support from institutions not bound to it by ties of party or any other loyalty: these institutions include Council and the European Court of Justice (ECJ) (Héritier and Moury 2008). Moreover, though not necessarily the Trojan horse of member states, the approval of the comitology committees is still required even for most significant pieces of the Commission's own delegated legislation.

The EU is not entirely unique in having an executive bureaucracy within a system of fragmented authority since the character of German federalism, for example, means that ministerial or cabinet support is not sufficient to guarantee the passage of legislation when the *Bundesrat* effectively has a veto and the weaker bonds of party loyalty within the executive and between the executive and legislative branches mean that top political executive support is not always enough to get agency proposals in the United States through hurdles of policy scrutiny within the executive (above all the Office of Management and Budget) and certainly not enough to get legislation adopted in the legislature (Page forthcoming). However, there is no doubt that the fragmentation of authority is severe in the EU and that it raises the question of how it is possible for a bureaucracy within it to appear to have such high levels of bureaucratic policy activity and output, especially where the authority of the Commission appears weak in relation to other institutions, in particular the Council.

Selck and Rhinard (2005: 134) show, on the basis of analysis of 174 issues contained in 70 legislative proposals, that where there are disagreements between the institutions – Commission, Council and Parliament – it is the Council that tends to have the greatest 'bargaining success'. They conclude that it 'is striking that the ... influence of both the Commission and Parliament are statistically almost non-recognizable' whether 'for the consultation procedure ... [or] for the codecision proce-dure ... In fact, it appears that it is the Council that acts as the domi-nant player under both legislative procedures'. How is it possible for the Commission to display such high levels of activism shaping policy when it appears to be encumbered by a highly fragmented system of authority? To answer this question, one must elaborate briefly on the problems that divided authority creates for a bureaucracy in the produc-tion of rules and how the Commission copes with them.

The bureaucrat's perspective

Low probability of success for bureaucrats' proposals to change a law makes them problematic. For an individual bureaucrat, wasting time on developing proposals which have no chance of being put into effect might be personally demoralising and even damaging for the career. Administrative leadership within the organisation suffers not only from the association with failure but also from the charge that financial and human resources are being wasted and they are unlikely to autho-rise their subordinates to develop such proposals. Put simply, if author-isation for bureaucratic activity does not mean a significant chance of success, then bureaucratic effort is potentially wasted. While it is not unheard of for civil servants in any system occasionally to indulge the potentially fruitless or Quixotic aspirations of ministers, Sancho Panza is an unlikely role model for bureaucrats and generally they try to avoid working ineffectually.

How do bureaucrats cope with this general disjuncture between success and authorisation in other systems where authority is fragmented? In Germany, one set of patterns (Page forthcoming) is to incorporate some kind of deal with the veto players whose agreement is required (above all representatives of the *Länder*) through prior political discussions before the matter is passed to the bureaucrats. In the United States, for example, officials proposing a regulation that will be examined by the Office of Management and Budget might try and cast the regulation before they submit it in such a way that the objectors to it are less likely to prevail (say, by some ground being given to them beforehand) or turn up at the Office of Management and Budget (OMB) and argue the case strongly. In France, the same argument could be made about the officials who seek to head off possible objections in the *Conseil d'Etat* or from the 'expert' supervisory bodies whose agreement is effectively required before a proposed decree can become law. In these negotiations, the support of the top political executives – ministers and agency heads – can be crucial in securing the success of executive proposals in systems where authority is divided.

In the European Union, inter-institutional negotiation is, of course, important, but the success rate of the Commission, especially when contrasted with that of Council, in bargaining on matters where there is disagreement, appears to be relatively low (Selck and Rhinard 2005). Yet the success rates for the Commission's legislative proposals seem to be quite high. These rates can only be calculated in the context of Commission proposals for legislation to be passed by others (Council or the Council and Parliament) and have generally been estimated at around 70 per cent (König and Bräuniger 2002), though this refers simply to the proportion of proposals that end up in legislation rather than the more complex question of whether outcomes reflect Commission preferences (discussed in Sullivan and Selck 2007).

In the European Commission, there appears to be a distinctive approach to the bureaucracy operating under fragmented authority. Broadly authorisation for Commission action appears to come less from the hierarchical structure of the Commission – through getting the support of the Commissioner or Directorate General (DG) – than through a range of authorisation procedures *external* to the Commission and not directly under their control – what I term 'prominent sources of authority'. Invoking these authorities might be expected to give the proposals greater chances of being accepted than proposals authorised through the political or administrative will of Commission officials, including Commissioners, alone.

Prominent sources of authority

To illustrate this point, a random sample of 31 of the 238 COMDOCS in Eur-Lex classed as 'preparatory acts' was examined. COMDOCS usually give background to the proposal and, in particular, pay attention to setting out the authorisation basis for the proposal. COMDOCs are official Commission documents that, among other things, convey to the Council and/or the Parliament the proposals that it would like to see turned into legiuslation. The 31 COMDOCs referred to 15 proposed decisions (14 Council and one Council and Parliament), 5 directives (all bar one Council and Parliament) and 11 regulations (7 Council and Parliament, 4 Council). By reading the COMDOC, one can learn what might have led the officials concerned to believe they could spend their time working on the proposal contained in it: the sources of implied authorisation.

The most important form of implied authorisation (covering 13 of the 31) is *auto-authorisation*. This refers to the authorisation to act that comes of particular conditions set in existing legislation or constitutional arrangements being fulfilled that leads to Commission action. Thus a proposal on the use of phosphates in domestic detergents arose from a requirement in the original regulation that the Commission 'evaluate, submit a report on and, where justified, present a legislative proposal on the use of phosphates...'. The second most common form of authorisation in the small sample is through *international obligation*. Meeting international obligations served as the apparent authorisation for another 9 of the 31 proposals in COMDOCs: proposals for Council decisions in compliance with international obligations (including meeting World Trade Organisation (WTO) rules and implementing international agreements negotiated with non-EU countries). Thus a proposal for a directive on fruit juices arose from changes to the *Codex Alimentarius* developed in the United Nations system.

Third, a large number of COMDOCs are authorised at the *request of Council* (8 of the 31 COMDOCs). A proposal for a directive on the right to information in criminal proceedings was 'the second step in a series of measures in the Procedural Rights Roadmap, adopted in Council on 30 November 2009 inviting the Commission to put forward proposals on a "step by step" basis'. (2 COMDOCs had more than one main implied authorisation and so the total number of sources adds up to 33.)

The three COMDOCs without obvious 'prominent sources' authorisation were not proposals but reactions to the proposals of others. Surprisingly, given the presumed importance of 'expert' advice of legislation, an expert body with powers of its own to make recommendations, was a source of authorisation for only one COMDOC, though since the body concerned, the Chemical Review Committee, meets under the auspices of the Rotterdam Convention even this case is arguably more a result of international obligations than expert advisory bodies.

Only one of the 31 COMDOCs appeared to result primarily from authorisation within the Commission, that is to say, the Commission directly proposing legislation. This was a proposal that cited G20 obligations. That the Commission is not simply directly implementing G20 proposals is set out in the explanation that 'this proposal for a Regulation delivers the Commission's commitments to proceed rapidly and with determination'. For good measure it boosts its legitimacy by stressing that 'it takes also into account the strong support and many of the measures suggested in the Resolution of the European Parliament of 15 June 2010, on "Derivatives markets: future policy actions" (Langen-report)'.

Of course, the concentration on proposals for Council or Council and Parliament legislation leaves aside a substantial body of Commission secondary legislative activity through the exercise of powers 'delegated' to it in legislation (Héritier and Moury 2008) and exercised through the Commissions own legislative powers. We know far less about the exercise of this form of 'delegated' powers than we do about the Commission's role in its contribution to other EU legislation. The preparatory work for the Commission's own legislation is generally less systematically and less well documented. My own study (Page forthcoming) indicates that such delegated legislation constitutes a rather tightly circumscribed realm of independent action in two respects. First, the delegations appeared very tightly circumscribed by the empowering legislation and accompanying procedural arrangements. Second, and related, the regulations were circumscribed by the comitology supervision arrangements. With the exception of the Silkworm regulation made under special consolidating arrangements, for the three other regulations, knowledge that the comitology committee could veto it was an important constraint on what the regulations could contain even if in the end securing agreement or acquiescence was unproblematic.

Overall, the Commission tends to rest its activity in proposing legislation on authorisation from what might be termed diverse 'prominent sources of authority', prominent because in a system with fragmented authority like the EU, some sources of authority carry particular weight in different policy areas and different contexts, and the sources of implied authorisation tend to reflect sources of authority that are likely to carry a regulation through. Of course, something along these lines has long been recognised in the EU. Nugent (2001: 236) puts it succinctly when he argues '[m]ore often than not legislative proposals emanate from the Commission not because it has itself identified needs or problems that require tackling, but rather because it is honouring treaty or international obligations, it is adjusting or developing already established policy commitments or is responding to suggestions and requests of others' and he goes on to cite the work of others, including the Commission's own analysis of its policies that suggested that as little as 6 per cent of its proposals were 'its own idea'.

However, the important point about separating authorisation from other aspects of the policy process is that it merely establishes the right of the Commission, more specifically this usually means the unit within the relevant DG, to come up with a proposal. It does not necessarily determine the content of the proposal and Commission officials can indeed have a substantial role in shaping them. However, establishing the influence of Commission officials on the output of legislation is not, however, the central point of the argument in this paper, and neither is it possible to generalise about its influence.

Reinforcing the weakness of administrative leadership

The most important consequence of this from the point of view of the fragmentation of authority within the EU is that the prominent authorities pattern of working institutionalises the patterns of fragmentation found in the EU system as a whole within the DGs. Of course, all ministries in member states can to a significant degree be regarded as subject to internal divisions that reflect a fundamental division of labour – in transport ministries, for example, units dealing with sea transport might as well be in a different ministry from those dealing with rail for most purposes. Some states, above all Germany and France, are indeed known for their internal divisions through *Ressorts* and *corps*.

With prominent authorities authorising their actions, Commission bureaucrats rely less on the political leadership within the Commission for developing policy and instead look to the specific cues set out in earlier laws, international organisations, the Council or other outside sources of authority to shape which particular issues on the political agenda come on to the Commission's agenda. While it would be a mistake to argue that ministries in member states have their agendas defined by ministers or other political executives, the values and objectives of political executives form an important part of the calculations of bureaucrats as they shape policy proposals (Page forthcoming): on controversial issues they rely on them for support, they anticipate their reactions. In the Commission, authorisation comes from external sources of authority, or sources over which higher administrative and political levels have little control. Commissioner support, though sought, is no strong guarantee of success. Commissioners certainly have to sign off on proposals and they are expected where needed to help. In these circumstances and as hierarchical superiors, they have the ability to instruct officials what to do and how to frame their legislative proposals.

There are certainly examples of Commissioner leadership in setting Commission agendas and shaping the content of their deliberations, but the degree to which this is found appears more limited than might be expected in member states. Of the three proposals for Council or Council and Parliament Regulations in my study (Page forthcoming), one (the Stability Instrument Regulation of 2006) involved close supervision by the Commissioner (Patten) in key stages of its development. Yet on the other two, which in member states might be expected to produce stronger ministerial intervention, the fingerprints of the Commissioner were lighter. In a fishing quota proposal, it was the scientific evidence on stocks that formed the basis of the proposal as specified in the legislation governing the annual negotiations, and the Commissioner, although important in deciding how to frame the figures (in this case whether to present them as straight scientific evidence or seek to offer realistic recommendations more likely to be accepted in Council), had little direct impact on what the proposal contained. In the other, the development of a grant for integrated transport in Europe (Marco Polo II) the Commissioner was surprisingly uninvolved, key matters in the development of the proposal and its negotiation through the co-decision procedure being a matter for officials mainly at the level of Director and below, occasionally the Director General but the Commissioner only tended to 'get things when they were done' in the words of one official involved.

Conclusion

The Commission has all the signs of an activist bureaucracy, producing legislation in significant volumes that make significant changes to the everyday lives of citizens, firms and other organisations. It does so by tying its proposals closely to prominent sources of authority that increase the chances of its measures achieving some success and thus its work bearing legislative fruit. Of course, it also relies on other methods for securing success and actively lobbies and negotiates with other centres of authority in the European Union. However, the prominent sources of authority, whether set out in the procedures contained in old legislation, in international obligations, in requests from Council or specified supervisory bodies, appears to be the main staple of the success of the Commission as an activist bureaucracy.

Prominent sources of authority provide the authorisation for Commission action but do not, however, necessarily rob the Commission administration of its decision-making power. Using a couple of the examples above, while legislation might stipulate that the Commission should produce a report on aspects of the regulation of derivatives, it does not specify what should be in it, and while the Council might have called for the Commission to develop the Procedural Rights Roadmap, it did not prescribe what that map contained.

Rather than saying that the Commission is impotent or its bureaucracy faces constraints on its decision-making power even in areas of decision-making delegated to it (all bureaucracies face these constraints), three important consequences seem likely to result from this prominent authority approach to developing activism. First, as already mentioned, political control over the agenda of the Commission consequently appears limited. Where officials rely less on senior Commission approval for defining their workload and more on prominent sources of authority, units within the administration rely even less on cues from the political top about priorities than they do in most nation states.

Second, there is a camel's nose argument. An indication that the Commission should legislate or recommend legislation might form a minor part of a set of earlier provisions, possibly not particularly extensively debated. But once they are down on paper as a prominent authority commitment they can have a life of their own, and while this is not to ignore the subsequent scope for inter-institutional bargaining, this fixes and gives weight to a set of arguments that then become legitimated core components of a subsequent Commission push for policy action.

Third, the apparently most common form of invoking prominent authority, acting on the provisions of existing legislation, serves to create a tendency similar to what is known as 'deck stacking' (McCubbins et al. 1987) in the US literature – devising rules of decision making that protect or privilege over the longer term the constituencies that created these particular provisions. However, it appears unlikely to be the kind of deck staking envisaged by the theory, allowing politicians to favour certain interest groups over others, but rather also offering the prospect of giving longer-term priority to positions established by bureaucratic groups within the EU administration and the technical and supervisory bodies with which they interact.

Principles of sovereignty seem less important in the Commission's internal operation than might be expected, and the Commission has found ways to become an activist administration in an institutional environment in which sovereignty principles remain exceptionally powerful. In the terms used in this volume, this would appear to make the Commission a significant force of solidarity insofar as this refers to 'the collective capacity and cohesion to develop' common policies (Chapter 1 by Hayward this volume). Yet if the term refers to the character of the legal norms produced or of the deliberation that produces common policies coherence, such activism does not necessarily amount to solidarity – just as lowest common denominator policies do not reflect solidarity in its wider sense, neither do those produced through the path of least resistance.

Note

1. Including Iceland, Liechtenstein and Norway.

Bibliography

Ballmann A., D. Epstein and S. O'Halloran (2002) 'Delegation, Comitology, and the Separation of Powers in the European Union', *International Organization*, 56 (3): 551–574.

Belier, I. (2007) 'Les hommes et les femmes de la Commission', *Ceras Projet 296 Janvier 2007* (Paris: Centre de recherche et d'action sociales).

Coombes, D. (1970). *Politics and Bureaucracy in the European Community* (London: Allen and Unwin).

Egeberg, M. (2006) 'Executive Politics as Usual: Role Behaviour and Conflict Dimensions in the College of European Commissioners', *Journal of European Public Policy* 13(1) 1–15.

Falkner G,. O. Treib, M. Hartlapp and S. Leiber (2005) *Complying with Europe. EU Harmonisation and Soft Law in the Member States* (Cambridge: Cambridge University Press).

Geuijen K., P. 't Hart, S. Princen and K. Yesilkagit (2008) *The New Eurocrats National Civil Servants in EU Policy-making* (Amsterdam: Amsterdam University Press).

Héritier, A and D. Lehmkuhl (2011) 'Governing in the Shadow of Hierarchy: New Modes of Governance in Regulation' in, A. Héritier and M. Rhodes (eds.) *New Modes of Governance in Europe: Governing in the Shadow of Hierarchy* (Basingstoke: Palgrave).

Héritier, A. and C. Moury (2008) 'The European Parliament and Delegation to Comitology', *Lisbon CIES Working Paper n.39/2008*. http://repositorio-iul.iscte. pt/bitstream/10071/716/1/CIES-WP40_Moury_.pdf

Hill, M. and P.L. Hupe (2002) *Implementing Public Policy: Governance in Theory and in Practice* (London: Sage).

Hooghe, L. (2002) *The European Commission and the Integration of Europe: Images of Governance* (Cambridge: Cambridge University Press).

Kassim, H. (2003) 'The European Administration: between Europeanization and Domestication', in J. Hayward and A. Menon (eds) *Governing Europe* (Oxford: Oxford University Press).

König T. and T. Bräuniger (2002) 'From an Ever-Growing Towards an Ever-Slower Union' in M.O. Hosli, A.M. Van Deemen and M. Widgrén (eds) *Institutional Challenges in the European Union* (London: Routledge).

McCubbins, M.D., R.G. Noll and B.R. Weingast (1987) 'Administrative Procedures as Instruments of Political Control', *Journal of Law, Economics, and Organization* 3: 243–277.

Miller, V. (2011) 'EU Legislation: Government Action on "Gold-Plating"'. *House of Commons Library Standard Note Standard note SN05943* (London: House of Commons Library.

Nugent, N. (2001) *The European Commission.* (Basingstoke: Palgrave).

Page, E.C. (forthcoming) *Policies without Politicians* (Oxford: Oxford University Press).

Pressman, J. and A.W. Wildavsky (1984) *Implementation: How Great Expectations in Washington Are Dashed in Oakland* (3rd edn, Berkely, University of California Press).

Schäfer G.F. (2006) 'Demystifying Comitology', *EIPASCOPE* 25th Anniversary Special Issue 47–52.

Selck T.J. and M. Rhinard (2005) 'Pares inter pares? The Bargaining Success of the Commission, the Council, and the Parliament in European Union Legislative Negotiations', *Swiss Political Science Review* 11(3): 123–140.

Sullivan, J. and T. Selck (2007) 'Political Preferences, Revealed Positions and Strategic Votes: Explaining Decision-Making in the EU Council', *Journal of European Public Policy*, 14(7): 1150–1161.

Suvarierol, S. (2008) 'Beyond the Myth of Nationality: Analysing Networks within the European Commission', *West European Politics* 31(4): 701–724.

Suvarierol, S. (2011) 'Everyday Cosmopolitanism in the European Commission', *Journal of European Public Policy* 18(2): 181–200.

Thomson, R. (2008) 'National Actors in International Organizations The Case of the European Commission', *Comparative Political Studies* 41(2): 169–192.

Trondal, J. (2006) 'Governing at the Frontier of the European Commission: The Case of Seconded National Officials *West European Politics* 29 (1): 147–160.

Trondal, J. (2007) 'The Anatomy of Autonomy: Reassessing the Autonomy of the European Commission', *European Journal of Political Research* 47(4): 467–488.

Trondal, J. (2009) 'Administrative Fusion: Less Than a European "Mega Administration"', *Journal of European Integration*, 31(2): 237–260.

Trondal, J., C. van den Berg and S. Suvarierol (2008) 'The Compound Machinery of Government: The Case of Seconded Officials in the European Commission', *Governance* 21(2): 253–274.

Wessels, W. (1998) 'Comitology: Fusion in Action. Politico-administrative Trends in the EU System', *Journal of European Public Policy* 5(2): 209–234.

Wonka, A. (2008) 'Decision-Making Dynamics in the European Commission: Partisan, National or Sectoral?' *Journal of European Public Policy* 15(8): 1145–1163.

7
The Empowerment of Parliaments in EU Integration: Victims or Victors?

Maja Kluger Rasmussen

National parliaments are often seen as the victims of European integration. While closer integration in the European Union (EU) has led to an increased role of the European Parliament (EP), national parliaments have seen their powers curtailed. According to the so-called deparliamentarisation thesis, EU integration has led to the erosion of national parliamentary control over their national governments. The marginalisation of national parliaments in EU decision-making is linked to three issues: reduced national policy autonomy, a shift in the domestic executive–legislative balance, and information asymmetries (Jans and Piedrafita 2009).

Firstly, the transfer of legislative powers to the EU level has reduced the remit of national parliaments, whose power is largely confined to the transposition of EU law into national legislation. Secondly, the increased use of qualified majority voting (QMV) reduces national parliaments' ability to impose detailed ex ante commitments on national governments prior to Council meetings. National parliaments' powers are even limited on issues requiring unanimity, such as treaty changes. Treaty revisions often present national parliaments with a 'take-it-or-leave-it' deal, where national parliaments have the choice of either accepting the treaty revisions without amendments or rejecting it and risking an EU crisis, as witnessed when the French and Dutch people rejected the Constitutional Treaty in 2005 (O'Brennan and Raunio 2007: 3). Lastly, national parliaments are at an informational disadvantage compared to national governments as they do not have a seat at the EU's bargaining table nor do they have direct information about the EU policy process. National legislatures are often ill-equipped to engage in thorough domestic coordination efforts, which require extensive coordination between different ministries, parliamentary committees, and, in the case of federal systems, across policy levels to find a national position (Jans and Piedrafita 2009; Goetz and Meyer-Sahlinh 2008).

This weakness of national parliaments in the EU decision-making process is seen as one of the reasons why the EU is often said to suffer from a democratic deficit, although the existence of a democratic deficit is contested in the academic literature (see for instance Majone 2000; Moravcsik 2002). Some scholars (e.g. Born and Hänggi 2004) contend that the EU suffers from a double democratic deficit (also called a parliamentary deficit) as the shift of powers from the national to the EU level has not been balanced by increased democratic accountability of either the EP or national parliaments.

The EP's elevation to a genuine co-legislator, following the Lisbon Treaty, does not fully compensate for national parliaments' loss of influence. It is well known that Members of the European Parliament (MEPs) are not held directly accountable to the public. EP elections are fought on national, rather than European issues. They are often treated as mid-term national beauty contests used to punish an incumbent government. The EP has not so far sparked the interest and enthusiasm of voters in Europe. The lack of a direct link between MEPs and their electorates, combined with the low visibility of EU affairs nationally, means that MEPs are not constantly held accountable for their activities to the same extent as national politicians. EP elections do not translate into a clear choice between different welfare agendas or political majorities. The EU's budget remains miniscule (approximately 1 per cent of GDP) and the meagre size of the budget limits the EU's redistributive powers and capacity to exert fiscal solidarity during the Eurozone financial crisis. The EU is mainly a polity restricted to economic integration, and lacks the competence for direct taxation and redistributive social policies, which are often salient policy issues in national elections. The absolute majority requirement in the second reading under the ordinary legislative procedure means that the Social Democrats (S&D) and Christian Democrats (EPP) often vote together in an informal 'grand coalition'. The EP thus lacks the cut and thrust of debates between a 'governing' party and an opposition as there is no permanent coalition in the EP nor do any political groups hold a permanent majority. Increasing the role of national parliaments, both individually and collectively, in the EU decision-making process has, therefore, been seen as one way to increase the EU's democratic legitimacy.

Since 1995 all EU member states have set up European affairs committees (EACs) with the function of coordinating parliamentary work on
EU matters and hold the executive to account (Hix and Raunio 2000).
Even EU candidate countries, such as Croatia, have established EACs
to prepare for full EU membership and monitor their government's
activities on EU matters. Moreover, the Lisbon Treaty has sought to
alleviate the EU's democratic deficit by strengthening the role of
national parliaments, increasing the EP's powers and introducing a
citizens' initiative, whereby one million citizens from a significant
number of member states can ask the Commission to put forward a
proposal (see also Chapter 3 by Monaghan). The Lisbon Treaty gives
national parliaments a greater opportunity to make a direct input into
EU decision-making by introducing an early warning system whereby
national parliaments are given eight weeks to scrutinise whether
the European Commission's legislative proposals comply with the
principle of subsidiarity. If enough national parliaments object, a
Commission proposal can potentially be amended or withdrawn. The
early warning system gives national parliaments an important role
in ensuring that the EU does not overstep its authority by involving
itself in matters that can best be dealt with at the national, regional
or local level.

The new role ascribed to national parliaments in the Lisbon Treaty
shows that national parliaments are perceived as playing a key role
in reducing the democratic deficit and enhancing input legitimacy.
This raises an important question: are the new provisions under the
Lisbon Treaty likely to make a significant difference to the influence
of national parliaments in EU legislation? This chapter examines
national parliaments' different approaches to scrutinising EU documents and decisions, and discusses whether national parliaments are
in practice able to take advantage of the new powers given to them
under the Lisbon Treaty. Although Denmark and the UK have opt-
outs to the EU treaty and are known for their Eurosceptic popular
sentiments, they have very different ways of conducting parliamentary scrutiny. The chapter concludes that while the Lisbon Treaty
reduces the information asymmetry between national parliaments
and their governments, national parliaments' ability to play a significant role in EU decision-making is still rather limited as they have no
real power to block EU legislation. So national parliaments have not
significantly either strengthened member state sovereignty or weakened EU solidarity.

Intra-parliamentary coordination

None of the EU institutions are directly accountable to any national parliament. Instead national parliaments can exert influence indirectly through their national governments. The German Bundesrat (the legislative body representing the states (*Länder*) was the first parliament to introduce an EAC in 1957 to exercise scrutiny over their government. In 1962 and 1968 respectively, the Belgian Chamber of Representatives and the Italian Senate followed suit (Jans and Piedrafita 2009). However, in the early years of European integration, national parliaments played a rather marginal and passive role in the, then, European Community (EC). Although MEPs in the early years of European integration held a dual mandate as both MPs and MEPs (albeit prohibited in the 2004 EP elections), the EP was merely a consultative assembly with limited powers. The existence of the 'permissive consensus' meant that most European citizens and political parties were either supportive or uninterested in European integration, giving national governments free reign to negotiate in Brussels and take steps favourable to integration.

When Denmark, the UK and Ireland joined in 1973, the role of national parliaments in the EC policy cycle started to change owing to Denmark and the UK's more Eurosceptic parliaments and electorates. The UK's House of Commons put in place a 'parliamentary scrutiny reserve' system in 1980, whereby British ministers cannot give their consent to decisions in the Council of Ministers before the EAC has completed its scrutiny (see Chapter 16 by Norton). Denmark went even further and introduced a mandating system in which ministers are required to obtain a mandate from the Danish Parliament's EAC before signing up to any EU proposals.

The Danish scrutiny model represents a major step forward for national parliaments' ability to hold its executive accountable. The Danish model was, however, met with much scepticism by other member states, who feared that close national scrutiny of governments could potentially delay and block decisions in the Council (O'Brennan and Raunio 2007: 10). Despite this, several of the newer member states have followed the Danish example and set up strong EACs, while many of the old member states have changed their systems to strengthen parliamentary control of EU affairs (such as Italy and Ireland). While all member states have set up EACs, there are significant cross-country differences with regard to the scope, timing and impact of parliamentary scrutiny. Member states with single party majority governments tend to have national parliaments which are less involved in EU affairs, while parliaments with minority and coalition governments (such as Scandinavia) usually have parliaments, which are more involved in EU affairs (Hix and Høyland 2011: 41).

In most parliaments, EU scrutiny is mainly confined to the EACs with varying degrees of cooperation with specialised committees. The involvement of specialised committees has partly been necessitated by the increased workload of EACs. The delegation of authority to specialised committees has its pros and cons. While it mainstreams EU issues across parliament, sectoral committees may lack the necessary knowledge about EU institutional affairs and ability to see the broader European picture. In some member states – such as Finland, Germany, Estonia and Slovenia – the specialised committees are responsible for EU scrutiny of issues in their specific areas. In most parliaments, however, the involvement of specialised committees is sporadic, and the EAC remains the main, and often sole, forum for discussing EU matters. Even plenary involvement is rare with the EACs usually being authorised to speak for the whole Parliament on European affairs. Rather than involving the full parliament, parliamentary scrutiny of EU affairs takes place behind closed doors shielded away from any public criticism that might hamper the reputation of the government (Raunio 2009: 3–4). This might be seen as a politically rational strategy by political parties given that parties are often internally divided on issues regarding EU integration and out of tune with the public. Only parties on the periphery of the political spectrum (the extreme left or right-wing parties) tend to be in step with their voters and have an interest in making the discussions open to the public.

The British House of Common's plenary vote in October 2011 on whether or not to have a referendum on Britain's relationship with the EU shows just how divided some governments are over European integration (see also Chapter 16 by Norton). Prime Minister David Cameron faced the biggest rebellion since his election as 81 members of the Conservative Party defied Cameron's instruction to vote against a referendum on Britain's EU membership. The vote was prompted by a parliamentary committee after more than 100,000 British people signed an e-petition calling for a referendum on Britain's EU membership. The vote in the House of Commons came just a few days after the EU summit on the Eurozone debt crisis, in which David Cameron and French President Nicolas Sarkozy clashed over Britain's stance. The Tories have long been divided over Europe and their internal fragmentation on the issue proved costly to both Margaret Thatcher and John Major's authority as prime ministers. The example also shows that when the full chamber is involved in discussions over EU matters, it is mainly on 'big' issues such as membership and treaty changes rather than day-to-day EU politics. Each year, the European scrutiny committee in the House of Commons recommends around three documents, which it considers to be of importance for discussion in the chamber. A debate can however only take place if the government is prepared to find time for it (House of Commons' Information Office 2010).

The Conference of Community and European Affairs Committees (COSAC) – a conference of members of national parliaments and the EP – conducted a survey in 2011 on the various types of EU scrutiny methods used in the EU's member states, and found that most parliaments use either a document-based model or a mandating system, or a combination of the two (COSAC 2011). The document-based model mainly focuses on information processing and parliamentary discussions on European Commission proposals rather than on the actual decision-making process in and between the EP and the Council. The objective is not to impose binding voting instructions on the government, but rather to inform Members of Parliament (MPs) in the EAC. However, this does not mean that parliaments using a document-based method are without any influence. EACs regularly call upon ministers to clarify and explain their position and governments often anticipate the reactions of MPs. Many EACs, such as the British House of Common's European Scrutiny Committee, invest in considerable information gathering and expert hearings. Document-based systems are often underpinned by a scrutiny reserve, which prescribes that ministers should not sign up to any given EU legislation before the national parliament has finished debating it, and thus reinforces national sovereignty. However, governments may seek to override the scrutiny reserve to avoid delaying decisions in the Council. In the British House of Commons, the reserve resolution states that the government may give agreement to a proposal still awaiting scrutiny by the European scrutiny committee if it is regarded to be 'confidential, routine or trivial, or is substantially the same as a proposal on which scrutiny has been completed', or if the scrutiny committee has specified that agreement 'need not be withheld pending consideration' by the EAC (The House of Commons 2010: 9).

Under the mandate-based system, governments are obliged to present their negotiation position to the EAC, which may oblige the government to review its position. If a government diverges from the mandate, a clear justification and, sometimes, a new consultation with the EAC are needed. The Danish Parliament is particularly known for keeping a tight leash on its government on EU matters. The Danish EAC issues binding voting instructions to Danish ministers prior to meetings in the Council. The committee convenes with ministers on the Friday before a Council meeting and goes through the forthcoming Council agenda on a point-by-point basis. If more than half of the members of the Danish EAC oppose the government's position on a particular proposal, the government will have to change its position accordingly. Despite Denmark's tradition of minority governments, the EAC rarely opposes the government's position, which is partly due to the fact that ministers adapt their position to that of the EAC. It is not uncommon for ministers to establish their position during the EAC meetings. The existence of mandating power is often associated with strong parliamentary powers. However, the QMV requirements in the Council reduce both national and parliamentary control over EU nego-tiations and outcomes. Even if a parliament manages to influence its government's position, this position may not prevail as governments can be outvoted by other member states in the Council.

Several scholars have developed classifications to help evaluate and compare national parliaments' impact on governments. Maurer and Wessels (2001) distinguish four types of parliaments according to their policy-making strength: (1) strong policy-making parliaments, such as Denmark and Austria; (2) potential or latent national players, such as Germany; (3) would-be national players, but who are unable to chal-lenge their government, such as the UK and France; lastly (4) slow adapters. Building on Maurer and Wessels' work, Raunio (2005: 320) suggests a three-dimensional indicator including: the involvement of specialised committees in EU affairs, the access to information in terms of timing and scope and the power to mandate ministers through issuing binding voting instructions. He finds that countries with both strong parliaments and Eurosceptic public opinion tend to have tighter national scrutiny than countries with weaker parliaments and more EU supportive voters. Some scholars (such as Judge 1995) question whether or not thorough parliamentary scrutiny benefit national parliaments at all or merely strengthens governments rather than national parlia-ments. Goetz and Meyer-Sahling (2008: 8) argue that national govern-ments can use the need for parliamentary approval as a bargaining chip in Council negotiations. Others contend that 'national parlia-ments can wield considerably more influence than before' (Hix and Raunio 2000: 159).

A controversial question is whether or not EU decision-making would be more legitimate if all national parliaments imposed binding mandates on their governments. Legitimacy and efficiency are often seen as trade-offs – the more control, the less efficiency. As it stands now, national scrutiny procedures do not, in any serious way, hinder the efficiency of EU decision-making as only a few member states impose strict control on their governments. But would that also be the case if all member states adopted the Danish scrutiny model? This question is both very speculative and normative. It raises further questions, such as: what is the right balance between democracy and efficiency? To what extent should a more active participation of national parliaments and the possible delaying and blocking effects on EU decision-making be allowed to impede the efficiency of the EU's decision-making process? There is no single answer to these questions, but they show that democracy concerns cannot be seen in isolation from the question of cost (Smith 1996: 15).

Inter-parliamentary cooperation

National parliaments have also sought to act collectively through the inter-parliamentary 'Conference of Community and European Affairs Committee' (COSAC) established in 1989. COSAC promotes the exchange of information and best practice between national parliaments and the European Parliament. It assembles twice a year in the country holding the EU presidency and brings together members of EACs (six MPs from each national parliament) and MEPs (usually one or two vice presidents responsible for relations with national parliaments). It is one of the few EU forums where national parliaments can exchange best practice and discuss their role in EU integration. However, COSAC is often referred to as a 'talking shop' – a label previously applied to the EP before it gained co-decision powers – due to its lack of capacity to make binding decisions. A greater collective role for COSAC with the possibility of making binding decisions in the future would however be problematic for the legitimacy of national parliaments. As Bengtson (2007: 62) points out, national parliaments are expected to defend and protect their national constituents' interests. Enforcing binding decisions in COSAC might run the risk of compromising national parliaments' role, and conflict with existing rules and practices in national parliaments. For instance, in the UK, it is not possible for committees to commit either the House of Commons or the House of Lords to a decision taken outside the British Parliament (ibid).

Despite COSAC's limited political role, there has, since the early 1990s, been a gradual effort to give parliaments a stronger role in the integration process. The Maastricht Treaty (Declaration 13) envisaged that national parliaments should receive legislative EU proposals in good time for information and possible scrutiny. National parliaments were however dependent on their own government to transmit proposals to them. The Amsterdam Treaty established – by means of a protocol – a minimum of six weeks between the Commission's communication of a new legislative proposal and its appearance on the Council's agenda to give national parliaments time to embark on parliamentary scrutiny. In 2006, the so-called Barroso Initiative was launched with the aim of encouraging national parliaments to express their opinions on Commission initiatives (such as green and white papers, communications and draft legislative acts) not only concerning their compliance with the subsidiarity principle. The initiative required the Commission to submit all its legislative proposals and communications documents directly to all national parliaments (which previously had to rely on their national governments for the access to these documents) and invite them to react and to engage in dialogue on its proposals. The Barroso Initiative is closely related to the Commission's Plan D (denoting Democracy, Dialogue and Debate) aimed at improving the EU's existing structures, bringing Europe closer to its citizens and alleviating the democratic deficit (Sørensen 2008: 17; European Commission 2005; see also Chapter 3 by Monaghan). The Lisbon Treaty formalises the practice of direct transmission to national parliaments and broadens the scope to include draft legislative acts, Council agendas and minutes and the Commission's annual work program.

There have been differing views on how national parliaments should be involved in EU decision-making. These range from focusing on an increased scrutiny role of draft legislation nationally to ideas of creating an EU institution representing national parliaments to increase parliaments' collective role. Those in favour of an increased collective voice for national parliaments tend to associate the empowering of the EP with a further weakening of national parliaments, and thus increased powers to the EP is not seen as a way to tackle the democratic deficit. On the contrary, MEPs have often argued that the best way to tackle the democratic deficit is to increase the EP's powers in relation to the European Commission and the Council, and to strengthen the role of national parliaments on the national level vis-à-vis their governments.

During the discussions in the Convention on the Future of Europe (2001–2003), preceding the aborted Constitutional Treaty, the EP

strongly opposed the idea of introducing a second chamber representing national parliaments in the permanent EU institutional structure as it was seen as usurping the EP's role (Rideau 1996: 173–78). It is
dubious whether or not this is a sign of the EP not showing solidarity
with national parliaments as several national parliamentarians have
been much opposed to the idea of a second chamber. Rather than gath-
ering support from MPs, the notion of a second EU chamber has mainly
been supported by executives, such as former British Prime Minister
Tony Blair and former German Foreign Minister Joschka Fischer. An
oft-aired argument raised by MPs is that a second chamber will further
complicate the EU decision-making procedure rather than contributing
to increased legitimacy (Bengtson 2007: 58). The suggestion to establish
a chamber representing national parliaments has, however, posed more
questions than answers. Would such a chamber impede the efficiency
of the EU decision-making process? How would such an institution
function? How should national parliaments authorise a certain number
of their members to represent them at the EU level?

The role of national parliaments in European integration remains a
recurrent theme, most recently discussed in relation to the European
Commission's green paper of 23 November 2011 on the feasibility of
introducing stability bonds. These Eurobonds are likely to be accompanied by requirements of stronger budgetary discipline and surveillance
of national budgets, which might undermine national fiscal policy-
making. While Eurobonds are seen as a means to resolve the Eurozone
crisis and as showing solidarity with struggling economies, it is highly
questionable whether or not they will work in practice given the vast
differences in the quality in governance across the Eurozone and the
lack of a true EU political union. Eurobonds provide the real test of
member states' will to support fiscal EU integration and solidarity.
Will EU citizens agree that their tax payments might be needed to
support countries in economic hardship? Holding taxpayers in thrifty
countries liable for spending decisions in other countries might turn
into a poison pill for the Economic and Monetary Union (EMU) and
potentially lead to a break-up of the EMU.

The diversity of views on EU integration in different national
parliaments makes it difficult to determine what role national parliaments should play in future EU integration. Particularly majoritarian
democracies, such as the UK, have been more concerned about ceding
parliamentary sovereignty to the EU's supranational institutions
compared to constitutional democracies, such as Germany. Upon the
UK's accession to the EU in 1973, the British parliament was hesitant

to accept the supremacy of EU laws as it conflicted with the central concept of parliamentary sovereignty that acts of parliament immediately can overrule existing laws and legislation (Hix and Høyland 2011: 98; See also Chapters 8 and 16 by Birkinshaw and Norton, respectively). The issue was only solved when the House of Lords argued that the British parliament could at any time withdraw the UK from the EU. Political culture is far from uniform across the member states with the UK at one end of the spectrum, defending its parliamentary sovereignty, and Germany at the other end of the spectrum, wanting a European *Rechtsstaat* and a more federal EU legal system.

With its troubled history and lack of strong parliamentarianism, Germany is less committed to protecting the role of national parliaments than other countries. As a result, Germany has often supported a stronger role for the EP than countries with strong parliamentary democracies. The co-existence between two types of democratic legitimacies – the EP and national parliaments – suggests the risk of conflict and tension between MPs and MEPs. Studies on MEPs' contact with their national parties find that the relationship between MEPs and MPs is often strained by MEPs feeling of rivalry and lack of interest (Blomgren 2003; Rasmussen 2008). As one MEP noted

> a characteristic feature of working down here [the EP] is that you are very much on your own. The party back home knows very little about what you are doing and are not very engaged in your work. They helped me in making my party program for the European Parliament election, but that is about the only time that they have really showed any interest in my work (Rasmussen 2008: 16).

This situation might be due to different legislative focuses, with the EP mainly engaged in regulation and the national parliament mainly focusing on redistributive policies. Moreover, EU legislation is often processed in the EP long before it is scrutinised in national parliaments. For instance, when the Service Directive (also known as the Bolkenstein Directive) was discussed in the EP in 2006, the Danish Parliament only initiated its scrutiny of the directive one and a half years later than the EP. Rather than discussing the amendments put forward in the EP and the Council, the Danish EAC discussed the Commission's initial proposal, whereas the EU institutions were much further ahead in the process. The delay in national scrutiny can put MEPs in a difficult position. On the one hand, they are decision-makers who need to strike compromises in the EP and, on the other hand, they might be criticised afterwards for not being in line with the national party position (Rasmussen 2008: 16).

The Lisbon Treaty: a small step

The Lisbon Treaty is the first to make a direct reference to national parliaments in the main treaty text (Raunio 2009). As stated by Article 10(2), 'Citizens are directly represented in the European Council by their Heads of State or Government and in the Council by their governments, themselves democratically accountable either to their national Parliaments, or to their citizens'. The Lisbon Treaty gives national parliaments the opportunity to review the Commission's legislative proposals, and within eight weeks send a reasoned opinion to the Commission if they think a proposal violates the principle of subsidiarity. Each national parliament has two votes, which is split between the two houses in bicameral systems. If a significant number of national parliaments find that a proposal does not comply with the subsidiarity principle, the Commission must review its proposal. Depending on the number of votes, a national parliament can either raise a yellow card or an orange card:

- For the *yellow card procedure* to be invoked one third of parliaments, and one fourth in the areas of justice and home affairs, must cast a vote against a legislative draft proposal due to non-compliance with the subsidiarity principle. If this happens, the Commission is obliged to review its proposal and decide to amend, withdraw or maintain it. The Commission is however not obliged to follow national parliaments' objections when a yellow card is invoked, but must justify its decision.
- *The orange card procedure* covers proposals falling under the ordinary legislative procedure. If a simple majority of all the available votes given to national parliaments object against a Commission proposal, the Commission is obliged to review it. If the Commission decides to maintain its proposal, the reasoned opinions from national parliaments and the Commission's justification is forwarded to the Council and EP, who must consider whether or not the proposal in question breaches the subsidiarity principle. In order to withdraw a proposal, 55 per cent of the members in the Council and a simple majority in the EP must confirm a violation of the subsidiarity principle.

Most academic observers (see for instance Raunio 2007) consider the above provisions as a step in the right direction, albeit a small one. Several problems have been highlighted. Firstly, whether a proposal does or does not comply with the subsidiarity principle is a matter of political judgement rather than an entirely objective assessment. In the political debate, the word subsidiarity is used in a very general manner, namely that a policy should be implemented at the level where it is best achieved. While the principle has been invoked by the European Court of Justice (ECJ) several times, the principle has never been defined legally. It might seem counterintuitive to have a principle of subsidiarity for considering whether or not legislation can be adopted under policy competences already relinquished to the EU. However, there are examples from the past where the Commission has overstepped its competences by basing legislation on an incorrect legal basis, such as the 1998 tobacco advertisement and sponsorship directive. In this particular case, the Commission tried to harmonise tobacco advertising rules under Article 114 of the EC treaty, covering the harmonisation of laws for the completion of the single market (an exclusive EU competence). However, in 2000, the ECJ annulled the directive as it did not refer to the correct Treaty Article, which should have been based on Article 168 regarding setting public health standards (an exclusive competence of the member states). The Lisbon Treaty gives national parliaments the power to police these competence boundaries, together with the ECJ, and control the use of unanimity versus QMV (Hix and Høyland 2011: 95). Secondly, 'early warning' is somewhat of a misleading term as national parliaments are only involved when the Commission has put forward its proposal. The intense lobbying of the Commission during its drafting phase shows the importance of getting involved earlier in the process.

Between 2005 and 2009, COSAC tested national parliaments' ability to conduct substantive subsidiarity checks within the eight week time frame. These 'try-outs' suggest that the time limit of eight weeks is too short for substantive subsidiarity checks. Since the entry into force of the Lisbon Treaty, 29 national chambers have submitted at least one reasoned report to the Commission, the majority of which have been put forward by the parliaments of Poland, Sweden, Luxembourg, Italy, Denmark, Lithuania, the Netherlands and Romania in consecutive order. The most frequently questioned draft legislative acts, so far, have been the directive on seasonal work (determining the conditions of entry and residence of third-country nationals for the purposes as seasonal employment), and the Directive on a common consolidated corporate tax base, both of which were contested by nine parliaments. However, none of the EU draft legislations have gathered enough votes to invoke a yellow or orange card. National parliaments' unwillingness to grant third-country nationals minimal rights when undertaking seasonal work in the EU evinces that the creation of a 'social Europe' based on solidarity and sharing remains more of a meta-constitutional aspiration than a reality.

The new provisions under the Lisbon Treaty are unlikely to make a significant difference to the influence of national parliaments in EU decision-making. The yellow and orange card procedures only empower national parliaments to trigger the Commission to rethink its proposal, but they remain dependent on the Council and EP to block a proposal. Without introducing a 'red card' in the future – compelling the Commission to withdraw proposals breaching the subsidiarity principle – it seems unlikely that national parliaments can have any real voice in EU decision-making. Moreover, governments and national parliaments cannot necessarily be seen as inseparable. In parliamentary systems, such as the UK, the majority of the parliament is controlled by the government. This means that if a government strongly supports an EU proposal, it is likely to do anything it can to avoid its EAC objecting to it because of concerns over subsidiarity.

Conclusion

Most of the discussion of national parliaments depicts national parliaments as 'victims' of increased European integration. National parliaments' limited ability to legislate and control their executive branch properly in the areas devolved to the EU level has been a recurrent point of criticism of the EU's institutional system. However, EU integration is not just a story of increased deparliamentarisation, but has also been characterised by a process of parliamentarisation with increased powers conferred on the EP. The empowerment of the EU's only directly elected institution, the EP, has not been able to compensate for national parliaments loss of influence. The low turn-out in EP elections and the low visibility of EU affairs nationally suggest that national parliaments remain the main political institution voters relate to directly. Overcoming the EU's (purported) democratic deficit is therefore inextricably tied to giving national parliaments a greater voice in EU decision-making.

National parliaments have not been idle bystanders to the erosion of their parliamentary powers, but set up scrutiny mechanisms (e.g. EACs) to hold their governments to account. The organisation of EU scrutiny varies significantly between member states. MPs in parliaments with coalition and minority governments tend to be more powerful against their government than in member states where the governments hold the majority in parliament. This is why EACs in Nordic parliaments have been more powerful against their governments on EU matters than the British House of Commons.

The Lisbon Treaty has tried to increase the EU's legitimacy by increasing the possibility for national parliaments to ensure that the Commission does not overstep its authority. These new provisions are, however, no magic bullet against national parliaments' loss of powers. While the increased transmission of EU documents from the Commission to national parliaments reduces the information asymmetry between national parliaments and their governments, national parliaments' ability to play a more active role in EU decision making remains limited. Moreover, the often limited contact between MPs and MEPs suggests that national politicians already have their hands full and might lack the appetite to engage more actively in EU policy-making. While national parliaments have sometimes reinforced member state sovereignty, the EP has not been strong enough significantly to increase EU solidarity.

Bibliography

Blomgren, M. (2003), *Cross-Pressure and Political Representation in Europe. A Comparative Study of MEPs and the Intra-party Arena* (Umeå: Umeå University).

Bengtson, C. (2007) 'Interparliamentary cooperation within Europe', in J. O'Brennan, and T. Raunio (eds). *National Parliaments within the Enlarged European Union. From 'Victims' of Integration to Competitive Actors?* (Abingdon: Routledge), pp. 46–65.

Born, H. and H. Hänggi (2004) *The 'Double Democratic Deficit': Parliamentary Accountability and the Use of Force Under International Auspices* (Aldershot: Ashgate).

COSAC (2011) 16th bi-annual report: developments in European Union procedures and practices relevant to parliamentary scrutiny. COSAC Secretariat, October 2011.

European Commission (2005) *The Commission's Contribution to the Period of Reflection and Beyond: Plan-D for Democracy, Dialogue and Debate, Communication from the Commission to the Council, the European Parliament, the European Economic and Social Committee and the Committee of the Regions*, October 13, COM(2005) 494 final (Brussels: European Commission).

Goetz, K.H. and J.-H. Meyer-Sahling (2008) 'The Europeanisation of National Political Systems: Parliaments and Executives', *Living Reviews in European Governance*, 3(2) (www.livingreviews.org/ lreg-2008-2, 2008).

Hix, S. and B. Høyland (2011) *The Political System of the European Union*, 3rd ed. (London: Palgrave).

Hix, S and T. Raunio (2000) 'Backbenchers Learn to Fight Back: European Integration and Parliamentary Government', *West European Politics* 23(4), 142–168.

House of Commons Information Office (2010), EU Legislation and Scrutiny Procedures, Factsheet 11, September 2010 (London: House of Commons).

Jans, T. and S. Piedrafita (2009) The Role of National Parliaments in European Decision-Making, EIPASCOPE 2009/1 working paper.

Judge, D. (1995), 'The Failure of National Parliaments', *West European Politics*, 18(3), pp. 79–100.

Majone G. (2000) 'The Credibility Crisis of Community Regulation', *Journal of Common Market Studies*, 38(2), 273–302.

Maurer, A. and W. Wessels (eds) (2001) *National Parliaments on their Ways to Europe: Losers or Latecomers* (Cambridge: Cambridge University Press).

Moravcsik, A. (2002) 'In Defense of the "Democratic Deficit": Reassessing the Legitimacy of the European Union', *Journal of Common Market Studies*, 40(4), 603–34.

O'Brennan, J. and T. Raunio (2007) 'Deparliamentarization and European integration', in J. O'Brennan and T. Raunio (eds). *National Parliaments within the Enlarged European Union. From 'Victims' of Integration to Competitive Actors?* (Abingdon: Routledge), pp. 1–26.

Rasmussen, M. (2008),' Another Side of the Story – a Qualitative Case Study of How MEPs Vote', *Politics*, 28 (1), 11–18.

Raunio, T. (2005) 'Holding Governments Accountable in European Affairs: Explaining Cross-National Variation', *Journal of Legislative Studies*, 11(34), 319–342.

Raunio, T. (2009) 'National parliaments and European integration: what we know and what we should know', Arena Working Paper No. 2, January 2009.

Rideau, J. (1996) 'National Parliaments and the European Parliament – Cooperation of Conflict', in E. Smith (ed.) *National Parliaments as Cornerstones of European Integration* (Dordrecht: Kluwer Law International), pp. 173–178.

Smith, E. (1996) 'Introduction: 'Sovereignty' – National and Popular', in E. Smith (eds) *National Parliaments as Cornerstones of European Integration* (Dordrecht: Kluwer Law International), pp. 3–18.

Sørensen, C. (2008) 'Love me, love me not…A typology of public euroscepticism', EPERN Working Paper No 19, Sussex European Institute.

8
National Courts and European Union Courts
Patrick Birkinshaw

Despite early claims to the sovereignty of Community law, a process of mutual accommodation and support between legal systems has developed in which crude interpretations of a legal hierarchy have virtually disappeared. The sovereignty of Community law over national laws has long been accepted but that recognition is based in national constitutions which determine the conditions of constitutionality. The preliminary reference procedure under TFEU Article 267 has helped to achieve solidarity by providing a focal point for the uniform interpretation of EU law. The most dramatic illustration of solidarity has come with the dialogue and development of human rights protection where the EU courts have absorbed the influence of the common traditions of the member states' courts and the European Court of Human Rights (ECHR) to help forge a human rights law in the EU. It has also been seen in the development of principles of judicial review in national systems.

Community law and sovereignty

If there were ever any doubts about the central role that law would play within the nascent European Economic Community (EEC), these were soon put to rest by the European Court of Justice (ECJ)[1] in a series of judgments setting out the Constitutional dimension to the Community, the position of its law and the conferral of rights upon individuals by that law. The Community was built on French models of governance with a limited representative assembly and powerful, professional and expert executive organs. Judicial control was of a limited nature built on the French model of judicial review although the ECJ was charged with ensuring that the 'law is observed' in the application and interpretation of the Treaties [TEU Article 19(1)]. Nonetheless, the Community, proclaimed the ECJ in 1986, 'was built on the rule of law' (Case 294/83 *Les Verts* [1986] ECR 1339, para 23), a claim subsequently taken up in the EU treaty [TEU Article 2]. The ECJ has even advised that its role as guardian and interpreter of the treaties meant that there are limits to the means of amending the treaties to remove this power [*Opinion 2/94* [1996] ECR I-1759 para 30].

Early in its jurisprudence, and in spite of the constraints imposed by the parameters of the Treaty of Rome, the ECJ ruled that 'the EEC Treaty has created its own legal system' becoming an integral part of the legal systems of the member states and which their courts are bound to apply. Member states had limited or transferred their own powers in deference to this new legal order unlike any existing or previous international legal regime or municipal one [*Costa v ENEL* [1964] ECR 585]. Within its sphere of competence, the ECJ had established the sovereignty of Community law over national laws. Furthermore, this new legal system had established rights for individuals enforceable through their national courts. These were not simply treaties between nation-states. The law could be invoked by nationals before their own national courts and tribunals. Individuals as well as official organs and states could exercise vigilance over Community and member state activity under Community law by vindicating their rights through national courts [*Van Gend en Loos* [1963] ECR 13].

This judicial conceptualisation was not set out in the treaties. This was truly a momentous development and jurisprudence. Momentous: yet it passed by most UK politicians and lawyers in its full implications when the European Communities Act 1972 was being debated in the UK Parliament in the early 1970s. It took almost another 20 years before the full implications of this foundational jurisprudence were realised within the UK.

In the famous *Factortame* decision of the House of Lords in 1991, the Law Lords disapplied provisions of an Act of Parliament that contravened EC law and applied remedies against a servant of the Crown, the British government, which in an earlier hearing of the case they had established could not be issued against the Crown. It was a revolutionary UK judgment unequalled in its effects on legal sovereignty since English case law of the seventeenth century. It was a reflection of the changing nature and complexity of sovereignty in the contemporary world. Furthermore, as Lord Bridge so aptly expressed the point: far from being 'a novel and dangerous invasion by a Community institution of the sovereignty of the UK', the ECJ in its jurisprudence had long established the supremacy of Community law over national law. 'Thus, whatever limitation of its sovereignty Parliament accepted when it enacted the ECA 1972 was entirely voluntary' (*Factortame* [1991] 1 AC 603, 658). It was always clear that a domestic court issuing final judgment had to 'override' any rule of domestic law inconsistent with a 'directly enforceable rule of' Community law. What was to become clearer was that there was not a neat hierarchical gradation of legal orders but a novel, pluralistic and interactive relationship involving different systems of law. It is also clear that supremacy or sovereignty was to be further analysed in the light of national constitutional juris-prudence (see later). The sovereignty of Community law did not apply *tout court*. It applied where domestic law operated *within the sphere* of Community law. The Treaty of Lisbon refers to the 'primacy' of EC law in declaration no. 17 – a removal from its position in the Constitutional Treaty as an article in the first part on constitutional provisions (Article I-6) – a softer edged epithet than sovereignty.

Despite the rejection of the EU Constitutional Treaty in 2005, the ECJ had long before established the treaties as a constitution and the ECJ as a constitutional court guided by the letter and spirit of the treaties and general principles of law. This fact has not been without challenge. The basic foundations established by the court above in its interpretative role on references from national courts seeking clarification of Community law have remained in place ever since. Indeed, they have taken an ever widening ambit. They have also, I would suggest, been responsible for the deepening juridification of governance within the UK and in other member states. As emphasised on countless occasions, one must have one authoritative ruling on the meaning and content of EU law. Money and business and political direction depend on that. Nonetheless, it would be folly not to appreciate that the model set out in the ECJ's judgments has been subject to the interpretations of national courts drawing limits on the ECJ judgments. What obstacles have opposed the pathway to sovereignty set out by the ECJ?

What is 'sovereignty'?

Every new treaty brings forth a process of review and if necessary amend-ment of national constitutions to ensure compliance with the treaties before they are signed and ratified. Where necessary, a protocol will recognise a national position such as Ireland's on abortion. In this way, disputes of a constitutional dimension are hopefully avoided. However, the national processes of ratification of treaties allow for the review of measures approving of accession to the new treaty. Ratification of treaties is in accordance with national constitutional requirements. In those countries with constitutional courts, review is conducted by these courts. In the UK, the Supreme Court has no written constitution to safeguard – only the common law constitution. In England, attacks on government proposals for entering into treaties would be based on vires and jurisdiction – that the government is not complying with legislative requirements or that it is abusing prerogative powers. The European Union Act 2011 is likely to increase such challenges. But what if the implementing measures are themselves in breach of the national constitution? This is the situation that the German constitutional court had to address in the Lisbon judgment and before that in the Maastricht judgment.

National implementing laws recognise the sovereignty of EU law, said the *Bundersverfassungsgericht* (BVerfG) but those laws must conform to the German Constitution, the basic law. To the extent that they do not – by not fully recognising the guarantee in the Constitution for democracy or the protection of human rights – those measures are unconstitutional in Germany. Furthermore, if the treaties, which are the product of national will collectively exercised with other nations, seek advertently or inadvertently, to undermine Germany's Constitution so that no choice is allowed in their manner of incorporation, then the BVerfG would have to rule on the incompatibility of the treaties with German constitutional law. The EU organs can only operate within the powers conferred by member states. The Union has no power to create its own powers beyond those conferred. German ministers cannot agree to a breach of the German Constitution. Core areas of constitutional identity are 'particularly sensitive', requiring 'sufficient' national space. However, in *Honeywell* (2 BvR 2661/06: 2/7/10), the BVerfG stipulated that the Court of Justice of the European Union (CJEU) must have the opportunity to rule on the legality of EU measures first.

The position in France took a different line because of the initial refusal of the administrative courts to accept the supremacy of Community law and the overriding effect of ECJ judgments. The administrative courts ruled that they lacked the capability of assessing the validity of French *lois* and whether they were compatible with Community law. Any decision on compatibility and constitutionality had to be decided by the *Conseil Constitutionnel* (CC) before promulgation of a law. The civil courts accepted Community sovereignty in 1975 ruling that a properly ratified treaty took priority over a domestic law. It took until 1989 in *Nicolo* before the *Conseil d'Etat* (C d'E) accepted the full implications of sovereignty and their ability to assess French law's compatibility with Community law. The basis of that recognition was Article 55 and subsequently 88-I of the French Constitution. In *Arcelor,* the C d'E refused to rule on the compatibility of a decree with the French Constitution implementing a directive on emission trading schemes. It noted that the fundamental rights in question were given similar protection under EU law as under French law. If there were a clash between the French measure and Community law, a reference would be made to the ECJ under the Treaty. If such rights were not protected under EU law, the C d'E could assess the compliance of the domestic measure with the constitution. It showed a willingness to engage in 'dialogue' and be 'Euro-friendly'.

The CC examined the question of supremacy in its 2004 decision on the European Electronic Commerce Directive and its compatibility with the French Constitution. The CC stated that it would not assess the constitutionality of laws that simply implemented clear and precise terms of directives. By virtue of Article 88-I of the constitution, the legal system of the Community forms an integral part of the French Republic. While accepting the supremacy of Community law in EC law matters, the CC would, however, scrutinise the constitutionality of the national implementing measures of European secondary legislation to establish whether such acts were incompatible with the constitution. The CC has also ruled that where the provisions of a national law merely transpose the precise terms of a directive, these are not subject to a review in the CC unless there is express contrary provision in the Constitution or the directive is annulled by the Community courts. Self-denial has been evident in other CC case law although the basis of ultimate sovereignty resides in the Constitution (Dec No 2010–605 DC 12 May 2010).[2]

One odd result of the case law in France was that while the courts came to recognise the superiority of EU law over domestic law, French statutes once promulgated could not be challenged in any French court under the Constitution. This anomaly was corrected by Article 61-I of the Constitution in 2008 allowing for challenge to the constitutionality of legislation in the CC on a reference from the administrative or civil courts of appeal.

Britain of course has no written Constitution to amend and so avoids the complications involved with constitutional review or internal divisions in domestic municipal law which embrace fellow member states. Here, parliamentary sovereignty and the rule of law take the place of a written Constitution. We have no way of subjecting statutes to judicial review except to the extent described above, or that they do not conform with EU law and may therefore in their offending provisions be disapplied by national courts. The position seems reasonably clear: EU law is law within our system by virtue of s 2(1) ECA 1972. EU law, through the ECJ, has declared its own sovereignty. That has to be taken on board. Provision is made for the ECA not to be impliedly repealed by subsequent statutes. Subsequent statutes and regulations must therefore be read subject to Section 2(1) and are constrained by it. There is a voluminous case law on what we refer to as 'articulate consistency' in the interpretation of domestic norms so as to comply with EU measures. A myriad of circumstances may show that EU norms and domestic norms appear inconsistent. The domestic courts have basically maintained that domestic law should be held to conform with EU law. The jurisprudence is highly developed and has significantly modified judicially created English canons of judicial interpretation of statutes and regulations to achieve consistency. But, what if Parliament *expressly* legislates to disapply Section 2(1)? That is, Parliament legislates *specifically* and *precisely* against an EU obligation or obligations. Does Parliament's sovereignty allow it to do this? That depends upon how one defines sovereignty.

The answer to some of these points came before Sir John Laws in a case concerning the 'metric martyrs' – English market stall holders who wished to sell goods by imperial measures and not metric ones as required at the relevant time by EU law (*Thoburn v Sunderland City Council* [2002] 4 All ER 156). This is the most detailed account that we have in our judicial decisions of these constitutional essentials. In every crucial respect, the relevant parts of the judgment are *obiter dicta* – not strictly necessary for the decision in the case and therefore persuasive but not binding under the common law doctrine of precedent. Laws clearly took the opportunity to expatiate at great length on the common law Constitution.

At the heart of Laws' argument is the belief that the constitutional foundations of the relationship between the UK and the then EC are not to be found in the judgments of the ECJ. The basis of Community sovereignty is forged within Section 2(1) ECA and EC law takes precedence within its sphere of operation by virtue of Section 2(1). But the *overriding sovereignty* of Parliament cannot be ceded because it was not established by Parliament. It was established by the common law. Under the common law, Parliament is incapable of giving away its foundational sovereignty. One might add that it may transfer its sovereignty in limited and ever increasing areas which is what Section 2(1) has achieved. But it cannot abandon the power allowing for such transfer.

The common law will not allow for that. The common law is interpreted by the judges. The common law may develop. This, as stated in a subsequent case (*Jackson v Att-Gen* [2005] UKHL 56), may involve a judicial adjustment on establishing what the master rule of the system – Parliamentary sovereignty – entails. Limits may even be placed on what Parliament can do.

Sir John also argued that the common law recognised 'constitutional statutes'. It is true that judges have long treated constitutional statutes in a special way from the perspective of interpretation. But what is novel is to give them a higher status than 'ordinary statutes'. Constitutional orthodoxy states that *all* legislation is of the same status. Constitutional statutes are those that deal with governmental relationships or with government/citizen relationships. The ECA is one such statute. A practical result of a measure having the status 'constitutional' is that it is not subject to the doctrine of implied repeal. The actual scope of implied repeal is not precisely defined and rests on uncertain decisions but it basically means that a later provision in a statute repeals an inconsistent earlier provision in a statute. The ECA can only be *expressly* repealed by unequivocal, precise terms. Section 2(4) ECA actually has the effect of stating that all subsequent legislation after the ECA has to be read as if the words 'This statute must be read subject to the provisions of Section 2(1)' were included.

Finally, Laws added sentiments echoing those of the German constitutional court in *Brunner* (concerning the Maastricht Treaty) and repeated in the *Lisbon* judgment:

> In the event, which no doubt would never happen in the real world, that a European measure was seen to be repugnant to a fundamental or constitutional right guaranteed by the law of England (sic), a question would arise whether the general words of the ECA were sufficient to incorporate the measure and give it overriding effect in domestic law. [para 60]

The domestic courts, and I add the UK courts, would have the final word on ultimate sovereignty in such a case, argues Laws. A similar position has been reached in other member states' legal systems. The method of statutory interpretation to protect fundamental rights identified by Laws has been developed in leading UK judgments in the House of Lords appellate committee and its successor the Supreme Court. Only the clearest of words in a statute can remove fundamental rights' protection. There is no removal by implication.

What we see happening here and in other member state jurisdictions is not a crude 'Who is sovereign?' approach. As in other member states, the sovereignty of EU law and its limitations are defined by domestic law. What we see is a balancing process and one dependent on cooperation, confluence and mutual adjustment and not domination and hierarchy (Kirchof 1999, 227–228, 241). These are matters on which neither domestic courts nor EU courts may have the last say. That is a matter which may depend, argues MacCormick, on international tribunals (MacCormick 1999: 117–121). But this creates its own problems as we shall see below.

The sophistication of the judicial and academic debate on the judicial balance that has been achieved puts into stark relief the attempt by the Conservative–Liberal coalition government to re-emphasise the sovereignty of the UK Parliament by virtue of Section 18 European Union Act 2011. This section is simplistic in its content and says nothing that has not already been established within Laws' judgment, which despite being *obiter*, is likely to be shared by senior UK judges. Not all senior English judges accept the views on the limits of Parliament's powers expressed in *Jackson* (above). Lord Bingham makes it clear that Parliament is still the sovereign body (Bingham 2010, 168) and constitutional change must come through Parliament.

The 2011 Act confers national referendum breaks on future EU treaty reforms and Parliamentary approval for a variety of other issues. The Minister is given an opt out where, inter alia, '...the making of any provision...applies only to member States other than the United Kingdom' (Section 4(4)). He has to table a statement to this effect and provide his reasons for the belief. This will doubtless be subject to judicial review challenge and will not be protected by Parliamentary privilege. It involves legal powers and their exercise and interpretation, a matter for the courts.

Human rights protection within the EU

The first significant legal dispute between a member state and the ECJ emerged from a perceived failure on the part of the Community legal system to provide an adequate form of protection in the area of human rights. The central plank of Community law was the establishment of a common market and the promotion of the four freedoms. Early in the history of the ECJ, it became apparent that these policies might well interfere with an accepted human right, the right for instance to property and the right to human dignity. This caused particular difficulties for West Germany as it was at the time. The Constitution of Germany had placed human rights' protection at the head of its Constitution. They were jealously regarded by the BVerfG. After several cases commencing in the late 1960s, the ECJ developed a human rights protection under the 'general principles of law' as part of Community law. This built upon the constitutional traditions of member states and international obligations including the European Convention on Human Rights. The ECJ, far from rejecting the influence of member states' jurisprudence as it had initially, was now embracing the 'general principles of law', including human rights' protection, accepted by those states. The approach adopted by the BVerfG was that it would not review Community measures where there was an adequate protection of human rights within Community law.

However, in a famous case in the 1970, the ECJ ruled that while it could not invoke national law to judge the validity of Community measures 'because this would have an adverse effect on the uniformity and efficacy of Community law', it could invoke the general principles as a part of EU law to protect human rights. However, the 'protection of such rights ... must be ensured within the framework of the structure and objectives of the Community' (*Internationale Handelsgesellschaft mbh* Case 11/70 [1970] ECR 1125 para 4).

This approach caused difficulties for the German courts and the BVerfG ruled that the 'inalienable essential features' of the German Constitution such as protection of fundamental rights could not be amended by Community organs via a transfer of power to the Community under Article 24 of the German constitution. The BVerfG retained the right to rule on which features of the German Constitution were unalterable and to protect fundamental rights where they clashed with Community laws ([1974] 2 CMLR 540). As far as the BVerfG was concerned, the German Constitution took priority over conflicting Community law. The likelihood of clashes between German courts and the ECJ was considerably lessened by a ruling of the BVerfG in 1986, which ruled that *so long as* the Community had a system of human rights protection protecting the 'essential content of fundamental rights' the BVerfG would not exercise its jurisdiction to rule on the applicability of Community measures (and on actions by German courts and authorities based on those measures) by applying the standards of fundamental rights' protection in the Constitution ([1987] 3 CMLR 225). The conditional terms 'so long as' were crucial.

These points were revisited in the decision on the ratification of the Maastricht Treaty in 1994 in *Brunner* ([1994] 1 CMLR), which was discussed above and where the BVerfG reasserted its jurisdiction to review the compatibility of Community measures with the German constitution when, and if, necessary. Self-denial was conditional.

Actual conflict has been avoided in relation to human rights as the ECJ and then the CFI (now General Court) have developed their sophistication on human rights protection, most famously and recently in the decisions in *Kadi* and related case law (Case C-402P and C-415P *Kadi Al Barakaat* [2008] ECR I-6351 and Case T-85/09). In *Kadi*, the EU courts have asserted that EU law is an 'autonomous system of law' in which human rights have to be afforded full protection even when the object of criticism is UN Security Council (UNSC) resolutions, and their review by one of the UNSC's committees. The UNSC agreed to the resolutions in relation to the international war on terrorism.

Nonetheless, the words from the 1970 judgment of the ECJ still ring true: protection of human rights must take place within the framework of EU law. The EU courts have shown a careful and nuanced approach to balancing the competing interests to ensure action is proportionate and justified (*Schmidberger* [2003] ECR I-5659), that human rights including the Charter of Fundamental Rights (below) must be accorded full respect in the balance with EU substantive rights (*Promusicae* [2008] ECR I-271) and have shown particular sensitivity to national constitutional protection (*Omega* [2004] ECR I-9609).

Problems remain. In two highly criticised decisions, the ECJ ruled that rights to collective representation and action in industrial disputes did not override basic market freedoms protected by the treaties. It involves the clash between individual freedom (although the 'individuals' involved were not real individuals but corporate bodies) and competing claims to a decent standard of living protected through collective action (Case C-341/05 *Laval* and Case C-438/05 *Viking Line*).

The Court of Human Rights (CHR) has pronounced that when asked to rule on breaches of the ECHR by a member state acting under EC law, it will be slow to intervene to find fault given the developed system of human rights protection within the EU edifice (*Bosphorus* 45036/98 (30 June 2005)). The ECJ has itself invoked rulings from the CHR to justify its review of EU measures allegedly breaching the human rights of children. The protection offered to children was arguably very thin (*Family Reunion Parliament v Council* [2006] ECR I-5769).

The charter of fundamental rights

I have already referred to the most significant development in EU human rights protection the Charter of Fundamental Rights (CFR) 'solemnly proclaimed' by the European Parliament, the Council of Ministers and the European Commission at Nice on 18 December 2000. Since the Treaty of Lisbon the CFR is accorded the same legal status as the two treaties of Lisbon. The CFR is a legally binding EU document and takes direct effect as explained in the introduction to this chapter. Although a very ambitious code for the protection of human rights, it is derived from international conventions, the ECHR, EU law and national constitutional laws. Its ambitious scope has caused problems for some member states particularly the UK, Poland and the Czech Republic. It has to be said that the CFR is attended by legal difficulties and uncertainties not least as presented by its 'horizontal clauses' contained in Title VII and which deal with the application and interpretation of the Charter as well as the 'Explanations' drawn up by the Praesidium. The legal status of the Charter is expressed in a peculiar manner. Unlike the aborted EU Constitution, it is not a formal part of the Treaties. As a 'proclamation' of human rights, it seems more like a declaration to be attached to a treaty rather than an expression of legally binding rights. Be that as it may it is accorded a legal status which will have to be followed by the courts.

The CFR applies to the institutions of the EU (with due regard to the principle of subsidiarity (itself not an uncontested concept) and to member states when they are 'implementing' EU law. Although the explanation refers to the EU human rights' protection including the Charter only applying within the 'scope of EU law', this phrase has been extended by the ECJ and also by English case law. 'Implementing' is not a self-explanatory word in this context. Furthermore, the CFR draws a distinction, not always consistently, between 'rights' and 'principles', the latter of which are only 'judicially cognizable' ('justiciable', i.e. right conferring) when implemented by 'acts' of the member states transposing Union law. In the case of EU institutions, 'principles' are so cognizable only when implemented by legislative or executive acts. The phrase 'acts' is not clear in its meaning.

Despite all these qualifications and uncertainties, the UK and Poland negotiated a Protocol (No. 30) giving them what Prime Minister Blair referred to as an 'opt-out' from the Charter including the 'solidarity' clauses. It is no such thing. British governments are notoriously antipathetic to the concept of human rights. The Conservative–Liberal coalition government has accepted in domestic judicial proceedings that the protocol is not a measure that seeks to exclude the UK from its application but one which seeks to explain its effect (*Saeedi* [2010] EWCA Civ 990). For a short document, the protocol contains numerous ambivalences, tautologies and confusions. Crucially, it is skewed in its attempts to qualify the application of the CFR to human rights developments in the UK. If the CJEU were to rule that a right or principle in the CFR is an EU human right, under the 'general principles of law' that would be directly effective in UK law. Judges are no slower than any other groups in learning lessons. Furthermore, the Protocol has no effect whatsoever on the development of human rights protection under the common law of human rights or under the ECHR. It is true that both these schemes do not operate in as wide a dimension as the CFR. But both regimes have gained in influence and force in recent years. This takes us to the next point of complexity and possible conflict and confusion within the EU: the multi-headed nature of human rights protection and especially the duty under the TEU Article 6 for the Union to accede to the ECHR.

A multi-headed human rights system

The ECJ ruled over 15 years ago (Opinion 2/94 [1996] ECR I-1759) that the treaties then in force did not empower the Community to accede to the ECHR. The Treaty of Lisbon TEU Article 6 now requires accession to the European Convention on Human Rights making the EU a member of the Council of Europe. The consequence will be that the institutions, offices, agencies, etc. of the EU, and member states as explained above, will be subject to the human rights jurisdiction of the CHR in their legislative, executive and judicial functions. Individuals as well as member states will be able to take matters allegedly in breach of the Convention to the CHR. Some have seen this as an act to clarify possible confusion because of the varied and variable bases of human rights protection within member states (House of Lords (2007–08)). Within the UK, there are four separate legal regimes for protecting human rights in addition to resort to the CHR by individuals making claims against the UK. There is protection under the common law (preserved by Section 11 Human Rights Act (HRA)); there is the HRA. There is protection under the general principles of EU law. There is protection under the EU CFR.

At first blush, accession seems to offer simplification because one court (the CHR) will be able to make rulings on alleged EU breaches of the ECHR. The ECJ and CHR have varied on rulings involving the same rights – dramatically so. The TEU is careful to emphasise that nothing in the accession will augment the powers or competencies of the EU as set out in the treaties. The CFR states that where rights in the Charter are derived from the Convention their meaning will be based on the interpretation of the Convention by the CHR. Nothing prevents an interpretation by the CJEU of the Charter giving *greater* protection than under the Convention. The CHR has jurisdiction over 47 vastly different states. The ECJ has jurisdiction over 27 states with far less variability. They operate in different contexts.

At one time, the scope for disagreement between the ECJ and CHR seemed considerable. Differences were remarked upon earlier. In the *Kadi* case, which was referenced above, the ECJ ruled that EU law is an autonomous form of law in which protection of human rights must be observed. This was reinforced even more dramatically by the General Court in *Kadi No 2*. The subject of attack was EU regulations based upon UNSC resolutions and then procedures adopted by the UNSC to review the resolutions involving financial sanctions against suspected terrorists. *Kadi* has emphasised that different legal orders, here the EU and the UN, are not hierarchically structured or cantilevered. In a global context, the law of the UN has to comply with human rights fundamentals of the EU legal order if implementing measures are to be consistent with EU legal principles. The fundamentals are determined by the legal principles of the EU, the laws of the member states as well as the ECHR. The EU approach may well be more robust than that of earlier case law of the CHR.[3] What if the CHR maintained its previous position? It would open up the prospect of a clear chasm between the human rights regimes (*MSS v Belgium and Greece No 30696/09*, 21/01/11).

The problems occurred before the House of Lords and Supreme Court when discussing the extra-jurisdictional operation of the UK HRA. *Al Jeddah*[4] dealt with the extrajurisdictional application of the HRA in relation to the British armed forces in Iraq. The case had to address the very un-British question of the 'hierarchy of norms'. The norms in question were the Convention as implemented by HRA and a UNSC resolution operating in Iraq. The resolution authorised the detention of terrorist suspects and in the case in question no charge or trial was in prospect. Several questions were relevant: was Article 5 ECHR (concerning detention) qualified by the legal regime established pursuant to United Nations Security Council Resolution (UNSCR) 1546 (and subsequent resolutions) by reason of the operation of Articles 25 and 103 of the UN Charter? These basically give precedence to the UNSC resolutions over the ECHR. In the Court of Appeal this question was basically: was the ECHR displaced by UNSCR? The Court of Appeal ruled that the ECHR (and therefore the HRA) was so displaced. This position was upheld by the Law Lords. Despite attempts by Lord Bingham to give a residual role to the Convention the judgments reveal a more pusillanimous approach than that of the ECJ and General Court.

The appeal in *Al Jeddah v UK* to the Grand Chamber of the CHR has now been decided. In *Al Jeddah* ([2011] ECHR 1092), the CHR ruled that Article 1 ECHR applied and the UK was within Convention jurisdiction and the matter was justiciable before the CHR. The CHR determined that there is no presumption within the UNSC resolution for states to be under an obligation to breach fundamental human rights. This would require 'clear and explicit language' in the resolution in order to authorise breaches of human rights. The resolution did not, the court ruled, intend to impose an obligation of indefinite detention. States were mandated to uphold security in Iraq, but subject to the requirements of fundamental human rights' law, which had not been displaced under the resolution. The ECHR was operative and Article 5(1) had been breached by the UK. Indeed, the CHR seems to operate on a principle of construction similar to that invoked by the House of Lords to protect human rights under the common law where statutes on their face breach human rights and which was touched upon above. Any breach of a human right has to be *expressly* provided for in the statute.[5] There is no room for justified breach by *implication*.

In short, the ECJ and CHR seem to have travelled along very similar routes in providing meaningful protection for human rights. It is another example of cooperative, collaborative decision-making and not one built on hierarchy and domination. The CHR will respect the human rights regime of the EU, just as the ECJ has respected the human rights contribution of the ECHR.

The Human Rights Act and its reform

The last subject concerns the repeal or amendment of the Human Rights Act 1998 (HRA). Before coming to power in a coalition government, the leader of the opposition, David Cameron, promised to repeal the HRA and replace it with something 'English' – a legal solecism given the United Kingdom application and non-devolved nature of the HRA. A new UK Bill of Rights was proposed. Some high-profile decisions have been used by the HRA's adversaries to attempt to ridicule the HRA. What seems to be at the root of the complaints is the fact that the HRA gives the upper hand to judicial and not political decision-making. There are some matters that are simply not to be determined on the basis of mathematical democracy and the will of a majority. Protection of human rights is one of those subjects. In a democracy, *all* have the right to be under a human rights regime. The HRA involves all branches of government in the protection and promotion of human rights and the Act was drafted so as not to override Parliamentary sovereignty. On only one occasion has a Minister presented a bill to Parliament, a provision of which contravened the ECHR (Communications Act 2003). Ministers are duty bound to inform Parliament whether a bill conforms with the ECHR. Judgments declaring provisions of an act incompatible with the ECHR as implemented have invariably been acted upon and offending provisions amended (by a fast track procedure if necessary).

What specifically would be repealed? What specific rights are *un English*? English lawyers had a considerable influence drafting the Convention. But the principles it seeks to protect, while based on common law history, were elevated to positive rights. They were not left as residuary, and easily defeasible, liberties. Senior figures in the Conservative Party have argued that repeal of the HRA should lead to the cessation of UK membership of the ECHR – I think the Council of Europe was meant. This would make the UK a pariah state in global protection of human rights (Birkinshaw 2012). It would lead to serious questions on whether the UK was in breach of Article 6 TEU.

Europe looks on in amazement at the British response to human rights' protection. UK politics does not seem to be in 'solidarity' on this question. The part of the CFR on 'solidarity' was expressly stated not to create legal rights in the UK in Protocol 30 (above). Even if the HRA were significantly modified, the common law of human rights, EU law and the Charter would together fill the vacuum.

Conclusion

What we witness then is a Community built on law, its own autonomous law that could not be driven by national laws because this would deprive it of its independence. It was a legal system declared by the ECJ as 'sovereign'. Slowly but surely national influences have crucially assisted the development of EU law (Birkinshaw 2003). There is now a far more subtle, nuanced approach to 'sovereignty' and human rights' protection within Europe. This process has not seen courts at loggerheads with each other. It has seen a constructive process of mutual accommodation and influence. The uniform message is: sovereignty must not be abused; solidarity requires uniform application of EU law and human rights' protection.

Notes

1. The European Court of Justice became part of the Court of Justice of the EU by the Treaty of Lisbon. It comprises the Court of Justice, General Court and Specialised Courts.
2. The position in Italy, Spain, Poland and in other jurisdictions – the Netherlands is an exception – is generally that EU sovereignty is recognised subject to the national Constitution. The German case law has been influential in central and east European states. In central and east European courts, although details differ, the courts are powerful actors among less powerful political actors. Accession provided those courts with an opportunity to enhance their position by promoting the rule of law, human rights and democracy. Given the historical loss of national sovereignty under communism, there was a reluctance to cede a recently acquired national sovereignty to another external supra national order (Sadurski 2006). See the Czech Constitutional Court in Brno 15 February 2012 http://www.usoud.cz/clanek/6341 on Czech constitutional law and EU law. The Czech court criticised the EU Court of Justice for issuing a decision that was 'ultra vires' in Case C 399/09 Landtová.
3. *Behrami v France* etc (2007) 45 EHRR 10.
4. *R (Al Jeddah) v Secretary of State for Defence* [2007] UKHL 58.
5. *R (Simms) v Secretary of State* [1999] 3 All ER 400 at 412g–j.

Bibliography

Birkinshaw, P. (2012) 'The EU and National Constitutional Law' in Huber, P. (ed.) *Like Canute – Pushing Back the Waters of the Incoming Tides. The Prospects for Re-inventing UK Constitutionalism* (Boorberg Germany) pp. 187–210.

Birkinshaw, P. (2003), *European Public Law*, 4th ed. (Cambridge: Cambridge University Press).

Bingham, T. (2010), *The Rule of Law*, (London: Allen Lane).

House of Lords European Union Committee (2007–08), HL 62-I, *Tenth Report* (2007–08).

Kirchof, P. (1999), 'The Balance of Powers Between National and European Authorities', *European Law Journal*, 5, 225–242.

MacCormick, N. (1999) *Questioning Sovereignty* (Oxford: Oxford University Press).

Sadurski, W. (2006), 'Solange No 3 – Constitutional Courts in Europe', Working Papers No 2006/40 (Florence: European University Institute).

9
Defending the Euro: Unity and Disunity among Europe's Central Bankers

David Howarth

In February 2011, Axel Weber announced his resignation as president of the German Bundesbank. The former front-running candidate for the post of European Central Bank (ECB) president explained his imminent departure by noting his opposition to the ECB's purchase of Greek sovereign debt. On 9 September 2011, Jürgen Stark, the German Executive Board member of the ECB and its head of economic research, also resigned because of, it was widely assumed, his opposition to the extension of the bank's bond-buying (its Securities Market Programme) to include Italian and Spanish sovereign debt. The two resignations were the clearest indication of the depth of disunity in the Eurosystem of central banks since the start of European Monetary Union (EMU) in 1999. In late 2011, with the yields on sovereign debt in even the euro area's core rising and the ECB facing unprecedented pressure from governments to step up its bond-buying as a defence against financial market pressures, Bundesbank opposition to bond-buying remained stubbornly firm and the ECB cautious (*Financial Times*, 9 December 2011). Weber's successor, Jens Weidmann, publicly questioned the legality of the ECB's Securities Market Programme (*Financial Times*, 7 December 2011).

ECB monetary policy-making was designed to disguise real, and to counter imagined, disunity within the bank itself, and among its component national central banks (NCBs) and their governors. The legitimacy of the bank and its monetary policy relied in large part upon the perception that its inflation target was set for the entire euro area, without any national bias (Howarth and Loedel 2005). Given persistent economic divergence, and varying national rates of inflation in EMU, ECB monetary policy could never correspond to the economic interests of all euro area member states (Heinemann and Huefner 2004). Several mechanisms were put in place to shelter the ECB from accusations of bias: treaty guaranteed independence, a clear euro area mandate, a specific euro area inflation target, the *ad personam* (that is, independent and personal) status of its Governing Council's members, the non-transparency of monetary policy making and, after teething problems in the bank's early years, a rationalised communication strategy. Crucially, unity was achieved because the ECB's institutional design and monetary policy was based upon that of the Bundesbank. The unity of the Eurosystem of central banks and the appearance of unity depended upon the assumption that central bankers keenly supported the German model – which they endorsed in the Delors Report on EMU in 1989.

However, several features of the ECB undermined its unity and reputation for impartiality even prior to the start of EMU: notably, the greater representation of individuals from larger member states in the Governing Council. Crucially, though, the potential for disunity is in the Maastricht Treaty (Treaty on European Union) and the asymmetrical design of EMU. Euro area economic governance was insufficiently developed and, notably, fiscal policy rules were inadequately clarified and enforced. Similarly, in the Treaty, the responsibilities of the ECB to promote financial stability were left imprecise. Notably, due to central banker fears on the monetisation of debt, the ECB was not assigned the typical central bank function of 'lender of last resort'. The disunity in the Eurosystem of central banks that erupted during the sovereign debt crisis from late 2009 demonstrated that unity relied on consensus around German and notably Bundesbank preferences. Disunity stemmed above all from the absence of a road map for ECB policy-making in a context of severe existential crisis.

Unity under the German model with caveats

The institutional design of the ECB, notably the bank's complete political and operational independence, its low inflation target – unqualified by other macroeconomic policy goals – and other features of its monetary policy-making were based on the Bundesbank model. The ECB blueprint was designed and approved by the governors of all NCB governors in the Delors Committee and later clarified by NCB governors prior to the start of EMU in 1999. The design was the product of, some would have it, an epistemic community (Verdun 1999). Unity was the product of an overriding 'economic culture' of the ECB's membership (Howarth and Loedel 2005; Kaltenthaler 2006) structured by a strong interest in low inflation and fiscal rectitude as the preconditions to a sound European economy. Keynesian-inspired macroeconomic policy found little support among ECB Governing Council members: a short-term trade-off between more inflation and less unemployment only created difficulties for the future. Bolstered by economic analysis, all NCB governors were firm believers in the benefits of independent central banks. The design and goals of the ECB had a clear political function: they were the *sine qua non* of EMU, without which German Chancellor Helmut Kohl would have been unable to lend his support given domestic opposition (Dyson and Featherstone 1999). Although the source of unity among central bankers, independence and the prioritised goal of low inflation remained controversial in several euro area member states and political leaders frequently railed against ECB monetary policy making (Howarth 2008). The specification of the ECB inflation target and the publication of a monetary map to show markets how the ECB would tackle inflation dispelled disunity. The original Stability and Growth Pact (SGP) agreed in December 1996 was hailed by central bank governors as a crucial mechanism to ensure an appropriate policy mix in the euro area and to limit the future inflationary consequences and instability created by unsustainable debt burdens (Howarth and Loedel 2004).

The ECB's relatively small six-member Executive Board and its limited weight on the 21-member Governing Council, which also includes the NCB governors, demonstrates an important feature of the Eurosystem. Compared to other federal banking systems, the Eurosystem is decentralised: NCBs have more sway collectively than, say, representatives from the Federal Reserve District Banks. This reflects the Bundesbank model prior to EMU where Land bank governors dominated the Central Bank Council. It also reflects practical reality: the NCBs are well-established, whereas the ECB is a fledgling, small institution. Eurosystem NCBs perform several operations vital to the operation of the euro area. Notably, they conduct foreign-exchange operations and ensure the smooth operation of payment systems. The NCBs hold and manage the official foreign reserves of the member states (of which they can provide up to 40 billion euro to the ECB) and hold the capital of the ECB (just under €4 billion). However, unity is maintained through the requirement that NCBs follow the regulations, guidelines and instructions of the ECB in these and several other areas: buying and selling securities and other claims; borrowing and lending securities; dealing in precious metals; conducting credit operations with banks and other financial institutions based on adequate collateral; acting as fiscal agents for public entities (although they may not grant them credit facilities or buy their debt instruments directly from them). The ECB can also engage in these activities. The precise role of the ECB in relation to the NCBs depends on the kinds of open market operations selected (with regard to aim, regularity and procedures). NCBs are able to perform tasks beyond those specified in the statute on the ECB and the European System of Central Banks (ESCB), except if the Governing Council decides that these activities interfere with the work of the ESCB (which includes all EU central banks). The ECB president alone attends meetings of the Euro Group and Ecofin, respectively, the meetings of euro area and EU ministers of finance. ESCB NCB governors occasionally attended informal meetings of Ecofin with varying degrees of participation, as well as meetings of the EU's Economic and Financial Committee when macro-economic policy coordination issues discussed directly impinge on them. However, in 2003, euro area governors lost their right to sit in Economic and Financial Committee meetings – much to the opposition of several NCBs, including the Bundesbank (see Dyson 2008) – which reinforced the importance of the ECB in European economic governance.

The degree to which the Eurosystem is centralised will develop over time. The burgeoning research and analytical capacity of the ECB has reinforced its power, in relation to Eurosystem NCBs. Ottmar Issing was appointed from the Bundesbank to the Executive Board of the ECB in 1998 to lead the development of the fledging institution's research capacities. Under the leadership of Issing, who worked as an academic economist for over 30 years prior to joining the Bundesbank eight years earlier, the ECB developed an impressive research capacity. In 2010, 138 working papers were released – considerably more than the output of the US Federal Reserve. One of the direct effects of the reinforcement of the ECB's own research capacity was the development of the New Area-Wide Model – the principal inflation forecasting model for the euro area (Trichet 2007). The ECB also led and co-ordinated the research efforts of Eurosystem NCBs through four networks on monetary transmission, inflation persistence, wage dynamics and the euro area business cycle. This reinforcement of the ECB's role at the heart of Eurosystem research, and increasingly analysis, contributes to the unity of the Eurosystem, even though it was met with some reluctance in those central banks, notably the Bundesbank and the Bank of Italy, with a traditionally strong role in economic research (Dyson 2010; Quaglia 2010).

The relative importance of the NCBs in the Eurosystem arguably reflected the highly decentralised nature of the EU political system and the problematic legitimacy of the ECB and EMU in the eyes of many member state citizens (Howarth 2007). NCB governors had final say – thanks to their majority in the Governing Council – over monetary policy decisions and the allocation of functions. Any reform to strengthen the Executive Board at the expense of the Governing Council would be challenged on grounds of legitimacy: despite their *ad personam* status (and *not* as national representatives), the strong presence of the NCB governors on the Governing Council was considered vital to selling the EMU project to sceptical national publics (*ibid.*). The arrangements of the present US Federal Reserve Board were developed just under 70 years ago, around 160 years after the creation of the United States as a country and long after the conclusion of the Civil War successfully asserted federal government authority. There was obviously no parallel situation in the EU. European citizens were more likely to accept ECB monetary policy if they knew that they were represented, however indirectly and unofficially, by NCB governors.

Yet from 1998, the different treatment of member states was reinforced through their unequal representation in the ECB Governing Council. The largest member state governments repeatedly insisted that their nationals hold Executive Board positions and the periodic battles over these positions undermined the perception of the *ad personam* status of Governing Council members. The most notorious example of the perceived importance of the placement of nationals was the fudged appointment of the first ECB president in 1998. President Jacques Chirac – in a minority of one opposing the appointment of Wim Duisenberg – insisted that the first ECB president be a French national and forced the highly unusual compromise that Trichet would replace Duisenberg half-way through the latter's eight-year term. Chirac insisted upon Christian Noyer's appointment as vice-president as a compensatory stop-gap measure to ensure France's hold over a leading position prior to Duisenberg's replacement.

The 2002 Governing Council reform also undermined the ECB's legitimacy based on national representation and *ad personam* status (Council 2003). The reform ended permanent voting by NCB governors and legally entrenched their inequality. While all governors were to continue to attend and be able to speak at meetings, the reform capped the number of NCB governors exercising a voting right at 15. When the number of NCB governors in the Governing Council exceeded 15, voting rights were to be exercised on the basis of tiered rotation systems, which assigned the governors voting rights with different frequencies depending on the relative size of their home country economies (see

Howarth 2007 for further details). Setting representation according to national economic size was important to the legitimacy of ECB policy-making, even though the move ended full NCB voting rights and undermined the treaty-established *ad personam* status of the NCB governors (see Dyson 2008; Howarth 2007).

In several respects, the ECB lacked transparency compared to the US Federal Reserve and the Bank of England (Haan et al. 2005). Notably, the ECB opted not to publish its minutes. This in large part reflected an attempt to de-politicise monetary policy and the fear that NCB governors would come under pressure at home to justify where they had stood in intra-ECB debates. The lack of transparency came at a cost: to many economists, the ECB's interest rate setting process and economic analysis remain too opaque (OECD 2007: 7). Yet, the ECB still achieved a credibility-enhancing transparency with the markets through the publication of its monetary policy-making map.

The ECB Executive Board was very cautious in its interventions into the operation of NCBs. One of the most controversial developments during the first decade of EMU was the Banca d'Italia Governor Antonio Fazio's mishandling of the takeover battle for Banca Antonveneta (Quaglia 2010), in which Fazio blocked a takeover bid by a German bank for questionable reasons to favour a merger with an Italian bank. Despite much criticism, the ECB Executive Board initially took a 'hands-off' approach and warned of a dangerous precedent for Eurosystem central bank independence if the Italian government used legislation to remove Fazio (*Financial Times*, 16 September 2005). The ECB finally adopted a much tougher tone in mid-December 2005, after it was made public that Fazio had received gifts from the former head of the Italian bank involved in the merger (*Financial Times*, 17 December 2005). However, the ECB had no investigative powers and was unable to pursue matters further. Ultimately, Fazio's resignation saved the ECB further damage to its credibility and the danger of public battles between Governing Council members.

Members of the Governing Council were expected to speak with one voice on the basis of the agreed-upon forecasts, although there was no legal requirement to do so. Efforts were made to ensure a tight coordination of official statements on ECB monetary policy: the president was made spokesperson in the official press conference following the bi-weekly meetings, while the other members of the Council were to explain Eurosystem policy in the member states in their own languages. There were a number of incidents where different NCB governors made ambiguous remarks between Governing Council meetings that led to false predictions of monetary policy decisions (for examples, see Louis 2002; Howarth and Loedel 2005). However, prior to 2010, there were no publicly expressed substantive differences of opinion between members of the Governing Council.

The ECB's negligible role in prudential supervision

During the 1991 Intergovernmental Conference on EMU, it was decided to leave the ECB's role in the micro-supervision of banks and in the macro-supervision of financial markets very limited. The Maastricht Treaty grants the Eurosystem NCBs the responsibility 'to contribute to the smooth conduct' of prudential supervision and the monitoring of euro area financial stability. The so-called BCCI (Bank of Credit and Commerce International) Directive (96/25/EC of 29 June 1995) lays the foundations for cooperation (exchange of information) but does not contain specific provisions or institutional arrangements to this end. The ECB must be consulted on the adoption of EC and national legislation relating to prudential supervision and financial stability and has the right to perform specific tasks concerning policies relating to this supervision. Clearly, the ECB's limited powers in this area were the subject of considerable debate at the time and it was decided to establish a simplified procedure in the Maastricht Treaty (Article 105(6) TEC) making it possible, without amending the Treaty, to entrust specific supervisory tasks to the ECB.

The precise role of the ECB in prudential supervision remained the subject of periodic debate. It is not unusual that the ECB lacks control over banking supervision, in that the central banks in many advanced industrialised countries do not have this power or share it with ministries of finance (more often there are completely separate institutions responsible for supervision). However, the euro area is unique in that the areas of jurisdiction over monetary policy and over banking supervision – which remains nationally based – do not coincide. ECB Executive Board members thus argued in favour of improved cooperation between Eurosystem central banks (including the ECB) and national banking supervisors on the grounds that central banks are, because of their responsibilities, necessarily concerned with the health of the banking system, and central bank credit control is managed in 'a situation that is generated by problems of interest to the supervisor' (Padoa Schioppa 1999; see also Duisenberg 2002; ECB 2001). The Basel Committee on Banking Supervision assumed the task of promoting cooperation between the ECB, the NCBs, and national supervisory authorities. To give the EU members of this Committee a more specifically Eurosystem profile, their gatherings were officially labelled the Banking Supervision

Committee of the ESCB. The ECB pushed to develop this cooperation further: to ensure that the system of national supervisors could operate as effectively as a single authority when required, in particular when dealing with local or national banking problems which could have wider effects.

ECB Executive Board members tended to argue in favour of transferring full supervisory powers to the NCBs rather than centralising them in the ECB, due in part to the NCBs' role managing the TARGET payment system, which gave them much greater awareness of the situation of the banks. The precise role of the ECB in the handling of solvency crises remained unsettled, and the lack of crisis management capacity of the Eurosystem was repeatedly criticised (see IMF 1998 for an early example). The Brown-Eichel plan of April 2002 (subsequently approved by Ecofin) proposed the creation of an umbrella EU financial-sector supervisory body, which would seek to improve coordination between national regulatory authorities. The creation of such a Lamfalussy-style committee structure for banking and insurance markets was a blow to the existing ESCB Banking Supervision Committee, and ECB president Duisenberg warned that a sideline role of the ECB in bank supervision would risk violating the Maastricht Treaty (Engelen 2002).

Growing disunity in the uncharted waters of euro area stabilisation

From the outbreak of the international financial crisis in 2007, the ECB had to shift the focus of its policy-making from the maintenance of low inflation to measures to combat financial and economic instability. The fight against inflation and the agreement on a clear policy map prior to the start of 1999 created a unity among Governing Council members. However, the goal of euro area financial stability lacked a clear policy map and was the subject of strong differences among NCB governors.

The intensified debate over supervision

Following the outbreak of the crisis, the ECB asserted the need for its reinforced role in both the macro-supervision of financial markets and, up to a point, micro-supervision of single cross-border institutions. Executive Board members expressed the concern that warnings about threats to the euro area's national financial systems might not be passed on fast enough at times of crisis because of the fragmented regulatory system in the EU and the insufficient cooperation and exchange of information both between supervisory authorities in different member states and between them and central banks (Stark 2008). Executive Board members (Bini Smaghi 2008) claimed that the effective conduct of the Eurosystem's liquidity-boosting operations from August 2007 relied upon the ECB's access to necessary information concerning the liquidity and solvency problems of the markets and institutions. They argued that banking supervisors needed to strengthen their cooperation to 'exert strong pressure on financial institutions to disclose in a prompt and coherent fashion their balance sheet situations' (*ibid.*). The ECB also argued that member states – Germany was frequently cited – must be required to remove all national legislative obstacles preventing supervisors from providing information to the ECB about specific banking institutions. The international financial crisis reinforced government openness to the arguments made by the ECB and NCBs. The German government moved to transfer most responsibilities for prudential supervision back to the Bundesbank. The ECB was also given a greater supervisory role at the EU level: the ECB president was assigned the first five-year chair of the newly created European System Risk Board (ESRB), which began operating on 16 December 2010, and gained voting rights along with the ECB vice-president and NCB governors, forming all but eight members of the new body. The ECB also gained a position on the European Banking Authority – the London-based body responsible for EU-wide bank stress tests – established at the start of 2011.

Some NCBs continued to resist the idea of a centralised European supervisory body for banks. In particular, the Bundesbank advocated a decentralised system emphasising national control on the grounds that this best served the German financial industry. Axel Weber, then president of the Bundesbank, appeared to reject the de Larosière Committee's proposals (2009) for the 'authorities' on the basis of the asymmetries between supranational bodies, which would possess the power, and national supervisors, which had the fiscal responsibility (*EuroIntelligence*, 16 April 2009). Weber subsequently clarified the Bundesbank's position as more focused on ensuring greater harmonisation and coordination between national supervisors for cross-border firms in the short term, towards an 'internationalisation' of supervision over the long term (*Financial Times*, 21 April 2009). However, his initially voiced concerns over fiscal responsibilities revealed the generalised fear among German policy makers that, as the biggest contributor to the EU's budget, Germany could be unfairly burdened with paying for future banking crises were greater supervisory powers transferred.

Central banking in exceptional times

With the outbreak of the sovereign debt crisis, extraordinary monetary and other policy measures became the subject of intense disagreement among Governing Council members and euro area member state
governments. Debates focused on the ECB's liquidity boosting measures
(notably, the purchase of covered bank bonds) and the ECB's purchase
of sovereign and other debt from the euro area member states most at
risk of default and facing high bond yields. The ability of the ECB to
neutralise fully the inflationary impact of its sovereign debt purchases
was the subject of increased scrutiny. Despite the *ad personam* rule
assigned to Governing Council members, several 'Northern' European
members expressed concerns that were widely shared in their home
member states. Although the full details cannot be known because of
ECB secrecy, a growing number of unilateral public announcements by
Executive Board members and NCB governors that criticised ECB policy
could be seen as the clearest indication of discord.

The German Governing Council members and the Bundesbank, like
the German government, typically argued for further fiscal consolidation in the besieged Southern European member states and criticised
ECB action to reduce their bond yields. From the outside, Otmar Issing,
the former German Executive Board member, repeatedly challenged
the bank's purchase of Greek and other sovereign debt on the grounds
that it took pressure off governments to engage in reform (Bloomberg,
3 September 2011). The resignations of Axel Weber from the Bundesbank
and Jürgen Stark from the ECB's Executive Board demonstrated the
intensity of internal discord. In February 2011, Weber announced
his intended departure at the end of April. He publicly explained his
departure in terms of the impossibility of leading an organisation in
which his policy preferences placed him in a small minority (*Financial
Times*, 13, 16 and 21 February 2011). Weber publicly opposed ECB emergency bond buying from its start in May 2010 and was joined by up
to four other Governing Council members who remained anonymous
(*Financial Times*, 12 May 2010). Weber's opposition reflected widespread
German concern over what the conservative newspaper *Frankfurter
Allgemeine Zeitung* referred to as the 'Americanisation of monetary policy'
(10 May 2010). In early April 2011, the Dutch Nederlandsche Bank
Governor, Nout Wellink also went public with his concerns over bond
purchasing (*Central Banking.com*, 4 April 2011) and called for a reduction.
There were additional hints at deeper tensions within the Eurosystem.
Sources from within the Bundesbank complained that French banks –
the most heavily exposed to Greek debt – were using the ECB purchase

programme to clean their balance sheets of Greek debt, while German banks had reached an agreement with the German finance ministry to hold on to Greek debt until 2013 (*Der Spiegel*, 31 May 2010).

As the sovereign debt crisis intensified in the summer of 2011, the Bundesbank held firm in its opposition to the ECB's Securities Market Programme. Jens Weidmann publicly queried the legality of the ECB's 'monetary financing' of debt as contrary to EU Treaty provisions (*Financial Times*, 7 December 2011) and a German economist brought a case against the ECB to the EU's General Court. There was speculation that the Bundesbank could even move to undermine any possible ECB action on reducing bond yield differentials by casting doubt on its willingness to defend this action (*Financial Times*, 29 November 2011). Weidmann publicly argued that Italy could 'handle even an interest rate that remains over 7 per cent for a while' (*Financial Times*, 29 November 2011): its bond yield would lower in time following what Weidmann saw as long-overdue structural reform. Yet criticism has not all been in one direction. In the aftermath of Stark's resignation, the former Italian Executive Board member, Lorenzo Bini Smaghi, publicly challenged criticisms of the ECB's bond buying as the result of 'inadequate economic analysis' (*Financial Times*, 15 September 2011), a direct jab at German Governing Council members.

The difference in positions among ECB Governing Council members also potentially reflected their professional background – although it is impossible to dissect the relative importance of different influences. Jean-Claude Trichet (president from 2003 to 2011) came to central banking relatively late in his career, following lengthy service in the French Treasury and ministerial *cabinets* (support staff). His non-central banking background potentially made him more open to the kinds of extraordinary measures that the ECB adopted in response to the crisis from 2007 to boost liquidity and purchase sovereign debt. In early August 2011, Trichet led the controversial decision to step up, considerably, the ECB bond-buying programme. Yet Trichet also performed a delicate balancing act, insisting publicly that the ECB was not a 'lender of last resort' and that its Securities Market Programme was not driven by the goal of maintaining the government solvency but rather was a 'temporary and limited' measure adopted for monetary policy reasons and the need to restore a better transmission of the bank's interest rate decisions – a claim made necessary for legal reasons (Lee 2011). Trichet has similarly insisted upon the ECB's success, far greater than the Bundesbank prior to 1999, in maintaining low inflation (*Financial Times*, 8 September 2011).

The decision to temporarily halt the emergency purchase of bonds in late January 2011 was the ECB's response to the rise in inflation, especially in Germany. It also potentially reflected a battle within the Governing Council over the prioritisation of inflation. By early 2011, the bank's measure of inflation (HICP) reached 2.4 per cent, the highest level for over two years. The ECB had consistently insisted that it could 'sterilise' the purchase of Greek debt and that its monetary policy remained focused upon its core goal (*Financial Times*, 31 January 2011). However, there was concern over the repeated failure to neutralise fully the inflationary impact of the ECB's bond buying and that financial markets would not take seriously a threat to raise interest rates if the ECB was still intervening heavily in debt markets. A second temporary halt in late March 2011 reflected ongoing concerns. By May 2011, the ECB had failed five times to neutralise fully the inflationary impact of its debt purchases (*Financial Times*, 3 May 2011), thus reflecting directly the tensions between the two ECB roles of financial and euro area stability and combating inflation and, most certainly, between Governing Council members – as demonstrated most clearly in the resignations Weber and Stark. While some economists have insisted that the amounts involved in the debt purchases were very small in relation to the ECB's overall operations, 'sterilisation' was an important political message to the Germans that the bank's actions would not create inflation (*Financial Times*, 3 May 2011). The extension of sovereign debt purchases to additional euro area member states from August 2011 undermined further the thrust of this message. At the same time, the European bank pursued its traditional anti-inflationary interest rate policy. In early April 2011 and again in July, the ECB raised interest rates twice by 25 basis points. While the move reflected standard ECB reaction to inflationary pressures, it was widely criticised for having increased pressure on struggling euro area member states at risk of sovereign default.

Despite disagreements on the ECB's bond buying programme, Governing Council members embraced a uniform position on the fiscal policies to be pursued by the member states most at risk of default. The ECB criticised member states for engaging in insufficient austerity; it took a strong position on the operation of the European Financial Stability Facility (that it not be allowed to purchase debt directly from the markets); and it strongly opposed the move by member states to push for a 'selective' default on Greek sovereign debt. However, even on some of these highly sensitive policies, apparent disagreements appeared. In July 2011, Ewald Nowotny, the Austrian Central Bank Governor, announced in an interview with an American television news channel that a short-term 'selective default' by Greece might *not* have 'major negative consequences' (*Financial Times*, 19 July 2011). Nowotny subsequently retracted his statement.

Conclusion

Some observers have argued that the resignations of Alex Weber and Jürgen Stark, a former Bundesbank vice-president, and their replacement with economists without recent experience working in the Bundesbank, symbolically demonstrated a shift of the ECB out of the Bundesbank's historical shadow (*Financial Times*, 11 September 2011) and a shift in ECB policy-making. Jörg Asmussen, the new German member of the ECB's Executive Board, was previously the top civil servant in the German finance ministry and known to be less hawkish on monetary policy, with links to the opposition Social Democratic Party (SPD) (*ibid.*). The appointment of an Italian to lead the ECB – regardless Mario Draghi's competence as a central banker and credentials on fighting inflation – contributed to the sense of a permanent shift in the operation of Europe's monetary authority.

However, the shift in ECB policy making should not be exaggerated. Jens Weidmann – who had prior to his five years as Chancellor Merkel's economic policy advisor been head of the Bundesbank's monetary policy division – proved to be as hawkish on inflation and as critical of ECB bond-buying and government fiscal policy failings as his predecessor (*Financial Times*, 22 September 2011). He came out strongly against the 21 July 2011 agreement to relax the terms of the bailout packages for Greece, Ireland and Portugal and widen the use of the European Financial Stability Facility (EFSF), the euro area's bailout fund, and he publicly opposed the ECB's move to expand its purchase of sovereign debt to include Italian and Spanish government bonds (*ibid.*). The Bundesbank's position on these matters likely worked to constrain ECB action. It refused to commit to extending its bond-buying programme following the 9 December 2011 European Summit agreement on reinforced euro area fiscal policy rules. President Draghi deliberately referenced the Bundesbank in noting that it was necessary to respect 'not just the letter, but the "spirit" of the treaties' on the monetisation of debt (*Financial Times*, 9 December 2011). The Bundesbank's shadow continued to darken the corridors of the European bank.

By late 2011, it appeared that a delicate balance had been achieved in the ECB's Governing Council. The ECB disappointed many national governments in its steadfast refusal to commit even greater resources to bring down yields on sovereign debt. The bank's bond buying was not to be accelerated but would be maintained and officially described as 'temporary and limited' – with the Bundesbank audibly grumbling. The ECB held firm on its position that it was not a 'lender of last resort'. At the same time, the ECB extended its intervention massively with the launch of the Longer Term Refinancing Operation (LTRO) for euro area banks on 22 December 2011, followed by the LTRO2 of 29 February 2012, providing a total of over a trillion euros in cheap lending to struggling banks. Despite the bank's willingness to engage in a range of extraordinary manoeuvres that few predicted when the Maastricht Treaty was signed, the dominant 'economic culture' of the ECB remained intact. The ECB remained unified in its insistence that governments had to take the lead in tackling the sovereign debt crisis and restoring confidence through fiscal consolidation and their own reinforced support mechanisms. The almost inevitable intensification of the euro area's woes in 2012 could place the ECB in a situation where it would have to choose between holding to its principles and preserving the current membership of the euro area and even the single currency itself. The strong potential for damaging disunity with the Eurosystem of central banks remained.

References

Bini Smaghi, L. (2008) 'Financial stability and monetary policy: Challenges in the current turmoil', Speech, CEPS joint event with Harvard Law School on the EU-US financial system, New York, 4 April, http://www.ecb.int/press/key/date/2008/html/sp080404.en.html.

Council (2003) *Decision of the Council, meeting in the composition of the Heads of State or Government of 21 March 2003 on an amendment to Article 10.2 of the Statute of the European System of Central Banks and of the European Central Bank (2003/223/EC)*; see http://ec.europa.eu/economy_finance/publications/euro_related/2005/compendium/pdfs/a06_En.pdf.

Duisenberg, W. (2002) 'The role of the Eurosystem in prudential supervision', Speech at the conference organized by the De Nederlandsche Bank on the occasion of the 50th anniversary of Dutch bank supervisory legislation, Amsterdam, 24 April, http://www.ecb.int/press/key/date/2002/html/sp020424.en.html.

Dyson, K. (2008) 'The European Central Bank: Enlargement as Institutional Affirmation and Differentiation', in E. Best, T. Christiansen, and P. Settembri (eds.), *The Governance of the Wider Europe: EU Enlargement and Institutional Change* (Cheltenham: Edward Elgar), pp. 120–40.

Dyson, K. (2010) 'German Bundesbank: Europeanization and the Paradoxes of Power', in K. Dyson and M. Marcussen (eds) *Central Banks in the Age of the Euro* (Oxford: Oxford University Press), pp. 131–160.

Dyson, K. and K. Featherstone (1999) *The Road to Maastricht: Negotiating Economic and Monetary Union* (Oxford: Oxford University Press).

Engelen (2002) 'Central Bank Losers: The Inside Story of How the ECB and the Bundesbank Are Being Pushed Aside as Financial Regulators', *The International Economy*, Summer.

ECB (European Central Bank) (2001) 'The role of central banks in prudential supervision', http://www.ecb.int/pub/pdf/other/prudentialsupcbrole_En.pdf.

Haan, J. de, Eijffinger, C.W. Sylvester and S. Waller (2005) *The European Central Bank: Credibility, Transparency, and Centralization* (Boston: MIT Press).

Heinemann, F. and F. Huefner (2004) 'Is the View from the Eurotower Purely European? – National Divergence and ECB Interest Rate Policy', *Scottish Journal of Political Economy*, 51 (4), 544–558.

Howarth, D. (2007) 'Running an Enlarged Euro-Zone – Reforming the European Central Bank: Efficiency, Legitimacy and National Economic Interest', *Review of International Political Economy*, 14 (5), December 2007, 820–841.

Howarth, D. (2008) 'France in the Euro-Zone: the Management of Paradoxical Interests', in K. Dyson, (ed.), *The Euro at Ten* (Oxford: Oxford University Press), pp. 111–132.

Howarth, D. and Loedel, P. (2004) 'The ECB and the Stability Pact', in *Journal of European Public Policy*, Spring, 11(5), 832–853.

Howarth, D. and Loedel, P. (2005) *The European Central Bank: The New European Leviathan?* Revised, second edition (Basingstoke: Palgrave).

IMF (1998), 'International Capital Markets', September, (Washington: (International Monetary Fund), http://www.imf.org/external/pubs/ft/icm /icm98/index.htm.

Kaltenthaler, K. (2006) *Policymaking in the European Central Bank* (Plymouth: Rowman and Littlefield).

Lee, P. (2011) 'The end of the last resort', *Euromoney*, December.

Louis, J.-V. (2002) *The Euro in the National Context* (London: BIICL).

OECD (2007) 'Policy Brief', January (Paris: Organisation for Economic Development and Cooperation) http://www.oecd.org/dataoecd/32/28/37867660.pdf.

Padoa Schioppa, T. (1999) 'EMU and Banking Supervision', *International Finance* 2 (2), 295–308.

Quaglia, L. (2010) 'The Banca d'Italia: Between Europeanization and Globalization' in K. Dyson and M. Marcussen (eds) *Central Banks in the Age of the Euro* (Oxford: Oxford University Press), pp.183–199.

Stark, J. (2008) 'The agenda for the competitiveness of europe's economy and financial system', Speech delivered at Ambrosetti Finance Workshop Cernobbio, 5 April, http://www.ecb.int/press/key/date/2008/html/sp080405. en.html, accessed 3 June 2008.

Trichet, J.-C. (2007) 'The role of research in central banks and at the ECB', Award of the Germán Bernácer Prize, Madrid, 21 May; http://www.ecb.int/press/key /date/2007/html/sp070522.en.html.

Verdun, A. (1999) 'The Role of the Delors Committee in the Creation of EMU: an Epistemic Community?', *Journal of European Public Policy*, 6(2), 308–328.

10
Territorial Flexibility
Michael Keating

Containing space

Political science has long struggled with the concept of territory. Taking the nation-state as the normal or even natural unit of analysis, as a container of economic, social, cultural and political systems, it has divided politics into demarcated external and internal spheres. International relations focuses on relations among states, seen as territorially enclosed units and (constructivist efforts notwithstanding) have even extended their paradigm into the European debate in the form of intergovernmentalism. In comparative politics, on the other hand, territorial politics refers to the division of power and behavioural differences within the boundaries of states. In both political science and sociology, modernization was presented as a process of territorial integration and functional differentiation in which internal divisions were of ever lesser importance.

The resulting inconsistencies in the treatment of territory are troubling. The nation-state represents the triumph of territory in the external sphere and its extinction in the domestic sphere, often relying on the same modernization processes. The term nation-state is used to mean different things. For international relations (IR) scholars, it refers to the *sovereign* state, even though sovereignty is a different concept. For others, it distinguishes multinational or plurinational states. It is problematic to think of territorial politics stopping at the boundaries of states, to neglect the interpenetration of domestic and international spheres or to ignore the external activities of sub-state units. Globalization in its myriad forms and, especially, European integration, have brought these questions into sharp focus as they challenge the monopoly of the state as the definer of territory, open borders and encourage the emergence of new territorial actors. European space is increasingly differentiated, posing challenges to understandings of sovereignty, political authority, economic management and solidarity.

The state as territorial container

The state has indeed been the privileged container of territory but this has never been the whole truth. European states have different origins, some emerging from a process of consolidation over centuries, while others were spun off from larger empires or conglomerates. The latter is typical of the former Ottoman, Habsburg, Russian and German empires, but there are examples in western Europe, including Norway, Ireland and Belgium. These have left important historical legacies. In the consolidated states, integration has been more or less complete (France, Germany), less complete (Italy) or highly contested (Spain, the United Kingdom). In the breakaway states, borders are accepted or contested to differing degrees.

In all cases, state integration has proceeded across several dimensions. State-wide economic integration breaks down internal barriers to create single markets. Cultural and linguistic diffusion forge shared identities. The closing of borders turns politics inwards, creating nation-wide cleavages and party systems. The state becomes the framework for civil, political and social rights and for electoral representation and accountability. Social compromises are forged at the state level, becoming the basis for welfare states, which are further bolstered by shared national identity. Stein Rokkan and others showed, however, that this process is rarely complete and that territorial cleavages have persisted even in the most unified European states (Flora et al. 1999). Indeed such cleavages are not merely hangovers from the past but are produced and reproduced in modern industrial and post-industrial societies (Keating 1988). They may be economic, based on spatial disparities or different territorial modes of production; cultural in the form of language, tradition, identity and memory; and political, with diverging political preferences and electoral patterns. States have long had to practice strategies of territorial management to accommodate these cleavages (Rokkan and Urwin 1983; Keating 1988).

As the imposition of economic borders closed national markets in the nineteenth century, some regions and territorialized sectors were privileged while others lost out. Places that were central in maritime trading systems were marginalized by national boundaries, while landlocked areas became central. Tariff policy was thus territorially contested in Spain, Italy, Germany, the United Kingdom and else-where. After the Second World War, the main instrument for economic territorial management was regional policy and planning, to plan the spatial economy in a balanced way. 'Spatial Keynesianism' was presented as a zero-sum game to help poor regions by diverting invest-ment their way; wealthy regions by reducing congestion and infla-tionary pressures; and the national economy as a whole by putting idle resources to use. The political management of territory was achieved through institutional reforms, through local government or federalism and central-local intermediaries able to represent the centre in the periphery and the periphery at the centre. Successive crises of territo-rial representation were followed by adjustments in territorial manage-ment (Keating, 1988). Cultural differences could be accommodated by more flexible policies on minority languages, especially where these had ceased to be a threat to the state.

The end of territory?

During the 1990s, with the globalization debate, there was a lot of talk about the 'end of territory' (Badie 1995) or a 'borderless world'. This was a form of high modernism, in which the processes that created the nation-state through functional integration were breaking its bound-aries and taking on a global scale; it is no coincidence that it coincided with the 'end of history' debate and a revival of neo-functionalism in Europe. Yet this is sustainable only if we identify territory exclusively with the nation-state. Rather than seeing the end of territory, we have been witnessing its reproduction at new territorial scales. Some of these are supranational (above the states); some are sub-state; and some are transnational (working across states and borders). Within Europe, this process has taken a deeper and more institutionalized form. One reason is the very fact that within the wider Europe and especially within the European Union, most political borders are, for the first time in history, uncontested, allowing them to be penetrated and loosened and economic and cultural borders to be redefined. At the same time, states lose their capacity for territorial management.

The best documented example of this process is in the economy. Even as markets have Europeanized and globalized, territory has become a more important element in explaining and managing economic change. There is now a large literature on local and regional produc-tion systems and their relationship to world markets (Scott 1998). Some argue that regions are competing with each other for investment, markets and technology and, whatever the truth of this claim, competitive regionalism (within European and global, and not just national markets) has become a shared assumption of national, regional and European policy makers. States have lost much of their capacity to manage their spatial economies because of fiscal constraints and capital mobility. World Trade Organization and European Union (EU) competition rules prohibit many of the subsidies, tax breaks and cross-subsidies formerly used. Policy has come to focus on endogenous capacity, innovation and entrepreneurship, rather than on diverting investment. The economic and political foundations of spatial Keynesianism have thus been undermined.

A less obvious example of re-territorialization can be found in culture and language. With modern means of communication, minority languages could thrive in virtual communicative communities. Yet they have become more territorialized, since to prosper they need to be reproduced through educational systems and be used in public and, to varying degrees, private institutions, which are themselves territorialized. The language border in Belgium has been frozen for some decades. The Basque language is prospering with the Basque Autonomous Community but not in the wider historic Basque-speaking lands. French in Canada is strengthening in Quebec and weakening elsewhere.

There are varying degrees of political territorialization, resting on economic, cultural or social demands. Spatial disparities and fiscal transfers have become a major issue in Belgium, Spain, Italy and Germany. Territorial parties are rising in some countries while elsewhere state-wide parties are riven by territorial cleavages. In the United Kingdom, there are quite different party systems in England and the smaller nations, while in both Germany and Italy territory has reshaped patterns of party competition. Nationality claims are being revived or in some cases (such as northern Italy) invented.

Rescaling Europe

It is difficult to capture these effects using traditional political science concepts, in which territorial boundaries are fixed and enclose a range of economic, social, cultural and political expressions. Rescaling, rather, is happening in different ways and at different levels according to the domain of social activity. Newer understandings of territory within social geography emphasize the constructed and contested nature of territory, the fuzziness of boundaries and the way different scales might be relevant depending on the question being asked. Some dispense with the notion of boundaries altogether, preferring a 'topological' conception, in which specific processes are connected within global chains. This is perhaps less an empirical question than a conceptual one, with different frames being relevant depending on the focus of the inquiry. Our concern here is with the impact of rescaling on the European project and the new forms of politics which it engenders; and about the institutional response on the part of states and the EU to the new challenges of territorial management posed by the new dispensation.

One challenge stems from spatial inequalities within the single market. In the early days, there was an assumption that economic integration would itself eliminate disparities. Given the mobility of goods, services, capital and workers, regions would find their own niche in the division of labour on the basis of comparative advantage. It soon became apparent that such mobility was imperfect and that, just as states had needed to intervene to overcome such market imperfections, so might Europe. New understandings of regional economic development make the problem more acute, since they postulate that regions are in competition, which implies winners and losers. Not only might the wealthy regions win out (from economies of agglomeration and existing endowments in research and technology) but within regions the most mobile classes and individuals could be privileged. In a 'race to the bottom', regions, especially poor ones, would cut social spending in order to reduce taxes and attract footloose investment. This would not only have adverse social effects; it would also undermine the social investment needed for economic growth in the longer term. As wealthier regions are now preoccupied with their own competitiveness in global and European markets, they are less willing to sustain transfers to their poorer compatriots, especially as the transfers no longer come back in the form of purchases of their products within national trading circuits.

A second effect of European integration on territorial politics concerns federal and devolved states. Where matters domestically devolved to regions are defined as EU competences, the regions risk a double loss of power: to the EU; and to their national governments, since it is member states who are represented in the Council of Ministers. This has provoked a two-fold reaction within regions: a defensiveness towards the European project, especially in the early years; and a demand for a new role within the EU policy-making system.

A third effect concerns plurinational or culturally divided states. Although in the early years of the European project, some stateless nationalist movements were reticent, seeing Europe as even more remote than their host state, others have long embraced Europe as a new framework for their aspirations. National minority movements generally welcome the weakening and opening of state borders as an opportunity to forge links with their co-ethnics on the other side. In recent years, the support from nationalists and minorities for European integration has depended on their ideological affinity with its underlying liberal values and on tactical considerations (Keating 2004). Catalan, Basque, Scottish, Welsh, Breton, moderate Flemish and moderate Irish nationalists have been pro-Europe. The *Vlaams Belang* is anti-Europe and the Italian *Lega Nord* went through a pro-European phase before turning virulently anti-Europe as it traded increasingly on xenophobia, racism and the insecurities of small north Italian business in face of the single market. Sinn Féin has consistently been Eurosceptic. National minorities in central and eastern Europe have looked to Europe to open borders and secure their collective rights.

For some, notably the Scottish National Party, Europe lowers the threshold for independence by taking care of externalities and difficult issues like market access, borders, the currency and to some degree defence and security policy. Other movements have moved beyond this to a 'post-sovereignty' stance, arguing that the European project has made the traditional concept of sovereignty redundant and that the concept of shared and divided sovereignty is common to both them and to the European project (Keating 2001). Rhetorical themes of a Europe of the Regions of a Europe of the Peoples have been deployed as an alternative to the Europe of the States. The argument has particular resonance where there is a historical tradition or 'usable past' of doctrines of shared and diffused sovereignty. So the old Basque foral tradition has been refurbished and modernized, breaking with the radical separatism of Sabino Arana, founder of modern Basque nationalism in the late nineteenth century and emphasizing a European vocation that was first pioneered in the 1930s. Catalan nationalism has always been less separatist, at least in its mainstream, harking back to their history as a trading people within a federal state (the kingdom of Aragon) itself embedded in a wider Iberian confederation and with an active external engagement across the Mediterranean. Welsh nationalism also has a weak separatist tradition so could engage easily with Europe. In the former Habsburg domains, such traditions of shared sovereignty, which were widely canvassed from the late nineteenth century, were ruptured after the First World War and are more difficult to recover.

Territorialized nationalist movements have also been able to draw on the themes of the new regionalism in the economic domain, arguing that the new conditions emphasize precisely their values of territorial embeddedness, social cohesion and a capacity for collective action and that the state framework is no longer very relevant. Such economic nationalism is a prominent feature in Flanders, Catalonia and the Basque Country. At one time, the Lega Nord argued for a separate Padania within the European single currency, leaving the south of Italy to keep the lira. Nationalists have also made common cause with the demands of regional governments for a greater role European policy-making. In central and eastern Europe, on the other hand, nationality movements, focused on ethnic identities and culture and lacking the region-building experience of the post-war western states, tend to be less territorialized.

Managing European space

Europe itself constitutes a new economic, political, institutional and, to a lesser extent, social and cultural space. It is both above the member states and amidst them as European influences penetrate domestic politics and policies. The European Union is also an actor, forging its own policies and building its own institutions, along with its member states. The construction of a European space in some ways resembles that of the earlier construction of states, with its interlinking of economic, political and institutional projects but, in contrast to the visions of early neo-functionalists, these dimensions have not developed at the same pace, nor do they always cover the same space, giving rise to a differentiated order (Dyson and Sepos 2010). If we add to the European Union the other bodies, including the Council of Europe, the Organization for Security and Cooperation in Europe (OSCE) and North Atlantic Treaty Organization (NATO), the institutional landscape is still more complicated.

Similarly, at the sub-state level, there is no uniform level or organization. Rather there are different meanings and contents to territory, some of which coincide in some cases while others do not. Spatial levels include cultural and historic regions and nations, functional regions created by states, city-regions and towns. Their economic significance, political salience and institutional strength vary within and between states. Then there are new spaces emerging at the borders of existing states. This is not just a matter of functional or economic determinism. This makes a strategy for managing territory at a European scale very difficult; but the problems sketched out above are forcing some response and the EU now has a variety of institutions and policy for the purpose of territorial management.

Managing disparities

The creation of the single market has the potential to exacerbate spatial inequalities, which it seemed to point to the need for an active European regional policy, on the lines of the old national spatial Keynesianism. Funding a regional policy, however, required a winning coalition of member states, which was achieved with British accession in 1973, the United Kingdom getting regional policy in compensation for its net contributions and as a counterpart to the Common Agricultural Policy. In the early years, the European Regional Development Fund worked as a simple intergovernmental compensation device, awarding money to states on the basis of fixed quotas and allowing them a free hand to do more or less what they wanted with it (see Chapter 18 by Bull).

Gradually funding was increased and the Commission sought to convert it into a genuine instrument of Community policy. A major change occurred in 1988, again as a side-payment, this time for southern Europe's acceptance of the single market programme. A single European map of eligible regions was drawn up, with a single set of criteria and it was stipulated that funding had to be additional to existing national spending. Rules provided for more participation by regional actors in the elaboration and implementation of programmes. The regional and social funds and the guidance section of the agricultural fund were brought together as the Structural Funds. Since then, there has been some backtracking as national governments have got back into the act. Eastern enlargement has led to most of the funds being diverted to the new member states, although programmes (increasingly sectoral rather than territorial) are retained in the EU15. In recent revisions, the British and German governments have sought to renationalize the policy, keeping European funding only as a transfer mechanism for the central and eastern states, but this view has not prevailed.

The idea that the Commission was trying to use the Structural Funds to promote a Europe of the Regions in alliance with sub-state governments and to undermine member states has always been fanciful, confusing regional policy with institutional reform. Regional policy was intended to facilitate the single market by integrating lagging regions and to diffuse new ideas about regional development base on academic thinking. The Commission required that states have in place a mechanism for managing the funds at the appropriate spatial level (now NUTS2) but has never had a view on how it should be constituted. Indeed, during the 2004 enlargement, it insisted on central management of the Funds, distrusting the capacity of local and regional governments in the new member states (Keating and Hughes 2003) . In practice, programmes are managed at a series of spatial scales, usually local rather than regional. The Structural Funds did, however, give regional politicians enormous scope to claim that they were responsible for getting money from Brussels, by-passing national governments and playing in the European league.

Establishing the inter-regional transfer mechanism required that the Commission have both a policy rationale and a coalition of support within member states and this continues to be the case. As thinking on regional development has evolved, it has put less emphasis on assistance and more on competitive regionalism and the contribution towards the Lisbon and Europe 2020 agendas. The Directorate General (DG) for regional policy has sought to broaden the policy by taking a territorial perspective on EU policies across the board and a clause on territorial cohesion was inserted into the Lisbon Treaty alongside economic and social cohesion. Support has been retained by keeping some eligibility of wealthy member states instead of transferring all the funding to the east. Cohesion policy is perhaps the most explicitly redistributive policy in the EU arsenal, thus representing a gesture to 'social Europe' but the Commission has been at pains to avoid portraying it this way, insisting on its economic rationale as a contribution to the single market. In this way, it has retained a strong role in the definition and realization of spatial policy at a European scale, although the resources, while the second-largest item in the budget, pale beside the territorial transfers at national level. The regional policy directorate has also fought a series of battles against the competition directorate, which has a very different vision of the internal market. There is also tension between regional policy, whether European, national or local, and the jurisprudence of the Court of Justice, which has taken a very stern view of the requirements of market competition.

The evidence on success of cohesion policy is mixed. There has been some overall convergence among regions but this disguises a convergence at national level as countries from successive enlargements have caught up. Within states, disparities have remained or increased. At one time, people talked of the 'golden triangle' bounded by southeast England, the Ruhr and Paris. In the 1980s, this was challenged by a group of French economists who favoured the image of the 'blue banana', which excluded Paris and thus justified European aid for

France. Later, this was replaced by the image of a mosaic, in which metropolitan regions and doing better than smaller centres. In central and eastern Europe, there are huge disparities between capital cities and the rest of the state, and between eastern regions and those closer to core European markets (European Parliament 2007; Geppart and Stephan 2008).

Representing territory

Regional and local governments have sought representation in European policy making to regain influence over devolved competences and to secure economic advantages. There are two forms of access: directly acting within European space; and going via their host state governments. Regions have been active in Brussels, where over 200 have permanent offices, in addition to visits and other lobbying activities. There have been claims that this is about getting money from the Structural Funds but, given the way these work, there is little that an individual region can to do to increase its eligibility, as opposed to taking credit for money that is coming anyway. More important is that regional actors can get access to the policy-making process at an early stage so as to exert influence.

The issue of regional access reached its peak at the time of the Maastricht Treaty, which set up a Committee of the Regions (CoR), which has gradually acquired rights of consultation over a wide range of policy fields. The Lisbon Treaty allows it to go to the European Court of Justice over violations of subsidiarity. CoR's main weakness is its heterogeneous membership, including federated units, strong regions, stateless nations and municipal governments, who have very different interests in both substantive and institutional policy questions. The stronger regional governments have argued for many years that their legislative role should be recognized in EU procedures, both upstream in the formulation of policy and downstream, in implementation. In the run-up to the Convention on the Future of Europe, they formed their own body, the Legislative Regions (RegLeg), alongside CoR (causing some tensions within it); but they made little progress during the treaty reforms. There is also a conference of the assemblies of legislative regions (CALRE). CoR has also been weakened by its method of working, which consists of reaching consensus through wordy and complex compound resolutions, rather than focused policy advice. It is thus far from the 'third legislative' chamber of which some of its more enthusiastic supporters once dreamed.

The Maastricht Treaty provided that a regional minister could represent a member state in the Council of Ministers where regions had a ministerial structure; this effectively means in legislative regions. This does not give regions an individual voice, since the delegate must speak for the state as a whole. The clause is interpreted differently in various states. The strongest position is Belgium, where, if only regional or language community competences are involved, then it is these who represent the state; in other cases there is a mixed state-regions delegation. All concerned governments must agree on the line to be taken, so giving a veto to regions, although this is rarely invoked. In Germany there is a similar division between federal, regional and mixed matters, although the regional position on the line to take is ultimately subject to a majority vote in the Bundesrat. Spanish autonomous communities are entitled to participate in certain Council formations, but can only influence the Spanish line, with no veto power. There is a similar but weaker provision in Italy. In the United Kingdom, the Scottish, Welsh and Northern Ireland governments can participate in delegations at the invitation of the centre and, while they seek to influence the line to be taken, it is the UK government that has the last word.

All this means that regions are incorporated into European policy-making to varying degrees but falls short of a constitutionalization of the regional level. States remain masters of the game and, since the high point at Maastricht, the notion of a Europe of the Regions has fallen away. Yet tensions continue to exist as regional governments use the European framework to loosen the confines of national policy-making systems and to regain control of powers that have lost. The issue remains unresolved.

Challenging borders

The opening of European borders creates an obvious opportunity to construct new spatial systems. Economic regions divided by state frontiers might come together. Complementarities in production might be exploited. Historic communities or nationalities might be re-united without threatening the integrity of states. The European Commission, not surprisingly, has been very keen on cross-border co-operation and has put into place programmes and funding for it. There is an intuitive neo-functionalist logic to cross-border cooperation, in the idea that working together on practical matters can serve to defuse antagonisms and spill over into wider forms of integration, thus furthering the European project. In practice, cross-border programmes have served to reconfigure space but not always in this way and often to reframe the significance of the border rather than suppress it.

One problem is that, while territories on each side of a border may be complementary, they may also be in competition for economic development, with the opening of the border increasing competitive regionalism. Local and regional politicians, while often keen on the symbolic status conferred by external projection, have to deliver the benefits to their own constituents rather than to those on the other side. It is also difficult to define the scale for cross-border co-operation. Usually only part of the territory is on the border, so that citizens elsewhere do not even perceive that they live in a border region. Many of the actual programmes are very local and it is local politics that count, although they may not be related to a strategic vision for a wider space. Where the definition of the relevant region is contested, opening the border may illustrate these conflicting definitions rather than fostering agreement on a shared one. So in the Basque Country, cross-border cooperation has shown how Basqueness has been constructed differently in Spain and France and in particular how the presence of a nation-building project and strong devolved institutions on the Spanish side have in some ways widened the divide (Keating and Bray 2012). European-funded cross-border programmes have, ironically, in some ways, reified the border, since its existence is the condition of continued funding.

The nationalities question

The opening of European space has in some ways encouraged the politics of minority nationalism and national minorities, while at the same time containing it by providing a new framework and attenuating separatist demands. It has proved difficult to accommodate these pressures, however, given that Europe is still based on nation-states. A proposal from the European Free Alliance (of nationalist parties) for 'internal enlargement' did not make the floor of the Convention on the Future of Europe. Nor is there a constitutional status within Europe for a territory that is semi-detached from its own state. The plan of the Basque First Minister Ibarretxe to recast the Basque Country as 'freely-associated state' linked to Spain relied heavily on the European context and 'direct links' with the EU (Keating and Bray 2006). In early drafts, it mentioned the Lamassoure proposal[1] for partner regions, but this was designed as an administrative reform with a very different meaning. In other stateless nations, Europe now features less in the nationalist prospectus (Elias 2008). The failure of the Convention and the Lisbon treaty to provide a larger role for regions or to recognize legislative regions further diminished the attraction of a European third way. Kosovo might have provided an occasion to put into practice new understandings of sovereignty within Europe but member states failed to grasp it and opted for recognition or non-recognition of independence of a conventional kind.

Europe has played a role in the diffusion of tensions around national minorities. Austrian accession helped to resolve the South Tyrol dispute with Italy. British and Irish membership of the European Union has aided accommodation in Northern Ireland, even if the direct role of the EU has been slight. Hungarian minorities in neighbouring countries have been less restive than was once feared. Cross-border cooperation has provided ways for people to cooperate with kin states and extend rights across borders. Much here depends on the politics behind the crossing of borders. So the extension of some citizenship rights to co-ethnics in neighbouring countries might be seen as a constructive way of overcoming division and working around, but not challenging, frontiers, as in the case of Ireland or Austria. In the hands of a Hungarian nationalist government who talked of 'reversing Trianon', on the other hand, efforts to extend citizenship are seen as a form or irredentism.

Minority rights have also been addressed in the wider European architecture of the Council of Europe and the OSCE. The former has a Framework Convention for the Protection of National Minority and a Charter for minority languages, which represent a recognition of national pluralism. On the other hand, states are allowed to define their own national minorities and do this in more or less restrictive ways. The only real leverage the EU has is during the accession process. Respect for minority rights was incorporated into the Copenhagen criteria for membership and proved of some effect in the Baltic states and Slovakia, as well as in current discussions in former Yugoslavia. This, however, was the only one of the criteria that was not accommodated in the *acquis*, for the obvious reason that existing member states did not want it to apply to themselves. The idea of minority rights, moreover, has been interpreted in a restricted way, which excludes the idea of territorial autonomy and largely confines it to the rights of individuals belonging to minority groups rather than to the groups themselves. In the case of Cyprus, the EU allowed the Greek part to join in advance of a settlement of the communal conflict, even although it had been the Greek Cypriots who had voted down the

Annan settlement plan, while the Turkish side had accepted. In former Yugoslavia, the EU has inconsistently pushed for federal reforms and accommodation but accepted secession, while dividing over the recognition of Kosovo.

Conclusion

European integration has helped to remould territory across the continent, taking it out of the exclusive context of the state. This is not radically new, unless we take too seriously the Westphalian myth of an integrated and sovereign state, stretching back to the early modern era. The territorial state has always been a work in progress, always subject to stress and tensions. What is new is the existence of an over-arching framework and a project for the construction of a supra-national space on a continental scale. Far from eroding territorial distinctiveness, European integration has encouraged the reconstruction of territory on new lines. This has posed a series of questions about territorial equity, the capacity of states to manage their territories, about power and influence in multilevel systems of government, and about nationality, sovereignty and self-determination claims. It puts these issues into a new context and, potentially, provides new ways of dealing with them.

There is no functional determinism here, producing coherent new territorial configurations. Rather, rescaling offers opportunities to political entrepreneurs and institution-builders, drawing on local conditions and traditions. In some places, new territorial systems have emerged, with an economic, a cultural, a political and an institutional dimension, linked to state-wide and European networks. Elsewhere, the definition of territory is contested, for economic, historical or political reasons. The principles and practice of regionalism are, generally, stronger in the older member states, where they build on policy developments since the 1960s, than in eastern and central Europe, where state elites have been more centralizing and fears for the security of borders persist. This is a further cause of inequality, as some territories are better equipped to confront European competition on their own terms, while others are reduced to dependency on European and global economic circuits.

Europe's response has been partial. Cohesion policy represents a way of dealing with disparities and Europeanizing the policy field, but falls far short of what nation-states used to do in their heyday and territorial disparities are still increasing. The role of sub-state governments in

European policy-making has been recognized and mechanisms put in place but these do not challenge the fundamentally inter-state nature of the policy process. Europeanization raises the prospect of new and imaginative ways of addressing nationality questions but these have not been exploited to the full. European institutions in general have not adopted forms of territorial flexibility corresponding to the differentiated nature of territorial demands, policy issues and emerging systems of action. This is not an argument for Euroscepticism or a reason for despair. It merely reminds us that the territorial dimension to politics is ever-present and constantly changing, whether within the nation-state or in the broader European arena.

Note

1. Named after Alain Lamassoure, a French Basque (but not nationalist) politician, it proposed that such regions be given more leeway in applying European regulations, in a tripartite partnership with the European Commission and the member state.

Bibliography

Badie, B. (1995), *La fin des territoires. Essai sur le désordre international et sur l'utilité social du respect* (Paris: Fayard).

Dyson, K. and A. Sepos (2010), 'Differentiation as a Design Principle and as a Tool in the Political Management of European Integration', in K. Dyson and A. Sepos (eds), *Which Europe? The Politics of Differentiated Integration* (Basingstoke: Palgrave).

Elias, A. (2008), *Minority Nationalist Parties and European Integration. A Comparative Study* (London: Routledge).

European Parliament (2007) Directorate General Internal Policies of the Union Policy Department Structural and Cohesion Policies, *Regional Disparities and Cohesion, What Strategies for the Future?*, IP/B/REGI/IC/2006_201.

Flora, P., D. Urwin and S. Kuhnle (ed.) (1999), *State Formation, Nation-Building and Mass Politics in Europe. The Theory of Stein Rokkan* (Oxford: Oxford University Press).

Geppart, K. and A. Stephan (2008), 'Regional disparities in the European Union: Convergence and agglomeration', Papers in Regional Science, 87(2): 193–217.

Keating, M.(1988). *State and Regional Nationalism. Territorial Politics and the European State* (Brighton: Wheatsheaf).

Keating, M. (2001), *Plurinational Democracy. Stateless Nations in a Post-Sovereignty Era* (Oxford: Oxford University Press).

Keating, M. (2004), 'European Integration and the Nationalities Question', *Politics and Society*, 31(1): 1–22.

Keating, M. and J. Hughes (eds) (2003), *The Regional Challenge in Central and Eastern Europe. Territorial Restructuring and European Integration* (Presses interuniversitaires européennes/Peter Lang).

Keating, M. and Z. Bray (2006), 'Renegotiating Sovereignty; Basque Nationalism and the Rise and Fall of the Ibarretxe Plan', *Ethnopolitics*, 5, 4, 347–64.

Keating, M. and Z. Bray (2012), 'Territorial Autonomy in Nationally Divided Societies. The Experience of the United Kingdom, Spain, and Bosnia and Herzegovina', in J. McGarry and R. Simeon (eds), *Assessing Territorial Pluralism* (Philadelphia: University of Pennsylvania Press).

Rokkan, S. and D. Urwin (1983), *Economy, Territory, Identity. Politics of West European Peripheries* (London: Sage).

Scott, A. (1998), Regions and the World Economy (Oxford: Oxford University Press).

Part III

Policy Divergences and Convergences

11
Foreign and Defence Policy: The Sovereignty Obsession and The Quest for Elusive Solidarity

Anand Menon[1]

Any account of EU defence and foreign policies is inseparable from a discussion of the desire on the part of national governments to retain control over these sectors and the resultant dangers of dissensus. Indeed, these are arguably the sectors that best exemplify the tension highlighted by the editors of this volume. On the one hand, a context of intensifying interdependence makes it increasingly difficult for even the largest member states to pursue purely national policies. On the other, the 'persistence and exacerbation of divergent national interests,' has culminated in 'institutionalized confusion and inertia,' undermining the ability of collective action within the EU to compensate for the shortcomings of national policies.

This chapter illustrates the extent of divergent national interests in the area of foreign and defence policy. Drawing on the analysis of 'high politics' carried out by Stanley Hoffmann almost half a century ago, it provides some suggestions as to why this is the case, and speculates as to its possible impact, particularly given the absence of effective EU institutions able to mitigate the worst effects of dissensus. It is divided into four sections. The first outlines the claims made by Hoffmann regarding the unique nature of foreign and security policy and its implications. Section two argues that experience in these sectors confirms Hoffmann's insights, illustrating how continued dissensus continues to characterize the EU's foreign and security policies. The third illustrates the weakness of EU institutions in this sector. Finally, the fourth section teases out the impact that continued dissensus has had on the European Union's Common Foreign and Security Policy (CFSP) and Common Security and Defence Policy (CSDP).[2]

Explaining dissensus: 'high politics'

It has long been something of a truism in the international relations literature that foreign and defence policy are different from other policy sectors. The scholar most associated with applying these arguments to European integration is Stanley Hoffmann, who developed the notion of 'high politics.'[3] Central to Hoffmann's argument was his claim that divergences between member-state preferences in foreign and security policy were a crucial factor in stymieing attempts to achieve integration. Moreover, such differences were more deeply rooted than in other policy sectors, making them more difficult to reconcile and overcome.

For Hoffmann, securing interstate agreement on foreign and security policy is inherently problematic because the interests involved are less reconcilable, less amenable to bargaining and compromise than those in the socio-economic sectors where European integration had occurred. Thus:

> In matters of welfare, governments have been animated by a common will, to maximize wealth.... What has made this enterprise both successful and limited is the essential difference between economic behaviour and theory and political behaviour and theory. On one side of the fence we deal with quantifiable interests – capable of being calculated, compensated, bargained...On the other side of the fence we find those intangible interests of state which are of quite another order (Hoffmann 1964: 1274–75).

Not only are the interests involved more intangible and thus less negotiable than in other sectors, but differences between them tend to be more entrenched. Europe is made up of 'nation-states that pour into their foreign policy the collective pride, ambitions, fears, prejudices and images of large masses of people' (Hoffmann 1966: 862; see also Hill and Wallace 1996: 8). Conflicting foreign policy objectives are thus not mere differences of calculation over optimal solutions, but rooted in different worldviews built up over many years. Stubbornly divergent national responses to international politics limit the potential of the European integration process, throwing up a tension between the logics of integration and diversity (Hoffmann 1966).

Moreover, the traditional techniques of integration offer little prospect of success in this sector. The 'Monnet method' placed a heavy emphasis on process. It was a 'gamble on the possibility of substituting motion as an end in itself, for agreement on ends' (Hoffmann 1966:

883). However, policy makers cannot make use of a crucial technique that has been deployed to such good effect in other sectors, as ambiguity is not a workable strategy for foreign and security policy-related questions (Hoffmann 1966: 874). Simply put, decisions 'on foreign policy and membership and defense cannot be reached unless the goals are clarified' (Hoffmann 1966: 883).

Defence policy poses particular problems for proponents of integration. For one thing, the implications of dissensus are probably more far-reaching in the area of security than in other policy sectors. Security policy is of crucial importance in terms of the survival of the state, and 'in areas of key importance to the national interest, nations prefer the certainty, or the self-controlled uncertainty, of national self-reliance' (Hoffmann 1966: 882). Thus, even given similar levels of consensus as in other sectors, member states would be less willing to undertake cooperation in matters relating to security.

Moreover, and compounding such reluctance, the level of integration required to achieve effective cooperation in defence policy is higher than in other sectors. The deployment of military power requires rapid decision-making – what the public policy literature refers to as a 'heroic' policy style. The institutions necessary to provide this would thus require significant autonomy implying a zero-sum relationship between EU and member states (Hoffmann 1982: 37). Effective integration of defence, therefore, would be more constraining than in other sectors, which, given the factors inclining member states towards caution, further undermines its potential.

The implications of the analysis of high politics carried out by Hoffmann are clear and simply summarized. In both foreign an defence policy, dissensus is both more probable, more deep-rooted and potentially more damaging than in other sectors.

Dissensus

Hoffmann has been proven prescient in pointing to the resilience of contrasting national interests in foreign and security policy and the unwillingness of national governments to cede control over these sectors. Examples are not hard to find. One need only look at the difficulties the Union confronted in attempting to arrive at a coordinated position on the Palestinian bid for statehood at the UN in September 2011 to recognize the degree to which different histories have created contrasting approaches to key foreign policy questions. Moreover, and in line with Hoffmann's arguments concerning systemic determinants of a 'logic of diversity', the different geographical situations of member states themselves spawn different policy preferences. Those member states geographically closest to Russia have tended to adopt somwhat harder line attitudes towards Moscow than several of their more westerly partners. Whilst French President Sarkozy worked to secure a ceasefire between Georgia and Russia following the former's invasion of the latter in 2007, Estonia, Latvia, Lithuania and Poland were critical of his willingness to consider an agreement which did not mention the inviolability of Georgian territorial integrity. They also pressed for the imposition of sanctions on Russia, whilst their presidents, along with their Ukrainian counterpart, visited Tbilisi to demonstrate solidarity with the Georgian government.

As for defence, a number of scholars have identified several major cleavages between member states including between: states favouring European or and Atlantic institutional solutions to defence collaboration; states with different conceptions of the preferred balance of instruments in security policy, in particular between civilian and military and states with contrasting views on the role of the military, be it force projection or territorial defence (Giegerich 2006: 46; see also Rynning 2003: 482–3).

Moreover, conflicting interests afflict both larger and smaller member states. A defining feature of previous EU 'projects' has been the ability of larger member states to push these initiatives through. A broad consensus between Britain, France and Germany on the need for market liberalization paved the way for the single market. Germany, the country with the strongest national currency, was crucial in driving forward the process of monetary Union.

A cursory glance at events leading up to the invasion of Iraq in 2003 illustrates the stark differences that persist between the 'big 3' over foreign policy. In defence, meanwhile, their commitment to it varies significantly. For Britain and France, whilst European cooperation is desirable, support for it has been predicated on continued national control over the key elements of defence policy (including control over national armed forces, a capacity for autonomous action, and the existence of a strong and competitive national defence industry). Equally, London and Paris share a far more expeditionary conception of what defence policy is for than do their partners in Berlin, whilst British and French preferences regarding security cooperation were historically marked by a significant divergence over the appropriate responsibilities to be accorded to European and transatlantic institutions (see also Chapter 15 by Paterson).

Large state leadership is therefore not readily available as a means of overcoming a lack of consensus. On those rare occasions when it has been forthcoming, the Union has proven able to act more effectively than many would have predicted. French President Sarkozy played a leading role, as President-in-office of the European Council, in shaping EU reactions to the Russian invasion of Georgia, however mixed the results of this might have been (Dehousse and Menon 2009). Yet such instances have proven the exception rather than the rule, and, as we shall see below, reactions to the Georgian crisis do not bode particularly well for the ability of the Union to respond to future international events with the same alacrity.

Such rare episodes aside, moreover, it is 'far from obvious that EU member share sufficient foreign policy interests, traditions, goals and outlooks to automatically generate substantive common policies' (Toje 2008a: 125). Moreover, the difficulties inherent in reconciling these interests has meant that the Union has tended to rely on 'constructive ambiguity' (Heisbourg 2000: 5) in order to secure agreement between national capitals. The vague statement of broad principles that passes as the European Union's security strategy is one example. As for defence, more than ten years after the inception of the European Security and Defence Policy (ESDP), it remains unclear what EU defence policies are actually for. Whilst some member states favour more expeditionary military policies, others tend to view CSDP primarily as way of bringing stability – using both military and non-military means – to Europe's near abroad.

Institutional weakness

Clearly, an absence of consensus between member states hampers effective integration. Yet dissensus alone does not explain the kinds of problems that CSDP has confronted in attempting to secure more effective cooperation over foreign and security policies. These are hardly the only sectors marked by cleavages between national preferences. Helmut Kohl, François Mitterrand and Margaret Thatcher hardly shared a vision of the appropriate form a single market should take. Nor did Kohl and Mitterrand agree on the nature of any putative monetary union. For both the single market and monetary union, however, member states tolerated the loss of national control to relatively powerful EU institutions – the European Commission and European Court of Justice in the single market, and the European Central Bank for monetary policy. Strong central institutions, in other words, represent a potential means of overcoming, or at least mitigating the most deleterious consequences of, continued dissensus.

The contrast with foreign and defence policy could hardly be more striking. Illustrative of the problems inherent in securing consensus in these sectors are the provisions of the Lisbon Treaty. Intended, as Hayward points out (see Chapter 1), as a means of providing institutional reinforcement, defence and foreign policies represented its major target – with 25 of the 62 amendments it ushers in applying to treaty provisions in these areas.[4]

Perhaps the most eye-catching innovations have been the creation of a new post of High Representative for Foreign Policy held jointly with the position of Commissioner for External Relations, and of a new European External Action Service (EEAS). The purpose of both was to provide clearer leadership over foreign and security policy matters by overcoming the interstate and inter-institutional rivalries that had hobbled previous attempts to generate common EU policies.

Yet for all the optimism the reforms generated, there are good reasons to question their ability to achieve their stated objective. Both structural and more contingent factors militate against the High Representative managing to provide the kind of leadership expected of her. Structurally, Catherine Ashton's job involves not only representing the European Union in its international dealings, but also acting as Vice-President of the Commission in charge of external relations (a function that involves coordinating those other commissioners whose portfolios impinge on the Union's international dealings) and chairing the Council formation dealing with Foreign Affairs (a task formerly carried out by the Foreign Minister of the country holding the rotating EU Presidency). Not only does the sheer scale of the task appear daunting. Baroness Ashton also has dual loyalties (to Council and Commission) and the need to earn the trust of both institutions despite their frequent clashes about competence over foreign and security policy matters. The outcry generated by her innocuous decision to maintain her office in the Berlaymont bore eloquent testimony to the problems inherent in such a task.

Nor, moreover, is the High Representative alone in having pretentions to impose coherence and exert leadership over EU foreign policies. Whilst she has Treaty mandated roles in CFSP, CSDP and all other aspects of foreign policy, the Commission President ensures representation of the EU in all matters except CFSP, whilst the new President of the European Council is charged with ensuring the external representation of the EU on issues related to common foreign and security policies. The scope for inter-institutional discord has hardly been reduced.

More contingently, member states made it clear from the first that political expediency rather than any real desire to foster effectiveness would shape their attitudes towards the post of High Representative. The choice of Catherine Ashton was clearly – whatever her merits or indeed eventual success – based on considerations of politics rather than on any real debate as to who was best qualified for what is undoubtedly a hugely challenging role.[5] The remarkable degree of personal vitriol directed towards her during her first 18 months in post rendered a hugely challenging job more difficult still.

Baroness Ashton has emphasized the need to secure consensus between the member states prior to laying out clear EU positions. Consequently, she has been criticized for not 'leading from the front.' Yet it is not evident that larger member states in particular would welcome such leadership. British Foreign Secretary William Hague has voiced his concern about the possible encroachment of the EEAS upon member state prerogatives and has both warned British diplomats to guard against this, and made it clear in public that he would fight back against any such 'mission creep' (*The Telegraph*, 28 May 2011). Meanwhile, for all the apparent success of the Union in reacting to the Georgian crisis, this was accomplished because of the activism of the large member state holding the chair of the Council, and Sarkozy largely ignored Javier Solana (the previous EU High Representative) whilst negotiating in Moscow and Tbilisi. The French insistence on putting forward their own plan for Palestinian statehood alongside that proposed by Baroness Ashton hardly implies a renewed willingness on the part of Paris to defer to EU institutions in the realm of foreign affairs.

Insofar as the EEAS is concerned, it is far too early to be able to judge its effectiveness. Evidence from the period of its creation, however, strongly suggests that it may be denied the autonomy it requires to function effectively. The whole point of the External Action Service was to combine as much EU foreign policy as possible under one roof – and under the authority of the High Representative. Yet the European Commission, quick to see in this a challenge to its authority, moved first. President Barroso transferred two sections of DG External Relations – dealing with climate change talks and energy issues – to new DGs for climate change and energy – so keeping them outside the purview of the EAS (see also Chapter 14 by Wurzel). Neighbourhood policy was similarly entrusted to DG Enlargement, whilst a cumbersome fudge over development policy raises the prospect of continued incoherence when the EU attempts to deploy the full range of its instruments. The jostling of member states to ensure the placement of their nationals within the new systems suggests that merit will prove about as central as it did in the choice of High Representative.

Whilst in the area of foreign policy member states have created institutions intended to provide leadership and coherence, but hamstrung these in various ways, in defence they did not even go this far. The treaty in fact simply reinforces member state prerogatives in the defence sector. Indeed, these prerogatives are restated *ad nauseam*. Such undiluted intergovernmentalism serves merely to reinforce the need for consensus. Lengthy negotiations are necessary in order to secure agreement on potential missions, which in turn tends to militate against the effective deployment of hard power, which 'demands executive authority to make decisions and command resources' (Rynning 2003: 487).

The central focus of the Lisbon Treaty when it came to defence policy was an attempt to encourage European military capabilities developments. Central to capabilities development is the European Defence Agency (EDA), created in 2004 in order to improve European defence capabilities via the promotion of Research and Technology, of armaments cooperation and the creation of a European arms market. Under the Lisbon Treaty, the EDA was elevated to the status of a formal EU institution and tasked with assessing member state contributions in the light of the criteria laid down to allow small groups of member states to cooperate more closely. Based on these assessments, the Council can decide to suspend participants for failing to respect the criteria established. As this were not enough, the EDA is also charged with 'identifying, and, if necessary, implementing any useful measure...improving the effectiveness of military expenditure'.

However, the EDA lacks the institutional autonomy necessary to fulfill its ambitious mandate. Its steering board is made up of 27 Defence Ministers (plus a non-voting Commission representative). It in turn appoints the Chief Executive and two deputy Chief Executives. The Agency is thus prey to the whims of the national ministers that control it (and notably, for several months, failed to appoint a Chief Executive). It is thus hard to see it opting to suspend a participant in permanent structured cooperation, and harder still to see such a decision upheld by the Council.

As for effective monitoring of national defence spending, it is virtually inconceivable that member states will take the Agency's recommendations seriously. After all, even in apparently technical areas like the liberalization of the services sector, perceived intrusion by Community institutions has generated angry retaliation from national capitals. How much more angry would be the reaction of a state whose defence spending priorities are questioned? And this particularly in a time of recession, of savage cuts in defence spending across the Union, when 'rationalization' equates to redundancies. Already the siren voices are being raised, warning of desperate consequences if cuts are made.[6]

Dissensus and the limits of EU foreign and security policies

The question remains as to how continued dissensus and the absence of strong EU institutions have conspired to shape the Union's foreign and security policies. Whilst the Union has become an influential actor in terms of global trade, its influence in terms of the non-economic aspects of foreign policy has been more patchy. Certainly, the existence of CFSP and CSDP provide European states with another set of tools that they can, if they so choose, deploy in the event of a crisis. And small-scale deployments in sub-Saharan Africa have doubtless served to improve some lives and secure limited areas. Yet it is no coincidence that the one notable area in which the Union has successfully exerted continual influence over non-member-states – enlargement – has been one for which observers have coined the notion of 'normative entrapment' to describe the way in which member states find it increasingly difficult to dissent from enlargement decisions (Schimmelfenning 2003).

Further afield, EU policies rest on the ability of member states to secure consensus. In the case of the Arab Spring, the relative slowness of European reactions bore eloquent testimony to the divisions that marked national approaches. Well after the outbreak of unrest in Egypt, Silvio Berlusconi was arguing against any rupture with a 'wise man' like Mubarak, hampering any effective European approach. In the case of Libya, Italy and Malta – states with extensive trade ties with the country and which feared an influx of migrants in the event of unrest – staunchly opposed the introduction of EU sanctions in the face of pressure from other member states. As late as mid-February, Malta was seeking to arrange a special Heads of State level summit of the so-called Five plus Five group. The Maltese Prime Minster and Foreign Minster both travelled to Tripoli on 9 February to discuss regional stability with Colonel Gadaffi.

As for CSDP, from its inception, it was based on at best ambivalent agreement between national governments. Indeed, the Anglo-French Saint Malo Declaration of December 1998, widely seen as the founding document of CSDP, was predicated on the ability of its drafters to obfuscate the tension between French insistence on the development of 'autonomous' European forces and British demands that any incipient EU defence force be tightly coupled with The North Atlantic Treaty Organization (NATO).

These different attitudes entailed severe practical implications. From a French perspective, the assumption characterizing the genesis of CSDP was that 'at some stage in the future ... the EU will have developed sufficient advanced military capacity to be able to cope with, say, a Kosovo crisis without having recourse to either NATO or US assets' (Howorth 2000: 55). For the British, given the complementary nature of CSDP and NATO, the Union simply did not need to develop capacities on this kind of scale. As UK Defence Secretary Geoffrey Hoon remarked in Washington in January 2000: 'For meaningful large-scale military operations, NATO remains and will remain, the only game in town. It will be the sole organization for collective defence in Europe. It will be the organization that we expect to turn to for significant crisis management operations' (Howorth 2000: 60).

The first test of these competing conceptions came over the proposed EU take over of the NATO peacekeeping mission in the Former Yugoslav Republic of Macedonia (FYROM). Whilst there had been much talk of this – particularly since the Seville summit of July 2002 – a final decision was delayed as a result of the failure to solve the so-called Berlin plus dispute, which led first Turkey, and then Greece, to block agreement between the Union and NATO. In the light of repeated delays, several member states, including France and Belgium, argued that, because the operation was relatively small (the NATO force numbered only some 800 troops) the EU mission should go ahead even in the absence of any EU-NATO accords. Britain, Spain and Germany blocked agreement on an early EU intervention, partly through concerns about the implications for the transatlantic alliance, partly too because of concerns voiced by military commanders that, whilst the proposed mission itself was small, there was still the possibility of escalation, in which case the EU would need support from NATO. At the European Council meeting of 24–25 October 2002, the UK vetoed a decision on the deployment of an EU force. The following November, President Chirac tried to block the requested six-month extension to the NATO force in FYROM in favour of two-month extension after which an EU force would replace it (*The Daily Telegraph*, 20 November 2002). He was ultimately overruled, but the attempt bore eloquent testimony to the levels of bitterness characterizing intra-EU disputes over the NATO link.

The second area of discord centred on continued disagreements between what Heisbourg has labelled 'extroverts' and neutrals (Heisbourg, 2000: 7), which spawned uncertainty about the appropriate scope of the Union's military ambitions, and in particular the relative weight that should be accorded to 'soft' and 'hard' elements of security policy. The 27 have historically adopted very different attitudes towards the concept of defence, ranging from neutrality (Sweden fought its last war in 1813), to an acceptance of military engagement, often far from home, as an integral part of a nation's 'mission'.

Consequently, the early years of the development of ESDP were characterized by a lack of consensus over whether priority should be placed on the military or non-military end of the Petersberg spectrum. On the one hand, Sweden insisted on greater priority being given to including a significant police element in any EU reaction force, while Finland refused to contemplate participation in peace enforcement missions. On the other, Britain and France emphasized a military approach to EU security policy, involving the existence of armed forces capable of responding to military crises. One outcome of such continued uncertainty was the 'studied ambiguity [of the Helsinki Headline Goal] as to its ultimate size and purpose' (Howorth 2000: 71).

As Hoffmann explained, ambiguity is hardly an adequate basis for defence policy. Given the lack of clear consensus over the objectives of CSDP, it is hardly surprising that member states have struggled to endow it with adequate capabilities. And the weakness of the institutions intended to assist them in this task has further undermined progress. The European Defence Agency lacks even the ability to provide accurate data on member-state contributions to CSDP missions (Witney 2008: 16). Little surprise, then, that it has failed to get member states to live up to their oft-repeated pledges on capabilities and resources. Indeed, having set up a relatively toothless institution, the member states, just to be on the safe side, and indicatively of the jealousy with which they insist on control over their own security policies, side-stepped it and undertook to devote 2 per cent of defence spending to research funding 'on a voluntary basis' (Council of the European Union 2008).

In a coruscating critique, the former head of the European Defence Agency baldly characterized as a 'failure' attempts to enhance European capabilities (Witney 2008: 30). A recent report comments that 'institutional initiatives have generated flurries of bureaucratic activity, but achieved limited results' (International Institute for Strategic Studies 2008: 29).

The impact of problems experienced in enhancing capabilities has been reinforced by an economic climate that has seen significant cuts in defence budgets made throughout the EU (Valasek 2011; Selden 2011). In response to this, observers have called for member states to undertake greater 'pooling and sharing' of their military equipment in an effort to save on costs and improve the interoperability of national armed forces (Maulny 2008: 173ff; Matlary 2009).

Here again, however, an abiding problem remains the central role of member states and their insistence on retaining national control over defence policy. Whilst rationalization would fulfill a functional logic in a sector characterized by duplication and falling defence budgets, it requires that some member states agree to do without certain capabilities. This requires not only a decision to rely on partners for key military needs, but also to absorb the socioeconomic costs of shutting down national capacity. Thus, whilst negotiations amongst Nordic states progressed well on the need to rationalize military training and thus cut costs, they eventually stalled over the issue of whose capabilities would be closed (interviews, Stockholm, 2011).

An interesting comparison here is provided by the process of base closure undertaken in the United States after the Cold War. Ultimate responsibility for this process lay with the Independent Commission on Base Realignment and Closure, whose decisions could only be overturned by a Joint resolution of Congressional Disapproval. With politicians retaining only a minor role in the process, over 100 bases were slated for closure or realignment, along with over 200 smaller facilities (Mayer, 1995). In Europe, by contrast, decisions regarding any form of defence rationalization are the preserve of national governments, with EU institutions enjoying no autonomous role. Little wonder, then, that short-term political considerations take precedence over potential longer-term efficiency gains.

Above and beyond dissensus over the nature of CSDP and of defence policy itself, a broader lack of consensus over the appropriate objectives of foreign policy have also served to hamper the Union's effectiveness as a security actor. Hence, even if some member states can summon up the desire and capabilities to intervene, political agreement on the need for an intervention must be sought. This is difficult to achieve because member state interests vary so widely.

The Union is limited to interventions solely in those cases where consensus can be achieved (Toje 2008a: 132). Thus, military interventions can take place 'as long as the humanitarian rewards are high, the costs in blood and treasure are low – and twenty-seven states are able to agree that this is the case' (Toje 2008b: 206). Hardly surprising, then, that CSDP missions have tended to be small scale and of limited duration (Menon 2009). When potentially difficult missions reach the agenda – as in December 2008 when the UN Secretary General requested an EU intervention in the Democratic Republic of Congo (Menon 2009: 231–2) – the tendency has been for the Union not to act.

Similarly, because consensus tends to be hardest to achieve over issues central to state interests, and involving the great powers, EU interventions have tended to be on the margins of international politics. One scholar suggests the reason why Africa has been the location for so many of the EU's interventions is that it is relatively easy to deploy hard power there without impinging on the interests of great powers (Toje 2008b: 208). The fact that five ESDP missions have taken place in the Congo is hardly evidence of profoundly important EU interests in that benighted country.

Conclusion: sovereignty and decline

Given the high hopes that characterize many assessments of EU foreign and security policies on the one hand, and the persistent disagreements between member states about what the nature of that policy should be on the other, one observer has coined the term 'consensus–expectations gap' to characterize the continuing gulf 'between what the EU member states are expected to do in the world and what they are actually able to agree on' (Toje: 2008a: 121).

A perpetual quest for elusive consensus has, more often than not, ended by illustrating the depths of dissensus amongst member states when it comes to these sectors. Above and beyond the problems inherent in reconciling conflicting national positions rooted in different histories, cultures and geostrategic positions, the EU has failed to put in place an institutional structure capable of reconciling or overcoming these cleavages. In addition, different national policy-making structures mean that executives can struggle to deliver on their commitments even on those occasions when consensus might be achievable between them.

The persistence of dissensus, coupled with the absence of effective EU institutions, has led to the emergence of a vicious circle. Member states tend to be more willing to delegate authority to EU institutions in those areas where their preferences have converged sufficiently to reassure governments about the implications of any loss of control (Gordon 1997–1998). Equally, however, effective institutions represent perhaps the most effective palliative to a situation in which continued dissensus leads to constraints upon effective action. In the absence of both consensus and such institutions, EU foreign and security policies remain highly limited. To the extent they have been utilized, they has been characterized by the kind of risk aversion (Laïdi, 2010) that could be expected of a system in which 27 member states with differing policy preferences must approve all actions.

Perhaps the ultimate paradox resides in the fact that national concern for sovereign control over 'high politics' merely reinforces the secular decline of influence experienced by all European states. There is, in other words, a clear functional need for EU foreign and security policies. In a world of rising powers, where economic and increasingly political influence is slipping away from the 'old continent', the aggregation of power via international institutions would represent a functional response to a shifting international distribution of power. In this sense, an obsession with sovereignty serves merely to hasten the diminution of Europe's practical international influence. It remains to be seen whether this stark paradox will serve to motivate national governments to move beyond impotent national control towards a more effective multilateral approach to foreign and security policy.

Notes

1. The author wishes to gratefully acknowledge the invaluable support provided by ESRC standard grant RES-062-23-2717.
2. Launched in 1999 as the European Security and Defence Policy, this was rebranded the Common Security and Defence Policy by the Lisbon Treaty a decade later.
3. For a more detailed discussion of the relevance of Hoffmann's thought to the development of CSDP, see A Menon, Plus ça Change: Defence Policy as 'High Politics,' Paper prepared for the workshop on 'Beyond the Regulatory Policy. The Integration of Core State Powers,' Herthie School of Government, Berlin, 17–18 June 2011.
4. For a more detailed discussion of the Lisbon Treaty and its impact on EU defence policy, see Menon (2011).
5. Barber, T. (2010) 'The Appointments of Herman van Rompuy and Catherine Ashton'. *JCMS: Journal of Common Market Studies*, 48, 55–67.

6. Nick Butler and Jeffrey Sterling, 'Defence Cuts will hit Britain's Industrial Capacity,' *Financial Times*, 30 September 2010.

Bibliography

Barber, T. (2010) 'The Appointments of Herman van Rompuy and Catherine Ashton', *Journal of Common Market Studies*, 48, 55–67.

Council of the European Union (2008) *Declaration on Strengthening Capabilities*, Brussels.

Dehousse, R. and A. Menon (2009) 'The French Presidency'. *Journal of Common Market Studies, Annual Review*, 47, 99–111.

Giegerich, B. (2006) *European Security and Strategic Culture* (Baden-Baden: Nomos).

Gordon, P.H. (1997–1998) 'Europe's Uncommon Foreign Policy'. *International Security*, 22, 3, 74–100.

Heisbourg, F. (2000) 'Europe's Strategic Ambitions: The Limits of Ambiguity'. *Survival*, 42, 2, 4–15.

Hill, C. and W. Wallace (1996) 'Introduction: Actors and Actions'. In Hill, C. (ed.) *The Actors in Europe's Foreign Policy* (London: Routledge).

Hoffmann, S. (1964) 'Europe's Identity Crisis: Between the Past and America'. *Daedalus*, 93, 4, 1244–97.

Hoffmann, S. (1966) 'Obstinate or Obsolete? The Fate of the Nation State and the Case of Western Europe'. *Daedalus*, 95, 3, 862–915.

Hoffmann, S. (1982) 'Reflections on the Nation State in Western Europe Today'. *Journal of Common Market Studies*, 21, 21–37.

Howorth, J. (2000) *European Integration and Defence: The Ultimate Challenge?* (Paris: European Union Institute for Security Studies).

International Institute for Strategic Studies (2008) *European Military Capabilities: Building Armed Forces for Modern Operations* (London: IISS).

Laïdi, Z. (2010) 'Europe as a Risk Averse Power: A Hypothesis'. *Garnet Policy Brief,* November.

Matlary, J.H. (2009) *European Union Security Dynamics: In the New National Interest* (Basingstoke: Palgrave Macmillan).

Maulny, J.-P. (2008) *Pooling of Member States Assets in the Implementation of ESDP* (Brussels: European Parliament).

Mayer, K.R. (1995) 'Closing Military Bases (Finally): Solving Collective Dilemmas Through Delegation'. *Legislative Studies Quarterly*, XX, 3, 393–413.

Menon, A. (2009) 'Empowering Paradise? ESDP at Ten'. *International Affairs*, 85, 2, 227–46.

Menon, A. (2011) 'European Defence Policy from Lisbon to Libya'. *Survival*, 53, 3, 75–90.

Rynning, S. (2003) 'The European Union: Towards a Strategic Culture?'. *Security Dialogue*, 34, 4, 479–96.

Schimmelfenning, F. (2003) *The EU, NATO and the Integration of Europe: Rules and Rhetoric* (Cambridge: Cambridge University Press).

Selden, Z. (2011) 'Matching Ambitions to Resources: Paying for CFSP in an Era of Fiscal Restraint'. *Annual meeting of the American Political Science Association*, Seattle.2–5 September.

Toje, A. (2008a) 'The Consensus Expectations Gap: Explaining Europe's Ineffective Foreign Policy', *Security Dialogue*, 39, 1, 121–41.

Toje, A. (2008b) 'The European Union as a Small Power, or Conceptualizing Europe's Strategic Actorness'. *European Integration*, 30, 2, 199–215.

Valasek, T. (2011) *Surviving Austerity: The Case for a New Approach to EU Military Collaboration* (London: Centre for European Reform).

Witney, N. (2008) *Re-energising Europe's Security and Defence Policy* (London, European Council on Foreign Relations).

12
Economic and Monetary Disunion?

Kenneth Dyson

Economic and monetary 'disunion' is a problematic concept. It can refer to the absence of union. In this weaker sense of deficient solidarity, disunion means that the European Union (EU) lacks economic and fiscal union ('burden sharing'), domestic ownership of EU fiscal and economic reform commitments ('effort sharing') and shared allegiance to monetary union ('unitary integration'). Indicators of disunion include the asymmetry between economic and monetary union; absence of collective responsibility for public debts; lack of a cross-national bank crisis resolution mechanism; membership of only 17 out of 27 EU member states in the Euro Area; lack of support by euro outsiders for collective financial assistance through the European Financial Stability Facility (EFSF), from 2013 the permanent European Stability Mechanism (ESM); and the decision of four EU member states to remain outside the new Euro Plus Pact of 2011, which sought to coordinate domestic reforms to strengthen competitiveness and convergence. In this same weaker sense, disunion refers to the absence of decisive and timely collective action in the face of intertwined bank and sovereign debt crises and persisting excessive trade and financial imbalances. Most notably, the Euro Area lacked a lender of last resort to member state governments facing debt crisis. The first decade of the euro, and above all the evolution of the post-2007 financial and economic crisis, provided ample evidence of deficient solidarity (Dyson 2010).

Disunion in its stronger sense describes the reversal of union. The most striking forms would be euro exit or EU exit; or expulsion from union, provision for which was proposed in the German paper on a European Monetary Fund in February 2010. An early indication was the distancing of the UK government from the processes leading to closer fiscal union, by vetoing the use of the EU treaty reform method for this purpose at the European Council in December 2011. Disunion takes the form of sharpening dissension, sparked by the reassertion of sovereignty. It leads to a 'spill-back' of competences and legitimacy to national governments, which seek to retrieve greater domestic freedom of action. The aspiration of solidarity is replaced by the unravelling of the Euro Area, perhaps to a core around Germany, putting 'firewalls' in place to prevent contagion from peripheral debt-burdened member states and challenge to single market commitments. From 2010–11, the Euro Area was increasingly threatened by economic and monetary disunion in this stronger sense. Greater differentiation in sovereign credit ratings, widening bond yield spreads and rising costs of credit default swaps for a number of member states heightened the probability that their debts would become unsustainable, that the Euro Area would fall victim to interconnected bank and sovereign insolvency problems, and that a severe credit crunch would deepen austerity. The risk of contagion and disorderly defaults, propelled by volatile bond markets and spread through interconnected banks, gave a potentially new quality to economic and monetary disunion.

Crisis and the *longue durée*

Over the *longue durée* of post-1950 European integration, the gradual evolution of European economic governance supported a prevailing account of an historic shift towards union. The process of Economic and Monetary Union (EMU) provided ample historical evidence. Whilst the member states may remain the 'masters of the treaties', they have erected in the European Central Bank (ECB) a supra-national institutional structure of monetary union. It is flanked – if very imperfectly – by intimations of economic union. The member states delegated competences to the EU to establish and secure a single market and to conduct competition policy. They have also created procedures to monitor and sanction fiscal indiscipline, to subject member state economic policies to mutual surveillance on the basis of 'integrated guidelines' and common priorities (in Europe 2020), to correct excessive imbalances that result from differences in unit labour cost development and to coordinate domestic policies to promote economic competitiveness and convergence (Hodson 2011). The coincidence of the first decade of the Euro Area with a global political economy of 'good times', and more generally the absence of a prolonged and deep financial and economic crisis during the *longue durée*, gave credence to this dominant narrative of union.

The gathering momentum of global financial and economic crisis from 2007 and its transfiguration from banking to sovereign debt crises raised serious questions about the teleological narrative of union. The EU faced more than a series of discrete, country-specific crises. It was enveloped in a fast-evolving structural crisis, which centred on the tension between contending claims of solidarity and sovereignty and on fundamental redefinition of the relationship between member states and the EU, as well as of both to highly volatile global financial markets. Serious questions arose about the political and institutional capacity of the EU to reinvent itself as a decisive actor in crisis management and prevention, one capable of large-scale coordinated action to address interrelated sovereign debt crises, banking crises and competitiveness crises. The central problem was to put in place the conditions for sustainable public finances, financial market stability and correcting excessive imbalances whilst major states sought to defend sovereignty. Other than the ECB in monetary policy, and in emerging as lender of last resort to Euro Area banks, the EU lacked the attributes of 'actorness'. More profoundly, it did not possess the basis of democratic legitimacy that would enable it to make a qualitative leap to economic and fiscal union and behave as an economic policy actor. In economic policy coordination, the EU relied on intergovernmental forums and – outside the single market and competition policy – a relatively weak European Commission. The evolving crisis laid bare the asymmetry between economic and monetary union; the lack of agreement on underlying principles of economic solidarity; and a consequent bias to 'muddling through', to improvisation, and to integration by stealth. It left the ECB as an increasingly lonely and exposed crisis manager. The ECB became more and more critical of the failure of member states to live up to their responsibilities. It hesitated to being drawn into filling the resultant vacuum by unlimited liquidity provision on the basis of suspect collateral and by blurring the line between monetary and fiscal policies. Mutual blame assignment added to the sense of weak political and institutional capacity.

Above all, the evolving financial and economic crisis illustrated how acutely vulnerable the EU was to the structural power of highly volatile global financial markets in the absence of collective responsibility for debts and a clear lender of last resort that could inflict costs on speculators (cf. Dyson 1994). It also raised the political spectre of a resurgence of national populism in the face of the high economic and social costs associated with economic 'bad times', protracted austerity and heavy collateral damage to those least able to shoulder it. Asymmetric, country-specific shocks and prolonged and painful austerity fed a new principle-based and emotionally charged discourse around a different meaning of solidarity – 'unfair' burden sharing versus lack of effort sharing – and around sovereignty – enforcing responsibility versus protecting autonomy. This double-headed challenge of retaining fragile market confidence and sustaining political consensus around the integration process required a capacity for large-scale, resolute and timely action for which the EU was ill-prepared. It lacked independent fiscal capacity to stabilize markets, notably European-financed recapitalization of banks, Eurobond issuance and assumption of collective responsibility for sovereign debts. There was a collective failure to recognize the need for an extreme emergency exemption from the stability-oriented principles of EMU.

The post-2007 crisis showed that the EU remained behind the curve in crisis management, as earlier it had been complacent in crisis prevention. This complacency led to excessive bank risk exposure through weak financial market supervision and regulation, especially in states that faced high asset-price inflation; the failure to create domestic fiscal cushions to manage crisis, consequent on lack of attention to deficit–debt dynamics, especially in domestic contexts of elevated sovereign debt levels, high private-sector indebtedness and weak, or unsustainable, growth; and neglect of competitiveness indicators and consequent build-up of excessive trade and financial imbalances. At the root of this complacency was the belief that the single currency provided shelter from the global financial markets consequent on removal of the traditional vulnerability to exchange-rate shocks. However, as the post-2007 crisis showed, vulnerability to financial markets had not been removed. It had been displaced to sovereign bond markets and to the banking system. Credit ratings and bond yields differentiated member states into saints and sinners.

The 'union' account of European economic governance: path dependency

The prevailing teleological bias in accounts of European economic governance is captured in the term Economic and Monetary 'Union'. This bias finds its inspiration in certain constitutional, politico-historical and economic characteristics of the integration process. Constitutionally, from its inception in the Treaty of Rome in 1957, the European Economic Community (EEC) was pledged to 'ever closer union'. EMU became a foremost expression of this fundamental commitment, including – as a precondition – the single market in goods, services, capital and people. The Maastricht Treaty of 1993 embodied a legal commitment to make union 'irreversible'. In this spirit, the Euro Area heads of state or government pledged in 2010 to do 'whatever it takes' to safeguard the euro.

Politically, member state governing elites were driven by shared historical memories of the catastrophic economic and social costs of interwar disunion. These costs had been associated with the harsh, intransigent politics of war debts and reparations through the 1920s, the protracted fear and misery of the Great Depression from 1931, the competing currency blocs of the 1930s and the brutality of fascism and total war. A central historical lesson was that European states stood to realize mutual gains in growth and employment from opening their markets to trade. In this way, 'ever closer union' promised enhanced state power to promote domestic welfare. It also offered an external discipline to overcome domestic blockage to reforms. In addition, by accelerating economic and political union, member states believed that they could strengthen their capacity to project external influence in a refashioned international order in which the pivot of power had moved decisively away from Europe. This combination of historical memories and lessons with constitutional commitment generated a profound sense of a path-dependent character to EMU. Its central political drive was imparted by the Franco-German 'motor' and the collective historical memory and lesson-drawing that it fostered (see also Chapter 15 by Paterson).

Economically, the shared belief in mutual gains from open markets, above all from reduced transaction costs, was sustained by long postwar cycles of economic expansion. The first, failed launch of EMU in the early 1970s foundered on the rocks of the collapsed Bretton Woods system and of the oil crises. However, its relaunch from 1988 coincided with a much more benign international economic context, if disrupted by the costs of German unification. More importantly, the first decade after the transition to the final stage three of EMU was characterized by the political economy of 'good times'. EMU had a relatively easy first decade in which it could establish itself as a pole of attraction for EU non-members. It grew from 11 to 16 between 1999 and 2007 (Dyson 2010).

This constitutional, political and economic bias to teleological accounts of EMU as a process of union was reinforced by the existence of a hegemonic monetary power. Germany provided intellectual leadership through a combination of its relative GDP size, export prowess and huge current account surpluses. Above all, it possessed the foremost record of monetary discipline, which was exemplified in the strength of the D-Mark as a currency and in its price stability record, and which endowed the Bundesbank with the reputation of being the 'bank that rules Europe'. The D-Mark functioned as the European 'safe haven' currency, alongside the Swiss franc; German bond yields served as the European bench-mark. German cognitive power over EMU was illustrated by the extent to which the Werner Report on EMU of 1970 borrowed from the Schiller Plans. After the oil crises of the 1970s, German economic reputation was even more solid. In 1979 the D-Mark became the anchor currency of the new exchange rate mechanism (ERM). The ERM was, in effect, a D-Mark zone (Dyson 1994). The Delors Report on EMU of 1989 owed more to the Pöhl Paper, presented by the Bundesbank, than the previous Werner Report had owed to the Schiller Plan (Dyson and Featherstone 1999). The incentive to create a sound, sustainable basis for currency union by borrowing existing German monetary reputation, and thus market confidence, was overwhelming. Also, for the same reason, German polit-ical commitment to enter was so vital that its elites emerged as both central agenda setters and key veto players in negotiations. Hence the Maastricht 'constitution of EMU' in 1991 was founded on German ideas of 'sound' finances and money (Dyson 2000). Centrality was accorded to the principle of the independence of the ECB, to the principle of 'no bailouts' for member state governments, to no privileged access for governments to central bank financing, to the excessive deficit proce-dure (later formalized in the Stability and Growth Pact (SGP) of 1997), and to convergence criteria for entry into stage three that emphasized inflation, fiscal deficits, public debt and exchange-rate stability. EMU seemed to be a path-dependent process, governed by German Ordo-liberal ideas of sound money and finance and the strict separation of fiscal and monetary policies.

In short, EMU seemed to rest on an impressive edifice of structural power that set it on a path-dependent process of union. Germany gave intellectual coherence and policy direction based on its monetary power; the treaties, from Rome to Maastricht, offered clear legal mandates and political direction to 'ever closer union' and the 'irreversible' character of stage three of EMU (they enter 'irrevocably'); the privileging of the market in economic policy discourse supported beliefs in reducing transaction costs through a single market and a single currency; whilst considerations of domestic and external political power, combined with historical lesson-drawing, suggested shared elite interests in supporting the union project.

This bias towards teleological accounts was reflected in European integration theories, notably neo-functionalism and 'new' institutionalism. Even the more politically sophisticated and nuanced forms of neo-functionalist theories, which allowed for the possibility of 'spill-back' effects, were essentially optimistic (Lindberg and Scheingold 1971). They believed in the efficacy of the mechanism of 'spill-over' from existing integration projects into related policy areas. It created powerful incentives to 'ever closer union'. In relation to EMU, the chain ran from customs union, external trade and agriculture, through the single market (especially freedom of capital movement), to exchange rates and monetary union. Neo-functionalism entered the EMU literature through the so-called monetarist theory, which argued that acceleration of monetary union would drive forward economic convergence and create the conditions for its own success (Dyson 1994). It also figured in a much diluted form in the thesis of the 'inconsistent triangle': the combination of freedom of capital movement after 1990 with commitment to stable exchange rates in the ERM left no room for independent monetary policies (Padoa Schioppa et. al. 1987). In other words, the first two commitments entailed a shift to monetary union. The various forms of new institutionalism, above all historical and sociological, offered accounts that pointed in a similar direction. A clear and powerful cognitive script was institutionalized in the ECB and the wider Eurosystem and protected by the ECB-centric Maastricht Treaty. EMU was set on a track defined by the sound finance and money paradigm (Dyson 2000). Whether seen in terms of neo-functionalism or new institutionalism, powerful structural forces – the legacies of past choices – created a path-dependent process towards union.

This union bias was also reflected in accounts of European integration, which pictured differentiated patterns of membership, for instance in the ERM and in the Euro Area, as temporary expedients (Dyson and Sepos 2010). European economic governance remained essentially a unitary project in which eventually all member states shared the same obligations and responsibilities. The core of the unitary project was the single market, competition policy and external trade policy. Similarly, all member states subscribed to the post-2000 Lisbon process of economic policy coordination for achieving a qualitative leap in growth, employment, competitiveness and cohesion. Following the reforms to strengthen integrated economic governance in 2011, the 'European Semester' brought together the processes of Commission assessment and recommendation of member state action in domestic reforms and in fiscal policies to help correct EU-wide excessive imbalances and ensure sustainable public finances. The norm, with the exceptions of Denmark and the UK, was derogation from stage three of EMU until the convergence criteria had been met.

The 'disunion' account of European economic governance: horizontal and vertical dimensions

Disunion is far from new in the historical experience of EMU. From the 1950s onwards, Franco-German divergences of economic policy belief over *dirigisme* and open, competitive markets sowed distrust and dissension. They help explain the lack of incorporation of EMU in the Treaty of Rome as a clear legal requirement; the abortive European Commission attempt in 1963 to set out a programme for EMU; the rapid loss of momentum behind the Werner Report of 1970; and the difficult processes of crisis management that beset the ERM (notably in 1983, 1987 and 1992–93). The union process can be seen as triumphing on the basis of agreement on shared values of a 'stability culture' in the Maastricht 'constitution of EMU' (Dyson 2000). However, this normative code continued to co-exist with divergent policy preferences. The resulting tensions and contradictions were highlighted in 2003 when the German federal government engaged in coalition building with the French and the Italian governments to prevent the implementation of the Stability and Growth Pact with respect to itself. It helped launch a process that culminated in the 2005 SGP reform, which created more room of manoeuvre for domestic fiscal policies (Heipertz and Verdun 2010). This episode illustrated the lack of traction of the 'stability culture' code, not least under a Social Democrat-Green German federal government. It brought the German government into open conflict with the Bundesbank and the ECB.

Probability of disunion was increased by three long-term structural developments in the EU that predated the post-2007 crisis: broadening, deepening and widening. Broadening involved the delegation or coordination of an increasing range of policy areas at the EU level. EMU evolved to embrace the single market, financial market regulation and supervision, fiscal policy coordination, economic policy coordination, euro payments systems and the single monetary policy. Their different functional attributes meant varying patterns of incentive to participate (Dyson and Sepos 2010). In consequence, European economic governance evolved as a complex cocktail of unitary and differentiated integration. All EU member states participated in the single market (other than temporary derogations for new members). The

Lisbon process of economic reforms remained EU-wide. Euro payment systems were managed within the Eurosystem of central banks but had members across the EU. The SGP united all in shared rules on deficits and debt. However, there were differences between Euro Area members and non-members with respect to the nature of the programme to be monitored and to sanctions. Financial market regulation and supervision was not just EU-wide but also embedded in globally agreed rules. In all these cases, the costs of exclusion and attempting to free ride were outweighed by the mutual gains from market access, coordinated economic reforms, financial stability and efficient payment systems.

However, monetary union introduced a different structure of incentives. Its central objective of price stability could be achieved domestically through central bank independence and inflation targeting. Moreover, there were costs in giving up exchange-rate flexibility and interest-rate adjustment. In their absence, states were induced to pursue potentially slow and painful 'internal' devaluation to restore competitiveness; they also lacked the capacity to conduct counter-cyclical monetary policies or to tackle debt problems by printing their own money. Denmark chose to be in a *de facto* monetary union through a tight ERM II fluctuation band, while retaining the option of exit in emergency. In effect, Denmark was free-riding. Sweden and the UK chose to stay outside both ERM II and the Euro Area. The Czech Republic, Hungary and Poland also gave priority to domestic economic policy flexibility. In so far as the euro acted as a catalyst to trade integration through the single market, they were able to be silent partners in the bandwagon.

This broadening of the scope of policy integration also generated different patterns of 'leaders' and 'laggards' in EMU and a process of transverse integration (Dyson 2010; Dyson and Marcussen 2010). Some member states, above all Germany, stood out as leaders in monetary union. However, in the Lisbon process of economic reforms and in the SGP, the leaders were often outside the Euro Area, notably Denmark and Sweden. Greece, Italy, Portugal and Spain were Euro Area 'insiders' but clear laggards. Lisbon and the SGP united some Euro Area 'insiders' (notably Austria, Finland, Germany and the Netherlands) with 'outsiders' in tightly knit networks. As we shall see, they shared the attributes of creditor states.

Deepening was reflected in a delegation of competences to the EU level, including the increasing use of qualified majority voting in Council and, from 2011, higher barriers to blocking the European Commission in the excessive deficit procedure. Pressures to delegate competences made more visible the tensions and conflicts between sovereignty and solidarity. These problems were manifest in the resort to formal treaty 'opt-outs' of Denmark and the UK from monetary union. Similarly, the German Federal Constitutional Court in its ruling on the Lisbon Treaty made delegation of fiscal and welfare-state competences to the EU conditional on a European-level structure of democratic legitimacy and of protection of basic rights (see also Chapter 8 by Birkinshaw). It saw in the evolving structures of European economic government risks that democratic legitimacy would be enfeebled. To the extent that deepening was an elite-driven process driven by technocratic considerations of efficiency, it threatened disconnection from public opinion and the exploitation of political disillusionment by national populists. In consequence, any gains from deepening would be offset, even outweighed, once domestic political elites sought to neutralize risks from extremist politics by adopting more Eurosceptic policy positions.

Finally, EU widening, especially the predominantly eastern enlargements of 2004 and 2007, brought increased diversity of economic structures, cultures and levels of development. In particular, disparities of GDP per capita grew. These new member states faced significant economic and political incentives to prioritize rapid real convergence in living standards over compliance with the nominal convergence criteria for euro entry. Hence self-determined timetables for euro entry tended to be regularly revised and prolonged, even ignored, notably in the Czech Republic, Hungary and Poland (Dyson and Marcussen 2009). Economic 'catch-up' focused their policy priorities around matching funding to maximize access to EU Structural Funds, major infrastructure projects and supportive welfare policies to ameliorate social costs.

Successive waves of EU enlargement also gave credence to the notion of distinct state clusters, like the Nordic states, the Baltic states, the Visegrad states, the Clubmed states, Carolingian Europe and Anglo-America (cf. Dyson and Sepos 2010). The value of this type of analysis was put into question by difficult issues of definition, boundary drawing and categorization, along with awkward idiosyncrasies. Nevertheless, the attribution of specific sets of economic policy preferences and of institutional capacity to pursue effective reforms to each cluster offered tempting shorthand for dealing with increasing complexity and diversity of EU membership. In particular, the southern and eastern enlargements seemed to increase the number of prospective *demandeurs* for collective European fiscal and financial assistance and of states with weak institutional capacity to adjust to European fiscal and economic policy commitments. This sense of increasing institutional and cultural diversity sowed greater distrust, especially amongst the creditor states of Carolingian and Nordic Europe.

The horizontal dimension of disunion

The evolving post-2007 financial and economic crisis opened up space for narratives of disunion to take clearer shape, especially as it meta-morphosed into intertwined bank and sovereign debt crises of a conta-gious nature. Emerging divisions were not so much new as old, notably the creditor/debtor state divide and the problems posed by a 'one-size-fits-all' monetary policy in a non-optimal currency area. Crisis management exposed and sharpened these divisions and made trans-parent the lack of capacity for unified, timely and decisive action to 'shock and awe' markets.

Neither the Werner Report nor the Delors Report had given central place to optimum currency area (OCA) theory in thinking about the design of European economic governance. The Commission-sponsored *One Market, One Money* report of 1990 had explicitly critiqued the rele-vance of this type of theory. It had advocated an approach grounded in institutional economics, notably modern monetary theory with its stress on the combination of central bank independence, fiscal disci-pline and mechanisms of economic policy coordination. However, the onset of the crisis highlighted the significance of the EU having given birth to a non-optimal currency union. OCA theory evolved to identify a range of variables that affect the capacity to sustain a 'one-size-fits-all' monetary policy: most notably, compensatory fiscal trans-fers, trade openness, labour mobility and spreading of risk. Measured in these terms, the EU (even the 12 member states at the time of the Maastricht Treaty) was not an OCA. Also, the Euro Area did not qualify. Its sustainability depended on the will and capacity of its member states to offset the domestic effects of a 'one-size-fits-all' monetary policy by tax and spending adjustments and by making product, service, capital and labour markets more flexible. Greece, Ireland, Italy, Portugal and Spain illustrated the lack of this domestic political ownership.

A further compensatory mechanism was provided by the endogenous effects of currency union. By removing exchange-rate risk and reducing transaction costs, monetary union promised substantial trade effects. In turn, trade effects promoted economic convergence and closer synchro-nization of business cycles, thereby making a single monetary policy easier to sustain. However, again, endogenous trade effects proved asymmetric (Baldwin 2006). They proved stronger within a group of Euro Area economies closely linked to Germany. In short, the vestiges of the D-Mark zone continued within the Euro Area. Strikingly, this zone reflected the continuing significance of distance (from Germany) in trade creation. Greece, Ireland, Portugal and Spain had business cycles less synchronized with the rest of the Euro Area, less so than the Czech Republic, Denmark, Poland and Slovakia. The decisive factor was intra-industry trade and cross-national supply chains. Evidence about the endogenous effects of currency union supported arguments for a downsizing of the Euro Area in Clubmed Europe.

Lack of large-scale fiscal transfers, linguistic and cultural barriers to labour mobility, weak domestic political ownership of the implications of a single monetary policy and asymmetric endogenous effects of currency union combined to fuel potential for discord. This fragile infrastructure raised doubts in the minds of international creditors, and potentially of publics, about the long-term sustainability of the Euro Area in its existing form. Ultimately, OCA theory served as an incentive to assume that the Euro Area faced an existential choice: become a permanent fiscal transfer union, on the Belgian, German, Italian and Spanish models, or slim down by exit of peripheral economies. Sustainability depended on closer economic and fiscal union or on more tightly defined differentiation in Euro Area membership.

The idea of a fiscal transfer union as shelter for member states facing strong market pressures and adjustment challenges provoked heightened dissension as the post-2007 crisis exposed the differences in strategic interests and in policy preferences between creditor and debtor states. The sharpening of this classic creditor–debtor state division shifted intra-EU diplomacy from a persuasive to an adversarial and coercive mode (cf. Dyson 2013). In particular, faced by increasingly anxious public opinion, the Austrian, Dutch, Finnish and German governments began to demand much tougher conditionality for collective financial assistance and to frame it as a 'last resort'. The problems with the first Greek rescue and the need for a second Greek rescue provoked in 2011 the emergence of an informal creditor state grouping within the Euro Area, formed by the triple-A rated states. They defined common positions on Greece, stressing large-scale externally supervised privatization of state assets and intense direct surveillance of fiscal and structural reforms. The strategic interests of creditor states focused on limiting their taxpayer liabilities and their risks of exposure to debtor states. Their arguments from principle stressed moral hazard and the constraints of the 'no bailout' Lisbon Treaty clause. Correspondingly, Germany rejected a wide range of proposals: a French-sponsored idea for a European bank rescue fund, an Italian-sponsored proposal for collective euro bond issuance, provision of below-market interest rates for collective financial assistance, giving the EFSF/ESM the right to mount its own independent rescues, and leveraging the EFSF/ESM by giving it a bank licence and access to the ECB to multiply its firepower.

In contrast, the strategic interests of debtor states focused on gaining plentiful financial assistance in order to buy time for painful domestic adjustments. Their arguments from principle emphasized the systemic risks from contagious banking and sovereign debt crises in an increasingly financially integrated currency union. According to the Italian Finance Minister Giulio Tremonti in July 2011, creditor states were at risk of becoming like the first-class passengers on the *Titanic*. At the same time, solidarity amongst debtor states was at best tenuous. All of them sought to differentiate themselves from Greece, as well as from each other. Thus Spain was not Portugal, and Italy was neither Ireland nor Spain. Similarly, in east central Europe, the Czech Republic and Poland differentiated themselves from Hungary and Romania. The advantage of larger numbers that debtor states had over creditor states was outweighed by their lack of unity, their lack of intellectual self-confidence and the sense of guilt that attaches to excessive debt.

Because of the ever closer institutional, economic and financial interdependencies that they generated, and their multitude of repeated and nested bargaining games, the EU and the Euro Area acted as constraints in taming the mutually coercive use of creditor and debtor state power. Debtor states avoided resort to threats of unilateral defaults with punitive costs on creditors or to measures of financial protection. Creditor states hesitated from curbing the sovereignty of debtor states by installing their own public debt administrations with assigned tax revenues to debt servicing, as in pre-1914 Greece and Ottoman Turkey. On balance, however, the asymmetry of power favoured the agenda-setting and veto power of creditor states, above all Germany. Though there was a smaller number of creditor than of debtor states, creditor states demonstrated more solidarity. Power was tamed more on their terms.

The third horizontal division was rooted in the coexistence of different models of capitalism and of welfare states within the EU and the Euro Area. Anglo-American 'liberal market' capitalism seemed different from continental European 'cooperative' capitalism, with its belief in balancing employer and employee interests, in creating shared institutional structures through which vocational training and technology transfer could be delivered, and in commitment to consensus (Hall and Soskice 2001). Enlargement drew attention to other possible models: for instance, the Baltic, Mediterranean and Visegrad. Again, problems of definition, boundary drawing and categorization in the presence of a multitude of idiosyncrasies raised difficulties in handling these models: and, again, their shorthand value prevailed. It was possible to reduce complexity by attributing divergences in policy preference, and in notions about legitimacy of burden-sharing in economic adjustments, to different institutional structures of capitalism and welfare state provision. However, as we saw earlier, the post-2007 crisis revealed an increase in differentiation within these models: between Slovakia and the rest of Visegrad; between the Czech Republic and Poland, on the one hand, and Hungary, on the other; and between other Mediterranean states and Greece. Rivalry intensified in the face of the power of credit ratings and bond markets to inflict fiscal and economic damage. Individual states may have carried a certain institutional imprint, but became increasingly hybrid.

On the horizontal axis, the Franco-German relationship displayed signs of disunion. The German federal government initially rejected French proposals to institute regular formal Euro Area heads of state and government summits. It also indicated its irritation with President Nicolas Sarkozy's 'grandstanding' in EU crisis management during the French EU presidency in 2008. It blocked the idea of a European bank rescue fund and took a tougher approach to involving private creditors in sovereign bailouts. There were some achievements: Merkel and Sarkozy gave joint backing to the ESM and to tougher fiscal rules; they also proposed the Competitiveness (later Euro Plus) Pact. Above all, the French role shifted from high-profile, Sarkozy-led EU presidency initiatives in 2008, which produced few substantive results, to one of acting as mediator and consensus builder within the Euro Group and ECOFIN, seeking to soften German positions. The counterbalance to this shift was a stronger emphasis on Anglo-French defence, returning to the notion of a juxtaposition of German leadership in EMU with French leadership in defence.

EMU had been founded on the basis of Franco-German leadership, France on process, Germany on substance (Dyson and Featherstone 1999). Disunion within this relationship could prove fatal. It was apparent in the lack of a bold and comprehensive joint initiative that offered long-standing reassurance to highly nervous financial markets. Repeated European Council meetings, preceded by intense Franco-German diplomacy, failed to draw a line under the dangerously contagious and intertwined sovereign debt and banking crises. There was, not least a serious risk that French public debt problems were not being aggressively addressed, so that the contagion problem could infect this core relationship through France's loss of a triple-A rating. This down-grading would in turn undermine the credibility of the guarantees underpinning the EFSF and reduce its firepower.

The vertical dimension of disunion

The evolving post-2007 crisis also opened up the vulnerability of EMU to the vertical dimension of disunion: to a more explicit hier-archy amongst EU and Euro Area states; and to problems of domestic democratic legitimacy for European economic governance.

The sharpening of the divisions between creditor and debtor states risked a serious shift in perceptions and discourse within inter-state relations. These relations come to be seen as an informal hierarchy, in which creditor states are presented as the fiscal and economic 'saints' (frugal, hard working and reliable) and debtor states as 'sinners' (feckless, indolent and untrustworthy). Public opinion in creditor states bitterly resents having to support through transfers the 'profligate'. By 2011, the elements of a transfer union seemed in place as ECB sovereign bond purchases displaced risk to creditor states through the balance sheet of the Eurosystem of central banks. In turn, opinion in debtor states pictures creditor states as turning them into an EU 'protectorate' or 'vassal' and the Euro Area as a 'Germanization' project. Historical memories of pre-1914 and interwar Greece and of later wartime occu-pation experiences are available for use in populist mobilization. Debt crises readily become highly emotionally charged and risk introducing a poisonous quality into intra-EU and intra-Euro Area relations.

Disunion processes after 2007 were also reflected in evidence of growing gaps between political elites and public opinion. The painful fiscal and economic adjustments associated with European crisis management touch on highly sensitive, interconnected issues of social justice, consent and identity. Disconnection between elites and public opinion – evident in mass demonstrations, violent protests, new popular movements of indignant citizens and electoral gains for extremist polit-ical parties – undermines the political basis for sharing more sovereignty in economic union. In the process the European Commission and the ECB risk becoming increasingly lonely and exposed institutions. These dangers materialized in creditor states like Finland and the Netherlands in 2010–11, inducing their national governments to adopt harder-line positions in EU-level negotiations. Domestic elites faced new questions about how best to contain enraged public opinion and the flight to national populist mobilization.

The narrative of disunion seems to fit more neatly with inter-governmental theories of European integration, in which member states are seen as jealously guarding their sovereignty and using their power to block and shape the process. President Charles De Gaulle reined in the European Commission's attempt to launch EMU in 1962–63, as did Federal Chancellor Ludwig Erhard. President Georges Pompidou acted to limit the threats to French fiscal sovereignty posed by the Werner Report of 1970, whilst German negotiators resisted French efforts to develop the ERM into a concerted intervention mechanism that would bind more tightly the hands of the Bundesbank. The scale of the collective action problems that beset the EU in the post-2007 crisis seemed to bear out much of intergovernmental theory.

Intergovernmental theory had been less successful in explaining the enormously ambitious commitment of member states, notably Germany, to 'irreversible' EMU at Maastricht or the realization of stage three in 1999. However, its 'liberal' variant offered two elements that support a narrative of union. Growing economic interdependency heightened vulnerability to exchange-rate crises and created an incentive to seek shelter in monetary union. In addition, geo-strategic shift, notably German unification, strengthened incentives to demonstrate continuing loyalty to past commitments by firmly tying hands to an ambitious union project. Collective action constraints were, in consequence, loosened.

The post-2007 crisis opened up two possibilities for a revival of the narrative of union. First, financial as well as economic interdependency within a currency union shifted the source of vulnerability to sovereign bond markets and cross-nationally active banks. There was, accordingly, a new incentive to create shelter for sovereign states from heightened risks of contagion. Devices for this purpose include common euro bond issuance; a huge expansion of the EFSF/ESM's firepower and instruments of intervention so that it provides a lender of last resort; collective debt redemption at the Euro Area level; and collective bank recapitalization. Second, German political leaders continue to have an incentive to rally to 'do whatever it takes' both to ease negative perceptions that it was reverting to a narrowly self-interested role and to protect its overwhelmingly important long-term economic interests in the EU and the Euro Area. By September 2011, the Bundesbank and the German federal government were reviving the idea of pressing ahead with political and fiscal union and enshrining it in treaty form (Weidmann 2001). This shift reflected recognition that rulings of the Federal Constitutional Court had narrowed the range of outcomes that the federal government could negotiate in reforming European economic governance without treaty change.

Conclusions

Despite a prevailing union account, EMU has always rested on a delicate political balance between German concerns about long-term security and prosperity – resolved by binding herself to Europe – and French efforts to compensate for loss of relative power vis-à-vis the United States and Germany through a leadership role in Europe. These French concerns were magnified by resurgent German economic power from the mid-1950s, by the 1983, 1987 and 1993 ERM crises, and by the shock of German unification in 1990.

The result of this process of Franco-German political balancing was an EMU project that Europeanized German monetary power on strict Ordo-liberal conditions. Germany surrendered monetary sovereignty in exchange for credible treaty-based guarantees that the Euro Area would be based on 'solidarity of effort sharing' in securing a 'stability culture'. This outcome led, in turn, to an EMU in which Europeanization and Germanization of member states seemed to become interchangeable, an association that contained political risks of disunion. Furthermore, from the outset, the asymmetry between economic and monetary union added to the sense of a precarious imbalance at the heart of the project. It was vulnerable to asymmetric shocks, to cross-national banking crises, to fiscal indiscipline and to divergences in competitiveness. Monetary union lacked the supportive infrastructure of a political union. In particular, neo-Gaullist French presidents remained deeply reluctant to cede their own economic and fiscal powers for the sake of establishing economic union to parallel monetary union. This reluctance connected President Sarkozy to President Pompidou in 1970–71.

However, it took the post-2007 crisis to lay fully bare the dangers of becoming prisoner of a teleological account of EMU. Protracted structural crisis strengthened processes of disunion, horizontal and vertical. It underlined that the evolution of European economic governance was a contingent and not a one-way process. Cross-currents of union and disunion co-existed in a precarious relationship.

An evolving financial and economic crisis makes any assessment of disunion in European economic governance highly tentative and provisional. Disunion has grown in its weaker sense. There is an absence of union, especially in the economic/fiscal pillar and an absence of decisive and timely coordinated action to 'shock and awe' financial markets. Above all, the Euro Area lacks the institutional capacity to act in extreme emergency when its integrity and continuity is put at risk. There was also evidence of growing dissension, initially between the German government and the ECB about involving private creditors in sovereign debt bailouts (resolved by the end of 2011), and above all between the German Bundesbank and the ECB over ECB purchasing of sovereign bonds. However, in the stronger sense, disunion had not by December 2011 taken the form of euro exits or expulsions or of unilateral sovereign debt defaults, only of British distancing from moves to fiscal union. Not least, the core Franco-German relationship remained intact, though highly strained. Perhaps the clearest signs of the stronger form of disunion are in differentiation. There is an emerging cluster of semi-permanent Euro Area outsiders, some of whom also opted to remain apart from the Euro Plus Pact and potentially (like Britain) the intergovernmental treaty on fiscal union.

The complexity of underlying structural developments, the pressure of events, above all in volatile financial markets and the quality of decision-making leave open the possibilities of union or disunion gaining the upper hand. On balance, the risks will tilt to disunion as long as the Euro Area continues to lack an extreme emergency exemption from stability-oriented principles in order to underscore its commitment to ensuring the survival of the currency union and to tame financial market speculation (Dyson forthcoming).

Bibliography

Baldwin, R. (2006) 'The Euro's Trade Effects', ECB Working Paper No. 594. Frankfurt am Main.

Dyson, K. (1994) *Elusive Union* (London: Longmans).

Dyson, K. (2000) *The Politics of the Euro-Zone* (Oxford: Oxford University Press).

Dyson, K. (2010) 'The First Decade: Credibility, Identity, and Institutional 'Fuzziness'', in K. Dyson (ed.). *The Euro at 10: Europeanization, Power, and Convergence* (Oxford: Oxford University Press), pp. 1–34.

Dyson, K. (2013) *States, Debt, and Power: Saints and Sinners in European History and Integration* (Oxford: Oxford University Press).

Dyson, K. and K. Featherstone (1999) *The Road to Maastricht: Negotiating Economic and Monetary Union* (Oxford: Oxford University Press).

Dyson, K. and M. Marcussen (eds) (2009) *Central Banks in the Age of the Euro.* (Oxford: Oxford University Press).

Dyson, K. and M. Marcussen (2010) 'Transverse Integration in European Economic Governance: Between Unitary and Differentiated Integration', *Journal of European Integration*, 32, 1: 17–40.

Dyson, K. and A. Sepos (eds) (2010) *Which Europe? The Politics of Differentiated Integration* (Basingstoke: Palgrave).

Hall, P. and D. Soskice (eds) (2001). *Varieties of Capitalism: The Institutional Foundations of Comparative Advantage* (Oxford: Oxford University Press).

Heipertz, M. and A. Verdun (2010) *Ruling Europe: The Politics of the Stability and Growth Pact* (Cambridge: Cambridge University Press).

Hodson, D. (2011) *Governing the Euro Area in Good Times and Bad* (Oxford: Oxford University Press).

Lindberg. L. and S. Scheingold (eds) (1971) *Regional Integration: Theory and Research* (Harvard: Harvard University Press).

Padoa Schioppa, T. et al. (1987). *Efficiency, Stability and Equity* (Oxford: Oxford University Press.

Weidmann, J. (2011). 'Die Krise als Herausforderung für die Währungsunion', *Auszüge aus Presseartikeln*, Deutsche Bundesbank, 14 September: 3–8.

13
Social and Labour Market Policy: The (Re-)Emergence of Competitive Tensions

Nick Parsons

The European Union (EU) has never been a 'social union' in the sense that the eurozone, for example, is a monetary union. Nevertheless, national sovereignty over social and labour market policies has always been exercised under the constraint of external pressures for economic competitiveness. As a consequence, any pan-European social solidarity has been difficult to achieve as social and labour market policies have become a factor of national economic competitiveness. As a result, regime competition theories predicted a race to the bottom in social and workplace protections. This chapter will argue that, whereas there is little evidence for this race to the bottom in times of economic growth, the 2007–08 financial crisis kickstarted it, aggravating tensions arising from constrained sovereign state control of social and labour market policies on the one hand and notions of European social solidarity on the other, with potentially dire consequences for the whole European project.

Certain minimum labour market and social rights – particularly with respect to equality and non-discrimination – are enshrined in texts such as the Charter of Fundamental Rights, now part of the Treaty on the Functioning of the European Union (see also Chapter 8 by Birkinshaw). Beyond these, however, there are no formal institutions to control member state policies in the areas of labour markets or social protection, although the process of the open method of coordination (OMC) does attempt to promote coordination through benchmarking and policy-learning. In recent years, the European Court of Justice (ECJ) has been increasingly interventionist in the areas of social and labour market policies, but these interventions mainly aim at upholding the four fundamental freedoms at the heart of European construction – the free movement of goods, services, capital and labour. The content and focus of social and labour market policies are therefore entirely under the aegis of member state governments as long as they do not infringe these freedoms and adhere to some basic rights.

Despite the lack of any formal 'social union', one could talk about a certain unity of purpose articulated by the European social model, based around a convergence towards high levels of social and labour market protections for European workers, albeit along the lines of different national models. Thus, member states could be seen as *acting in union* through adherence to certain values that emphasize high standards of social and workplace protection, the role of unions and collective bargaining in negotiating compromises over social and labour market policy issues and so on. Until the 2007–08 financial crisis, there appeared to be some evidence of this, despite the continual problems that beset the financing of welfare regimes in all member states. These national expressions of social solidarity were complemented by mechanisms of solidarity operating at the EU level through institutions for 'soft' coordination such as the various OMCs and the redistributive mechanisms of structural funds and the like. However, this solidarity, at both national and European levels, was dependent upon economic growth to fuel and pay for social improvements. Below the surface, economic growth in the decade from 1997–2007 merely masked the underlying tensions between the competitive forces unleashed by the market-driven focus of European integration on the one hand, and the notion of transnational social solidarity on the other. From 2008, responses to financial and economic crisis brought these tensions to the surface, challenging the very notion of European solidarity.

This chapter will firstly examine the notion that member states act in union with respect to labour market and social policies. It will then analyse the impact of the 2007–08 financial crisis on social and labour market policies within the EU, before conclusions are drawn about implications for the future.

Acting in Union? Social solidarity in the EU

The establishment of the European social model has never been a unitary project involving the transfer of competencies to a supranational level. Over the long term in the EU, from the signing of the Treaty of Rome in 1957 to the outbreak of financial crisis in 2007, there was a shift from a neglect of social and labour market policies to an attempt to coordinate developments in these areas. At the outset, with the European Economic Community (EEC) being essentially a customs union comprising six Bismarckian welfare states and with the competitive pressures of globalization not on the political agenda in a period of welfare expansion, harmonization of labour market and social polices was not a concern. Although Jacques Delors promoted the idea of a 'social dimension' to European integration in the mid-1980s, the successive enlargements of 1973, 1981 and 1986 rendered any harmonization impossible due to the sheer diversity, complexity and differing institutional and financial capacities of the various welfare state and industrial relations models present in the EU. Further enlargements in 1995, 2004 and 2007 have only exacerbated this variety. Furthermore, the link between welfare states, citizenship and national identities has meant that the cross-border sacrifices and compromises necessary for wealth redistribution on a pan-EU scale have been historically impossible to legitimize, and even to seriously consider (Parsons and Pochet 2010).

Successive enlargements have further reduced the incentives for a harmonization of tax and spending policies across member states. Firstly, the free movement of labour and principles of non-discrimination have weakened the link between the boundaries of the nation and of the welfare state, increasing the risk of welfare migration and the importation of unemployment to high-standard welfare states from low-standard ones. Secondly, there is the risk that low-standard welfare states could undercut high-standard ones, thereby reducing costs for industry and attracting investment and employment. In effect, in a context of regime competition, low-standard welfare states can free-ride on more advanced welfare states, effectively exporting unemployment to the latter. Thus, although high-standard welfare states may have an incentive in promoting an upwards harmonization of social provision, the leakage of positive external effects to non-participants in this upwards harmonization gives the latter an incentive to reject it. A similar argument can be made about the failure to construct an EU-level system of collective bargaining.

For the above reasons, social and labour market policies have been resistant not only to a unitary approach, but also to integration, defined as the sharing of competences (Dyson and Sepos 2010: 11). Even inter-governmental cooperation is difficult to achieve due to the 'asymmetric' nature of European integration over the long term (Scharpf 1998), and the issue linkage between economic integration on the one hand and social and labour market policies on the other.

Even before the introduction of the euro on 1 January 1999, many commentators feared that globalization and the financialization of the economy would require states to adjust through policies of tax reduction, welfare recalibration – if not retrenchment – employment flexibility, wage moderation and a general dismantling of labour market and social protections to attract the internationally mobile investment capital necessary for job creation (Martin, 1999; Rhodes, 1998). Through market integration, the EU has internalized these pressures, while competition policy and rules on public procurement and state subsidies to industry have robbed states of a major means of promoting domestic employment. The introduction of the euro and the conditions of entry for the 2004 and 2007 accession states further constrained national economic sovereignty by placing limits on public deficits and debts and, for eurozone countries, depriving governments of currency devaluation as a macro-economic tool to restore competitiveness. Even for eurozone outsiders, similar pressures were felt as financial markets, investors and ratings agencies placed a premium on non-inflationary growth and low levels of public debt. Under these constraints, the search for national economic competitiveness focused on wage moderation and unit costs, and by extension on welfare reform to reduce spending on what was seen as a burden for economic competitiveness.

As a result, certain general trends are clearly discernable across European welfare states: active labour market policies and an activation of welfare benefits, the promotion of active ageing and pension reform, a greater use of targeting in the distribution of benefits to fight poverty and social exclusion, the greater use of in-work benefits to overcome the 'poverty trap' and 'make work pay', an emphasis upon education and training, and the flexibilization of labour markets to facilitate economic adjustment and employment creation. There was, however, little evidence of the welfare retrenchment predicted by regime competition theories. On the contrary, trends around the turn of the present century saw a rise in welfare benefit generosity in the traditionally least generous European states – Britain, Ireland and Italy – and a slight decline in the most generous – Scandinavian – states, although differences between these extremes remain significant. Nevertheless, there was evidence of the recalibration of welfare regimes to make them more compatible with notions of economic competitiveness. Thus, the Bismarckian states of France and Germany introduced new social provisions funded from general taxation rather than their traditional work-related social insurance systems (Wincott 2008) in an effort to shift the burden of financing provision from business to households in order to reduce unit costs for the former.

In other words, integration in the field of social policy has been minimal and restricted to creating basic economic, social and political rights at the European level, but certain common trends are perceptible. It is a moot point, however, whether such convergence is a product of any unified action among member states. Such trends can also be explained by the need for domestic economies to adapt to the new realities of economic globalization and this is certainly part of the story. However, to the extent that processes of OMC and social dialogue are articulated with and frame domestic debates over labour market and welfare reform, one could argue that policy convergence is a result of normative integration through soft coordination. This, however, is open to question. OMC is primarily an intergovernmental process resulting in rhetorical compromises that reflect member state interests, approaches and political agendas, with member states negotiating texts that are compatible with domestic policies and maintaining what domestic level sovereignty they have. Thus, any integration through the OMC is purely superficial and has a limited impact upon domestic policies (Barbier 2007). At best, OMC would appear to provide leverage to 'modernizers' in their interactions with other actors in domestic settings (Barbier et al. 2006; Erhel et al. 2005).

The same assertion of national interests can be seen in collective bargaining in Europe. The main development of the 1990s and 2000s was the re-emergence of tripartite bargaining in the form of social pacts (Parsons and Pochet 2008). These pacts link wage moderation to issues such as economic growth, employment, labour market flexibility, vocational training and welfare reform. The focus of reform where qualitative or welfare issues are dealt with aims at improving economic competitiveness, rather than income redistribution, by focusing on supply side issues such as vocational training, more flexible working time and activation programmes (Donaghey and Teague 2005: 483). Indeed, social pacts have been described as 'competitive corporatism' (Rhodes 2001). Indeed, they have contributed to a more general trend across the EU to wage moderation and declining unit costs. Thus, unions across the EU appeared to be locked into a cognitive framework that accepts wage moderation and welfare reform in the name of economic competitiveness (Parsons and Pochet 2008).

Aware that this could lead to competitive underbidding, trade unions in some states have attempted to coordinate wage bargaining across borders. In 1999, the ETUC advanced a 'solidaristic wage bargaining policy' based upon an inflation plus productivity formula, designed to eliminate wage dumping. However, unions rarely have the political leverage to impose the terms of the European bargaining formulae, with the result that 'the co-ordination initiatives of the European trade unions have hardly any discernable bearing on national collective bargaining disputes' (Shulten 2004: 18). Indeed, pressures for domestic trade-offs between wage moderation on the one hand and welfare reform and/or employment creation on the other are more likely to be felt by unions that are still nationally embedded than vague calls to European solidarity. Moreover, domestic competitive pressures need to cause only one participant to withdraw from European coordination of collective bargaining to give others an increased incentive to do the same (Traxler 2003). As with welfare reform, the free-rider problem and the leakage of positive external benefits to non-participants act as a serious brake on unified action. As a result, the competitiveness orientation of national collective bargaining and welfare reform is at odds with any moves towards, or logic of, a putative European solidarity, let alone 'social union', through social dialogue, OMC or collective bargaining (Parsons 2007).

Asymmetric integration means welfare and labour market policies are one of the few remaining areas in which states can operate to gain competitive advantage and therefore become the adjustment variables for increased competitiveness. For unions to refuse this would be to risk a rise in unemployment, and their strategy therefore appears to be one of damage limitation through cooperation with governments. The sphere of social and labour market policy is therefore characterized by competition between states. These competitive pressures have been reinforced by European Court of Justice (ECJ) judgements, such as those in the Viking and Laval cases. These have established the supremacy in European law of the freedom of establishment over national terms and conditions of employment, with the result that companies can post workers from abroad to undercut local pay rates in the name of the freedom to establish services, such as in the Laval case, or can replace workers of one nationality with those of another to reduce wages, as in the Viking case (see also Chapter 8 by Birkinshaw). The effect of all these, and other similar, judgments has been to move from a 'non-discrimination approach' to a 'market access approach' to the treatment of service providers and posted workers in which the freedom to provide services takes precedence over the principle of equal treatment of all workers within a given territory (Barnard 2008). Disputes around the use of Italian and Portuguese construction workers at the Lindsey oil refinery in the UK in 2009 demonstrated the capacity of such decisions to provoke nationalist reactions

(Parsons 2012). The effect is to reinforce competition between social models and to reinforce the view that high levels of social and labour market protections are anathema to the efficient workings of the market in a context of market integration. When financial crisis mutated into sovereign debt crisis in several eurozone countries, the effects of this view and its implications for European solidarity became evident, both in terms of the social and welfare reform required to restore competitiveness within some member states, and in terms of solidarity across member states.

Crisis and the re-emergence of tensions

When financial crisis hit EU member states in September 2008 as a result of contagion from the US sub-prime mortgage market, it was first felt in the banking system. The vast sums required for governments to bail out banks deemed too big to fail resulted in a sovereign debt crisis in some states (Ireland, Greece), and increased debts and deficits in others (UK). Contagion effects were felt in yet more as speculative bubbles, particularly in property, burst. International investors moved money out of more vulnerable member states, particularly in Central and Eastern Europe, while the cost of borrowing on international money markets to support their increased debts rose considerably for those countries considered to be risky investments, particularly Spain, Italy and Portugal. At the European level, the reaction was, on the one hand, the presentation to member states' governments of the European Economic Recovery Plan, which aimed to maintain labour market participation rates and household income. It also amended the European Social Fund and reformed the European Globalization Adjustment Fund in order to improve access to monies for retraining and labour market integration (Euzéby 2010: 77–8). On the other, and more importantly, it involved a relaxation of competition policy and of the Stability and Growth Pact to allow states to prop up ailing banks, a reduction of interest rates by the European Central Bank to facilitate inter-bank borrowing and the establishment of the European Financial Stability Facility to enable state bailouts with International Monetary Fund (IMF) and World Bank participation. The general thrust of intervention was thus towards debt containment and reduction. The terms imposed by donor organizations for bailouts, moreover, were of far greater significance than the 'social' response of the EU, and had major implications for systems of labour market and social protection, as well as for commitment to the European project on the part of European citizens.

Social protection

Although Ireland, and particularly Greece, hit the headlines due to the scale of the interventions and the possibility of sovereign default in those countries, the first states to require recourse to international funds to prop up their economies and stabilize their currencies were Central and Eastern European countries highly exposed to the withdrawal of foreign direct investment. Hungary is, perhaps, the prime example. Spending cuts of up to $1.4 billion (€1.1 billion) were reported to be the price to pay for a package of up to $12.5 billion in financial support from the IMF, as part of a $25 billion rescue package also involving the EU and World Bank (*Financial Times*, 28 October 2008). This translated into cuts in public sector pay, public investments, the freezing or reduction of many welfare benefits and a rise in personal taxation, particularly through value added tax (ETUC, 2011).

The picture in Hungary was repeated in many other member states, with the most severe measures taken in those states exposed to sovereign debt crises. Thus, the *quid pro quo* of the Greek bailouts saw pension cuts of 20 per cent and a rise in the retirement age as well as pay cuts and reductions in state spending in areas such as education, hospitals and local government. In Ireland, following three deflationary budgets that had taken €14.5 billion out of the economy, a four-year plan to reduce public spending by €10 billion and raise taxes by €5 billion was announced in November 2010. This involved a pension levy and pay cut for public employees, a loss of 25,000 public sector jobs (10 per cent of the government workforce), and cuts in a range of social welfare benefits, in the health budget and in transfers to local government. Similar measures could also be seen in Spain, Portugal and Italy (ibid.). In these eurozone countries, when financial crisis hit, adjustment could not take place through currency devaluation, but occurred through reductions in public spending as a response to external constraints.

Elsewhere in Western Europe, the picture was more patchy. In the UK, although not threatened by a sovereign debt crisis, vast sums had been spent by the Labour administration bailing out banks. In response, the Conservative-dominated coalition with the Liberal Democrats, elected in May 2010, used the backdrop of the global financial crisis and the crisis in the eurozone to push through harsh policies of welfare reduction, public sector pay freezes, tax rises (VAT) and reductions in government spending of €98 billion, equivalent to 14 per cent of public spending. In France, as well as pushing through a pension reform that had been planned before the onset of crisis, the Fillon government announced a reduction of public sector employment by 31,000 by only replacing one departure in two, reduced transfers to local authorities of €3 billion a year and increases in taxation. It also, however, announced countercyclical stimulus measures in the form of a €27 billion investment in public works programmes and the extension of the minimum income to the under-25s. In Finland, countercyclical measures predominated, with minimal welfare benefits tied to the consumer price index to protect their purchasing power, and no investment cuts or lay-offs in the public services, although the non-replacement of retired staff aimed to produce productivity gains and reduce staff by nearly 10,000 between 2007 and 2011. Finally, Germany was the first country to come out of recession following the financial crisis. German unions and workers had understood the implications of the single currency for international competitiveness and employment, and engaged in wage moderation throughout the 2000s. This restored and increased the competitive advantage of German manufacturing industry, resulting in export-driven growth. Nevertheless, German public sector workers still faced job losses of 10,000 to 15,000 by 2014, and cuts of €20.5 billion from the budget for labour market policy were announced, along with cuts in transfers to local authorities of €15 billion and in some welfare payments (ibid.).

Among the 2004 and 2007 accession countries, government debt was not the problem, as it was relatively low compared to EU15 countries, with public finances generally sound. However, in the wake of financial crisis, capital flight and/or exposure to foreign debt along with declining exports to recession-hit Western Europe resulted in falling revenues and solvency problems, while growing budget deficits put spending cuts on the agenda. Some states (Hungary, Latvia, Romania, Poland) turned to the EU and IMF for credit. Exposure to foreign debt – particularly high in the Baltic states – meant that governments attempted to defend the exchange rate in order not to increase the cost of borrowing, rather than devalue the currency to restore price competitiveness in an attempt to protect output and employment. The result was 'socially costly' adjustment, particularly in the Baltic states, with Latvia, the worst case, implementing €712 million of cuts and tax increases in an attempt to reduce the budget deficit by 10 per of GDP over four years, in June 2009 (Drahokoupil and Myant, 2009: 17). In these countries, welfare regimes are essentially 'minimal', as in the Baltic states, or 'residual', as in the Visegrad countries (ibid.: 10), so the brunt of adjustment was borne by public sector employees through draconian pay cuts (an average of 10, 25 and 50 per cent in the Czech Republic, Romania and Latvia respectively), while a range of social benefits were also cut (ETUC 2011).

Labour market institutions

Inevitably, these adjustments fuelled tensions, with riots and protests against rising unemployment and budget cuts taking place in many states. In some instances, this saw innovative action (for example, *los indignados* in Spain and later, to a lesser extent, Greece) or the re-emergence of radical forms of action, such as 'bossnapping' in France. Cooperative strategies were unattractive to unions as they had little to gain from governments unable or unwilling to compensate the losers in reform. The ETUC (2011) articulated the concerns of many European trade unions in arguing that governments had to maintain consumption – and therefore wages and employment – as a pre-condition of economic growth, or risk a downward spiral in terms and conditions of employment, rising unemployment, welfare retrenchment and prolonged recession due to the deflationary effects of austerity policies.

This lack of common ground at the European level was also reflected at the national level although developments here were more nuanced due to the need to find concrete solutions to crisis, and, particularly for the unions, to stem the tide of job losses. Thus, on the one hand general strikes were threatened in some countries, although they only occurred in those with a tradition of such action: Italy, France, Greece, Spain and Portugal, with threats in Ireland and Finland coming to nothing (Hyman and Gumbrell-McCormick 2010). Nevertheless, protest and union opposition to cuts were a common reaction across Europe. In Ireland, the recent tradition of signing social pacts came to a halt. Firstly, employers withdrew from a 2008 agreement to raise wages by 6 per cent over 21 months, then unions opposed the government's November 2010 National Recovery Plan over a reduction in the minimum wage, having agreed to a public sector pay freeze in exchange for job security and the maintenance of pensions the previous July.

On the other hand, macro-level concertation continued in many countries. In Belgium, a December 2008 agreement traded wage moderation for increased benefits to the unemployed and pensioners and reduced business taxes, and was followed in April 2009 by a tripartite agreement for white-collar workers allowing for a 25 per cent reduction in working time, compensated for by public funds. Glassner and Keune (2010) identified similar policy outcomes, involving combinations of short-time working schemes, training measures, labour legislation and welfare benefits, agreed to or discussed in tripartite settings, in Austria, the Netherlands, Hungary, Italy, Slovenia, Slovakia, France, Lithuania, Estonia and Luxembourg. Discussions also took place in Poland, Ireland and Romania, but ended in disagreement. To these, one can add the 2011 social pacts signed in Portugal and Spain following intense conflict involving general strikes (Lima and Artiles 2011). For Glassner and Keune (2010: 6–7) the crisis stimulated tripartite concertation, but only in a few cases did this result in formal agreement rather than merely consultation (agreements in their data are only mentioned in the cases of Belgium, Italy, Lithuania and Estonia, although Spain and Portugal subsequently signed pacts). Indeed, the negotiation of social pacts proved conflictual and difficult, with those signed being narrow in focus (Rychly 2009).

At sectoral and company levels, there were inevitably a wide range of responses to the crisis, addressing issues such as the restructuring and reorganization of companies, wage adjustment, flexibility, vocational training and reskilling (Glassner and Keune 2010). One of the key initiatives in macro-level dialogue was taken up in lower levels of bargaining. Thus, the dominant cross-national trend in collectively bargained responses to crisis was the recourse to short-time working, often with full or partial compensation for lost pay through public funds, with incentives for training included in almost all cases. Short-time working schemes were introduced on a temporary basis to stabilize employment in nine member states where none existed previously (Bulgaria, the Czech Republic, Hungary, Latvia, Lithuania, the Netherlands, Poland, Slovakia and Slovenia). In almost all countries with well-established short-time working schemes, they were extended to previously excluded workers, extended in duration, their generosity improved or rules for use relaxed (Austria, Belgium, Denmark, France, Italy, Germany, Luxembourg, Portugal and Spain) (EIRO 2010). Despite this, early analyses pointed to a difference in approach between Eastern and Western Europe, with Central and Eastern European countries more likely to experience large-scale redundancies and the more widespread use of agreements for short-time working in the west (Glassner and Galcóczi 2009).

Where unions were involved in negotiating solutions, the main effort was to stem the tide of unemployment. Thus, while collective bargaining appeared to have survived the crisis, collective agreements could hardly be said to represent win-win outcomes as unions were on the defensive. This, plus the lack of exchange resources on the part of governments in national bargaining explains the unions' generally weak response to the above reforms. In effect, unions found their hands tied – conflict would not prevent job losses, but co-operation could offer few, if any, gains. All unions could sell to their members was the notion that they prevented things from being even worse. With unions poorly placed to stall, let alone reverse, the restructuring of welfare states and labour market protections in their own countries, transnational coordination appeared more necessary than ever, but was even more problematic due to the need to protect jobs within the national territory.

European social solidarity in crisis?

The European social model has never been a formal construct giving concrete reality to a European 'social union'. At best, the aspirations to high standards of social and workplace protection and rights contained in various treaties and charters amount to an implicit social contract between governing elites and populations in Europe. At worst, they could be seen as a cynical legitimizing discourse for market integration. Reactions to the 2007–08 financial crisis challenged the more benign interpretation. Indeed, the precarious nature of any implicit social contract was revealed in 2009 when Article 151 of the Treaty of Lisbon downgraded the aspiration to high levels of social protection to the 'more vague and less ambitious' 'proper social protection' (Euzéby 2010: 81).

Indeed, under conditions of market integration, social and labour market policies became the adjustment variables for national economic competitiveness. This explains why states have sought to retain control of these policy areas while, in the case of eurozone countries, pooling sovereignty in the field of monetary policy. However, in reality, despite any formal autonomy, any sovereignty exercised over social and labour market policies was severely constrained for both euro insiders and outsiders due to the competitive pressures unleashed by asymmetric integration and economic globalization. The financial crisis of 2007–08 has further constrained this sovereignty, particularly for those states suffering sovereign debt crisis, due to the externally imposed deficit reduction programmes that have accompanied bailouts. Under the watchful eye of ratings agencies, other states are more or less constrained to follow suit in order to stabilize their own public finances and/or competitive position within the global economy as demand slumps.

It is not only sovereignty that has been eroded, but solidarity too. Transnational coordination and solidarity had always been problematic for European labour due to the asymmetry between economic and social integration at the heart of the EU, but was rendered even more so by the need to preserve domestic employment in the face of global economic crisis. While bailouts of countries on the verge of bankruptcy may demonstrate some form of solidarity, this was, at best, economic rather than social solidarity. Even this economic solidarity was difficult to bring to fruition, particularly in the case of the July 2011 bailout of Greece. The problem here was not just one of coordinating different national approaches to the problem of Greek sovereign debt. It was also apparent that national leaders, particularly Merkel in Germany, were fearful of how they would be able to sell another transfer of funds from the taxpayers of their own state to the government of another, when the latter was seen as suffering the effects of its own past profligacy. The rise of the True Finns in Finnish elections around the same time served to confirm a growing reluctance on the part of the wealthy northern European states to financially support their poorer southern counterparts. However, such bailouts also served national economic self interest. The exposure of German and French banks, for example, to Greek debt meant that default would have dire economic consequences in donor countries. The conditionality attached to bailouts also clearly demonstrates that these were not socially redistributive transfer payments. Indeed, the populations of indebted southern European states appeared increasingly reluctant to put up with the social consequences of eurozone discipline and the socially disastrous conditions attached to them.

Thus, formal sovereignty in the area of social and labour market policies is highly constrained and cannot shelter governments and labour movements from external competitive pressures. Such pressures look set to continue, further eroding not only effective sovereignty but also solidarity. Under the 'Euro plus pact' – adopted in March 2011 with the aim of fostering competitiveness, employment and financial stability – progress in fostering competitiveness will be assessed on the basis of wage and productivity developments, through the monitoring and comparison of unit labour costs. As well as the usual calls to promote flexicurity through labour market reforms, there are also pressures towards greater decentralization in wage setting as 'where necessary, the degree of centralization in the bargaining process' should be reviewed, with the aim of ensuring that wage costs are contained in line with productivity increases (EC 2011: 16). Using unit labour costs as benchmarks of competitiveness while encouraging the further decentralization of bargaining carries the risk of encouraging competitive undercutting rather than improving the terms and conditions of Europe's workers.

During times of economic growth, such pressures could be contained, but they were present. Pressures for increased competitiveness and wage moderation in this period were compatible with at least the maintenance of, if not improvement in, living standards, wages, social protection and welfare provision. However, as all member states feel the consequences of a global crisis, with cuts in employment and welfare provision in nearly all states, fiscal transfer occurs only in emergency cases and is increasingly contested, resulting in a rise in nationalist feeling. In effect, the external constraints upon the exercise of sovereignty in social and labour market policies threaten a European solidarity that already has little in the way of any institutional underpinning that could represent a bulwark against unraveling on two fronts. Horizontally, tensions are growing between member states, while vertically, elite visions of ever closer union are increasingly rejected by the populations to whom they are electorally answerable. As the financial crisis has transformed the pressures for competitiveness into pressures for financial stability, it has acted as the starting pistol for the long-predicted race to the bottom in labour market and social protection systems. European unity, and belief in the European project, can only suffer as a consequence.

Bibliography

Barbier, J.-C. (2007) *The European Social Model and Cultural Diversity in Europe.* Working Papers, Department of Economics, Politics and Public Administration (Aalborg: Aalborg University).

Barbier, J.-C. with N. Samba Sylla and A. Eydoux (2006) *Analyse comparative de l'activation de la protection sociale en France, Grande-Bretagne, Allemagne et Danemark, dans le cadre des lignes directrices de la stratégie européenne pour l'emploi* (Paris: DARES).

Barnard, C. (2008) *Employment Rights, Free Movement Under the EC Treaty and the Services Directive.* Mitchell Working Paper Series 5/2008 (Edinburgh: Europa Institute).

Donaghey, J. and P. Teague (2005) 'The Persistence of Social Pacts in Europe', *Industrial Relations Journal*, 36, 6, 478–93.

Drahokoupil, J. and . Myant (2010) 'Varieties of Capitalism, Varieties of Vulnerabilities: Financial Crisis and its Impact on Welfare States in Eastern Europe and the Commonwealth of Independent States', *Historical Social Research*, 2, 35, 266–95.

Dyson, K. and A. Sepos (2010) 'Differentiation as a Design Principle and as a Tool in the Political Management of European Integration' in K. Dyson and A. Sepos (eds) *Which Europe? The Politics of Differentiated Integration* (Basingstoke: Palgrave Macmillan).

EC (2011) *European Council 24/25 March 2011 Conclusions* (Brussels: EC).

EIRO (2010) *Short-time working prevalent across Member States.* Available at: http://www.eurofound.europa.eu/eiro/2010/10/articles/eu1010021i.htm. Accessed 3 August 2011.

Erhel, C., L. Mandin and B. Palier (2005) 'The Leverage Effect. The Open Method of Co-ordination in France' in J. Zeitlin and P. Pochet (eds) with L. Magnusson, *The Open Method of Coordination in Action. The European Employment and Social Inclusion Strategies* (Brussels: P.I.E.-Peter Lang).

ETUC (2011) *Austerity Watch.* Available at: http://www.etuc.org/r/1598. Accessed 22 July 2011.

Euzéby, A. (2010) 'Economic Crisis and Social Protection in the European Union: Moving beyond Immediate Responses', *International Social Security Review*, 63, 2, 71–86.

Glassner, V. and B. Galcóczi (2009) *Plant-level Responses to the Economic Crisis in Europe*, ETUI Working Paper, January 2009 (Brussels: ETUI).

Glassner, V. and M. Keune (2010) *Negotiating the crisis? Collective bargaining in Europe during the economic downturn.* Dialogue Working Paper No. 10 (Geneva: ILO).

Lima, M. and A.M. Artiles (2011) 'Crisis and Trade Union Challenges in Portugal and Spain: between General Strikes and Social Pacts', *Transfer: European Review of Labour and Research*, 17, 3, 387–402.

Hyman, R. and R. Gumbrell-McCormick (2010) 'Trade Unions and the Crisis: a Lost Opportunity?' *Socio-Economic Review*, 8, 364–72.

Martin, A. (1999) *Wage Bargaining under EMU: Europeanization, Re-Nationalization, or Americanization?* DWP 99.01.03 (Brussels: OSE/ETUI).

Parsons, N. (2007) *Collective Bargaining in an Enlarged Europe: Undermining the European Social Model?* Paper presented to the ECPR General Conference, Pisa, September 2007.

Parsons, N. (2012) 'The EU and Posted Workers: Industrial Relations Consequences in the UK' in S. Smismans (ed.) *The European Social Dialogue: New Procedures, New Contexts* (Cheltenham Glos: Edward Elgar).

Parsons, N. and Pochet, P. (2008) 'Wages and Collective Bargaining' in K. Dyson (ed.) *The Euro at Ten: Europeanization, Power and Convergence* (Oxford: Oxford University Press).

Parsons, N. and P. Pochet (2010) 'Social Europe' in K Dyson and A. Sepos (eds) *Which Europe? The Politics of Differentiated Integration* (Basingstoke: Palgrave Macmillan).

Rhodes, M. (1998) 'Globalisation, Labour Markets and Welfare States: A Future of "Competitive Corporatism"?' in M. Rhodes and Y. Mény (eds) *The Future of European Welfare: A New Social Contract?* (London: Macmillan).

Rhodes, M. (2001) 'The Political Economy of Social Pacts: "Competitive Corporatism" and European Welfare Reform' in P. Pierson (ed.) *The New Politics of the Welfare State* (Oxford: Oxford University Press).

Rychly, L. (2009) *Finding better solutions: Social dialogue in times of crisis.* Working Paper No. 1 (Geneva: ILO).

Scharpf, F.J.W. (1998) 'Negative and Positive Integration in the Political Economy of European Welfare States' in M. Rhodes and Y. Mény (eds), *The Future of European Welfare: A New Social Contract?* (London: Macmillan).

Schulten, T. (2004) *Foundations and Perspectives of Trade Union Wage Policy in Europe*, WSI Discussion Paper, No.129 (Dusseldorf: WSI).

Traxler, F. (2003) 'Co-ordinated Bargaining: a Stocktaking of its Preconditions, Practices and Performance', *Industrial Relations Journal*, 43, 3, 194–209.

Wincott, D. (2008) 'Welfare Reform' in K. Dyson (ed.) *The Euro at Ten: Europeanization, Power and Convergence* (Oxford: Oxford University Press).

14
From Environmental Disunion towards Environmental Union?

Rüdiger K.W. Wurzel

The EU's environmental policy is widely seen as a success story (e.g. Jordan 2005; Weale et al. 2000). In contrast to most other EU policies (e.g. Economic and Monetary Union (EMU) (see Chapter 12 by Dyson), environmental policy is not – or at least no longer – merely an elite-driven common policy without public support. On the contrary, EU environmental policy is one of the most popular common policy areas amongst European citizens. A 2011 Eurobarometer public opinion survey, which was conducted in all 27 member states, found that an average 81 per cent of EU citizens thought that 'European environmental legislation is necessary for protecting the environment' (Eurobarometer 2011: 7 and 38). This represented a drop of only one per cent compared to the previous environmental awareness survey in 2007 despite the difficult economic situation in the aftermath of the 2008 financial crisis (Eurobarometer 2008, 2011: 7).[1] In 2011 an average 64 per cent of EU citizens supported the view that decisions on protecting the environment should be made jointly by national governments and the EU (Eurobarometer 2011: 7, 37), a drop of only 3 per cent compared to the 2007 survey (Eurobarometer 2008: 46). There are, however, significant national differences as regards public support for joint environmental policy action. While more than 70 per cent of the populations in Cyprus (81), Estonia (78), Germany (73), Portugal (73), Belgium (72), Luxembourg (72) and the Netherlands (72) were in favour of joint action, support remained below 50 per cent in Austria (48), Finland (48) and the UK (40) in 2011 (Eurobarometer 2011: 37).

Considering the general success and popularity of EU environmental policy, it is unsurprising that the European Parliament (EP) and various Environmental Commissioners (e.g. Dimas, 2007) have called for an 'Environmental Union' to advance further the protection of the environment *and* to rejuvenate the stalled European integration project. Because Britain is usually portrayed as an awkward European partner (see Chapter 16 by Norton), which has failed to act as a leader state for EU environmental policy – climate change being one important exception (e.g. Wurzel and Connelly 2011) – it is surprising that even some British Secretaries of State have made a plea for 'Environmental Union'. While Secretary of State for the Environment David Miliband (2006) argued that:

> Europe needs a new raison d'être. For my generation, the pursuit of peace cannot provide the drive and moral purpose that are needed to inspire the next phase of the European project. The environment is the issue that can best reconnect Europe with its citizens and re-build trust in European institutions. The needs of the environment are coming together with the needs of the EU: one is the cause looking for a champion, the other a champion in search of a cause.

Miliband later repeated his call for 'Environmental Union' when he served as Foreign Secretary (Miliband 2009).

Importantly, issues of international and intergenerational solidarity have also provided a certain, albeit limited, justification for the adoption of EU environmental policy in general and EU climate change and energy policies in particular (e.g. Hilson 2010: 138). An EP commissioned 2011 Eurobarometer survey entitled *The Europeans and Energy* showed that within the EU-27 an average 79 per cent of citizens agree with the following statement: 'It is desireable that (OUR COUNTRY) provides assistance to another EU Member State facing significant energy supply problems in the name of European solidarity between Member States'. There was even a majority in favour of this statement in the three member states in which the publics showed least solidarity, namely the UK (67), Romania (66) and Malta (51).

Environmental policy requires cooperation between states because pollution does not stop at national borders. Even the most powerful (member) states are unable unilaterally to resolve transnational environmental problems such as acidification and climate change. Even in cases where the EU is not the optimal environmental regulatory arena (e.g. for global issues like climate change), a common policy stance by the European Union provides member states with increased bargaining power in international relations. Moreover, common EU targets in international environmental agreements grant member states greater flexibility. A classic example is provided by the Kyoto Protocol on greenhouse gas emissions. It sets a collective EU reduction target of 8 per cent by 2012 (compared to 1990). However, while some member states have national greenhouse gas emission reduction targets that far exceed the collective 8 per cent target (e.g. Luxembourg (28), Denmark (21), Germany (21) and the UK (12.5)), the economically less developed Southern European member states were actually allowed to increase their greenhouse gas emissions under the EU's internal so-called burden sharing agreement.

At first sight, EU environmental policy therefore does not seem to be a particularly promising common policy area for exploring the concept of European disunion and the hypothesis that 'the EU is exacerbating its adversarial rather than its consensual characteristics' (see Chapter 1 by Hayward). On the other hand, if there is empirical evidence for creeping or increased disunion even in the common environmental policy, which has often been identified as a core driver for further integration (Jordan 2005; Weale et al. 2000), then it would be perturbing for the European integration project, which, according to the preamble of the 1957 Rome Treaty, strives towards 'ever closer union'. (Perhaps David Miliband's own political fortune might serve as a warning. In 2010, he lost in the British Labour Party's leadership contest to his younger brother Ed Miliband who showed less commitment towards Europe and the environment.) Similarly, if the EU has been unable to sustain common efforts to take into account inter-state and intergenerational solidarity to tackle environmental pollution, which does not stop at national borders and often produces long-term effects, then this could be interpreted as a sign of European integration stalling or even reverting to European disunion.

In trying to assess the degree to which 'European disunion' exists in EU environmental policy, this chapter starts with a brief assessment of the meaning of European disunion. The next section provides an overview of the history of EU environmental policy, which pays particular attention to instances of European disunion. This is followed by an analysis of disunion between EU and member state actors (vertical disunion) about domestic and foreign EU environmental policy issues. The next section teases out disunion within and between core EU environmental policy actors (horizontal disunion). Finally, the concluding section provides a summary analysis of the evidence presented.

European environmental union and disunion

Over the years, a wide range of competing theories of European integration and politics have emerged, which have tried to elucidate the degree and direction of European integration. In the early years of the EU, disunion seemed to be more prevalent between proponents of the dominant classic integration theories – neofunctionalism and inter-governmentalism – than amongst leading politicians and bureaucrats involved in the European project. This is certainly true for the environmental policy field, which is not to downplay De Gaulle's use of the national veto to delay British EU membership and to slow down the expansion of supranational powers for the Commission in particular (see Chapter 5 by Hayward). Nevertheless, since the early 1970s, EU environmental policy has progressed 'from silence to salience' at surprising speed (Weale 1996: 596).

While intergovernmentalists pointed out that environmental policy is essentially a highly technical 'low politics' area, which receives only the sporadic attention of member states heads of state and government, neofunctionalists argued that EU environmental policy constitutes a classic case of functional 'spill over' (which eventually leads to political spill over) because the negative externalities of the single European market (e.g. environmental pollution due to transport) triggered the need for the adoption of common measures in a policy area for which the EU did not possess explicit legal competences under the founding Treaties. However, while rejecting as overly simplistic the dichotomous explanations of intergovernmentalism and neofunctionalism, Weale (1996: 602) pointed out that '[a]lthough EU rule making institutions can be said to have a life of their own in the field of environmental policy, they still need to be connected to the life-support machine of the nation states if they are to function at all'.

In order to overcome 'joint decision traps' (Scharpf 1988) in EU environmental policy-making, concurrent majorities are required for which agreement is needed from a large proportion of participants on different levels of decision-making (i.e. primarily the EU and member states levels, although the international level is also important for environmental policy, which is a highly internationalised policy field) (Weale 1996). Veto actors often dropped their opposition to EU environmental policy proposals only after arduous and drawn out negotiations, leading to EU laws which were riddled with exemptions, derogations, phased in deadlines and vague compromises that were open to different (national) interpretations. Moreover, at the implementation phase, member states once again questioned the consensus which they had achieved during the adoption phase of the EU environmental policy-making process.

While the fits and starts of European integration have been assessed extensively, relatively little attention has been paid to the precise meaning of the terms 'European Union' and 'ever closer union'.[2] As Dinan (2000: 225) has pointed out, 'European Union was an ill-defined terminus. Despite many exhortations over the years, there was never a clear idea of what a union would look like'. The 2009 Lisbon Treaty has not brought about clarification on this issue although it strengthened the Treaty base for the EU's climate change policy. It is therefore a challenging task to analyse whether multidimensional power struggles have led to 'European Disunion', which is also a contestable term, in the environmental policy field and/or incidents of solidarity, which is a similarly contested concept within the context of the EU (Ross and Borgmann-Prebil 2011).

Disunion implies the absence or reversal of union (see Chapter 12 by Dyson). In contrast with EMU, there has never been a formal 'environmental union' although it has been advocated by politicians, as shown above. Between the early 1970s and 2000s, the degree of integration in EU environmental policy increased to such an extent that academics have also started to use the term 'environmental union' or 'ecological union' (e.g. Liefferink and Jordan 2005; Weale et al. 2000). The absence of union covers a wide analytical spectrum, which ranges from weak to strong forms of disunion. It can stretch from relatively minor disagreement, which can easily be papered over at the adoption phase with vague compromise deals, to fundamental dissent that produces joint decision traps from which escape is usually possible only with the help of costly side payments (e.g. funding for sewerage facilities through the structural funds) and complex package deals. The reversal of union infers a roll back – or 'spill back' in the neofunctionalist terminology – which includes the repatriation of EU environmental policy measures and/or competences to the member state level.

From environmental disunion towards environmental union?

Although EU environmental policy is a relatively young common policy, which was not even mentioned in the 1957 Rome Treaty, it matured speedily since the early 1970s. Broadly speaking, the following five phases of EU environmental policy can be identified (Wurzel 2008): (1) 1958–72: infant phase; (2) 1972–87: adolescent phase; (3) 1987–92:

mature phase; (4) 1992–2005: sedate phase; (5) since 2005: selective activism. Rather than assessing the main environmental policy measures adopted in the various phases, this chapter concentrates on major instances of 'environmental disunion' while also flagging up EU environmental policy measures which explicitly make reference to solidarity.

Taking a bird's eye view, it can be argued that disunion in EU environmental policy was most prevalent during the adolescent phase and in the early sedate phase. The infant phase passed without major disagreements largely because EU environmental policy was not a salient policy issue prior to the early 1970s. In other words, there was an absence of environmental union in the 1950s and 1960s when political reconciliation and economic recovery were the main political priorities which provided the main drivers for 'ever closer union'.

Neither the European Coal and Steel Community (ECSC), European Atomic Energy Community (EURATOM) and European Economic Community (EEC) Treaties, which all came into force in the 1950s, made explicit reference to a common environmental policy. The need to protect the environment and human health was mentioned in the ECSC and EURATOM Treaties but the relevant legal provisions dealt almost exclusively with the work environment in the steel, coal and nuclear industries (Bungarten 1978: 119–21). The EEC Treaty did not mention the word environment although it stated the goal of 'accelerated raising of the standard of living' (Article 2 EEC Treaty), which, at the time, was not yet automatically linked to an unpolluted environment. On the contrary, the dominant view was that there was a trade-off between economic prosperity and environmental protection with priority given to the former.

The EU's heads of state and government gave the starting signal for a common environmental policy at their Paris meeting in October 1972, which took place a few months after the first United Nations (UN) conference on the environment in Stockholm where the member states had spoken with different voices (Bungarten 1978). Failure by the EU to present a common position in international environmental negotiations became something of a habit which member states found difficult to change. In the UN climate change conference in Copenhagen in 2009, a cacophony of member state voices did not help to advance the EU's relatively progressive climate change policy proposals (Jordan et al. 2010; Wurzel and Connelly 2011). The 2009 Lisbon Treaty, which created a High Representative of the Union for Foreign Affairs and an elected President for the European Council while maintaining the rotating Presidency for the Council, has not made representation in international environmental negotiations easier (see Chapter 5 by Hayward).

The declaration by the heads of state and government at the 1972 Paris summit stopped short of mentioning explicitly the term solidarity when it stated that

> economic expansion is not an end in itself: its first aim should be to enable disparities in living conditions to be reduced. It must take place with the participation of all social partners. It should result in an improvement in the quality of life as well as standards of living. As befits the genius of Europe, particular attention will be given to intangible values and to protecting the environment so that progress may really be put at the service of mankind (cited in *Official Journal*, C 112/5 of 20.12.1973).

There was, however, considerable inter-institutional disagreement about how to put into practice the grand rhetoric. The EP had been demanding a common environmental policy since the late 1960s but member states achieved consensus on the need for the adoption of an EU environmental policy only in 1972 (Bungarten 1978: 161). However, serious disagreements erupted about the need for a revision of the 1957 Rome Treaty, which was devoid of any explicit environmental policy provisions. Attempts by Germany and the Netherlands, which favoured both ambitious common environmental policy measures and the deepening of European integration to bring about the revision of the Rome Treaty, were vetoed by France, which was opposed to the extension of supranational powers (for the Commission in particular) into a new policy area (Bungarten 1978).

Because it was not possible to overcome the French veto, the 1969 information and standstill agreement was amended in 1973 to include also draft national environmental laws. It was a legally non-binding gentlemen's agreement, which obliged member governments to inform the Commission about draft national legislation that potentially impacted on the functioning of the internal market with a view to adopting EU legislation instead. The 1973 standstill agreement increased the internal market bias of the early common environmental policy measures and allowed member governments to exert significant influence on the EU's environmental policy agenda.

A legally non-binding first Environmental Action Programme, which was adopted in 1973, listed the main environmental objectives and policy principles while stating that the task of

the European Economic Community is to promote throughout the Community a harmonious development of economic activities and a continuous and balanced expansion, which cannot now be imagined in the absence of an effective campaign to combat pollution and nuisances or of an improvement in the quality of life and the protection of the environment (*Official Journal*, C 112/1–2, 20.12.1973).

The lack of an explicit treaty foundation for common environmental policy measures was sidestepped by basing most of the early EU environmental policy proposals on the internal market provision (then article 100 EEC Treaty) with the argument that different national environmental (product) standards needed to be harmonised to prevent the creation of barriers to trade (Bungarten 1978). The pro-integrationist European Court of Justice (ECJ) backed the wide interpretation of existing Treaty provisions, which helped to pave the way for the adoption of a wide range of common environmental policy measures (Weale 1996: 597). The EU was therefore able to adopt more than 100 common environmental laws before the 1987 Single European Act (SEA) finally introduced explicit environmental policy provisions into the EEC Treaty.

Jordan (2005: 1) has argued that

[o]ne of the more puzzling characteristics of EU environmental policy is its remarkable capacity for steady growth. For the most part, it has been (and remains) largely unaffected by the political and economic vicissitudes, periodic budgetary crises and recurrent waves of Euro-pessimism that have continually frustrated European integration in cognate policy fields.

However, in the aftermath of the 'no' vote in the first Danish referendum on the Maastricht Treaty in 1992, Britain and France drew up a 'hit list', which proposed the repatriation of more than 100 EU laws including 24 environmental laws (Wurzel 2002, 2008). Environmental groups were up in arms because they feared a 'roll back' (Hey 2005: 24), which would have brought about a significant reversal of the fledgling 'environmental union'. Hey (2005: 24) identified the following three main explanatory factors for the attempted roll back of EU environmental policies: (1) the unwillingness of some member states to follow the proposed policy changes put forward by the Commission; (2) economic recession and ratification problems of the Maastricht Treaty; and, (3) the fact that post-unification Germany lost some of its environmental zeal. According to Hey (2005: 24), in the early 1990s, 'it became obvious that the Commission was overly optimistic on the willingness of Member States to follow "paradigmatic change"'.

In the end, none of the EU environmental laws earmarked for repatriation on the Anglo-Franco hit list was scrapped (Wurzel 2002). However, there was a subtle shift in EU environmental policy away from detailed ambitious 'command-and-control' regulation towards more flexible procedural measures (e.g. environmental impact assessment). It clearly represented a move towards greater differentiation (Holzinger and Knoepfel 2000; Wurzel and Zito 2010). Until then, differentiation in EU environmental policy measures were primarily short-term, granting some member states additional time to implement the otherwise uniform obligations of EU environmental laws.

The inability of the Environmental Council to adopt an EU-wide carbon dioxide/energy tax led to the resignation of the outspoken Environmental Commissioner, Ripa di Meana, a few months before the 1992 UN Rio summit.[3] The Commission was therefore only represented in Rio by an acting Environmental Commissioner and Commission President Delors who, however, showed overall little interest in environmental issues.

However, di Meana's sudden departure was greeted with relief by some member states, particularly the British government, which had become unhappy about his strategy of shaming member states into improving their implementation record. This strategy raised di Meana's media profile and gave him added legitimacy, as he could claim to be acting on behalf of EU citizens whom the Commission encouraged to use an informal complaints procedure for flagging up alleged breaches of EU environmental law to the Commission's Directorate General (DG) for the Environment (Wurzel 2002: 68).

Being taken to the ECJ for breaches in EU environmental law was particularly embarrassing for British governments, which consistently maintained that the UK had an excellent implementation record (see Chapter 16 by Norton). However, for much of the 1990s, the UK's transposition record of environmental directives was only mediocre in the environmental policy field, which stood in marked contrast to the UK's excellent transposition record of internal market directives (Wurzel 2002: 68–69).

While environmental NGOs praised Ripa di Meana's actions, others identified his adversarial style vis-a-vis member governments as one of the main reasons why EU environmental policy was pushed into a defensive phase in the early 1990s. Ripa di Meana, was nicknamed 'Ripa the Ripper' by the British Prime Minister, John Major, for allegedly singling out Britain for the incorrect implementation of EU environmental law (Wurzel 2002: 68). Shortly after Ripa di Meana's departure, DG Environment's legal unit was downgraded and its head of unit, Ludwig Krämer, moved sideways, against his will (Wurzel 2002: 70). The highly regarded *Environment Watch: Western Europe* reported on 3 February 1995:

> Krämer's effective demotion after 10 years in the job and the downgrading of his unit are widely seen as politically motivated revenge by national governments for his strict interpretation of EU environmental laws and his uncompromising pursuit in the European Court of Justice of member states that fail to properly transpose or implement them.

In the early 1990s, the Commission shifted its preference for ambitious uniform emission limits derived from the best available technology (BAT) principle, which mirrored the German environmental regulatory approach, towards more flexible framework directives, cost-effectiveness appraisals and procedural measures that were closer to the British environmental policy style (Héritier et al. 1996). In other words, although the adoption rate of EU environmental laws did not slow down – at least not initially – the underlying regulatory philosophy on which these policy measures were based altered significantly.

The early 1990s also witnessed the absence of 'environmental union' when member states failed to adopt a proposal for a common carbon dioxide emission/energy tax, which the Commission wanted to present as the EU's flagship policy instrument in the fight against climate change at the 1992 UN Conference on Environment and Development (UNCED) in Rio, which negotiated the UN Framework Convention on Climate Change (UNFCCC). The Commission's proposal for an EU-wide carbon dioxide/energy tax was strongly supported by the EP and the EU's green trio made up of Denmark, Germany and the Netherlands, which later expanded to a green sextet when Austria, Finland and Sweden joined the EU in 1995 (Wurzel 2008). However, it was vetoed by Britain, which opposed the adoption of any taxes at the EU level on sovereignty grounds, although the Southern European member states (and Spain in particular) were also opposed for fear that EU-wide eco-taxes might have serious negative repercussions for their national economies.

Ten years after the EU had failed to agree unanimously on a common carbon dioxide/energy tax, it adopted under qualified majority voting (QMV), the world's first supranational emissions trading scheme (ETS) for greenhouse gases. However, the EU became a somewhat reluctant ETS pioneer (Wurzel and Connelly 2011). It had initially opposed proposals by the United States (under President Clinton) to include emissions trading during the Kyoto protocol negotiations. The United States (under President George W. Bush) later abandoned the Kyoto protocol although the EU managed to keep alive the Kyoto protocol, which entered into force in 2005. In the same year, the EU ETS, which quickly developed into a flagship policy instrument for reducing greenhouse gas emissions from large industrial installations, became operational. Although the EU ETS is a market-based instrument, its implementation has not been completed devoid of efforts by the more affluent member states to show some solidarity with the less affluent member states. It is arguably most obvious with regards to the use of revenues from the auctioning of allowances during the third EU ETS trading period (2012–2020) when

> [t]en per cent of these revenues are to redistributed from the member states with high per capita income to those with low per capita income to strengthen the capacity of the latter to invest in climate-friendly technologies (Skjærseth and Wettestad 2010: 206).

Importantly, the EU implemented its collective greenhouse gas emission reduction target (i.e. 8 per cent by 2012 compared to 1990 emissions) under the 1997 Kyoto Protocol with a so-called burden sharing agreement according to which the richer Northern European member states had to achieve significantly higher reduction rates than the poorer Southern European member states. In other words, the more affluent member states showed solidarity with economically poorer member states although the differentiated burden sharing agreement was strongly criticised by many non-EU member states including the United States and China. There was a significant change in rhetoric when the EU adopted in 2010 a similarly differentiated agreement to implement its so-called climate and energy package, which, amongst others, proposed 20 per cent unilateral greenhouse gas reductions by 2020 that was meant to pave the way for a Kyoto Protocol follow-up agreement (Wurzel and Connelly 2011). It became officially known as an 'effort sharing agreement', thus toning down significantly the reference to solidarity between member states, which the term burden sharing agreement implied.

Environmental disunion: vertical disunion

The leader-laggard-swing state dimension

The importance of environmental leader states has long been acknowledged for the development of EU environmental policy (Bungarten 1978; Héritier et al. 1996). Broadly speaking, three categories of member states can be identified in EU environmental policy. First, environmental leader states want to see the adoption of stricter environmental measures. The group of environmental leader states can be subdivided into 'forerunner' states, which aim to maximise the freedom to develop their own ambitious domestic environmental policy, and 'pusher' states, which try to export to the EU (and international) level their domestic standards and regulatory philosophies (Liefferink and Andersen 1998). While forerunner states are keen to set a good example, pusher states will not act unilaterally because they insist on a level-playing field. Second, environmental laggards drag their feet and may even use the national veto to stop other member states from advancing. The third intermediate category is made up of swing states, which do not hold strong national preferences but are swayed by side payments (e.g. increased EU structural funds), promises of future support on other policy issues (i.e. package deals) or simply by the intellectual weight of the best arguments advanced during the Environmental Council negotiations.

The classification into environmental leader, laggard and swing states may vary over time or even from issue to issue. Nevertheless, there is relatively wide agreement that the group of environmental leader states initially consisted of a green trio, which was made up of Denmark, Germany and the Netherlands, that expanded to a green sextet when Austria, Finland and Sweden joined in 1995 (Andersen and Liefferink 1997). Although the green sextet still holds a blocking minority (under QMV), its influence has diminished since the EU's Eastern enlargement because most of the Central and Eastern European states are often more concerned about catching up economically rather than on the adoption of ambitious environmental standards.

The Southern European member states (Greece, Portugal and Spain) and Ireland are often grouped together as environmental laggard states. However, the domestic environmental problems of these member states often differ from those of the more highly industrialised Northern European member states who tend to set the agenda for EU environmental policy (Börzel 2000; Weale et al. 2000). The Southern as well as the Central and Eastern European states also have weaker domestic environmental groups and Green parties. Up to the 1980s, the UK was widely considered an environmental laggard state (Weale 1992).

Alliances on particular environmental issues can cut across the leader–laggard divide as can be seen, for example, from the highly contentious issue of nuclear power. Out of the current 27 member states, the majority of member states has either never used nuclear power or is phasing out its use. Importantly, some environmental leader states (i.e. Finland, the Netherlands and Sweden, which has delayed the implementation of a referendum in which the majority of Swedish people voted for the phasing out of nuclear power) favour the continued use of nuclear power while some environmental laggards are opposed to nuclear power. The EURATOM Treaty never had any significant impact on member states' use of nuclear power with the exception of the work environment within nuclear power stations. In other words, the leadership that France, which relies heavily on nuclear power, offered for a nuclear power union was largely rejected by other member states.

Major disagreements in EU environmental policy initially occurred largely between an environmental advocacy coalition (made up of the EP, the Commission's DG for Environment, environmental leader states and environmental NGOs) and an economic feasibility coalition (made up of the Commission's Directorate General (DG) for Industry, environmental laggard states and corporate actors). However, the dividing lines became fuzzier as EU environmental policy matured and the EU expanded from 6 to 27 member states.

The absence of an EU environmental regulatory style

The EU does not have a single policy style but a patchwork policy style (see Chapter 1 by Hayward; Héritier et al. 1996). In the adolescent phase the main disputes about EU environmental policy centred not only around the level of stringency of particular environmental standards but also on dominant environmental regulatory approach. In particular, the island states (Britain and Ireland) insisted on environmental quality objectives (EQOs), which define the desired quality of the receiving environment (such as a river), while most continental states (and Germany in particular) were adamant about the need for uniform emission limits (UELs), which are set at the source of pollution (e.g. the exhaust pipe of cars). At an Environmental Council meeting in October 1975, the British Environment Minster stated uncompromisingly: 'Environmental quality standards – yes. Product standards – yes. Uniform emission limits – no' (cited in Bungarten 1978: 219).

Anglo-German differences were aggravated by the fact that British environmental policy was informed by the best practicable means (BPM), best practicable environmental option (BPEO) and best available technique not entailing excessive costs (BATNEEC) principles, which all emphasised the importance of cost-effectiveness considerations, while German environmental policy was informed by the best available technology (BAT – *Stand der Technik*) principle, which, in combination with the precautionary principle *(Vorsorgeprinzip)*, allowed German government to justify more stringent environmental standards while taking a longer-term perspective of the environmental and economic advantages of particular abatement technologies. In the 1970s, there were bitter Anglo-German rows about the best approach to EU environmental policy in general and the common water policy in particular. EU environmental legislation subsequently resembled a patchwork containing both EQOs and UELs rather than expressing a clear preference (Wurzel 2002: 25). EU environmental laws also made use of the BATNEEC principle, which, in some laws, was defined as best available *technique* not entailing excessive costs, in which case it resembled the British BATNEEC principle, while in others it was referred to as best available *technology* not exceeding excessive costs, which was closer to the German BAT principle. The directive for air pollution from industrial plants stipulated both the BATNEEC and BAT principles and made use of both EQOs and UELs (Wurzel 2002). However, one former Environmental Commissioner, Stanley Clinton-Davis, warned that, 'in too many ways the BATNEEC principle has been replaced by another acronym – CATNIP, the Cheapest Available Technology Not Involving Prosecution' (cited in Wurzel 2002: 30).

It would be wrong to present serious disputes about EU environmental laws merely in terms of national interests. The disagreements about EU car emission regulations in the 1980s, which threatened to develop into a trade war, cut across national boundaries because they essentially reflected conflicts between the producers of large cars (e.g. BMW, Mercedes and Porsche) and small cars (e.g. Fiat, Peugeot, Renault and Volkswagen).

Environmental horizontal disunion

Early conflicts about EU environmental policy were not confined to disputes between EU, member state and societal actors; they frequently cut across EU institutional boundaries and European interest organisations. One of the earliest EU inter-institutional conflicts about EU environmental policy broke out within the Commission between the Dutch Agricultural Commissioner, Mansholt, and the French Industry and Finance Commissioner, Barre. The left-leaning Mansholt, who briefly became interim Commission President in 1972, pleaded for an immediate u-turn in the EU's common economic policy. He was so impressed by the findings of the Club of Rome's *The Limits to Growth* (Meadows et al. 1972) that he advocated a 'clean and recycling' economy based on a system of central planning and the extensive use of environmental taxes (*The Guardian* 11 May 1972; *Süddeutsche Zeitung* 25 February 1972). The market-minded and growth-oriented Barre issued a strongly worded statement in which he accused Mansholt of putting at risk European competitiveness and jobs (*Handelsblatt* 20 June 1972). Mansholt appealed for support to a wider audience by repeating his ideas at the 1972 UN Stockholm conference, which he attended as Commission President. However, he failed to gain the backing of Luxembourg's Interior Minister who spoke on behalf of the EU Presidency in Stockholm (*EC Bulletin* 1972, No.7: 37–8).

EU environmental policy was initially largely a low politics area, which was driven forward by an environmental advocacy coalition that was primarily made up of the EP's environmental committee, a highly activist DG Environment, and an Environmental Council, which was relatively insulated from the other technical Council formations as well as the European Council. National Environmental Ministers were sometimes able to champion ambitious environmental policy measures, which they would have had great difficulties getting accepted within their national cabinets. However, as environmental policy issues became politically more salient and in some cases, for example, climate change, developed into high-politics issues, opposition grew from the economic feasibility coalition. Up to the late 1990s, the European Council dealt only sporadically with environmental issues. However, since the early 2000s, the heads of states or governments regularly focus on EU climate change policy for which they have tried to set the overall strategic goals, particularly in international climate change politics (Wurzel and Connelly 2011). Occasionally, this has led to disagreements about the most appropriate EU goals and best strategies between the environmentally concerned Environmental Council and the European Council, which tends to put a stronger emphasis on competitiveness issues.

Conclusion

Unlike European integration in general EU environmental policy has not been driven by a Franco-German alliance (see Chapter 15 by Paterson) because France and Germany have different environmental policy preferences. However, German Chancellor, Merkel, instigated an 'unholy alliance' between Germany and France in 2008 in order to prevent the adoption of stringent carbon dioxide emission standards to which the German car industry was opposed.

The strong emphasis on the harmonisation of national environmental product standards initially allowed only for temporary differentiation in EU environmental policy. Considering the marked national differences in geography (e.g. island states vs. densely populated continental states), environmental regulatory styles (e.g. EQOs vs. UELs and BAT vs. BPM), economic development (e.g. affluent Northern European vs. poor Southern and Central and Eastern European states) and environmental awareness (e.g. high levels of postmaterialism vs. low levels of environmental awareness), it is not a small achievement for the EU to have adopted a large number of environmental laws.

This is not to argue that EU environmental policy-making has been devoid of major disputes and disagreements, most of which have taken place along national lines, although some have occurred also between EU institutional actors (e.g. the environmentally minded EP vs. the cost-conscious European Council) or even within EU institutions (e.g. between Environmental Commissioners and Industry Commissioners) and member governments (e.g. Environmental Ministries vs. Economics Ministries). However, environmental union has often broken down when it came to the correct implementation of EU environmental laws. Some member states have advocated the repatriation of a significant number of EU environmental laws when the Commission enlisted the help of environmental NGOs to take them to the ECJ for failing to implement correctly EU environmental laws.

The roll-back of EU environmental policy has not taken place. However, there has been a subtle shift in EU environmental policy towards more flexible and less interventionist instruments (e.g. environmental impact assessment) as well as less detailed environmental laws (e.g. the water framework directive). Moreover, implicit references to solidarity have been toned down as can be seen, for example, with the renaming of the climate change burden sharing agreement as an effort-sharing agreement. These developments do not amount to overall disunion in EU environmental policy. The effort sharing agreement still puts forward a differentiated approach, according to which the more affluent member states need to make a larger contribution in reducing greenhouse gas emissions compared to the less affluent member states. However, the establishment of an 'ever closer environmental union' has become even more difficult particularly since the Central and Eastern European enlargements.

Notes

1. It should, however, also be mentioned that the survey was conducted only a few months after BP's Gulf of Mexico oil spill and the Fukushima nuclear reactor melt down.
2. The EP's *Draft Treaty on European Union* constitutes one of the few efforts by EU institutional actors to define European Union. Federalist politicians and theorists often define European Union as a federal state-like entity.
3. Ripa di Meana took up a ministerial post in the Italian government shortly after his resignation.

Bibliography

Andersen, M.S. and D. Liefferink (eds) (1997) *European Environmental Policy. The Pioneers* (Manchester: Manchester University Press).
Börzel, T.A. (2000) 'Why There Is No Southern Problem. On Environmental Leaders and Laggards in the European Union,' *Journal of European Public Policy*, 7 (1), 141–162.
Bungarten, H. (1978) *Umweltpolitik in Westeuropa* (Bonn: Europa Union Verlag).
Dimas, S. (2007), 'Celebrating the Environmental Union', *BBC News Viewpoint*, 23 March 2007, http://news.bbc.co.uk/1/hi/sci/tech/6476273.stm, accessed date 5 September 2011.
Dinan, D. (2000) *Encyclopedia of the European Union* (Basingstoke: Palgrave /Macmillan).
EP (2011) *European Parliament Eurobarometer. The Europeans and Energy* (Brussels: European Parliament).
Eurobarometer (2008) Attitudes of European Citizens Towards the Environment (Brussels: Commission of the European Communities).
Eurobarometer (2011) Attitudes of European Citizens Towards the Environment (Brussels: Commission of the European Union).
Héritier, A., C. Knill and S. Mingers (1996) *Ringing the Changes in Europe* (Berlin: Walter de Gruyter).
Hey, C. (2005), 'EU Environmental Policies: A Short History of the Policy Strategies', in S. Scheuer (ed.) *EU Environmental Policy Handbook* (Brussels: European Environmental Policy).
Hilson, C. (2010) 'EU Environmental Solidarity and the Ecological Consumer: Towards a Republican Citizenship', in M. Ross and Y. Borgmann-Preble (eds)

Promoting Solidarity in the European Union (Oxford: Oxford University Press), 136–50.

Holzinger, K. and P. Knoepfel (eds) (2000), *Environmental Policy in a European Union Variable Geometry?* (Basel: Helbing & Lichtenhahn).

Jordan, A. (2005) 'Introduction: European Union Environmental Policy – Actors, Institutions and Policy Processes', in A. Jordan (ed.) *Environmental Policy in the European Union*. 2nd edn (London: Earthscan), 1–15.

Jordan, A., et al. (eds) (2010) *Climate Change Policy in the European Union* (Cambridge: Cambridge University Press).

Liefferink, D. and M. Andersen (1998), 'Strategies of the "Green" Member States in EU Environmental Policy-making', *Journal of European Public Policy*, 5 (2), 24–70.

Liefferink, D. and A. Jordan (2005) 'An "Ever Closer Union" of National Policy? The Convergence of National Environmental Policy in the European Union', *Environmental Policy and Governance*, 15 (2), 102–113.

Meadows, D.H., D.L. Meadows, J. Randers and W.W. Behrens (1972), *The Limits to Growth* (New York: Universe Books).

Miliband, D. (2006) *Building an Environmental Union*. Speech by David Miliband, Berlin on 19 September 2006 (Berlin: British Embassy Berlin), http://ukingermany.fco.gov.uk/en/news/?view=Speech&id=4615999, accessed 12 September 2011.

Miliband, D. (2009) 'EU's Next Big Project an "Environmental Union"', Commentary in *EurActiv*, http://www.euractiv.com/climate-change/eu-big-project-environmental-union/article-185311, accessed 12 September 2011.

Official Journal (various years) (Brussels: European Economic Community).

Ross, M. and Y. Borgmann-Prebil (eds) (2010) *Promoting Solidarity in the European Union* (Oxford: Oxford University Press).

Scharpf, F.J.W. (1988) 'The Joint-Decision Trap: Lessons from German Federalism and European Integration', *Public Administration*, 66, 239–78.

Skjærseth, J. B. and J. Wettestad (2010), 'Fixing the EU Emissions Trading System? Understanding the Post-2012 Changes', *Global Environmental Politics*, 10 (4), 101–23.

Weale, A. (1992) *The New Politics of Pollution* (Manchester: Manchester University Press).

Weale, A. (1996), 'Environmental Rules and Rule-making in the European Union', *Journal of European Public Policy*, 3 (4), 594–611.

Weale, A., et al. (2000) *Environmental Governance in Europe* (Oxford: Oxford University Press).

Wurzel, R.K.W. (2002) *Environmental Policy-making in Britain, Germany and the European Union* (Manchester: Manchester University Press).

Wurzel, R.K.W. (2008) 'Environmental Policy: EU Actors, Leader and Laggard States', in J. Hayward (ed.), *Leaderless Europe* (Oxford: Oxford University Press), 66–88.

Wurzel, R.K.W. and A.R. Zito (2010) '"Green" Europe: Differentiation in Environmental Policies', in K. Dyson and A. Sepos (eds) *Which Europe? The Politics of Differentiated Integration* (Basingstoke: Palgrave), 265–78.

Wurzel, R.K.W. and J. Connelly (eds) (2011) *The European Union as a Leader in International Climate Change Politics* (London: Routledge).

Part IV
Adjusting to the Receding Sovereignty of Member States

15
A Contested Franco-German Duumvirate

William Paterson

Until relatively recently the leading role of the Franco-German duumvirate was normally accepted by other member states and the United Kingdom, which sometimes challenged it, was never able to raise significant counter support. Internally it was sometimes contested but until relatively recently, Germany was prepared to accept French leadership at least in presentational terms. The duumvirate was strengthened in the Maastricht negotiations .This period came to an end with the grand enlargement of 2004, which has greatly reduced the traction of the Franco-German relationship and narrowed Germany's *marge de manoeuvre*. Enlargement has also reduced the legitimacy of the Franco-German duo by forcing it into a defensive posture where it is often the brake rather than the motor of European integration.

The Franco-German relationship relied on the assumed objections to a solo German leadership position and Germany's 'European vocation', which required an ally. In the last years, other member states have often pressed Germany to lead and Germany has lost much of its European vocation. This loss of European vocation is associated with the loss of the internal autonomy traditionally enjoyed by the German political elite in European policy making and the growth of 'compelling demands' from domestic German institutions and public opinion (Bulmer and Paterson 2010). These developments have threatened to destabilise the Franco-German relationship in the Eurozone where the ongoing crisis has placed Germany in the position of 'reluctant hegemon' (Paterson 2011).

The founding years

The catastrophic failure of two German attempts at hegemony in the short century from 1870 to 1945 required that any post-war European construction had to possess a built in anti-hegemonial character, however unlikely it looked that West Germany would ever attain the position of hegemon. This was achieved in the various institutions leading to the European Union (EU) by over-weighting votes in favour of smaller members, the insistence on the unanimity rule until the Single European Act and most originally by delegating powers to a supra-national authority/Commission, which was expected to continually grow in power. While such a construction may have satisfied the anti-hegemonial test, it was unlikely of itself to have been able to provide dynamic leadership. The leadership of the authority/Commission was potential and would have had to rely on very skilful leadership if it were to be transformed into a key leadership position. Moreover, the further it progressed the more serious would have been the legitimacy problems. It was therefore clear that in the self-imposed absence of the United Kingdom, leadership would ultimately depend on cooperation between France and the Federal Republic.

The preconditions for such cooperation were present in the founding years. For France, such cooperation offered the chance of structuring European integration in a fashion that created the leading position for France not only at the point of creation but which would over the longer term guard against a German Gulliver unbound.

Participation in supranational institutions allowed the Federal Republic to gradually transform its subject status, to flourish economically through being granted access to export markets and to strengthen an impaired and weak state identity. These gains were contingent on French agreement. Germany was the *demandeur* and the partnership could not be of equals but it was rather a leader–follower relationship. Despite its junior status the material and status benefits that the Federal Republic derived from the arrangement were such as to create a 'Europeanised identity'. This identity was easier to create than in other large member states, as uniquely in the Federal Republic national consciousness was not focused on the existing state but on a United Germany that seemed unlikely to re-emerge.

Post-Wall Europe

The collapse of communism and the achievement of a unified Germany led many to expect a slackening of European integration and the end of the reflexive coordination between France and Germany. William Wallace (1991) wrote that the effect would be to reinstate Germany as 'the natural hegemon of any European political system'. In fact, European integration and the Franco-German relationship experienced a golden half decade and the 'future proofing 'of the community institutions by its founders appeared to be wholly vindicated. Other member states apprehensive about the effects of a Gulliver Unbound were concerned to ameliorate the impact of increased German power: for all of them with the exception of the United Kingdom, the answers lay in deepening European integration. This option was especially attractive to Mitterrand since it offered France a continued leadership role. In particular, it offered the prospect of wresting monetary policy away from the unilateral control of the Bundesbank.

Deeper integration around a reinforced Franco-German core was also the preferred option of Helmut Kohl and the German government. The successful achievement of German unity had if anything strengthened German's Europeanised identity and support in Germany's political class for pursuing a European vocation remained strong though public opinion in Germany remained suspicious of European monetary union, the keystone of the Maastricht settlement. Fears of an over mighty Germany were also shared inside Germany and the remedy was seen as binding Germany in through European integration and continued membership of North Atlantic Treaty Organization (NATO). In framing his policy choices in favour of deeper integration and Franco-German cooperation, Kohl owed a great deal to Jacques Delors. As communism collapsed, Delors asserted the priority of deepening rather than widening. He also played a key strategic role in facilitating the simultaneous entry of a united Germany into the EU and the achievement of German unity.

The degree to which the Kohl–Mitterrand dynamic duo dominated the EU in the first half decade after the fall of the Berlin Wall led Thomas Pedersen to advance a theory of cooperative hegemony (Pedersen 1998). This theory starts from the perception that Germany is the potential hegemon and France was offered a share in its evolving regional hegemony and the opportunities for regional hegemonic rule, which such a continental leadership offers both countries (ibid.). Whilst it can be queried as to whether a semi-sovereign Germany fits Pedersen's realist assumptions (Paterson 2005), he is surely correct in underlining that the choice as to the depth of the Franco-German relationship has rested with Germany.

The declining effectiveness of the Franco-German relationship

The period from the 1950s till the Kohl–Mitterrand era was one in which the Franco-German relationship had assumed increasing importance though this had been punctuated with periods of stasis (Paterson 2008).

Reviewing this process, it is possible to isolate a number of underlying factors which shape the impact of the Franco-German relationship. The first element is the perception by German decision makers that an exclusive or even manifest exercise of German leadership would not be acceptable .The second element was the French perception that Europe in conjunction with Germany offered a leadership role. A third element was the degree of popular and elite support for the relationship and European integration. A fourth element was the absence of other potential leaders. Fifth, the legitimacy of their leadership role had to be accepted by other member states. Sixth, the constellation of personalities was important and the relationship progressed furthest under 'dynamic duos' who made the Franco-German relationship an important element in their leadership. Seventh, leadership roles usually have to be backed by material resources and the relationship relied on the economic strength of the two partners, trade concentration on the EU and that the disparity between their own economic strengths not be too great. A final factor is the changing composition of the EU. In the following section, the declining effectiveness of the Franco-German relationship will be traced through the shifting impact of these factors in recent years before we turn to a case study on the Eurozone crisis.

The perception that Germany should not exercise an exclusive leadership role has been a staple of German leadership style and indeed so strong was this reflex that it was possible to write of a 'leadership avoidance reflex' (Paterson 1993). German leadership only emerged as a possibility in the Schmidt period but he was very careful to avoid any impression of exclusive leadership as he believed that any significant move in that direction would be unacceptable to Germany's partners. Kohl was wholly committed to a joint Franco-German leadership and Chancellor Schröder came around to the idea of Franco-German leadership after being diplomatically isolated on Iraq. During the Schröder chancellorship, the so-called Blaesheim meetings of heads of government and foreign ministers were introduced in 2001 alongside the bi-annual joint cabinet meetings. His influential Foreign Minister, Joschka Fischer, was consistent in his support of the Franco-German relationship. Chancellor Merkel's natural political style, honed in German coalition politics, is to lead from behind internally and externally. In the salvage of the Lisbon Treaty however, she successfully responded to demands from partners to exercise a more up front leadership, a policy made possible by the high degree of consensus and the high calibre of the leading ministers in the

Grand Coalition, which freed her from a concentration on domestic politics. Caught between domestic pressures engendered by domestic opinion and institutions and external expectations, she has disappointed both constituencies in her handling of the Eurozone crisis, where her leadership has been seen as cautious and over-responsive to domestic cues.

Closely connected with the avoidance of exclusive leadership was the precept that Germany should always be predictable. This was a precept that was generally adhered to though less consistently by Schröder whose opportunism led to him sometimes being referred to as the 'great occasionist'. Chancellor Merkel's deliberate style did not include surprises before the onset of the Eurozone crisis where under the pressure of the markets she has made some unexpected moves, though she has been criticised more for sticking to a deliberate style, which is seen as too slow and ponderous by the markets. The loss of the autonomy that used to be enjoyed by the German executive on European policy has significantly reduced predictability and the former Chancellor Kohl has recently delivered a stinging rebuke to his one-time protégé Angela Merkel (Gathmann, *Der Spiegel* online 19 May 2011).

France

The Franco-German relationship was the one which allowed France to pursue a European political strategy in a context which would ensure France a leadership role in a manner which no other relationship could deliver. This strategy potentially came under pressure with German unity, which was expected to result in an economically much more powerful Germany but Chancellor Kohl chose a strategy of even greater closeness to France. Pressure on the Franco-German core increased after the Kohl era but German isolation in the Iraq crisis meant that President Chirac was for a time able to reassert French leadership. The French position was weakened by defeat in the 2005 referendum and Germany took the leading position on the salvage of the Lisbon Treaty. As the Eurozone crisis developed, it had a double negative impact on French aspirations. The crisis further eroded Germany's European vocation, which provides much of the glue in the Franco-German relationship and German economic power in relation to France greatly increased. The result is that the partnership no longer appears as between equals. It has become much more important to France than to Germany, which is now a more 'awkward partner'.

Popular and elite support: The paradox of Maastricht

Whilst the Maastricht Treaty greatly strengthened the EU institutional complex, it also gradually eroded public support for European integration (Eichenberg and Dalton 2007), a support which was further weakened by the 2004 enlargement. This decline in support was manifest in the 2005 French referendum and more recently in declining public support for European integration in Germany. This decline in popular support for European integration in both France and Germany has had a negative effect on their European policies and the effectiveness of their leaders to cooperate with each other.

Firstly, they (increasingly negative views on European integration) change their domestic cost–benefit calculations with regard to the proactive and pro-integration stance of their European policies: and secondly, the perceived lack of domestic support undermines the states' power positions in European negotiations (Schild 2010: 1377).

The absence of other potential leaders

Franco-German leadership has depended on the absence of alternative poles of leadership and the absence of a UK presence was a founding condition. Occasionally a Directorate of the Big Three emerges as in dealing with Iran but the advent of a Conservative-led government in Britain, which is actively uninterested in any leadership role except on a bilateral basis (Libya) means this is off the agenda at present. The alternative of supranational leadership under the Hallstein Commission was seen off by De Gaulle in the 1966 crisis. Jacques Delors was very careful to embed his leadership in the Franco-German relationship and his presidency coincided with the high watermark of Franco-German leadership. As President of a weaker Commission, Jose Maria Barroso has neither been able to establish an alternative leadership pole nor add much value to the Franco-German leadership.

The post-Lisbon leadership structures are something of a mixed bag. Baroness Ashton has struggled and Herman Van Rompuy has done a decent job and was entrusted to produce suggestions for dealing with the eurozone crisis for the October 2010 European Council Summit. Chancellor Merkel invested political capital in securing Uwe Corsepius the post of Secretary General of the European Council with the hope that the new structures would meld better with the key national leaders but the bureaucratic setting means his influence is likely to be long-term. The new and unplanned for leadership pole that has emerged is Germany itself as in the Lisbon salvage operation and the Eurozone crisis.

Acceptance by other member states

Franco-German leadership clearly depends for its legitimacy on acceptance by the other member states. This was a test that the De Gaulle–Adenauer version failed. The Mitterrand–Kohl version succeeded for three principal reasons. As Commission President, Delors added huge value to the relationship and helped win over other member states. The opposition to the Kohl–Mitterrand leadership was headed by the United Kingdom but this opposition was neutralised by the provision of 'opt-outs' for the United Kingdom. Support was also attracted by significant 'side payments' paid for by Germany. Support was easier to attract when as in the Kohl–Mitterrand case the leadership could plausibly be presented in 'motor mode' where the Franco-German couple were acting as the avant garde of European integration. The legitimacy of Franco-German leadership suffered a severe knock when they acted as an rear guard as in the Chirac–Schröder deal on agriculture and perhaps more importantly in their breaching of Stability and Growth rules in 2003.

The grand enlargement brought in new members whose experience of supranational organisations in the Soviet bloc had been deeply negative and they found the Franco-German leadership less instinctively comfortable than those members who had grown up with it. This reaction was very visible in the post-Iraq split, where the failure of France and Germany to consult in advance and their expectation that it was the duty of lesser members to fall in behind the leadership caused real tensions. The material inducements in the form of side payments that had been there for the earlier peripheral members were also now much less in evidence.

The Franco-German relationship has normally been associated for fairly self-evident reasons with' dynamic duos'. It would clearly not be acceptable to base an interstate relationship on one pole. In broad terms, one might have expected the relationship to work. Sarkozy and Merkel both come from the centre right and could agree on the line to take on Turkish accession. Neither of them were Europeans of the old style and both of them rejected the choice between the Atlantic and Europe, which had been endorsed by their immediate predecessors. Despite these favourable preconditions, the Sarkozy–Merkel duo has generally malfunctioned. Most obviously there is a contrast of styles. Sarkozy's self-dramatising, hectic, actionist style grates on the studiedly calm, deliberate, evidence-based (she is a physicist) Merkel style. Sarkozy is a politician with many policy ideas on the EU while Merkel has brought only a small number of projects to the table. Where they had a common goal, as in the salvage of the Lisbon Treaty, the relationship worked well though Merkel was clearly the dominant partner. In general, it has not worked well in tackling the eurozone crisis though this is a crisis which contains many further surprises and shocks.

Material strength

France and Germany were from the beginning the dominant economies in the European Community. Currently they constitute 48 per cent of the GDP of the EU. There was a complementarity about their economies with their differing core sectors. Crucially both economies were overwhelmingly centred on intra-European trade. French fears of an over-mighty German economy post-unity were initially calmed in the 1990s when the French economy did well and the German economy to some extent stagnated. The reinvention of the German economy in recent years, the introduction of the euro and globalisation has altered these parameters. In the wake of the (so-called Hartz 4) labour reforms and the moderation of German wage levels, German firms significantly improved their performance. This much improved German performance transmitted through the Eurozone allowed Germany to build up ever-increasing surpluses in intra-European trade. These imbalances led to a crisis for the weaker peripheral members but France also emerged weaker.

Alongside an increasing asymmetry, the direction of German trade has been altering. Whilst the greater proportion of German trade is within the Eurozone the fastest growing element is with China and the BRICS (Brazil, Russia, India, China and South Africa) where the demand for capital goods and expensive consumer products like luxury cars has played to German strengths. The changing patterns of German trade mean that while the Eurozone and the Franco-German relationship remain important to German business they are losing the absolute centrality they once had (Webber 2011). German business was largely mute as the eurocrisis developed but came out with a strong statement of support for the eurozone in the run up to the key vote on the July summit recommendations on 29 September 2010.

It might be thought that Germany's burgeoning trade surpluses would make it more ready to indulge in the side payments that were an important sustaining element in earlier periods. The continuing high costs associated with German unity and Germany's very high social costs had resulted however in a weak budgetary position. This prompted the German government in 2009 to introduce a new balanced budget rule represented by Article 115 of the Basic Law, which entered into force in 2011. This new rule which Germany wants to see exported throughout the eurozone will make side payments in the manner of the past extremely problematic.

Enlargement

The Franco-German relationship was born in the Europe of the six. It was always anticipated that a major enlargement would weaken the gravitational pull of the Franco-German core. It was this perception that accounted for British enthusiasm and the decision by Kohl, Mitterrand and Delors to attempt to hard wire the dominance of a centralising core through the Maastricht Treaty before undertaking the grand enlargement. Enlargement has resulted in 'a shrinking core and an expanding periphery' (Dyson and Goetz 2003) of smaller and poorer states who have been very effective in the Council of Ministers (Thomson 2010). This pressure has resulted in France and Germany being more defensive, being less prepared to trade off leadership against a narrow defence of national interests and the Franco-German relationship losing traction.

The pattern of influence in the Franco-German relationship has rarely been straightforwardly linear but the cumulative trend line of these shaping factors points to a much greater asymmetry between the partners and the decreased effectiveness of this relationship.

The ultimate test: the Franco-German relationship and the eurozone crisis

The creation of the Eurozone represented the highpoint of Franco-German cooperation. One notable feature is the manner in which it was pressed ahead with in Germany by the political leadership against a hostile public opinion and the reservations of the Bundesbank. German experience of the Eurozone until the outbreak of the Global Financial Crisis in 2008 had been overwhelmingly positive and despite differences on governance issues, one might have expected the Franco-German relationship to cooperate well in dealing with crisis and for the German leadership to display the same boldness in dealing with a hostile public opinion and a sceptical economic orthodoxy that it had in launching the euro. Somewhat unexpectedly, given the degree to which Germany had profited from the eurozone, its ideational leadership in the establishment of the Eurozone and the boldness of Chancellor Merkel's leadership in the Lisbon salvage process, the German government has often preferred to adopt a very cautious and defensive role while France has been more active and responded with a much greater sense of urgency. Despite some successes including joint backing for the European Stability Mechanism (ESM) and the Competitiveness Pact (see Chapter 12 by Dyson), the Franco-German relationship has been unable to cap the crisis and has not yet lived up to rhetorical statements about doing whatever it takes to save the euro.

Rather than give an account of the crisis (Bulmer and Paterson 2010; Paterson 2011; Chapters 9 and 12 by Howarth and Dyson, respectively), a range of factors which have impeded the operation of the Franco-German relationship are identified. The first factor is that sovereign debt crises have a brutal logic pitting the interests of the creditor nations very sharply against those of the debtor nations .This implies that Germany's natural allies are Austria, Finland and the Netherlands, with a common interest in restricting aid and imposing strict conditionality in any aid given, rather than France. This also explains why Chancellor Merkel's preference was for including the International Monetary Fund (IMF) from the beginning rather than restricting the search for a solution to the Eurozone members, which might have privileged the debtors and the more statist member states. It also corresponds to a consistent German aspiration that as many as possible, including states outside the eurozone contribute to any rescue.

France was in a rather ambivalent position with fears that its relatively high debt level would mean that its AAA status might be imperilled if France was required to contribute too high an amount to any bailout mechanism while on the other hand it has an elemental interest in the survival of the eurozone. One of the strengths of the Franco-German relationship is that Germany often aggregates the interests of the northern states and France those of the southern states in grand bargains. In the case of the eurocrisis, France was understandably reluctant to place itself unequivocally on one side or the other. The existential self-interest necessarily involved also made it difficult for the Franco-German couple to make the appeal to the higher European interest of the kind that had been successful in the past. There was also the moral hazard issue raised if it involved a bail out.

Another structural factor involved the appropriateness of the Franco-German relationship for dealing with issues in which the financial

markets were major players. It is the most institutionalised bilateral relationship in the world, an institutionalisation which has been further
thickened since 2001. It has also sometimes been effective where the
partners started from widely differing positions. Its modus operandi
therefore is basically deliberate and slow moving. Progress between
Ministerial meetings follows the so-called *Feuilles de Route*. This makes
it very ill adapted to the sort of speedy crisis management needed to
respond to the financial markets. It can and has been at points in the
Eurozone crisis effective at compromise building including a widening
acceptance of treaty change, a position on which Germany had been
isolated but at a glacial pace, which means the response has been seen
as behind the curve. Not all of the problem here resides with a malfunc-
tioning Franco-German couple. Even when they come to an agreement
implementation is sometimes delayed by the necessity for necessarily
time-consuming ratification procedures.

The structural drag inherent in such an institutionalised relationship
might have been overcome if there had been a 'dynamic duo' at the
top in France and Germany who were focused on economics. Helmut
Schmidt has argued that he would immediately have phoned Giscard
and developed a strategic plan (*Baseler Zeitung* 29 May 2010). Such a relationship depends on a very high level of mutual trust and confidence,
which is absent despite the profoundly institutionalised relationship.
One of the features of this crisis has been that delay has pushed up
the costs and made the solution ever more intractable. By not crafting
a solution, they are in danger of having one imposed on them by the
financial markets.

In establishing the eurozone, it had been possible to appear to transcend long-standing differences of outlook and approach in relation to
economic governance on the part of France and Germany. The eurozone
crisis has reopened these differences, which never really went away. A
defining element in German economic policy conditioned by memories of the great inflation has been the attachment to sound money.

'Ever since the Federal Republic was founded, Germany has had two
over-riding strategic objectives: sound money and European integration.
These were the twin imperatives learned from the calamities of the early
twentieth century. The euro embodies these aims. Now they conflict
with each other.' (Martin Wolf, *Financial Times* 10 March 2010).

German fears were calmed by the design of the European Central
Bank, the Stability and Growth Pact and the strength developed by the
euro. The sound money reflexes revived with the onset of the eurocrisis and have been an important framing factor in the German policy

response. The defenders of Ordoliberalism and sound money concentrated in the German academic economics profession, the Economics Ministry and above all in the Bundesbank. Having been on something of a backfoot in the flat years of the German economy when they were exposed to lots of scorn by their Anglo-American peers, now recovered their voice. It had been assumed that with the creation of the European Central Bank that the Bundesbank had lost its bite but in the crisis it has continued as the key defender of the sound money principle. Chancellor Merkel had placed a great deal of political capital in Axel Weber, the President of the Bundesbank succeeding Jean-Claude Trichet as the President of the European Central Bank (ECB) but concerns about the policy of the ECB led him to withdraw his nomination and resign as Bundesbank President in February 2011. He was replaced by Jens Weidmann, Chancellor Merkel's economic adviser but the signs were that Weidmann had gone native. Perhaps even more strikingly, Jürgen Stark, former Vice President of the Bundesbank who was responsible for Economics and Monetary Analysis in the ECB, resigned in September 2011 over worries about the ECB's purchase of government bonds. Of course, attachment to sound money is not confined to Germany but its strength and doctrinaire character have had a negative effect on attempts to put together a Franco-German position.

This attachment to sound money was associated with strong German resistance to the concept of EU economic government, which would in German eyes open up the possibility of other objectives crowding out the sound money objective. Following the injunction of never wasting a good crisis, the French government from the beginning attempted to push the economic government idea and has had some limited semantic success but it remains very vague with little idea of what competences would be transferred from the national to the European level.

A third factor reflects significant changes in the shaping elements of German European policy. It is the changes in the factors that condition German European policy alongside the usual debtor state reflexes and economic doctrine that cast light on the failure of the Franco-German relationship to come up with the grand bargain, agenda-setting step that might succeed in capping the crisis. The changes in the framing factors of German European policy include generational change, the waning power of Europeanist discourse and an increasingly sceptical public opinion (Paterson 2010; Bulmer and Paterson, 2010). Further constraints are added by compelling demands from the Federal Constitutional Court (see also Chapter 8 by Birkinshaw) and the Länder (states) governments (see also Chapter 10 by Keating). A federal government, which has regained sovereignty at the international and European level, has lost a lot of the executive autonomy in European policy, which allowed German governments to be the masters of coalition building (Maull 2008). The contrast with the position of the German government at the time of the eurozone launch is very striking.

The stark imperatives imposed by a sovereign debt crisis and Germany's position as the creditor of last resort has pushed Germany into the position of 'reluctant hegemon'. Participants at summit meetings refer to Angela Merkel being regarded by others as the headmistress. What is surprising is that this position was not anticipated in Germany. In a monetary union where one member state builds up huge surpluses there must be corresponding deficits. These deficits can only be remedied by making the debtors more competitive or being bailed out by the creditor countries. The competitiveness route runs into the obstacles constituted by Germany's position 'as an extraordinary trader' (Hager 1980) adopting a single-minded hyper-export orientation. When Christine Lagarde suggested that this was a problem and Germany might do more to stimulate internal demand she was met with incomprehension and irritation (Lagarde, *Financial Times* 14 May 2010). This leaves Germany in an unsought hegemon position for whose obligations elite and public opinion appear ill-prepared.

Alongside a developing hegemon position, the eurocrisis was initially associated with a grave weakening of the supporting pillars of Germany's European vocation and a growth of compelling demands from German institutions. Both processes made Germany much more of an awkward partner, much less able to operationalise the Franco-German relationship to deal with the eurocrisis. Whilst the compelling demands of the Federal Constitutional Court and the Bundesbank continue to present obstacles, the direction of travel of the main political parties has reversed itself and they are all now at least at a declaratory level more 'European' than they were at the onset of the crisis. The redevelopment of a European vision is seen as necessary to reengage a much more sceptical German public and to soften Germany's image in southern Europe where it has been seen as smelling like a hegemon and dressing like an accountant (Peel, *Financial Times* 11 April 2011).

In the course of the crisis, Chancellor Merkel has increasingly stressed the Franco-German relationship, but this emphasis remains more at the level of presentation than substance. There have been an endless succession of summit meetings, none of which has proved to be conclusive. The markets expect that the key players, especially Germany, will make huge resources available to deal with the deficit economies but this hope is always disappointed with the emphasis being placed on measures to prevent a future crisis rather than dealing with the current one.

At the European Summit of 8–9 December 2011, the basic German emphasis on competitiveness, budgetary consolidation and the balance of adjustment including increased surveillance of budgets falling on the stricken economies was preserved. The arrangements for increasing the funds beyond the €500 billion available to the European Stability Mechanism from July 2012 remained unclear and a lot of hope was invested in the IMF and other outsiders without any indication that the required volume of funds could be delivered. The Eurobonds option was, with reluctant French support, decisively ruled out although the ECB made new funding available for banks. Whilst prepared to concede a little on the haircuts to be imposed on investors in view of the wall of bond issues due in the first months of 2012, Chancellor Merkel stuck to her insistence on the necessity of a new treaty. Prime Minister Cameron's calculation that she would be prepared to pay a high price for UK agreement quickly proved to be mistaken. Its most prominent effect was to hand President Sarkozy a get out of jail card from the accusation that France had had little input on what was essentially a German design where his influence was restricted to the decisions on future budgetary autonomy and the severity of the haircuts to be imposed on private investors.

There is an argument that the harsh conditions imposed on debtor countries are necessary to produce the long-term transformation of these economies and the minimum required for domestic German opinion to agree to the expenditure of German treasure that many see as inevitable. In the meantime, the crafting and ratification of a treaty for 26 will be time-consuming and replete with elephant traps including legal uncertainties about the status of a treaty that does not include all 27 members, probable referenda in a number of member states and nervous legislatures in others. Further difficulties were posed by the rating agencies and the threat they represented for France's AAA status, a threat that engendered a huge amount of nervousness in the French governing elite and did little to calm the markets that were underwhelmed by the less than decisive results of the election.

Conclusion

In the troubles in Northern Ireland, each fresh atrocity would raise the fear that we were on the edge of the abyss, which was never quite reached. In dealing with the eurozone crisis, the Merkozy duo[1] was adept at 'moving the abyss' through endless ultimately inconclusive summit meetings but at some point the exigencies of the markets will prove inescapable and the edge of the abyss will be reached. One element of this situation is the reduction in the France's AAA rating, which occurred in early 2012. An even graver element would be an investors strike. At this point, the decision will lie with Germany. The key decision will be how much German taxpayers money will go into the rescue. President Sarkozy provided cover for Chancellor Merkel by endorsing her rejection of Eurobonds. François Hollande, the Presidential candidate of the French socialists, undertook before his election to renegotiate the fiscal pact. In a joint paper on the eve of the Brussels Summit of December 2011, the SPD and the Greens issued a joint critique of the government's austerity policy and endorsed the recommendations of the German Council of experts in favour of a common European debt repayment fund (Bündnis 90/The Greens and SPD 9 December 2011).

There is of course no certainty that the left will take part in government after the 2013 election in Germany. There is of course no certainty that the left will be elected in either country or that they would maintain these positions if they were in power. It is also possible that faced with the choice Chancellor Merkel would retreat from her austerity policy. What does appear more inevitable is that if Germany did underwrite a massive bail out for the eurozone as at present constituted then the price would be a greatly increased level of budgetary surveillance and significant moves towards a more open hegemon position for Germany. That this would not be unwelcome to many member states is indicated in the speech by Radoslaw Sikorski, just before the summit.

> I demand of Germany that, for its own sake and for ours, it help the eurozone survive and prosper. No one else can do it. I will probably be the first Polish foreign minister in history to say this but here it is: I fear German power less than I am beginning to fear its inactivity. You have become Europe's indispensable nation. You may not fail to lead: not dominate, but to lead in reform (Sikorski, *Financial Times* 28 November 2011).

One alternative scenario would see the eurozone shed a number of its weaker members and German dominance would be less explicit as there would not be the same need for German resources to prop up the system. In such a construction, the Franco-German asymmetry would be less pronounced and their relationship would continue under

German leadership. A final and still unlikely scenario would be a disorderly collapse of the eurozone.

For most of the history of the EU, the Franco-German relationship was seen as the inevitable relationship since there was a general assumption, entertained especially strongly by German governments, that singular German leadership was unacceptable. This taboo would have been expected to apply especially strongly in Poland. It is therefore of huge significance that the Polish Foreign Minister pins all his hopes not on the Franco-German relationship but on Germany as the indispensable nation. Such a view carries with it enormous implications for the governance of the eurozone. A project, embedded in Franco-German cooperation, which was intended to guard against hegemony, has resulted in Germany being even more firmly installed in the driving seat than in pre-eurozone times. That, of course, is only part, albeit a central part of the picture. Germany is not the indispensable nation in relation to the European Security and Defence Policy (ESDP) (see Chapter 11 by Menon) where France and Britain play the key roles. In an EU future of increased differentiation the Franco German relationship will endure.

'Like ageing sopranos they refuse to retire. Their technique remains impressive even if their voices grow feeble and their repertory more restricted' (Calleo 1980).

Note

1. The appellation Merkozy is rather flattering to President Sarkozy who was rarely seen as the co-equal partner.

Bibliography

Bündnis 90/The Greens /SPD 'The Euro area must not founder on the narrow mindedness of the German Government', http://www.gruene-bundestag.de /cms/english/dok/399/399059.the_Euro_area_must_not_founder_on_the_ na.html, accessed on 9 December 2011.

Bulmer, S. and W. Paterson (2010) 'Germany and the European Union: From "Tamed Power" to "Normalized Power"?', *International Affairs*, 86, 1051–1073.

Calleo, D. (1980), *The German Problem Reconsidered: Germany and the World Order 1870 to the Present* (Cambridge: Cambridge University Press).

Dyson, K. and K. Goetz (2003) *Germany, Europe and the Politics of Constraint* (Oxford: Oxford University Press).

Eichenberg, R. and R. Dalton (2007) Post Maastricht Blues: The Transformation of Citizen Support for European Integration 1973–2004', *Acta Politica*, 42, 128–152.

Gathmann, F. (2011) 'Mahnung eines alten Europäers' *Spiegel* online, 19 May 2011, http://www.spiegel.de/politik/deutschland/0,1518,762881,00.html, accessed on 4 June 2012.

Hager, W. (1980),'Germany as an Extraordinary Trader ' in W. Kohl and G. Basevi (eds) *West Germany: A European and Global Power* (Lexington MA: Lexington Books), pp. 3–43.

Lagarde, C. (2010) 'Lagarde Criticises Berlin Policy' *Financial Times* 14 March 2010.

Maull, H. (2008) 'Germany and the Art of Coalition Building', *Journal of European Integration*, 30/1,131–152.

Paterson, W. (1993),'Muss Europa Angst vor Deutschland haben?' in R. Hrbek (ed.) *Der Vertrag von Maaastricht in der wissentschaftlichen Kontroverse* (Baden-Baden: Nomos), pp. 1–9.

Paterson, W. (2005) 'European Policy Making: Between Associated Sovereignty and Semi Sovereignty' in S. Green and W. Paterson (eds) *Governance in Contemporary Germany* (Cambridge: Cambridge University Press), pp. 261–282.

Paterson, W. (2008) 'Did France and Germany Lead Europe? A Retrospect' in J. Hayward (ed.) *Leaderless Europe* (Oxford: Oxford University Press), pp. 89–112.

Paterson, W. (2010) 'Does Germany Still Have a European Vocation?', *German Politics*, 19, 41–52.

Paterson, W. (2011) 'The Reluctant Hegemon? Germany Moves Centre Stage in the European Union', *Journal of Common Market Studies*, 49, Annual Review, 57–75.

Pedersen, T. (1998) *Germany, France and the Integration of Europe* (London: Pinter).

Peel, Q. (2011) Germany: A trial Of Strength, *Financial Times,* 11 April 2011.

Schild,J. (2010) 'Mission Impossible? The Potential For Franco German Leadership in the Enlarged EU', *Journal of Common Market Studies*, 48, 1367–1390.

Sikorski, R. (2011) 'I Fear Germany's Power Less Than Her Inactivity' *Financial Times* 28 November 2011.

Thomson, R. (2010) 'The Relative Power of Member States in the Council: Large and Small, Old and New', in D. Naurin and H. Wallace (eds) *Unveiling the Council of the European Union: Games Governments Play in Brussels* (Basingstoke: Palgrave Macmillan), pp. 238–260.

Wallace, W. (1991) 'Germany at the Centre of Europe' in E. Kolinsky (ed.) *The Federal Republic of Germany: The End of an Era* (Oxford: Berg), pp.167–174.

Webber, D. (2011) 'How Likely Is It That the European Union will Disintegrate? A Critical Analysis of Competing Theoretical Perspectives ', unpublished manuscript.

Wolf, M. (2010) 'The Eurozone crisis is now a nightmare for Germany' *Financial Times* 10 March 2010.

16
Opt-Out: Britain's Unsplendid Isolation

Philip Norton

The UK became a member of the European Communities on 1 January 1973. Her journey to becoming a member was tortuous and her membership has been far from being trouble-free: it has been dubbed 'the awkward partner' (George 1990). Indeed, the UK can be characterised not so much as an awkward partner as a reluctant bride, delaying saying 'yes' because her heart still yearned for others and unhappy in a domestic relationship that does not allow her to play the role she expected. Though pressed at times to end the relationship, and experiencing a particularly fraught relationship at the end of 2011, she remains wedded to the institution and, despite having opted out of certain domestic chores, nonetheless deals efficiently with those that remain.

The fault line of British politics

The issue of European integration has been a contentious one in British politics throughout the post-war era. The two main political parties have witnessed major changes of policy. In the 1950s, both were sceptical of participating in moves towards integration. In the 1960s, the Conservative Party switched to support membership of the European Community – Conservative Prime Minister Harold Macmillan submitted the first application for membership in 1961 (see Camps 1964) – and was followed by the Labour Party (Kitzinger 1968). In the 1970s, membership was achieved by a Conservative government but was opposed by the Labour Party. In the 1980s, the Conservative Party under Margaret Thatcher adopted a more sceptical approach and the roles changed in subsequent decades as Labour became more supportive of the European Union and the Conservatives more hostile.

Conservative Prime Minister John Major (1990–97) was an active participant in the negotiations producing the Maastricht Treaty, but Conservative leaders since 1997 (William Hague, Iain Duncan Smith, Michael Howard and David Cameron) have been notable opponents of moves towards further integration. Hague ran the party's campaign in the 1999 European Parliament elections under the slogan 'In Europe, not run by Europe'. The party's election manifesto in 2010 committed a Conservative government to providing that any further transfers of power to the European Union (EU) would be subject to a referendum, and adding 'A Conservative government would never take the UK into the Euro' (Conservative Party 2010). The European Union Act 2011 gave effect to the former pledge.

Complicating the picture is the fact that neither party has been able to maintain a united stand on the issue. Each has committed supporters and opponents of integration. The changes of party policy have meant that at times supporters of integration have moved from being the dominant force within the party to occupying a minority role, or vice versa. When the Conservative government of Edward Heath applied successfully for membership, the measure to give legal effect to membership in UK law was vehemently opposed by a minority of Conservative MPs (Norton 1978: 64–82, 2011). Since the time of Margaret Thatcher's leadership of the Conservative Party, supporters of further integration have been in a marked minority. Labour leader Hugh Gaitskell led his party in opposition to Britain's first application for membership. (See, for example, his Godkin Lecture at Harvard; Williams 1979: 703). Today, opponents of European integration are in a minority within the ranks of the parliamentary Labour party.

The extent to which both parties have been divided has been reflected in notable votes in the House of Commons. In October 1971, the House spent six days debating a motion supporting 'Her Majesty's Government's decision of principle to join the European Communities on the basis of the arrangements which have been negotiated'. Labour opposed the motion, but 69 Labour MPs voted for it and a further 20 abstained from voting (Norton 1975: 395–8; Kitzinger 1973: 400–5). On the Conservative side, 39 MPs voted against it. When the Bill to give effect to membership in UK law, the European Communities Bill, came up for Second Reading in February 1972, the Prime Minister declared it a vote of confidence. Despite that, 15 Conservative MPs voted against it, and a further 5 abstained. The vote was only won, by a majority of 8, because of the votes of 6 Liberal MPs and abstentions by 4 Labour MPs (Norton 1975: 404–6).

John Major had especial difficulty in 1992 in achieving the support of Conservative MPs for the Maastricht Treaty. The Bill to give legal effect in domestic law to its provisions took up 163 hours in committee in the House of Commons and passed into law a year later than planned by government. Major also had trouble mobilising his MPs to support the 1994 Bill to increase the size of the EU budget. It was only passed after he made the vote one of confidence. Eight Conservative MPs who failed to support the government had the party whip withdrawn (Norton 1996a: 106).

Further adding to a complicated picture is the fact that attitudes within the parties are not simply split between support and opposition to further integration. Within Conservative ranks, for example, there are four broad groupings (Norton 2010: 266–7). There are *anti-Europeans* who opposed UK membership of the European Community and favour withdrawal from the EU. There is a somewhat larger group of *Euro-sceptics*, who support membership but, especially since a speech by Margaret Thatcher in 1988 at Bruges (Thatcher 1988), take the line of 'so far and no further' and oppose further integration. There are *Euro-agnostics*, comprising the largest group in the parliamentary party, who have no strong view and support whichever line they feel is best for the country and the party. Finally, there are *Europhiles*, who have a principled commitment to further integration. Since the 1990s, the Euro-agnostics have tended to swing against further integration, thus isolating the Europhiles within the party.

The inconsistencies and divisions shown by the two main parties have been reflected in, and may have been in part a consequence of, uncertainty among the public. There were deep divisions among the British public when Britain joined the European Community. Polls suggested that opinion in the 1970s was generally hostile, but in a UK-wide referendum held in 1975, on the terms renegotiated by a Labour government, there was a substantial 'yes' vote in favour of continued membership: 17.3 million against 8.4 million voting no (Butler and Kitzinger 1976; King 1977). However, opinion since has not been consistent and certainly not as supportive. In the 1980s, opinion polls suggested stronger support for membership. In the 1990s, the gap narrowed and ever since there have been notable swings in opinion. Between 1977 and 2007, the percentage of those wanting the UK to remain as a member ranged from a low of 26 per cent (March 1980) to a high of 63 per cent (June 1991). Those wanting to withdraw in 1980 comprised 60 per cent of those questioned. The volatility was marked in 2000. In June, 53 per cent of those questioned favoured staying in, against 32 per cent in favour of withdrawing. In September, 43 per cent supported staying in against 46 per cent who favoured withdrawal (Ipsos MORI).

Any majority support for membership has been more than offset by opposition to joining a single currency. Here views have been more consistent. Both main parties committed themselves to a referendum in the event of a decision to join the single currency and the potential of losing a referendum on the issue appears to have contributed to government reluctance to contemplate such a move.

Delayed membership

The UK had the option to participate in the negotiations leading to the Treaties of Paris and Rome but declined to do so. In 1950, Conservative leader Winston Churchill moved a motion in favour of participation in the talks leading to the Treaty of Paris, but the motion was defeated. The Labour government of Clement Attlee was not prepared to support supranational control of the European Steel and Coal Community. It was happy to encourage its European neighbours to come together but, as Attlee recorded, 'we could not enter into engagements to the full extent possible to the Continental Powers' (Attlee 1954: 173). The government did participate in the formation of the Council of Europe 'but we were unable to accept the views of the extreme federalists' (Attlee 1954: 173).

The succeeding Conservative government declined to participate in the proposed European Defence Community and in the negotiations leading to the Treaty of Rome. Sir Anthony Eden as Foreign Secretary resisted American pressure to participate (Eden 1960: 157–74) and as Prime Minister declined to send anyone to participate in the Messina conference. 'Nothing would induce him to contemplate Britain pooling sovereignty with other European nations or entering a customs union subject to supra-national control' (Lamb 1987: 69). Britain instead, on the prompting of Chancellor of the Exchequer Harold Macmillan, pursued the option of a European Free Trade Area (EFTA). Even this proved a step too far for some, not least *The Daily Express,* owned by former Conservative Cabinet minister Lord Beaverbrook, who was vehemently opposed to any moves towards European integration.

When the British government did come round to the view that it wished to join the European Communities, it was late in the day and by then dependent on the existing members to be admitted. Britain had enjoyed economic prosperity in the 1950s, but it then witnessed a downturn. It did so at a time when Atlantic and Commonwealth links were not delivering the benefits expected of them. The Commonwealth was not proving as reliable in political and trading terms as Conservative leaders may have wished. The sudden cancellation by the US administration of the Blue Streak missile, on which UK had rested for its forward nuclear defence programme, demonstrated the UK's junior status in the trans-Atlantic relationship.

Prime Minister Harold Macmillan sought ways of restoring Britain's position. He decided that membership of the European Communities was the answer, informing the House of Commons on 31 July 1961 that the UK was applying for membership. French President Charles de Gaulle vetoed the application in January 1963. He also blocked the second application submitted in 1967, this time by the Labour government of Harold Wilson. Membership was achieved, following de Gaulle's succession by Georges Pompidou, under the succeeding Conservative government of Edward Heath.

As a member, the UK has proved somewhat detached and on occasion combative. Margaret Thatcher fought for a budget rebate. John Major for a time adopted an 'empty chair' policy. Labour Prime Minister Gordon Brown notably turned up late to sign the Lisbon Treaty. The move in the twenty-first century away from the presumption of moving toward 'an ever closer union' has seen no great shift in the stance of the UK, but rather others moving towards a position that it has always taken.

Why, then, the reluctance to join and the continued uncertainty over membership?

The key to Britain's reluctance to join can be found in its island status, its military history and its colonial heritage. The first two are essentially conjoined, though all three came together to induce a particular view of Britain's role in the world. As Anthony King recorded, 'Its preoccupations, its national interests, and its self-image ... combined to keep Britain apart from Europe' (King 1977: 6). Even King's language is instructive: the rest of the continent was 'Europe'. Britain was historically an island maritime nation with few natural resources. It had gone overseas to trade and to acquire resources and in the course of doing so developed overseas possessions and in time an Empire. It was a major player on the world stage. It had lost battles overseas but it had not been invaded since 1066. As Jean Monnet summarised the situation: 'Britain has not been conquered or invaded. She felt no need to exorcise history' (Monnet, *Memoirs,* quoted in Hennessy 1992: 364). It was not therefore subject to the same psychological appeal to a united Europe as existed among other European nations.

Despite having become dependent on the United States during the Second World War, the UK still saw itself as a major player on the world stage. It remained attached to the Commonwealth – successor to the British Empire – and saw itself as having a 'special relationship' with the United States. In its stance towards the rest of Europe, it had a tradition of acting as a power broker, seeking alliances as appropriate in order to prevent a great European power emerging (Norton 1996a: 92). It was therefore wary of any permanent engagement with other European nations. It did not regard itself as on a par with those nations and could see little substantial benefit to engagement.

Reinforcing the reluctance to participate were factors specific to the political parties as well as the nation's relative economic position. The post-war Labour government was wary of a body that it viewed as essentially anti-socialist. Sovereignty had to be preserved in order to deliver the government's programme of democratic socialism. When informal talks were held to discuss some economic co-operation, Foreign Secretary Ernest Bevin 'felt that even these would go too far in the direction of a surrender of British sovereignty' (Edwin Plowden, quoted in Hennessy 1992: 361). For the Conservatives, the attachment was to maintaining the nation's world role and a hankering after Empire. The Commonwealth was seen as something of a substitute, certainly a means to the UK remaining a world leader. There was therefore resistance to calls for a European customs union or moves that meant loosening its global ties.

Nor was there any clear economic imperative to get involved. The UK initially was stronger than its European neighbours and did not need them for its own economic recovery.

> Not only did the continentals' talk of 'building Europe' not seem to have anything to offer Britain; almost no one in Britain believed that much would come of it. The dream of the Continent was a united Europe; the reality was economic chaos and unstable minority governments. (King 1977: 5)

Finally, but in many respects crucially, underpinning the reluctance to join and participate in the European Commission (EC) was the constitutional implications (see also Chapter 8 by Birkinshaw). Sovereignty was involved in two respects. One, which we have covered, was national sovereignty. The other was parliamentary sovereignty. Under the British Constitution, according to Dicey in his classic work of 1885, only Parliament had the right to make or unmake any law whatever; furthermore, 'no person or body is recognised by the law of England as having a right to override or set aside the legislation of Parliament' (Dicey 1959: 39–40). Not only was the UK used to determining its own stance in relation to the rest of the world, Parliament was not open to challenge in the law that it passed. The UK, in postwar years, was viewed as having a settled Constitution; indeed, the outcome of the Second World War appeared to confirm the virtues of its parliamentary system of government (Norton 1998a: 46–9). Membership of the EC would constitute a fundamental challenge to Parliament's omnipotence. Opposition on constitutional grounds to British engagement was marked, underpinning much of the argument put forward by many anti-Europeans.

There were thus historic, political, economic and constitutional objections to Britain becoming embroiled in negotiations leading to any form of European body under supranational control. Indeed, some of these were seen as so self-evident that there seemed little point in devoting time to them. The consequence, as King observed, was not that the UK chose not to participate in creating a united Europe but rather that it never seriously considered engaging on the subject (King 1977: 7). It was essentially distant from the process.

The reluctant suitor

This narrative points to the double-edged nature of the motivation for the UK's application for membership. The reasons for joining were proffered as being political and economic. The EC offered a large, tariff-free market as well as a medium through which the UK could again play a leading role on the world stage. However, the reason for joining was as much because other possibilities had not delivered and so the EC was the remaining best option, possibly the only remaining option. This was reflected in Heath's 1968 Godkin Lectures at Harvard: 'I had argued that Europe was now alone in both enhancing its political stature and remaining open to British influence. The Commonwealth was fissiparous, and the United States was increasingly beset by internal problems and a crisis of confidence abroad' (Heath 1998: 361). This was said by the one Prime Minister who eschewed sovereignty in favour of solidarity.

The UK, in short, was suitor to the EC because others had proved a disappointment. As we have seen, there was no element of love at first sight. If anything, it was a case of 'you will have to do'. The reluctant nature of Britain's membership was reflected in the position taken by the Labour government returned in 1974. It had committed itself to renegotiating the terms of membership and submitting the result to a referendum. It did so, not out of a principled stance on the issue of membership (or the use of referendums) but in order to hold a divided party together.

The troubled marriage

The concerns that had underpinned Britain's reluctance to join the EC were not abated once it became a member. The Labour government of Harold Wilson was badly divided, hence the renegotiation and referendum. The new Conservative leader, Margaret Thatcher, appeared alongside Edward Heath in the referendum in arguing for a 'yes' vote, but once in Downing Street in 1979 she took a highly nationalist stance. She argued that Britain's financial contribution to the EC was too high and pressed for a reduction. After several fraught meetings, in which she did not endear herself to other heads of government, agreement on a rebate was reached in 1984, and was to prove a running sore in EC relationships thereafter. Thatcher agreed in 1986 to the terms of the Single European Act, seeing it as a means of achieving a single market. When it appeared to be used to go beyond that, she signalled her opposition, articulating a role for the EC that was at odds with that taken by other leaders.

Thatcher's successor, John Major, sought to adopt a more conciliatory approach and was characterised as playing a productive role in the 1991 negotiations leading to the Maastricht Treaty. This was the high point of Conservative engagement and was quickly undermined in the new Parliament returned in 1992. The 'no' vote in the Danish referendum in 1992 emboldened Conservative critics of the EC. They opposed the Bill to give effect to the Treaty and its passage was fraught, not to say uncertain (Norton 1998b: 82–6). Thereafter, Conservative attitudes towards the EC were more detached, especially on the issue of a single currency. The government adopted an approach of 'negotiate and decide' (or wait and see), a stance that divided Tory MPs. During the 1997 election campaign, a substantial number declared their outright opposition to UK participation in a single currency. Following defeat in the election, the party elected leaders who were Euro-sceptics: indeed one, Iain Duncan Smith, had been a leading opponent of the Maastricht Treaty. David Cameron, elected leader in 2005, took the view that European integration had 'gone too far and in the wrong direction. We need a European Union that works as a looser and more flexible, open organization' (in Jones 2008: 255–6).

In the early 1980s, the Labour Party embraced withdrawal from the EC and embodied it in its 1983 election manifesto. The next Labour government, it declared, 'committed to radical, socialist policies for reviving the British economy, is bound to find continued membership a most serious obstacle to the fulfilment of those policies' (*The Times* 1983: 328); it therefore proposed to achieve withdrawal within the lifetime of the Parliament. However, after its decisive defeat in the election, the new leader, Neil Kinnock, modified the party's position. In 1992, he was succeeded by a leader, John Smith, who had been one of the 69 Labour MPs who had voted in 1971 in support of the principle of British membership. He led a badly divided party. Labour MPs were even more divided over the Maastricht Treaty than the Conservatives (Stuart 2005: 271) and Smith had to walk a political tightrope, seeking to embarrass the government while accepting that the Treaty was the best that could be achieved in the circumstances (Stuart 2005: 281).

Smith's leadership represented the high point of Labour support for European integration. Following his death in 1994, the party acquired a more pragmatic leader in Tony Blair. Smith had favoured the UK joining the single currency. Blair shifted the policy from being 'in favour in principle' to one of 'not opposed in principle'. 'By the time he was elected Labour leader, he said only that there were "potential benefits" in joining and was starting to set conditions' (Rentoul 2001: 473). The government decided against joining the Euro in the first wave of membership. Commitment to a referendum in the event of a decision to join acted as a restraint and the official line became one of joining if five economic conditions were met. Chancellor Gordon Brown set himself as the guardian of the tests and was not minded to concede the case (see Seldon 638–9; Lee 183–211). The tests were not met and Blair failed to give a decisive lead in support of joining the Euro. After the Iraq war, his political capital was limited. 'He had failed to persuade Brown. He accepted that he would fail to persuade the nation also. In his heart of hearts he did not mind that much' (Seldon 2004: 640).

Brown succeeded Blair as Prime Minister in 2007 and he was in no mood to move in a more positive direction towards European integration. Far from wanting the UK to move towards the EU, he wanted the EU to move towards Britain. His vision was for the EU 'to move on from the older, inward-looking model to become a more flexible, reforming, open and globally-orientated Europe' (quoted in Lee 2007: 184). The government set various 'red lines' for the discussions on the proposed constitutional treaty. The government had promised a referendum on the treaty but the rejection of it in referendums in France and the

Netherlands saved it from the potential embarrassment of producing a similar result. The salvaging of the treaty in the form of the Lisbon Treaty enabled the government to claim that it was a different document and thus avoid a referendum and a potential defeat. 'For most voters, however, Europe was, by now, an unimportant issue. Calls for a new referendum never fired the public imagination' (Allen 2011: 19).

Following Labour's election defeat in 2010, a Conservative–Liberal Democrat coalition was formed under David Cameron. The need to craft a coalition constricted his desire to adopt a more Eurosceptic approach but even so agreement was reached on the measure providing for referendums on any further transfers of power to the EU. The Liberal Democrats, long-standing advocates of greater European integration, had moved to a more detached stance. In the coalition negotiations, they had accepted that there was no chance of Britain joining the Euro. As one Liberal Democrat negotiator recorded, 'I shouted out "Hurrah!" as I have never been a big fan of Britain joining the euro, and have never thought that there was the slightest chance of the British people supporting the euro in a referendum' (Laws 2010: 118). The coalition held in the face of David Cameron's exercise of his veto during treaty negotiations in 2011. His action upset his Liberal Democrat partners but proved popular with the electorate. The UK may be in a marriage, but the stance was more one of resigned acceptance than enthusiasm.

Domestic chores

Although the UK is in a marriage that many may regard as loveless, it nonetheless accepts that so long as it is a member then it is necessary to abide by the rules. Indeed, we can identify two levels of her engagement with the EU. There remains the high-level debate over the merits of membership of the Union – the discussion we have adumbrated – and a more understated but important low-level involvement in the day-to-day running of the Europe. This involvement can be identified in respect both of government and Parliament.

Despite the brief 'empty chair' policy adopted by the Major government, the British government has played its role in the Council and civil servants have been active in their engagement with EU institutions. Though sometimes seen as a berth for politicians who have failed or completed their political careers at home, the posts of Commissioners from the United Kingdom have generally been filled by senior political figures. These have included those who have held senior Cabinet rank – including most notably Sir Leon Brittan, Chris Patten and Peter Mandelson – and, in one case, a former Labour party leader (Neil Kinnock). One Commissioner appointed by the UK, Lord Cockfield, was the architect of the 1985 White Paper on *Completion of the Single Market* (Norton 1996b: 5). Indeed, one former civil servant, Sir Roy Denman, said Cockfield 'will long be remembered in Brussels, with both affection and respect, as one of the great public servants of a uniting Europe' (*Guardian*, obituary, 11 January 2007). As Commissioners, they have been active and generally respected members of the college, often given leading portfolios. Mandelson referred to 'the warmth and camaraderie' among members (Mandelson 2010: 395). 'In the Commission', he wrote, 'technically every decision is taken by the college. So, at every step of the way I had to learn to carry key colleagues with me, starting with José Manuel [Barosso]' (Mandelson 2010: 396).

Officials contribute to the Committee of Permanent Representatives (COREPER), the UK ambassador being supported – as with other ambassadors – by a team of diplomats and civil servants seconded from the home civil service. Indeed, it has been argued by a former Director-General of the European Commission that the engagement of UK officials is indistinguishable from that of other delegations. 'If you took away the nameplates of the delegations', he said, 'it would be impossible to work out which member state they represented' (former Director-General of the EC to author, interview, 2011). The task of the delegation is to negotiate and to ally with other member states in pursuing a particular stance on a proposal emanating from the Commission. The engagement by government applies to output as much as input. Directives have been transposed into UK law, on occasion with a little too much enthusiasm, the government being accused of 'gold-plating' measures, for example by stipulating an earlier date for enactment than that stipulated by the directive.

The second is at the level of Parliament. In the event of a debate on EU membership, there will be an argument about the merits and demerits of the EU and Britain's continued membership. Tory backbenchers were especially vocal in 2011–12 in calling for greater detachment and, in some cases, withdrawal. However, a more pervasive engagement is maintained through a systematic scrutiny of EU documents. The UK is a document-based rather than a mandating system (see Chapter 7 by Rassmusen). Bergman (2000) ranked the UK 6th out of 15 in terms of the level of parliamentary scrutiny in EU matters. Each House has a committee dedicated to scrutiny (Norton 1996a) and the work undertaken by the two is extensive.

The work of each complements the other, the House of Commons going for breadth (examining every document) and the House of Lords for depth (examining in detail the documents deemed significant in political and legal terms) (Norton 1996a). Each is assisted by an explanatory memorandum compiled by the government that accompanies every document deposited, as well as by the scrutiny reserve, under which the UK government is committed not to agree a proposal (except in exceptional circumstances) until it has cleared scrutiny in both Houses.

The House of Commons operates through the European Scrutiny Committee, which in staff terms is the best resourced of select committees in the House. The House of Lords operates through the European Union Committee, which has six sub-committees, each with 10 to 12 members, resulting in over 70 members of the House being engaged in regular scrutiny of EU documents. Members are appointed on the basis of their experience or expertise. (Of the 19 members of the main committee in 2011, one was a former EC Commissioner, another a former EC Assistant Under-Secretary and Ambassador to the United Nations, and five had served as members of the European Parliament.) The committee not only examines the documents that are deposited, engaging in regular dialogue with ministers prior to Council meetings, but can and does undertake inquiries into particular developments within the EU, producing detailed and evidence-based reports – disseminated to EU institutions – generally regarded as authoritative and sometimes portrayed as more substantial than reports from the relevant committee of the European Parliament. At the end of 2011, for example, the sub-committees were examining the European rail market, EU military capabilities, freshwater policy, drugs strategy, a financial transaction tax, criminal procedure and the EU's contribution to the modernisation of higher education in Europe.

Both Houses have also adapted their procedures in the light of the Lisbon Treaty and have been among the more active chambers in scrutinising proposals to ensure compliance with the principle of subsidiarity. (In 2010 the Commons certified three and the Lords two proposals that it deemed to conflict with the principle.) Both have also been active in engaging with other national parliaments and EU institutions. In addition to contributions to the Conference of Community and European Affairs Committee (COSAC), the committee of members of European affairs committees of national parliaments, committee officers regularly visit Brussels and the member state holding the EU presidency. Commission officials and Members of European Parliament

(MEPs) have variously given evidence to Lords sub-committees and members of the EU committee or sub-committees have on occasion given evidence to committees of the European Parliament, as for example as part of the examination of the proposal to establish a Fundamental Rights Agency.

Though the UK may be an uncertain member of the EU, it nonetheless accepts the obligation to ensure that what is being proposed is subject to scrutiny. The two approaches are not necessarily incompatible in that there is a reluctance to concede scrutiny solely to the level of the European Parliament.

Coming in from the cold – or being left in the cold

The UK has, in short, always been a reluctant as much as an awkward partner. Its history has meant that it has always embraced sovereignty rather than solidarity. It has taken membership and the rules of membership seriously, but it has pursued membership for essentially strategic purposes. Its detached stance has, if anything, been reinforced by the fact that membership has not delivered all that was expected of it, at least not in economic and political terms: critics, primarily anti-Europeans, would argue that it has proved them right in terms of its constitutional implications.

One aspect of European development, though, that has been supported by successive governments is enlargement of the Union. Drawing in more members has been seen as a way of avoiding 'fortress Europe' in economic terms and diluting the influence of the Franco-German alliance (see Chapter 15 by Paterson). Enlargement has also brought in states who are more towards the sovereignty rather than the solidarity end of the spectrum, bringing in some member states who have been sympathetic to the British approach. The UK has on occasion been able to garner allies in a way that was not possible in the first decades of membership. 'The hopeful signs' declared David Cameron, 'are that now that countries from Eastern and Central Europe have come in, having just rediscovered their national identity, they are less likely to want to subsume it into a European nation state' (Jones 2008: 256).

The UK has been keen to harness support for moving away from what it sees as an overly statist approach. 'Some regulation', opined Cameron in 2008, 'is inevitable in creating a single market, but it's far too prescriptive as it is now. But there are also signs of hope, actually. If you listen to President Barroso, the current head of the European Commission, he's making all the right noises and actually abolishing some regulations' (Jones 2008: 255). This is seen as confirming the rightness of Britain's approach. It has tended to be endorsed by business leaders in the UK, previously keen advocates of EU membership. The turmoil in the economic markets, and especially the Eurozone, in 2010–11, was seen as also confirming the UK's wisdom in staying out of the single currency.

Enlargement and deregulation have nonetheless not served to dispel the position of the UK as the reluctant bride. David Cameron's veto of a new treaty in 2011 attracted no support from other EU leaders. Some viewed divorce as a possibility, as indeed did some UK politicians. However, the reality was one of a largely loveless marriage, exacerbated by some marital spats but a relationship that, however rocky, was expected to endure.

Bibliography

Allen, N. (2011), 'Labour's Third Term: A Tale of Two Prime Ministers', in Nicholas Allen and John Bartle (eds), *Britain at the Polls 2010* (London: Sage).

Attlee, C.R. (1954), *As It Happened* (London: William Heinemann).

Bergman, T. (2000), 'The European Union as the Next Step of Delegation and Accountability', *European Journal of Political Research*, 37 (3): 415–29.

Butler, D. and Kitzinger, U. (1976), *The 1975 Referendum* (London: Macmillan).

Camps, M. (1964), *Britain and the European Community 1955–1963* (Oxford: Oxford University Press).

Conservative Party (2010), *An Invitation to Join the Government of the United Kingdom* (London: The Conservative Party).

Dicey, A.V. (1959), *An Introduction to the Study of the Law of the Constitution* (first pub. 1885), 10th ed. (London: Macmillan).

Eden, A. (1960), *The Memoirs of Sir Anthony Eden: Full Circle* (London: Cassell).

George, S. (1990), *An Awkward Partner* (Oxford: Oxford University Press).

Heath, E. (1998), *The Course of My Life: My Autobiography* (London: Hodder & Stoughton).

Hennessy, P. (1992), *Never Again: Britain 1945–51* (London: Jonathan Cape).

Jones, D. (2008), *Cameron on Cameron: Conversations with Dylan Jones* (London: Fourth Estate).

King, A. (1977), *Britain Says Yes* (Washington, DC: American Enterprise Institute).

Kitzinger, U. (1968), *The Second Try* (Oxford: Pergamon).

Kitzinger, U. (1973), *Diplomacy and Persuasion* (London: Thames & Hudson).

Lamb, R. (1987), *The Failure of the Eden Government* (London: Sidgwick & Jackson).

Laws, D. (2010), *22 Days in May* (London: Biteback).

Lee, S. (2007), *Best for Britain? The Politics and Legacy of Gordon Brown* (Oxford: Oneworld Publications).

Mandelson, P. (2010), *The Third Man* (London: HarperPress).

Norton, P. (1975), *Dissension in the House of Commons 1945–1974* (London: Macmillan).

Norton, P. (1978), *Conservative Dissidents* (London: Temple Smith).

Norton, P. (1981), *The Commons in Perspective* (Oxford: Martin Robertson).

Norton, P. (1996a), 'The United Kingdom: Political Conflict, Parliamentary Scrutiny', in P. Norton (ed.), *National Parliaments and the European Union* (London: Frank Cass).

Norton, P. (1996b), 'Introduction: Adapting to European Integration', in P. Norton (ed.), *National Parliaments and the European Union* (London: Frank Cass).

Norton, P. (1998a), 'Winning the War but Losing the Peace: The British House of Commons during the Second World War', *The Journal of Legislative Studies*, 4: 33–51.

Norton, P. (1998b), 'The Conservative Party: "In Office but Not in Power"', in Anthony King (ed.), *New Labour Triumphs: Britain at the Polls* (Chatham, NJ: Chatham House).

Norton, P. (2010), *The British Polity*, 5th ed. (Boston MA: Longman).

Norton, P. (2011), 'Divided Loyalties: The European Communities Act 1972', *Parliamentary History*, 30: 53–64.

Rentoul, J. (2001), *Tony Blair: Prime Minister* (London: Little, Brown and Company).

Seldon, A. (2004), *Blair* (London: The Free Press).

Stuart, M. (2005), *John Brown: A Life* (London: Politico's).

Thatcher, M. (1988), *Britain and Europe* (London: Conservative Political Centre).

The Times (1983), *The Times Guide to the House of Commons 1983* (London: Times Books).

Williams, P.M. (1979), *Hugh Gaitskell: A Political Biography* (London: Jonathan Cape).

17
The Nordic Countries: The Causes and Consequences of Variable Geometry

Nick Sitter

The Nordic states all participate in European integration, but to different degrees and through somewhat different institutional arrangements. Finland has been a full European Union (EU) member since 1995, and it is the only one of the four states discussed in this chapter that has adopted the EU's single currency. Sweden has been a full EU member since 1995, but it decided unilaterally not to adopt the Euro. Denmark, an EU member since 1973, has a formal opt-out from European Monetary Union (EMU) and three other policy areas (citizenship, civil law and defence). Norway is perhaps best describers as a 'quasi-member' of the EU: despite two referendum decisions against joining the EU, the country is closely involved in most aspects of EU policy through the European Economic Area (EEA) and Schengen. The fifth Nordic country, Iceland (which is not covered in the present chapter), applied for full EU membership in 2009 (and is in the EEA and Schengen). The four 'mainland' states have all held referendums on European integration, and all but Finland have seen their governments defeated by popular vote. This chapter explores the political processes and patterns of Euroscepticism that have produced these different forms of participation in European integration, and some of its practical consequences.[1]

The European question – whether and to what extent each state should participate in European integration – has been an important question in the region since the early 1960s. However, its political salience has varied considerably over time, depending on a combination of domestic and international politics. The establishment of European organisations that sought to deepen the interdependence between Europe's non-communist states put the European question firmly on the agenda in the 1960s. The realities of the Cold War meant that only Norway and Denmark could seriously consider European Economic Community (EEC) membership. When the collapse of communism changed this in the 1990s, it prompted a second wave of debates on European integration. Denmark's 'no' to the Maastricht Treaty, Norway's second 'no' to the EU and the closely run Swedish 'yes' vote resulted in a patchwork of improvised arrangements that still characterises the EU's Nordic dimension. The opt-outs that permitted a sufficiently large number of Danish Eurosceptics to approve the modified Maastricht Treaty in 1993 have since developed into a more or less permanent fixture of the EU system. The same holds for the EEA arrangement, which most Norwegian (and EU) negotiators initially saw as a stepping stone towards full EU membership. A third wave of decisions in the 2000s, linked mainly to Economic and Monetary Union, helped institutionalise this pattern of variable participation in European integration. More than any other sub-set of EU states, the Nordic states thus illustrate the phenomenon that is sometimes labelled 'differentiated integration' or variable geometry (Andersen and Sitter 2006).

The chapter is organised along three themes: (i) the politics of European integration, (ii) the regular and ad hoc institutional arrangements that this has resulted in and (iii) the policy consequences of Nordic variable geometry. The first section traces the four states' responses to European integration, from the first time the issue was raised in 1961 through party politics and referendums up to the present day. The central theme in this volume, the relationship between sovereignty and solidarity, has also been a core issue in Nordic politics. However, in these four cases, it has been a matter of several parties perceiving EU membership as a threat to solidarity at the national level; a fear that the Single European Market might undermine the Nordic welfare model in the long run. The second section covers the resulting institutional arrangements, and the different ways the four states participate in European integration. These arrangements reflect efforts to reconcile concerns about sovereignty and solidarity with the aim of participating in European integration; in effect the four countries' welfare regimes (and Norwegian agriculture and fisheries) have largely been shielded from the effects of European integration. The third section assesses and evaluates the consequences of these patterns of differentiated integration in terms of public policy.

Contesting Europe: patterns of popular and party-based Euroscepticism

To date, 20 major decisions about participation in European integration have been taken in these four states.[2] The contest between the pro- and anti-integration forces has been played out in referendums 11 times and in parliamentary votes 9 times (see Table 17.1). The governments have won all nine parliamentary votes, but lost almost half the referendums: two Norwegian governments' efforts to join the EU were defeated in 1972 and 1994; Danish governments saw their effort to ratify the Maastricht Treaty defeated in 1993 and to join EMU defeated in 2003; and the Swedish government was defeated when voters rejected it plans to join EMU in 2000. However, the different ways the Nordic states participate in European integration is not simply a reflection of popular sentiment towards the EU in the four states (see Figure 17.1). During the 1990s a higher percentage of Danes saw the EU as a 'good thing' than Swedes or Finns; and support for EU membership in Norway was not consistently lower than in the other three states (although it dropped substantially in the late 2000s). The explanation for the differences in how these states are linked to the EU lie in the nature of party politics and the dynamics of government

Table 17.1 Major decisions on European integration: yes/no ratio in referendums

	Denmark	Norway	Finland	Sweden
EEC membership	1972: 63.4/36.6	1972: 46.5/53.5		
Single European Act	1986: 56.2/43.8			
Maastricht Treaty	1992: 49.3/50.7			
	1993: 56.7/43.3			
To join EEA		Parliamentary decision only	Parliamentary decision only	Parliamentary decision only
EU membership		1994: 47.8/52.2	1994: 56.9/43.1	1994: 52.3/46.8
Amsterdam Treaty	1998: 55.1/44.9		Parliamentary decision only	Parliamentary decision only
Nice Treaty	Parliamentary decision only		Parliamentary decision only	Parliamentary decision only
To join EMU	2000: 46.8/53.2		Parliamentary decision only	2003: 42.0/55.9
Constitutional Treaty	Referendum (cancelled)		Parliamentary decision only	Parliamentary decision only (suspended)
Lisbon Treaty	Parliamentary decision only		Parliamentary decision only	Parliamentary decision only

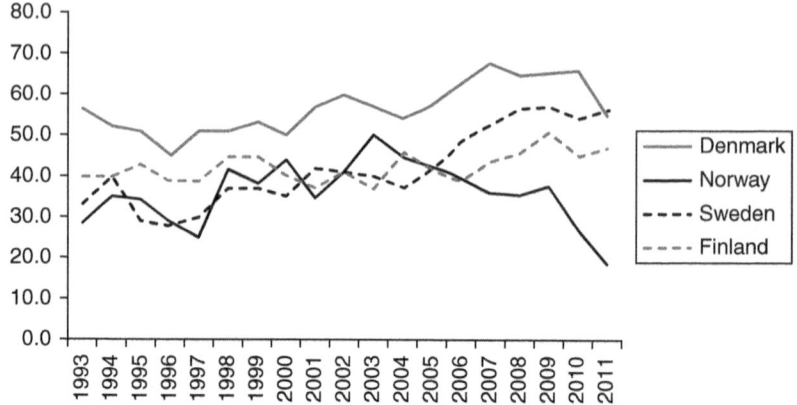

Figure 17.1   Pro-EU opinion 1993–2011: share of Danish, Swedish and Finnish voters who regard EU membership a 'good thing', and Norwegian voters who favour EU membership

Sources: Sweden, Denmark and Finland: Eurobarometer (Sweden 1993 and 1994 from Widfeldt 1996); Norway: yearly averages of polls reported by NTB and the Norwegian press 1993–2011 (calculated by the author).

and opposition, as much as in popular support for or opposition to the EU. In each of these states, the politics of European integration has very much been the art of the possible: an effort to balance policy objectives with coalition management and the constraints that referendum results impose. The remainder of this section therefore focuses on party politics and the European question.

As for party positions on the European question, the most striking feature is that opposition to European integration cannot easily be associated simply with left or right, the centre or the flanks. The centre-left Swedish and Finnish parties opposed participation in European integration during the Cold War, but reassessed their positions when it ended. Soft Eurosceptic parties have been found in the centre and on the left wings, but several of them modified their positions after their country joined the EU. Most Eurosceptic parties in Denmark, Finland and Sweden are by and large committed to maintaining the status quo, and no longer argue for withdrawal from the EU altogether. The parties that have changed their stances on European integration have generally changed it in favour of closer cooperation with the EU; the single exception is the right-populist Progress Party in Norway, which has become more ambivalent over the last two decades. Current party positions are set out in Table 17.2.

Table 17.2   Nordic Parliamentary (and some ex-parliamentary) parties

Party Family	Finland (2011 election)	Sweden (2010 election)	Denmark (2011 election)	Norway (2009 election)
Far, Socialist left and Greens: new politics	Left League – VAS (8.1) Green League – VIHR (7.3)	Left Party – Vp (5.6) Swedish Greens – Mp (7.3)	Unity List – E (6.7) Socialist People's Party – SF (9.2)	Socialist Left – SV (6.2)
Social Democrat: socioeconomic left-right	Social Democrats – SDP (19.1)	Social Democrats – SAP (30.7)	Social Democrats – SD (24.9)	Labour – DNA (35.4)
Centre (Christian, liberal, agrarian): territorial and/or socioeconomic left-right	Centre Party – KESK (15.8) Christian Democrats – KD (4.0) Swedish People's Party – SFS (4.3)	Centre Party – C (6.6) Christian Democrats – KD (5.6) Liberals – FpL (7.1)	*Radical Liberals – RV (9.5) Liberal Alliance – LA (5.0) *Liberals – V (26.7)	Centre Party – Sp (6.2) Liberals – V (3.9) Chr. People's Party – KrF (5.5)
Conservative: socio-economic left-right	Conservatives – KOK (20.4)	Moderates – M (30.7)	Conservatives – KF (4.9)	Conservatives – H (17.2)
Far right: new populism	**True Finns – PeruS (19.1)**	**Swedish Democrats (5.7)**	**Danish Peoples Party – DF (12.3)**	Progress Party – FrP (22.9)

Note: Eurosceptic parties in bold, formerly Eurosceptic parties underlined, percentage of votes in recent elections in brackets.

* RV and V hardly count as 'centre' except in genesis, the former being close to the SD and the latter generally perceived as to the right of KF on the socioeconomic left-right dimension.

Source: Current and past party programmes; country chapters in Taggart and Szczerbiak (2008).

The key characteristic of all four party systems is the lack of party-based Euroscepticism among the mainstream conservative and social democratic parties. All the catch-all parties that compete along the main left–right dimension favour EU membership. When the mainstream Swedish and Finnish parties opposed EEC membership during the Cold War, this was predominantly a matter of foreign policy and neutrality (Aylott 2008). To be sure, this overall picture masks significant internal divisions in the social democratic parties, particularly in Norway and Sweden, which draw partly on fears that EU (or EMU) membership might undermine the welfare state (Christensen 1996; Saglie 2000a; Aylott 2002). A persistent theme has been the fear that the EU represent a free-market model that is not compatible with the high-tax, large public sector and redistributive Nordic welfare states. This question featured particularly strongly in the Swedish and Danish EMU referendum campaigns. On the other hand, the conservative parties (including the Danish Liberals) have advocated EU membership since the 1960s, even in Sweden, mainly for economic and geopolitical reasons (Svåsand and Lindström 1996). Because of the country's consensual foreign policy, the Finnish parties hardly needed to adopt positions regarding EU membership until 1990, when the Conservatives, Swedish People's Party and Social Democrats all came out unambiguously in favour of their country joining the EU (Tiilikainen 1996).

The Nordic political centre has a more mixed past, and until the 1990s it featured a form of centrist Euroscepticism that was uncommon elsewhere in Europe. To be sure, the 'centre' hardly constitutes a proper party family in strict ideological terms. Nevertheless, most Nordic centre parties share common roots in the nineteenth century liberal left and are classified by von Beyme (1985) as part of the 'liberal and radical', 'agrarian' or 'regional and ethnic' party families. This group includes parties that represent farmers' interests, all of whom (except the Danish Liberals, an agrarian party only in historical terms) have at one point opposed European integration (Batroy and Sitter 2004). The group also includes dissident or fundamentalist Christian parties, which in the early 1990s opposed EU membership in Norway, Sweden and Finland on the basis of national identity, sovereignty and social policy. During the 1990s, however, all the Swedish and Finnish parties of the centre abandoned hard Euroscepticism. Only Norway is left with a persistently Eurosceptic centre, and of the three Norwegian centre parties only the Centre Party opposes both EU and EEA membership. The Christian People's Party continues to oppose EU membership, but favours the EEA-based status quo; as does the somewhat more neutral Liberal Party. Only in Denmark and in the case of the Swedish Liberal People's Party has the centre a long-standing pro-EU tradition dating back to the 1960s, although the Danish Christian Democrats oppose EMU (Knudsen 2008). With the Norwegian Liberals' recent adoption of a neutral stance on European integration, the region no longer features any Eurosceptic liberal parties.

With the exception of the Norwegian Centre Party, the strongest opposition to participation in European integration can be found at the right and left flanks of the party systems. Perhaps predictably given the EU's long-standing focus on the common market, the far left has traditionally opposed European integration as a capitalist plot. Only in Finland is this no longer the case, and even here the Left and Green Leagues' formal neutrality on the EU issues masks considerable internal opposition to participation in European integration (Raunio 2008). Moreover, some of the left flank parties were born as anti-EU or -NATO dissenters from the mainstream Social Democrat left, much as the Christian parties were born as dissent against the secularising and socially permissive mainstream consensus (Karvonen 1994; Madeley 1994; Christensen 1996, 1998).

The far right, however, has been less cohesive on the European question. While the current Swedish, Danish and Finnish far right conform to the European pattern of far right scepticism towards European integration, their sister party in Norway is caught between its national and populist focus on one hand and advocacy of less interventionist government and lower taxes on the other (Sitter 2008). In 1994, the Norwegian Progress Party advocated a 'yes' in the EU referendum, as did the short-lived New Democrats in Sweden (1991–94); whereas the populist Danish Progress Party was the only parliamentary party not to accept the 'national compromise' over the Maastricht Treaty. The Danish People's Party, which split from the Progress Party in 1995 and eventually eclipsed it, takes an even more uncompromising Eurosceptic stance.

From an overall EU perspective, the Nordic states have thus been exceptional inasmuch as political parties (or in the social democrats' case, factions) across the spectrum have adopted Eurosceptic positions. Membership debates and debates on further integration have always pitted at least one parliamentary party against the government of the day; and Eurosceptic parties have had considerable success in mobilising disproportionate numbers of voters in referendums. Although Cold War neutrality provided an important part of the basis for centre-left Euroscpeticism, the most salient and enduring twin themes have been defence of national sovereignty (across the political spectrum) and the solidarity mechanisms built into the Nordic welfare states (on the centre and left). Coalition governments have relied on the support of Eurosceptic parties to an extent almost unheard of elsewhere in the EU. The result has been a series of ad hoc compromises, particularly in the shape of the EEA and the Danish opt-outs. Nevertheless, over the last two decades all four states have established something of a consensus on the process whereby decisions on European integration are taken. In Denmark and Finland, there is even a degree of consensus on substance, and in Norway and Sweden both pro-EU and Eurosceptic parties have grown to accept temporary second-best solutions as semi-permanent arrangements. The next section turns to the individual decisions about EU membership and further integration, and how these 20 contests brought about variable geometry.

The Nordic states and European integration
1961–2011: improvised variable geometry

The question of EU membership first became salient in Denmark, Norway and Sweden when the UK announced its application for EU membership in 1961, barely a year after the establishment of the European Free Trade Area (EFTA). Denmark's centre-left government followed the British Conservatives' lead, while the Norwegian minority Labour government prevaricated and was relieved of the need to make a decision when French president De Gaulle vetoed UK membership (Frøland 1998). No Finnish politician was prepared to issue the kind of challenge to the USSR that an effort to join the EEC would entail; and (partly in solidarity) Sweden's majority Social Democrat government rejected membership on the grounds that it would be incompatible with neutrality (Widfeldt 1996; Ryden 2000). The Swedish centre-right was more open to joining the EEC, but it would remain in opposition until 1991 (except for a six-year period from 1976–82 during which the European question lacked any salience at all). De Gaulle's second veto in 1967 closed the debate until his departure from French politics two years later, whereupon the Norwegian and Danish parties returned to the question. This first phase was brought to a halt after the Danish 'yes' and Norwegian 'no' in 1972 referendums, which settled the matter for almost two decades.

The decisions to hold referendums were effectively taken in the 1960s, voluntarily in the Norwegian case and by consensus in Denmark (in the end the decision to join the EEC was in any case approved by less than a five-sixths majority in parliament needed to avoid a referendum; Bjørklund 1982). The Eurosceptic parties demanded referendums because they feared they might not be able to block accession in Parliament, the divided parties favoured them as a means of avoiding party spits, and in both countries the governing parties and/or coalitions were divided on EEC membership at the time. The contest centred on a combination of national identity, sovereignty and economic interest, including historical narratives that linked these states to each other in opposition to continental (German) Europe (Knudsen 2008; Sitter 2008).

During the 1970s and 1980s, the European question remained off the political agenda in three of the four states. In Sweden and Finland, the debate was limited as long as the Cold War lasted, and in Norway political parties (particularly the Liberals and Labour) was well as blocs (the centre-right) were recovering from damaging splits and had little appetite for a new round of debates. The European question only resurfaced in Denmark with the ratification of the Single European Act. In 1986 the minority government consisting of the Conservatives, Liberals, Centre Democrats and Christian People's Party could not secure ratification in parliament (the Social Democrats and Radical Liberals opposed the Single European Act (SEA), as did the smaller left-wing parties), and invoked a referendum to circumvent parliament and avoid calling fresh elections (Svensson 2002). The Danish 'yes' avoided a crisis, and left Denmark fully involved with all aspects of the EU.

The second wave of EU debates came in the 1990s, as the end of the Cold War reopened the question for Sweden and Finland and thereby also set the scene for a second round in Norway. The fact that the Swedish Social Democratic governments of the 1970s and 1980s continued to oppose membership principally on the grounds of neutrality, meant that questions of sovereignty and socioeconomic policy were played down. In the early 1990s, the solidarity dimension of the European question thus played a lesser role than it did in Norway and Denmark, although this dimension would return to Swedish and Finish politics when they debated EMU towards the end of the decade. Once the neutrality question became obsolete, there was therefore little to prevent the Swedish centre-left from moving swiftly to advocacy of EU membership. The Finnish mainstream parties soon followed suit. Both countries joined the EU in 1995 after referendums, the 'yes' side polling 57 per cent in Finland and a less comfortable 52 per cent in Sweden. In Sweden, only the Left Party and the Greens opposed membership, but the Social Democrats, Centre Party and Christian Democrats all had higher shares of 'no' voters than 'yes' voters among their supporters (Aylott 2008:190). In Finland, only the Christian Democrats and the True Finns advocated a 'no' vote, but the two left-wing parties (the Green league and the Left Alliance) were so divided as not to make a recommendation either way (Raunio 2008:170). The consequence was that both countries signed up to accept the full *acquis communautaire*, down to and including the commitment to join EMU.

By contrast, Norwegian voters opted once again not to join the EU. It was politically impossible to overturn the 1972 result without a second referendum (Pettersen et al. 1996; Saglie 2000b). The 1993 election saw a surge in votes for the Eurosceptic parties, and the 1994 referendum yielded a 'no' that was more resounding than in 1972. No party had changed its position: the Conservatives and Labour favoured member-ship (the latter managing its divisions somewhat better than in 1972), and were joined by the somewhat ambivalent Progress Party (formed in

1975); the Socialist Left and Centre Party firmly opposed both EEA and EU membership, and the somewhat more pragmatic Christian People's Party and Liberals came out in favour of the EEA but against the EU. However, the big difference between 1994 and 1972 was the alternative: this time the country was a member of the European Economic Area, which had become operational in January 1994, and had thus secured access to the single market (minus agriculture and fisheries) in return for adopting new relevant EU legislation. Although the EEA arrangement formally accords Norway the right not to apply new EU legislation, the severity and asymmetry of sanctions in case of dispute has made most parties reluctant to test this. Moreover, Norway has also secured access to a number of other EU-related activities, from ad hoc participation in education policy, military and police initiatives to almost full membership of Schengen, in a system sometimes described as 'buy-ins' because it mirrors the EU states' opt-outs but comes with a price-tag (Eliassen and Sitter 2003).[3]

The third set of decisions about European integration involved further participation beyond the original membership debates. The first instance of this, Denmark's ratification of the SEA, has been discussed briefly above. The next step, the Maastricht Treaty, proved far more controversial. Because previous governments had opted to call referendums in 1972 and 1986, the government had little choice but to repeat this when seeking to ratify the new treaty (Siune 1993; Svensson 1994). To the shock of her EU partners, Danish voters said 'no'. This set in motion the negotiations that concluded with the Edinburgh summit and the opt-outs from participation in EMU, common citizenship, defence, and supranational decisions in Justice and Home Affairs. The participation of the Eurosceptic parties (minus the Progress Party) in this deal secured a 'yes' in the second referendum, in 1993. Subsequent EU treaties have retained the Danish opt-outs, and consequently, after its other EU partners reach decisions by majority voting on policies on asylum, immigration and civil law, Denmark chooses which of the decisions to adopt (this arrangement is not unlike the one enjoyed by non-Schengen members UK and Ireland). In 2000, Danish voters implicitly confirmed this arrangement, when they voted in a referendum to reject the governments' recommendation to join EMU. Successive Danish governments have planned referendums to end some or all of the opt-outs, but none had been scheduled by the end of 2011.

Sweden joined Denmark and Norway (and Britain and Ireland) on the list of states that voluntarily opted out of part of the EU system in 2003, when it held a referendum on whether to join the Euro and

Table 17.3 European integration

	Finland	Sweden	Denmark	Norway*
Single Market (EEA)	X	X	X	X
Schengen	X	X	(X)	X
Full EU membership	X	X	X	
EMU	X			

(X) indicates participation on an intergovernmental basis only.

*Norway has no voting rights in EU decision making.

saw the 'no' side carry the day with 56 per cent of the vote. Although Sweden had signed up to join EMU, the Swedish government simply unilaterally assumed a British/Danish-style EMU opt-out. The government claimed that its right to do this had been recognised by its EU partners, but the legal status of its commitment became a moot point after the referendum.[4] Consequently, when EMU was launched Finland became the only Nordic state to participate fully in all aspects of the EU (Table 17.3). It joined the Euro without a referendum and against the opposition of the Centre Party, the government arguing that the membership referendum had already cleared the way for EMU.

By the mid-2000s, participation in European integration thus entailed something different in each of the four cases. All participate in the core of the EU's activity: the Single Market and its flanking policies. All participate in Schengen, although Denmark only does so on an intergovernmental basis. Norway also participates in some of the EU's international operations, but only on an ad hoc basis of invitation after decisions have been reached. Only Finland participates fully in what is sometimes called the EU's only fully federalist arrangement – EMU. The next section turns briefly to the consequences of this variable geometry.

The effects of differentiated integration: consensus or adversary politics?

In the mid-1990s, the literature on variations in European integration began to expand, driven primarily by debates about the UK's role in the EU and the potential consequences of enlargement to the former communist states. One review classified the alternatives as 'multi-speed', 'variable geometry' and *à la carte* integration (Stubb 1996). The Nordic experience with European integration suggests that there are indeed a number of options for states to participate in the EU on bases other than full participation in all policy areas. However, whereas the policy debates in the 1990s sought to classify different and distinct *types* of integration, the point here has been precisely *not* to settle the issues once and for all. Most of these agreements are seen as more or less temporary arrangements; as second-best solutions that 'will do' for a while. The Nordic states simply participate in some of the EU's policy areas to different extents, some through more formal arrangements than others. Denmark's formal opt-outs and Norway's non-membership stand at one end of the spectrum; Sweden's self-proclaimed EMU opt-out and Norway's ad hoc 'buy-ins' on the other. The remainder of this section turns briefly to the workings of these arrangements, and their implications for politics and policy at both the state and the EU-level.

First, in terms of the effects of European integration on domestic politics, the most striking development is the relatively low salience of the European question in day-to-day politics. Although all four states feature relatively strong Eurosceptic parties and questions about European integration flare up on a more or less regular basis, the mainstream political parties have successfully disentangled EU questions and national coalition politics. In Norway, no government has ruled without the support (direct or indirect) of Eurosceptic parties since the 1980s, and it has not been uncommon for minority or coalition government to rely on Eurosceptic parties for support in the other three states either. Given the relatively high percentages of Eurosceptic voters, domestic party politics has been surprisingly bereft of EU issues in all four states.

Second, the effect of variable geometry on domestic policy has been remarkably limited, or at least remarkably un-disruptive. Academic analyses and government reports (national and EU) regularly document evidence of widespread 'Europeanisation' across the board in all fours states, including Norwegian policy sectors that are not covered by the EEA agreement (Claes and Tranøy 1999; Emerson et al. 2002).[5] But political contestation is generally limited. For example, central banks in Norway, Sweden and Denmark all operate in accordance with the principles that guide the European Central Bank (ECB); both formal mandates and informal norms are closely aligned with those of the EU and draw on similar ideas and concepts. At the same time the EU remains far removed from the most salient political issues in domestic politics, such as redistribution and the welfare state, the organisation of public services, and (at least on the far right) immigration. When EU-related issues are contested, the response tends to be a quest for compromise. The most dramatic example came in April 2011, when the Norwegian Labour Party conference defeated the leadership and instructed the governing party not to implement the third EU postal directive. The core arguments were related to welfare and solidarity questions the national level: maintenance of local post offices, service quality and job security. If this 'veto' were carried through, the consequence might be the termination of the EEA agreement. At the time, however, both the Prime Minister and policy analysts expected that drawn-out negotiations would produce a face-saving compromise.

Third, the other side of the coin is the effect of Nordic Euroscepticism and variable geometry on EU policy. While the effects in each individual sector might be limited – Danish and Swedish participation is hardly crucial to the success (or otherwise) of EMU – the cumulative effect of a series of countries opting in and out of policy areas has been an EU system that is somewhat less homogeneous that it looked in the 1980s. The question in terms of European union or disunion is: does this matter? The Nordic arrangements seem to add up to a strategy that might be describes as 'homogeneity where necessary, heterogeneity where possible'. All four states participate in the EU single market, have reformed their competition laws and policies in line with the EU regime, and regularly score top results on the Commission's score cards for implementation.[6] So far, no government has sought the kind of clash with the European Commission or EFTA Surveillance Authority that might precipitate a serious crisis over a policy issue (all crises have been over membership of treaty ratification); there have been no episodes comparable to the 1996 'beef crisis' in the UK (see also Chapter 16 by Norton). The most likely candidate for this kind of crisis remains non-EU member Norway: if a government decides not to implement a new EU directive (e.g. the above-mentioned postal directive) there is no precedent to guide the outcome, and the potential implications of the treaty rules are hotly debated.[7]

Fourth, however, the effect on *EU politics* is perhaps the most important and dramatic aspect of Nordic contestation of European integration. The requirement that all new treaties must be supported by a supermajority of the Danish parliament or ratified by referendum imposes clear limits on the scope for dramatic steps forward in European integration. Something similar holds for decisions that require unanimity, since in some cases Nordic governments might simply not be able to deliver their consent. The most dramatic example in 2011 was the effect of the Finnish election on the EU's effort to build a rescue package for Greece, when the electoral success of the Eurosceptic True Finns threatened to derail the process (and in the end the Finns secured a deal on collateral that differed somewhat from the other Eurozone member states).

Conclusion: sovereignty, solidarity and variable geometry

Although the Nordic states' experience with European integration reinforces many of the central themes of this book – the story set out in this chapter has certainly been characterised by fraught consensus, compromise, crises and contestation – this also points to a different trade-off between sovereignty and solidarity than many of the states on the continent face. In the Nordic context, sovereignty and solidarity have been two sides of the same coin: most parties that equate sovereignty with democracy *at the national level* also emphasise that this is important in order to defend solidarity in the form of the (national) welfare state. The trade-off is thus between *integration* and *solidarity*, not between sovereignty and solidarity. The central issue in all four states has been how to combine substantial participation in European integration on one hand with sovereignty *and* solidarity on the other. A large number of voters and parties have seen European integration as a straight trade-off between national and EU-level decision making, on issues from agriculture to defence and from competition policy to public service delivery. This has limited the pro-EU parties' room for manoeuvre, even when they make up majority governments. Consequently all four states have sought to establish a degree of consensus, often centred on improvised compromises designed as temporary fixes that have developed into solid institutions over time. Nordic variable geometry does not point so much to a theory of tension or disunion, let alone disintegration, as to a basis for theorising about how states manage differences in their relationships with the EU.

Notes

1. For the sake of simplicity the term EU is used also to include the European Economic Community before the Maastricht Treaty entered into force in November 1993, except where reference is only to the pre-Maastricht EEC.
2. If the Greenland's decision, by referendum in 1982, to leave the EEC is counted, the total is twenty-one. See Knudsen (2008). At the time of writing it was not clear whether ratification of Icelandic membership might be by parliamentary vote or referendum.
3. Norway (and Iceland) takes part in most Council meetings that are Schengen relevant, but without voting rights.
4. For a good review of Sweden's EMU policy see e.g. "The Swedish Referendum and the Euro", *House of Commons Research Paper 03/68*, 15 September 2003.

5. In 2009 an independent Norwegian Review Committee was appointed to carry out a research-based root-and-branch review of Norway's relationship with the EU (published 17 January 2012 as *NOU 2012:2 Utenfor og innenfor*). This prompted a Council review of the EU's relationship with the EFTA states published as *Council conclusions on EU relations with EFTA countries*, 14 December 2010.
6. See the European Commissions yearly reports, e.g. *Internal Market Scoreboard December 2010*.
7. The optimistic reading of the EEA treaty is that if Norway uses its right to reserve itself against the new directive only the relevant part of the EEA treaty will be suspended and the Single Market operate as usual in all other respects; a more pessimistic reading suggests that EU member states might retaliate under the reciprocity clause by closing their postal (or communications!) markets to Norway, or even that EU might use its right to terminate the EEA treaty. Both trade unions and government offices published some of their legal advice on the internet.

Bibliography

Andersen, S.S. and N. Sitter (2006) 'Differentiated Integration: What Is It and How Much Can the EU Accommodate?', *Journal of European Integration*, 28:4, 313–330.

Aylott, N. (2002) 'Let's Discuss this Later: Party Responses to Euro-Divisions in Scandinavia', *Party Politics*, 8:4 (441–461).

Aylott, N. (2008) 'Softer but Strong: Euroscepticism and Party Politics in Sweden', in P. Taggart and A. Szczerbiak (eds) *The Comparative Party Politics of Euroscepticism* (Oxford: Oxford University Press).

Batory, A. and N. Sitter (2004) 'Cleavages, Competition, and Coalition-building: Agrarian Parties and the European Question in Western and Eastern Europe', *The European Journal of Political Research*, 43:3, 521–544.

Bjørklund, T. (1982) 'The Demand for Referendum: When Does it Arise and when Does It Succeed?', *Scandinavian Political Studies*, 5:3, 237–259.

Christensen, D.A. (1996) 'The Left-Wing Opposition in Denmark, Norway and Sweden: Cases of Euro-Phobia?', *West European Politics*, 19:3, 525–546.

Christensen, D.A. (1998), 'Foreign Policy Objectives: Left Socialist Opposition in Denmark, Norway and Sweden', *Scandinavian Political Studies*, 21:1, 51–70.

Claes, D.H. and B. S. Tranøy (1999) *Utenfor, annerledes og suveren? Norge under EØS-avtalen* (Bergen: Fagbokforlaget).

Eliassen, K.A. and N. Sitter (2003), 'Ever Closer Co-operation? The Limits of the "Norwegian" Method' of European Integration', *Scandinavian Political Studies*, 26:2, 125–144.

Emerson, M., M. Vahl and S. Woolcock (2002) *Navigating by the Stars: Norway, the European Economic Area and the European Union* (Brussels: the Centre for European Policy Studies).

Frøland, H. O. (1998) 'Ambiguous Interests: Norway and the West European Market Formations 1959–62', *Arena Working Paper*, 25.

Karvonen, L. (1994) 'Christian Parties in Scandinavia: Victory over the Windmills?', in David Hanley (ed.) *Christian Democracy in Europe: A Comparative Perspective* (London: Pinter).

Knudsen, A.-C. K. (2008) 'Euroscepticism in Denmark', in P. Taggart and A. Szczerbiak (eds) *The Comparative Party Politics of Euroscepticism* (Oxford: Oxford University Press).

Madeley, J. (1994) 'The Antinomies of Lutheran Politics: The Case of Norway's Christian People's Party', in D. Hanley (ed.) *Christian Democracy in Europe: A Comparative Perspective* (London: Pinter).

Pettersen, A., A. T. Jenssen and O. Listhaug (1996) 'The 1994 Referendum in Norway: Continuity and Change', *Scandinavian Political Studies*, 19:3, 257–281.

Rauino, T. (2008) 'The Difficult Task of Opposing Europe: The Finnish Party Politics of Euroscepticism' in P. Taggart and A. Szczerbiak (eds) *The Comparative Party Politics of Euroscepticism* (Oxford: Oxford University Press).

Ryden, L. L. (2000) *Ett Svenskt Dilemma: Socialdemokraterna, Centren och EG-Frågan 1975–1994* (Göteborg: Avhandlingar från Historiska institutionen i Göteborg).

Saglie, J. (2000a) 'Between Opinion Leadership and 'Contract of Disagreement': The Norwegian Labour Party and the European issue (1988–1994), *Scandinavian Political Studies*, 23:2, 93–113.

Saglie, J. (2000b) 'Values, Perceptions and European Integration: The Case of the Norwegian 1994 Referendum', *European Union Politics*, 1:2, 227–249.

Sitter, N. (2008) 'The European Question and the Norwegian Party System since 1961: The Freezing of a Modern Cleavage or Contingent Opposition?' in P. Taggart and A. Szczerbiak (eds) *The Comparative Party Politics of Euroscepticism* (Oxford: Oxford University Press).

Siune, K. (1993) 'The Danes Said NO to the Maastricht Treaty: The Danish EC Referendum of June 1992', *Scandinavian Political Studies*, 16:1, 93–103.

Stubb, A. (1996) "A Categorization of Differentiated Integration", *Journal of Common Market Studies*, 34:2, 283–295.

Svåsand, L. and U. Lindström (1996) 'Scandinavian Parties and the European Union', in J. Gaffney (ed.) *Political Parties and the European Union* (London: Routledge).

Svensson, P. (1994) 'The Danish Yes to Maastricht and Edinburgh: The EC Referendum of May 1993', *Scandinavian Political Studies*, 17:1, 69–82.

Svensson, P. (2002) 'Five Danish Referendums on the European Community and Union: A Critical Assessment of the Franklin Thesis', *European Journal of Political Research*, 41:5, 733–750.

Taggart, P. and A. Szczerbiak (2008) (eds), *The Comparative Party Politics of Euroscepticism*, two volumes (Oxford: Oxford University Press).

Tiilikainen, T. (1996) 'Finland and the European Union', in Lee Miles (ed.), *The European Union and the Nordic Countries* (London: Routledge).

Von Beyme, K. (1985) *Political Parties in Western Democracies* (Aldershot: Gower).

Widfeldt, A. (1996) 'Sweden and the EU: Implications for the Swedish Party System', in Lee Miles (ed.) *The European Union and the Nordic Countries* (London: Routledge).

18
Southern Europe and the 'Trade Off': Architects of European Disunion?

Martin J. Bull

The global economic downturn and ensuing Eurozone crisis has focused attention on the traditional 'periphery' of the European Union (the 'old' southern Europe of Portugal, Italy, Greece and Spain) and revived an age-old fear that Europe, in the words of the *Financial Times*, 'is economically and politically divided between a northern hard core and a flaky southern fringe' (quoted in Verney, 2009: 1). Excepting Ireland (which might be described as a 'periphery' of the North), the Eurozone crisis stood out both for the public indebtedness of the four 'old' south European states and the collapse in confidence of the markets in their capacities to repay those debts.[1] With the Greek government close to default on its debts in the summer of 2010, the Eurozone, in a first-ever bailout of a debt-laden country, negotiated a €110 billion rescue package. This was followed, in late 2010, by Ireland, and, in April 2011, Portugal. This coincided with a re-emergence of the Greek crisis when it was evident that the bailout was failing, requiring a further €109 billion rescue package on new (easier) terms and conditions described by Jean-Claude Trichet (then head of the European Central Bank), as a form of expected 'selective default' of temporary duration; a package, however, that took months to negotiate and was not accepted until November 2011. During this process, the fear of contagion became real as the economies of Spain and Italy came under severe pressure in the autumn of 2011, with Italy in the subsequent months entering a dramatic crisis of borrowing, which took the crisis to an entirely different level (since the size of the Italian economy and its public debt make it effectively not subject to rescue).

This situation, not unanticipated in some general approaches to European integration (e.g. Dyson and Marcussen 2010), prompted a political crisis at two levels. The first was in economic governance in the European Union (EU), resulting from an inability to provide decisive leadership and management of the Greek and southern European situations and therefore the Eurozone overall. The second level was the domestic. March 2011 saw the resignation of Portugal's Prime Minister, José Sócrates. Shortly after, the Spanish Prime Minister, José Zapatero, announced that he would stand down and elections in November saw the Socialists effectively wiped out on the back of a massive centre-right majority on a programme of austerity. In October, the Greek Prime Minister, George Papandreou, having caused a veritable political storm by unexpectedly announcing that the second rescue package he had agreed with the Eurozone leaders would be subject to a referendum before it could become formally accepted (a position that was subsequently rapidly abandoned), was forced to resign and was replaced by an economist, Lucas Papademos. In November, the crisis of market confidence enveloping Italy took with it the Berlusconi government, Berlusconi being replaced by a non-party government of technocrats headed by an economist and former EU Commissioner, Mario Monti.

This chapter views the southern European enlargement in the 1980s and the EU–southern European relationship as based on a form of 'trade-off' between 'solidarity' on the one hand and 'sovereignty' on the other. It suggests that, while the trade-off appeared to work well until the launch of the single currency in a period which might be described as a 'golden age' in the EU–Mediterranean relationship (e.g. Tsoulakis 2006), in the 2000s it began to deteriorate through a combination of different factors (launch of the Euro, enlargement, reform of cohesion policy, prospective reform of the common agricultural policy, economic crisis) of which the Eurozone crisis became the most critical reflection. This has produced a third level of crisis (between the EU and the southern European states themselves) that could produce new forms of solidarity and discipline embodying much tighter restrictions on economic sovereignty than in the past.

'Solidarity' and southern Europe: rise and fall

It could be argued that the southern European democracies, in contrast with their northern counterparts, have been characterised by using European integration in three complementary ways: first, to support and reinforce their (at one time) fragile democracies; second, to obtain 'solidarity' through funds to support their economic development; and, third, to help resolve problems and impose fiscal and economic discipline where the political classes proved unable or unwilling (the EU as a welcome 'external constraint'). In short, the membership of the EU involved a 'trade off', which went to the heart of the *raison d'être* of the integration process: democratic consolidation and solidarity (in the form of cohesion) in return for better economic and fiscal discipline, which itself would be assisted through European economic rules. For existing members, entry of the southern European states would be a mixed blessing. One the one hand, it would provide greater security on its southern border, while, on the other, it introduced peripheral economies, which might constrain European Community ambitions into being no more than a free trade area; hence, the importance of cohesion and convergence policies to the European framework.

It is therefore no surprise to find that the introduction, development and extension of cohesion policies mirrored the enlargement of the EU (although even in the period before the launch of a regional policy in 1973, Italy benefited from a form of spatial policy through the European Social Fund). The introduction of regional policy and the creation of the European Regional Development Fund (ERDF) that followed two years later was a product of the deal negotiated over accession of the UK and Ireland. The Mediterranean enlargement of the 1980s (Greece – 1981, Spain and Portugal – 1986) led to the adoption of the Integrated Mediterranean Programmes, larger funding and the creation of a Cohesion Fund. This fund began to operate in 1993, the budget rising to about 3 per cent of the overall EU budget by 1999, with the 1995 Scandinavian enlargement leading to the adoption of further objectives particularly relevant to these countries (regions with sparse populations). In the course of the new millennium, the Fund was expanded and reformed again (in relation to budgetary redistribution and policy substance) with the entry of new members from the former communist states in 2004 and 2007. By 2010, cohesion policy was the largest item in the EU budget, surpassing even the Common Agricultural Policy (Begg 2010: 77).

As Begg (2010: 78) argues, cohesion (and specifically territorial cohesion), while 'tending to be equated operationally with regional divergence in economic indicators, such as GDP per head, and (in a less easily calibrated way) social conditions.... is ultimately a political notion'. Its political nature was seen not just in its nature as a goal (that the nation-states should 'converge') and in the negotiations at different phases that led to its implementation, but also in convergence being a fundamental part of the longer-term goal of economic and monetary union. This was in the form of a *quid pro quo*, which was made explicit as early as 1973 in a European Communities *Report on the Regional Problems in the Enlarged Community* where it was stated that: 'No Member States can be expected to support the economic and monetary disciplines of Economic and Monetary Union without Community solidarity involved in the effective use of such instruments; equally Member States must be prepared to accept the disciplines of Economic and Monetary Union as a condition of this Community support' (quoted in Manzella and Mendez 2009: 9). For this reason, despite the fact that cohesion policy, over the years, developed multiple goals that were not easily reconcilable (equity, solidarity, sustainable development, competitiveness, good governance) the redistributive bias towards less prosperous states was consistent, and led critics to argue that the policy, in fact, amounted to little more than a form of 'side payment' to certain countries to 'buy' their support for other objectives: 'In this... view, the Cohesion Fund could be seen as the price extracted by the (then) four cohesion countries – Greece, Ireland, Portugal, Spain – for acquiescing in the establishment of economic and monetary union' (Begg 2010: 82).

If this was a 'trade off' there can be little doubt that, at least in the initial period, the southern European states reaped its benefits. Their fledgling democracies were consolidated under the EU umbrella, and their economies underwent a process of opening out and change, supported by significant financial assistance from agricultural, regional development, training and cohesion programmes. Empirical analyses up to 2000–01 concluded that convergence of the Mediterranean countries with the European average had occurred (notably after 1986) and that structural funds had had a clear impact on this process (Beugelsdijk and Eijffinger 2005; Barry 2003).

In the millennium, however, the issue of solidarity with southern Europe was gradually (if not inevitably) called into question, largely as a result of the enlargement to Central and East Europe that occurred. In 2004, eight Central and East European former communist countries (Czech Republic, Estonia, Hungary, Latvia, Lithuania, Poland, Slovakia and Slovenia) and two more Mediterranean countries (Malta and Cyprus) entered the EU, and 2007 saw the addition of Bulgaria and Romania. The accession of these 12 countries transformed the nature of the EU and specifically its periphery, widening regional disparities considerably. In 2005, the 14 regions with the lowest GDP per head were from three countries: Bulgaria, Poland and Romania. Moreover, countries such as Poland entered with large agricultural sectors.

The Cohesion Fund was reformed (in line with the Lisbon Agenda's aims) for the period 2007–13 and, while southern European states were still allocated substantial allocations of structural funds, the likelihood of this into the post-2013 period is unclear. Depending on how the funds are allocated, countries such as Italy and Spain may find themselves in the positions of being net contributors. More generally, European regional policy faces dilemmas in relation to member-state expectations, which may not bode well for southern Europe, as the debate on the future of structural funds suggests. For the least prosperous member states, convergence is about raising GDP per head nationally, and the most effective method is to invest in growth poles with the greatest returns (e.g. in capital regions such as Warsaw or Bratislava); for more prosperous member states, the concern is more with territorial imbalance both across Europe and specifically within their own states. Consequently, 'an especially contentious issue is how to interpret the Treaty commitment to cohesion for richer states; or to put the question starkly: should the EU try to deal with regional problems in eastern Germany, northern England or the Mezzogiorno, or should they be left to the Member States?' (Begg 2008: 8). Finally, 2013 will mark the year when the member states, which acceded in 2004 and 2007, will be entitled to full support from the Common Agricultural Policy (the European Council having decided on this delay back in 2002). In short, by 2011 solidarity with the European southern periphery, as traditionally defined and implemented, was becoming a thing of the past.

'Discipline' or restricted sovereignty and southern Europe: rise and fall

If 'solidarity' was part of a trade off, the other side involved accepting new economic rules related to sound money and financial discipline. These were first represented in the five Maastricht criteria, which had to be met for any nation-state to participate in the single currency. The benefits involved in such a trade off were: removal of exchange rate uncertainty; greater transparency in relative prices across national borders; reduction of transaction costs; lower inflation; and falling risk premia in interest rates, leading to long-term gains in trade and growth and a consolidation of public finances. The challenges involved accepting restrictions on one's economic sovereignty, specifically in the form of an economic regime, which ruled out nation-states recovering loss of competitiveness through devaluing the exchange rate and made sound public finances essential. The trade off was hardly questioned in southern Europe, especially as it was recognised that a model of the economy based on competitive devaluations (which fuelled inflation and further devaluations) and large public sector deficits was unsustainable in the long-term (Bardone and Reitano 2009: 37–8). Yet, while the first would be imposed by the single currency itself (i.e. a sovereign currency was removed), the second required action by the nation-states both *before* (and as a condition of) entry to the single currency and *after* as an economic model based on sound finance.

In view of the likely benefits, as well as the negative implications of being left out of the 'core' single currency group, the southern European states were more than willing to accept the external constraint in the 1990s and to use it domestically (even by technocrats against hesitant politicians) to drive through the measures necessary to bring about fiscal adjustment (Dyson and Featherstone, 1996). Consequently, and against expectations, all four of the south European states met the Maastricht criteria and entered the single currency (Italy, Spain and Portugal in 1999 and Greece in 2001). Yet, the nature of this achievement did not in and of itself guarantee that these countries' fiscal adjustment would continue into the post-entry phase, for three reasons.

First, rigid as the Maastricht criteria were, they 'gave more emphasis to fiscal consolidation rather than fiscal sustainability' (Blavoukos and Pagoulatos 2008: 233) and such consolidation could be achieved through methods (especially raising tax revenue), which avoided the more difficult to achieve structural reforms essential to the foundation for sustainability in the future. Moreover, the one criterion which might have provided a better foundation for future progress (reducing the public sector debt to 60 per cent of GDP) was, in the run-up to the deadline, relaxed to 'a steady decrease of the public debt rate' (ibid., 250).

Second, since there was no supranational prescription for the means by which fiscal consolidation should be achieved it was left to the choice of the individual nation-states to develop their own approaches. While existing evidence suggested that 'budget consolidations relying too heavily on the revenue side by raising taxes rather than on the expenditure side by cutting spending are likely to be successful and sustainable' (ibid., 234), only in the case of Spain was a programme of fiscal consolidation based on a reduction in government expenditure and extensive structural reform (pensions reforms, labour market reforms, welfare reforms, privatisations) (ibid., 241–42; Royo 2009). In contrast, Portugal, Greece and Italy successfully achieved fiscal consolidation primarily through increasing tax revenue (and at least in one case through some creative accounting[2]) with little or no reduction in government primary expenditure and limited structural reforms – those which were begun (in Italy and Greece) remained partial and incomplete (Blavoukos and Pagoulatos 2008: 236–41; Torres 2009; Pagoulatos and Triantopoulos 2009; Bardone and Reitano 2009).

Third, once participation in the single currency was secured and once the currency was launched, the rules of the game changed somewhat. The (spirit of the) pre-entry implications about sustainability were meant to be enforced through the Stabilty and Growth Pact (SGP)'s Excessive Deficit Procedure for those countries in breach of the 3 per cent rule, and, in 2002, Portugal fell foul of this and had to enact urgent measures. However, shortly after, with the French and German economies similarly struggling but arguing for more flexibility in the policy, the rules effectively became 'softer' and the credibility of the SGP was undermined, thus reducing the pressure on the southern European states to continue with fiscal consolidation (see also Chapter 12 by Dyson).

As a consequence, fiscal consolidation was relaxed in Italy, Greece and Portugal, and structural reforms, where they had been commenced, were given less priority (where not abandoned). This situation was reflected in both the primary balances (in the cases of Greece and Portugal dropping into deficit for some years) and general governmental balances (with all three either breaching or coming very close to breaching the Stability Pact's threshold of 3 per cent of GDP), situations usually met through one-off corrective measures. In contrast, Spain managed to run consistently healthy surplus primary balances and to keep within the Stability Pact's threshold, actually producing surpluses in two years (Blavoukos and Pagoulatos, 2008: 242–44). Public debt as a percentage of GDP remained largely unchanged in Greece, Portugal and Italy, while it was brought down in Spain.

At the same time, there were two common effects of operating within a single currency. First, due largely to high rates of inflation and the strengthening of the Euro, there was a decline in their competitiveness (which could not be offset through devaluing the currency), reflected in a worsening state of their current accounts. The average figures for the decade 1999–2008 (in per cent of GDP) were, for Spain, –5.90 (against –1.73 for the previous decade), for Greece –8.75 (against –3.28), for Italy –1.26 (against 0.49) and for Portugal –9.13 (against –2.01), with the average for the Euro area 0.31 (against 0.26 for the previous decade) (Le Cacheux 2010: 51). In theory, this should have led to a reduction in wage rates and the development of a more flexible labour market in order to maintain the GDP growth rate and employment levels. However, second, the single nominal interest rate set by the European Central Bank (ECB) for all Euro area countries brought down real interest rates (i.e. accounting for inflation), helping to boost economic growth by making investment and debt less costly (and providing an alternative to the enforcement of wage restraint). The average real long-term interest rates for 1999–2008 were 1.16 in Spain (against 5.03 for the previous decade 1989–98), 0.66 in Greece (against 5.58), 2.22 in Italy (against 6.18) and 1.55 in Portugal (against 6.76), and were 2.2 for the Eurozone as a whole (Le Cacheux 2010: 51). This meant that, despite the loss of competitiveness, growth was able to be maintained through easier credit (reinforced by liberalisation of banking regulations under the single market programme) and more manageable deficits. Nevertheless, Italy and Portugal were sluggish compared with Greece and Spain, where average growth rates for the decade 1999–2008 were 3.54 per cent in Spain and 4.15 per cent in Greece (in contrast with 1.70 per cent in Portugal and 1.36 per cent in Italy, and an average growth rate of 2.12 per cent for the Euro area overall) (Le Cacheux, 2010: 50).[3] However, gross national income showed convergence with the Euro area average in these years for Spain, Greece and Italy, and unemployment fell and was kept at the Euro area average, except for Spain (which nonetheless had come from a high figure of 20 per cent in the mid-1990s).

In short, this combination (non-structural approach to fiscal consolidation, relaxing of the rules and easy credit) laid the basis for increased (or over) borrowing by governments, banks and households and thus a rise in demand and potential overheating of the economies. In Blavoukos and Pagoulatos' words (2008: 242), 'Once membership was achieved, the ... [four south European states] ... could potentially free ride on the common currency's credibility without being individually penalized by financial markets.' Low interest rates contributed to a boom based on private consumption (and in countries undergoing rapid growth such as Spain, a housing bubble), masking at the same time other economic weaknesses (low productivity, growth based in areas not exposed to international competition, decline in competitiveness, high labour costs, family indebtedness, unresolved structural issues). The Euro moreover helped to sustain severe demand imbalances through German banks lending to the southern European states and creating demand for its own exports. This exporting of credit dependence increased the divergence between German surpluses and south European deficits (Featherstone 2011: 200). As Tombazos (2011: 34) argues, '....the euro, in the short term encouraged the expansion of some "peripheral" economies, where the markets failed sufficiently to enforce "obligatory reforms" in the labour market and in the public sector...The financial markets, instead of imposing "discipline", displayed a greater propensity for immediate and uncertain profits'. The four south European states were therefore ill-prepared to cope with the world economic downturn in 2008 and the sovereign debt crisis, which began in 2010.

Crisis and southern Europe: new forms of solidarity and restrictions on sovereignty

The sovereign debt crisis of southern Europe was dramatic, at the heart of which was a collapse in market confidence in their capacities to repay their public debts, with Greece, Portugal (and Ireland) requiring bailouts, and the Greek bailout failing and requiring, therefore, a second. The management of the crisis by EU and Eurozone leaders was characterised by a mixture of weakness, division and procrastination, thus exacerbating the financial plight of the Eurozone (Underhill 2011). The first Greek bailout, when it came, failed largely because it loaned Greece €110bn at *market rates* as a means of tiding the country over until it could borrow on the markets again. The delay on negotiating the second bailout, the evident divisions in the German political position combined with the effects of successive downgrades of the crediting ratings of the four southern European countries by the international ratings agencies (Standard & Poors, Moody's, Fitch) were a recipe for a further collapse of confidence, as well as for contagion. Spain and notably Italy were dragged into difficulties, with Italy's situation changing the whole nature of the debate. The run on the Italian markets began in August 2011 and was characterised by dramatic increases in the 'bond spread' (the difference between the German and Italian 10-year bond yields), which touched historical highs in November (in November the Italian bond yield surpassed 7 per cent, the threshold at which bailouts for Greece and Portugal had been necessitated) and suggested that the markets had serious doubts about Italy's capacity to repay its public debt.

European and international elites responded to the crisis in two ways, both of which were attempts in vain to reassure the markets. The first was to try to prevent contagion by transforming the bailout fund into a much more ambitious financial instrument (European Financial Stability Facility [EFSF]), which would have the power to buy bonds of struggling debtor countries, to take pre-emptive action before a debt crisis developed too far and to provide loans to Eurozone countries to support their banks. Yet, once the crisis reached an economy of the size of Italy's (where its public debt amounted to approximately a third of all Eurozone debt), it was clear that no EFSF 'firewall 'would be big enough for that. Worse, by late November, contagion was beginning to affect both France and Germany, the core countries of the Eurozone, with France being warned by the credit-rating agency Fitch that it could lose its triple-A credit rating if the debt crisis deepened, and Germany, on 23 November, finding investors shunning its bonds, as it was forced to retain nearly €2.4 billion of a planned €6 billion sale (and subsequently faced with yields on its 10-year bonds higher than those of the UK).

The second response was to drive through a spate of emergency austerity budgets at the national levels, these involving a mixture of tax increases and draconian cuts to the public sector. These emergency budgets were not only demanded of the 'errant' states by the EU, ECB and International Monetary Fund (IMF), but were also closely overseen. In situations where national governments appeared incapable of carrying them through (Greece, Italy), the lack of political confidence at the European and international levels in them was made sufficiently apparent as to exacerbate the country's market position, the governments fell and were replaced by technocrats. Although there were few alternatives, critics were quick to condemn the EU for 'rushing to plunge the euro area peripheral economies into recession ... ' (Tombazos 2011: 34), which, of course, would exacerbate and not alleviate their public debt problems.

It is clear that the depth and protracted nature of the crisis was not just caused by the 'errant' behaviour of the southern European states (as well as Ireland) and EU 'mismanagement' of the crisis. It was also an inevitable consequence of structural flaws in the Eurozone edifice, and especially those related to the nature and management of sovereign debt. Adair Turner (2011), adopting Charles Goodhart's distinction between 'fully sovereign debt' (where fully sovereign bonds are issued by a sovereign authority which is also a currency issuing authority), and 'subsidiary sovereign debt' (where the bonds are issued by political units which are not themselves currency issuing authorities), argues that the Eurozone nations were, with the single currency, transformed from fully to subsidiary sovereign bond issuers. However, the institutional precautions necessary to offset the greater risks this change embodied were not acted upon. Fully sovereign debt can, at the extreme, be monetised. This carries with it risks (inflation, currency depreciation) that are of a more manageable nature than default. Subsidiary sovereign debt, on the other hand, carries with it a nominal and real repayment risk, and where, as in southern Europe, situations arise where the nominal debt cannot be re-paid, it cannot (under the existing arrangements) be monetised. The European governance framework separates responsibility for monetary stabilisation (European level) from fiscal, invariably distributive policies (at member-state level). While this placed it in a position to manage the 2008–09 crisis (which was about financial liquidity), it could not deal with the 2010–11 sovereign debt crisis where member state autonomy had prevailed (Schelkle 2011: 381–2).[4] The Eurozone model, therefore, was highly ambivalent about 'bailouts' of errant states, excluding them on the one hand but failing to provide any effective instruments for dealing with those states on the other: 'the logic was of stability increasing the credibility of the arrangements' (Featherstone 2011: 202). Finally, to exacerbate matters, the banks were incentivised by regulation to become major investors in sovereign bonds, making it easier to continue issuing those bonds until unsustainable levels were met and thus increasing the risk to the banking system as a whole.

Yet, if these problems suggested obvious solutions, they were far from easy to introduce, largely for political reasons. The idea of Eurobonds and the European Central Bank acting as the lender of last resort, proposed formally by the President of the European Commission was flatly rejected by Germany both for fear of inflation (embedded in the German psyche from the 1920s) and 'moral hazard' (that southern European nations would fear indebtedness even less in the knowledge that their debts would in the end be bought out by somebody else). The crisis therefore raised a fundamental issue of EU governance, which the richer nations (and specifically, Germany) had been avoiding until then: whether European Monetary Union (EMU) should be a 'debt union' based on solidarity and burden-sharing, in which the richer nations would guarantee the borrowings of the poorer nations. It had proved elusive in the original model, Dyson describing 'the prospect of people being asked to make sacrifices for others with whom there was a weak sense of identity' as the Achille's heel of the EU (cited in Featherstone 2011: 211). The dilemma, therefore, was to find an appropriate set of arrangements, which would satisfy different member-states and the electorates their governments represented. Such arrangements could only be based on closer ties between the Eurozone economies entailing new forms of solidarity in exchange for restrictions on national economic sovereignty, e.g. binding limits on borrowing. The profligacy of the southern European states, in short, had exposed the cracks in the Eurozone edifice and was forcing a significant reform of European economic governance as a consequence.

Yet, such moves would not only have to overcome the deep reservations of the peoples of the richer nations towards burden-sharing in
relation to southern Europe, it would also have to address reservations
from the periphery, for whom it was not clear how acceptable European
'tutelage' (depending on the form it took) would be in the long-term.
For Tombazos (2011: 41), 'Today the feeling in Greece is that the country
is now under occupation. The IMF, the European Commission and
the ECB not only dictate policy, but also oversee its implementation.
More generally, the attempt to tighten the supervision of nation states
by European bodies is perceived in southern Europe as an attempt of
the European core to place the European periphery under check.' The
Italian government, for example, overseeing one of the largest economies in the world, was, in the latter part of 2011, essentially placed
under a form of EU 'tutelage', being ordered to bring forward by a year
its goal of balancing the budget and being informed what measures
had to be incorporated in order to do so. And Berlusconi's supporters
did not hide their feelings that the centre right government had effectively been forced out of office through a collapse in confidence not just
of the markets but of Chancellor Merkel, President Sarkozy and other
European elites.

This raises the critical issue of whether we may be witnessing the
beginning of an unexpected 'falling out' between the peoples of
southern Europe and the European Union, and this during a time when
Europe generally is undergoing a shift in support for the EU from a
'permissive consensus' to a 'constraining dissensus' (Hooghe and Marks
2009). The peoples of southern Europe have (albeit with periodic exceptions, notably in relation to Greece) been fairly reliable and consistent
supporters of the integration process. The most recent detailed analyses
of Euroscepticism in southern Europe largely pre-dated the economic
crisis (Verney 2011a), and concluded that, in the period until then
(2008–09), southern Europe did not make up the mainstream drift
towards a 'constraining dissensus'. Nevertheless, the analyses also
revealed evidence of more nuanced forms of Euroscepticism in the past,
a rise in Euroscepticism in the 2000s and relatively high percentages of
those in some countries currently indifferent to, or ignorant, about the
EU. These findings suggested that there is the potential for negative
views about the EU to grow (Verney 2011b). The 2010 *Eurobarometer*
survey on popular attitudes to the Euro revealed that, apart from France,
only the four southern European states fell below the Eurozone average
of those who thought that having the Euro was a good thing for Europe,
even if the percentages were still high (from 61 per cent in Portugal to

65 per cent in Italy against an average of 65 per cent for the Eurozone as a whole) (Eurobarometer 2010: 10). True, the violent protests that have been witnessed in countries such as Greece and Italy have, until now, been directed primarily against the failings of their national governments. Yet, the severe austerity is effectively being imposed on these countries from above and it is not inconceivable for the protests to be directed against the EU in the future, the more the supranational level concerns itself not just with monitoring national governments' finances but regulating, if not dictating, their budgets. By the end of 2011, therefore, the southern European states faced a watershed: having lost the trust of their Eurozone counterparts, they could no longer expect to receive European financial solidarity without increased externally imposed discipline and restrictions on their economic sovereignty.

Conclusion

The 'golden era' that characterised the Mediterranean enlargement and the Mediterranean–EU relationship of the 1980s and 1990s has disappeared. The 'trade-off' between 'solidarity' and 'discipline' appeared to function well until the launch of the single currency, under the guise of the EU as an 'external constraint'. However, the particular mode of economic governance that developed under the single currency was (even if unwittingly) predicated on the idea that the 'external constraint' had, somehow, been 'internalised'. The flexibility this allowed, combined with the new challenges of operating in a single currency led the southern European states into a situation where they were poorly prepared for the world economic downturn that began in 2008. The result is a crisis in the EU–southern European relationship whose resolution has pulled the EU towards two opposing extremes: either towards some southern European states defaulting and exiting the Euro; or towards a debt union and full supranational economic governance. Whether a middle of the road route ('a fudge, well short of fiscal union' – Münchau 2011) is possible remains open to question, but all three scenarios signal a dramatic change in the EU–southern European relationship, and the definitive end of the golden era.

Acknowledgement

The author is grateful to Leonardo Morlino for his suggestions and advice.

Notes

1. And in stark contrast with other EU 'regional' groupings, albeit partly (but not only) because of the fragmentation within these groupings between Euro and non-Euro countries (see Dimitrov 2012; Sitter 2012).
2. An audit conducted in 2004 by a former Finance Minister, George Alogoskoufis, concluded that Greece had never, in fact, met the Maastricht criterion of the public deficit being within 3 per cent of GDP (Featherstone 2008).
3. The Portuguese economy, in fact, experienced a small boom before entering the single currency, based also on increasing indebtedness (Torres 2010: 56–9).
4. This heightened risk explains why, even though the aggregate Eurozone percentage of debt to GDP was, in 2011, lower than for the UK, United States or Japan, the average interest rate paid on its debt was much higher.

Bibliography

Bardone, L. and V.E. Reitano, 'Italy in the Euro Area: The Adjustment Challenge', in M. Buti (ed), *Italy in EMU: The Challenges of Adjustment and Growth* (Basingstoke: Palgrave).

Barry, F. (2003), 'Economic Integration and Convergence Processes in the EU Cohesion Countries', *Journal of Common Market Studies*, 41: 5: 897–921.

Begg, I. (2008), 'Cohesion in the EU', *CESifo Forum*, 1/2008: 3–9.

Begg, I. (2010), 'Cohesion or Confusion: A Policy Searching for Objectives', *Journal of European Integration*, 32: 1, January: 77–96.

Beugelsdijk, M. and S. C. W. Eijffinger (2005), 'The Effectiveness of Structural Policy in the European Union: An Empirical Analysis for the EU-15 in 1995–2001', *Journal of Common Market Studies*, 43: 1: 37–51.

Blavoukos, S. and G. Pagoulatos (2008), 'The Limits of EMU Conditionality: Fiscal Adjustment in Southern Europe', *Journal of Public Policy*, 28: 2, 229–53.

Dimitrov, V. (2012), 'The Central and East European Countries: From Weak Latecomers to Good Citizens of the Union', this volume.

Dyson, K. and K. Featherstone (1996), 'Italy and EMU as a *"vincolo esterno"*: empowering the technocrats, transforming the State, *South European Society and Politics*, 1 (2), Autumn.

Dyson, K. and M. Marcussen (2010), 'Transverse Integration in European Economic Governance: Between Unitary and Differentiated Integration', *Journal of European Integration*, 32: 1, January: 17–39.

Eurobarometer (2010), *The Euro Area 2010. Public Attitudes and Perceptions. Analytical Report* (Brussels: European Commission).

Featherstone, K. (2008), 'Greece and EMU: A Suitable Accommodation?', in K. Dyson (ed), *The Euro at Ten: Europeanization, Power and Convergence* (Oxford: Oxford University Press).

Featherstone, K. (2011), 'The Greek Sovereign Debt Crisis and EMU: A Failing State in a Skewed Regime', *Journal of Common Market Studies*, 49 (2): 193–217.

Hooghe, L. and G. Marks (2009), 'A Post-Functionalist Theory of Integration: From Permissive Consensus to Constraining Dissensus', *British Journal of Political Science*, 39: 1–23.

Le Cacheux, J. (2010), 'How to Herd Cats: Economic Policy Coordination in the Euro Zone in Tough Times', *Journal of European Integration*, 32: 1, January: 41–58.

Manzella, G.P. and C. Mendez (2009), 'The Turning Point of EU Cohesion Policy', Report Working Paper, ec.europa.eu/regional-policy, accessed 12 May 2011.

Münchau, W. (2011), 'Eurobonds and Fiscal Union Are The Only Way Out', *Financial Times*, 18 September.

Pagaloutos, G. and C. Triantopoulos (2009), 'The Return of the Greek Patient: Greece and the 2008 Global Financial Crisis', *South European Society and Politics*, 14 (1): 35–54.

Royo, S. (2009), 'After the Fiesta: The Spanish Economy Meets the Global Financial Crisis', *South European Society and Politics*, 14 (1), March: 19–34.

Schelkle, W. (2011), 'A Tale of Two Crises: the Euro Area in 2008/09 and in 2010', *European Political Science*, 10 (3), September: 375–83.

Sitter, N. (2012), 'The Nordic Countries: The Causes and Consequences of Variable Geometry', in J. Hayward and R. Wurzel (eds), *European Disunion: Between Sovereignty and Solidarity* (Basingstoke: Palgrave).

Tombazos, S. (2011), 'Centrifugal Tendencies in the Euro Area', *Journal of Contemporary European Studies*, 19 (1), March: 33–46.

Torres, F. (2009), 'Back to External Pressure: Responses to the Financial Crisis in Portugal', *South European Society and Politics*, 14 (1), March: 55–70.

Tsoulakis, L. (2006), 'The JCMS Lecture: Managing Diversity and Change in the European Union', *Journal of Common Market Studies*, 44: 1: 1–15.

Turner, A. (2011), 'Debt and deleveraging: Long term and short term challenges', Presidential Lecture, 21 November, Centre for Financial Studies, Frankfurt: http://www.fsa.gov.uk/pages/Library/Communication/Speeches/2011/1121_at.shtml (accessed 24 November 2011).

Underhill, G. (2011), 'Paved with Good Intentions: Global Financial Integration and the Eurozone's Response', *European Political Science* 10 (3), September: 366–74.

Verney, S. (2009) 'Flaky Fringe? Southern Europe Facing The Financial Crisis', *Southern European Society and Politics*, 14:1: 1–6.

Verney, S. (2011a) (ed), 'Euroscepticism in Southern Europe: A Diachronic Perspective', Special Issue, *South European Politics and Society*, 16 (1), March.

Verney, S. (2011b), 'Euroscepticism in Southern Europe: A Diachronic Perspective', *Southern European Society and Politics*, 16: 1, March: 1–29.

19
The Central and East European Countries: From Weak Latecomers to Good Citizens of the Union

Vesselin Dimitrov

This chapter investigates how the Central and East European countries (CEECs) dealt with the challenges posed by their membership of an increasingly complex, over-extended and crisis-prone European Union (EU). The chapter focuses on two key areas: the capacity of these states to coordinate EU policy, including the management of the affairs of the Union as a whole when acting as rotational presidencies of the Council of Ministers, and their ability to maintain fiscal discipline and thereby avoid being swept into the Euro Area crisis. The analysis in the chapter demonstrates that the CEECs were relatively effective in dealing with both of these challenges, albeit with significant variations. The key factor that enabled these states to act as 'good citizens' of the Union in these two areas was the relatively high coordination capacity of their national executives, forged mainly in the context of the post-communist transition. The 'good citizenship' of the CEECs was, however, of a rather passive kind. In terms of the unifying theme of this volume, sovereignty and solidarity, these states could be seen as practising a limited form of solidarity, focused primarily on keeping their own houses in reasonable order and on transposing Union legislation. They acted largely as policy-takers rather than policy-makers within the Union, and did not play a prominent role in the shaping of Union institutions (with the notable exception of Poland). This form of limited solidarity was something that they shared with the Nordic states and the United Kingdom, though the latter countries were more successful as policy-makers in certain specific areas, such as the environment in the case of the Nordic states and the single market in the case of the UK (see Chapters 14, 16 and 17 respectively by Wurzel, Norton and Sitter in this volume). An even more important difference between the CEECs, on one hand, and the Nordic states and the UK, on the other, was that the former tended to place a less emphatic and sustained emphasis on sovereignty than the latter: the role of Euroscepticism in their party systems was less marked, and their concerns about the path-dependent progress towards 'ever closer union', with the Economic and Monetary Union at its core, tended to centre on problems of temporal management rather than on normative issues or structural economic incompatibilities (Dyson 2007).

Based on its findings, particularly with regard to the relatively high coordination capacity of national executives in the CEECs and the ability of these states to act as 'good citizens' of the Union, this chapter argues for a fundamental reinterpretation of the relationship between the CEECs and the EU. It challenges the view that has prevailed in the extensive literature on this topic, which has stressed 'hierarchical' aspects of 'adaptation' to EU requirements and has paid special attention to the impact of EU 'conditionality' (Grabbe 2003). While some authors have studied the domestic obstacles to externally driven reform (Goetz 2006), for instance in regional policy (Brusis 2002; Hughes et al. 2004a, 2004b) or budgetary policy (Dimitrov et al. 2006), or have examined the impact of the organisation of national executives on the effectiveness of transposition (Zubek 2008), Falkner and Treib (2008: 208) are right in arguing that the field has been dominated by the 'external incentives' or the 'conditionality' model. According to this model, rule adoption has been successful due mainly to the membership incentive offered to the CEE applicants by the EU as an external actor (Falkner and Treib 2008: 294). Oft-cited arguments in support of this model include the pronounced asymmetry of power between the EU and the CEE applicant states; the weakness of institutional 'cores' in the post-communist countries, which are less likely to offer resistance to 'adaptive pressures' than are the deeply embedded institutions of most of the old (pre-2004) member states; evident crises of performance and legitimacy of domestic institutions, which encourage policy transfer and learning from foreign experiences; and the existence of institutional and policy 'voids', so that Europeanisation involves not so much adaptation but rather the *ab ovo* creation of new actors, institutions, and policies (Dimitrov et al. 2006; Goetz 2006). Furthermore, the EU adaptive pressures on the CEECs were considerably greater than in previous rounds of enlargement, such as the one involving Greece, Spain and Portugal, since the *acquis* had expanded very substantially since the 1980s, and the Union required the CEECs to adopt it in full (with some temporary derogations) before accession (Goetz 2006). The condition-ality model predicted that with the attainment of membership, compli-ance in the CEECs might be slowed down, halted or even reversed, as the Union would no longer be able to offer an 'external incentive' (Schimmelfennig and Sedelmeier 2004, 2005a, 2005b; Schimmelfennig et al. 2005; Falkner and Treib 2008).

The coordination of EU policy: backsliders or good citizens of the Union?

As members of the Union, the CEECs had to deal with a considerably wider range of functional pressures than they did as candidates. They needed not just to concern themselves with transposition, but to partic-ipate in the work of the Council of Ministers and the European Council across the full range of Union activities. They had to establish a commu-nications infrastructure linking their national capitals to Brussels and to other member states. They needed to organise their input into EU decision-making processes and respond to the rhythm of individual institutions. They had to ensure that national negotiation positions were prepared and defended, effectively and on time. In addition to coordinating their own relations with the Union, they faced the task of managing the affairs of the Union as a whole, as rotational presidents of the Council of Ministers.

While success is a problematic concept in regard to the national coordination of EU policy (Wright 1996; Sepos 2004), since the extent to which a member state is able to secure favourable policy outcomes depends on factors that are independent of the efficacy of the coordina-tion system – the decision rule in Council, the positions taken by other governments, and the size and weight of the member state in question – no consideration of coordination systems would be complete without a discussion of how well they perform.

A research project led by the author and Hussein Kassim carried out the first systematic comparative investigation of national EU policy coordination in the CEECs after their accession to the Union (Dimitrov and Kassim forthcoming). The research did find some evidence for the impact of the EU functional requirements outlined above on the CEECs, but these requirements tended to exert only general pressures on the national coordination systems. How governments responded to those pressures was governed primarily by domestic factors, and especially the coordination capacity of the national executives. This finding goes against the expectations of the conditionality model. On the other hand, it chimes with the literature on the national coordination of EU policy in the old (pre-2004) member states, 'the major theme' of which has been 'the tenacity of nationally rooted factors' (Kassim et al. 2000: 19).

In examining the impact of the CEECs' executive institutions, this chapter tests the hypothesis that centralised executives have greater success in the coordination of EU policy (investigated in this section) and in achieving fiscal discipline (explored in the next section) than decentralised executives. The configuration of national executives can best be analysed through the concept of the 'core executive', that is, 'all those organizations and structures which primarily serve to pull together and integrate government policies, or act as final arbiters within the executive of conflicts between different elements of the government machine' (Dunleavy and Rhodes 1990). Since its introduction by Dunleavy and Rhodes in 1990, this concept has shaped the study of central governments (Dunleavy and Rhodes 1990; Rhodes and Dunleavy 1995; Weller and Bakvis 1997; Dimitrov et al. 2006; Zubek 2008; Elgie 2011; Zubek 2011). Based on this concept, a comparative analysis by Zubek (2008) tested the hypothesis that centralised executives were more effective than decentralised ones in the transposition of the *acquis* in the CEECs before EU accession, and found strong evidence in support of the hypothesis. This chapter extends this hypothesis in two major directions: first, it applies it to the post-accession period, i.e. the period in which the CEECs had to cope with the demands stemming from membership of the Union, and secondly, it applies it to the national coordination of EU policy (which includes transposition but goes considerably beyond it – see above) and to fiscal policy. In relation to fiscal policy, Hallerberg (2004) has argued, based on the assumption that budgeting has the characteristics of a 'common-pool' problem, that centralised executive institutions are likely to produce lower fiscal deficits than decentralised institutions.

In the CEECs, the configuration of the national executives was shaped primarily by the experience of post-communist transition (Dimitrov et al. 2006). Under communism, political decision-taking had been the prerogative of the Communist Party, which had enforced its domination through its formations that run parallel to, and penetrated, all state, economic and societal institutions. Since the ruling Communist Parties had served as the chief integrative institutions within the political system, when these parties gave up their monopoly of power in 1989, the CEECs were left with a 'hollow crown' (Weller and Bakvis 1997) at the very top of their new democratic order. One of the key challenges for these countries after the transition to democracy was, therefore, to fill this 'hollow crown', i.e. establish effective government institutions, able to perform the policy coordination functions, which had previously been carried out by the Communist Parties.

In the period since the fall of communism, only some CEECs, such as Hungary and Poland, succeeded in establishing relatively stable centralised institutions within their executives. However, it is notable that even countries such as the Czech Republic and Bulgaria, which did not set up centralised institutions on a long-term basis, were nevertheless able to develop relatively effective centralised arrangements when faced with a serious crisis, such as the transition from a centrally planned to a capitalist market economy, or the challenging process of EU accession (Dimitrov et al. 2006). For instance, when negative reports from the European Commission on the Czech Republic's progress towards accession (1998, 1999) threatened the country's chances of joining the EU, the executive rose to the challenge by establishing a centralised Government Council for European Integration, headed by the Social Democratic Prime Minister Zeman. This centralisation was based mainly around the person of the prime minister, rather than on institutions. A central part in the system was played by career diplomat Telička, who held dual roles as head of the negotiation delegation (established in 1998) and as First Deputy Foreign Minister (1999–2003). The prime minister and Telička held weekly meetings and supervised the links between the Permanent Representation and the line ministers. This mechanism was successful in improving the effectiveness of the transposition process and in securing the Czech Republic's membership of the Union. Once accession had been guaranteed, the Council for European Integration abolished itself in 2003. However, the emphasis on transposition survived in the post-accession period (Kabele forthcoming; Dimitrov and Kassim forthcoming). To sum up, nearly all the CEECs developed quite a high executive coordination capacity in the post-communist period; that capacity was more firmly based in the countries with stable centralised institutions, though even in the countries where such institutions were not established on a long-term basis, centralisation could be developed in times of crisis, and, once the crisis had been resolved, could leave some positive legacies.

The varying success of the CEECs in developing stable centralised institutions in their executives after the fall of communism had a notable impact on their ability to deal effectively with the coordination of EU policy. Countries such as Poland and Hungary, with relatively stable centralised institutions, performed relatively well both in projecting their national interests at the EU level and in coordinating the work of the Union as rotating presidents (though the Hungarian presidency in the first half of 2011 was thrown off course by some specific party political factors). Slovenia and Estonia had less stable and sharply defined configurations than Poland and Hungary, but nevertheless tended to maintain sufficient centralised institutions in their executives to achieve relatively effective coordination. By contrast, the other CEE states – the Czech Republic, Latvia, Lithuania, Bulgaria and Romania – did not develop stable centralised institutions and therefore found it more difficult to project their national positions at the EU level and to run the affairs of the Union when their turn came to serve as presidents of the Council of Ministers (Dimitrov and Kassim forthcoming). These countries tried, in the run-up to their presidencies, to increase the coordination capacity of their executives through centralisation, but generally with mixed results. In the Czech Republic, for instance, a new 'Committee for the EU' headed by the prime minister – in fact a duplicate of the government – was created in preparation for the Presidency in 2009. Furthermore, a new Deputy Prime Minister for European Affairs became responsible for coordinating EU-related government activities, and his secretariat at the Office of the Government also became the secretariat of the Committee for the EU. However, just as the Czech Presidency was getting into its stride, the Topolánek government was brought down by a no-confidence vote. In the end, the only aspect of the Czech Presidency that was not subjected to criticism was its organisational capacity, which held up reasonably well despite the change of government (Kabele forthcoming; Dimitrov and Kassim forthcoming).

In the area of transposition, nearly all the CEECs proved themselves to be 'good citizens' of the Union. The research project led by the author and Kassim found that, contrary to the expectations of the conditionality model, the effectiveness of transposition in these countries did not change significantly once the 'external incentive' of membership was no longer operating (Dimitrov and Kassim forthcoming). This finding is supported by other research on post-accession transposition in the CEECs (Epstein and Sedelmeier 2008; Falkner and Treib 2008). Furthermore, research by Steunenberg and Toshkov (2009) indicates that the transposition records of the CEECs compare favourably with those of many of the pre-2004 member states, especially (but not only) the southern European states. The research project led by the author and Kassim found that there was a clear emphasis on transposition across the CEECs, as a coordination ambition and as a priority of their coordination systems. Particularly striking was the commitment and the record of the CEECs with decentralised executives in this regard. In the EU-15, those member states with good transposition records, such as Denmark and the UK, tended to be strongly centralised. Germany, by contrast, as an institutionally (and territorially) fragmented state, was relatively poor in this area. This difference between the CEECs and the pre-2004 member states could be explained mainly by the lengthy pre-accession process experienced by the former, in which the EU not only insisted on the transposition of the *acquis* as a condition of membership, but also assisted with the development of administrative capacity and closely monitored performance, an experience distinguishing the CEECs even from member states that had joined the Union in the preceding waves of enlargement. Transposition thus became a political priority for the CEE acceding states, systems were created that were geared to ensuring that the process was managed effectively, and the mechanisms and associated culture survived into the post-accession period (Dimitrov and Kassim forthcoming). Of course, transposition is only the first step, and there could be serious shortcomings in enforcement and application (Falkner and Treib 2008), but as Zubek (2011) notes, 'timely and effective transposition constitutes a precondition for full implementation'.

Fiscal policy: candidates for bailout or islands of stability?

Building on previous work by the author (Brusis and Dimitrov 2001; Dimitrov et al. 2006; Dimitrov 2006a, 2006b), this section investigates the capacity of the CEECs to achieve fiscal discipline. The functional pressures from the EU in this area were relatively low with regard to the CEECs, at least until the European Council in December 2011 (see Conclusion). While on entry to the EU, the CEECs undertook an obligation to join EMU, the time of entry was not specified. These states thus had considerable scope to decide when and whether to adjust to EMU conditionality (Dyson 2007). This meant that domestic factors played a primary role in determining whether the CEECs achieved fiscal discipline. As noted above, the theoretical prediction tested in this section, based on Hallerberg (2004), is that centralised national executive institutions are likely to produce lower fiscal deficits than decentralised institutions.

There were significant variations among the CEECs in relation to the centralisation of their executives in the area of fiscal policy, and more specifically, with regard to the stability of the centralised institutions operating in this sphere. The first cluster of countries included states with relatively stable centralised institutions. In this cluster, we could identify three groups of countries, based on the type of centralised institutions that they employ: a currency board (Estonia, Latvia, Lithuania and Bulgaria); delegation to the prime minister and/or finance minister (Poland and Hungary); and commitment based on tripartite institutions (Slovenia). In the countries with a currency board, the governments' discretion in fiscal policy was substantially restricted, as they were prevented from financing the budget deficit by printing money or by borrowing from the national central bank. Governments could still borrow on the international financial markets, but they tended to use this option only as a last resort. The countries in this group were generally successful in maintaining strict fiscal discipline, with low fiscal deficits and debt-to-GDP ratios, even in the context of the post-2007 crisis. In order to anchor their domestic stability-oriented framework, they sought an accelerated entry into the Euro Area (Dyson 2007), an objective that Estonia achieved in January 2011, while Lithuania and Latvia had been members of ERM II since 2004 and 2005, respectively.

Poland and Hungary were successful in establishing relatively stable centralised fiscal institutions, based on delegation of authority to the prime minister and/or finance minister. However, the centralisation of fiscal institutions did not necessarily lead to lower deficits. Contrary to Hallerberg's (2004) argument that party policy preferences do not affect fiscal performance, the fact that since the late 1990s all the major parties in Poland and Hungary, both on the centre-left *and* on the centre-right, competed for votes mainly by emphasizing their welfare credentials (although all of them accepted the ultimate need for fiscal discipline, as a result of the entrenchment of the 'sound money and finance' paradigm– see below), had a negative effect on the fiscal deficit. The centralised fiscal institutions did have the advantage, however, that in a crisis situation, the government could push through a tough austerity programme and re-impose fiscal discipline. This happened, rather dramatically, in Hungary after 2006, in the second term of the Socialist-led government, with the budget deficit falling from over 9 per cent of GDP in 2006 to 4.2 per cent in 2010 (Eurostat). The austerity measures were followed, however, by the heavy defeat of the Socialists in the 2010 elections, and the succeeding centre-right government was less consistent in the pursuit of fiscal discipline. In Poland, the budget deficit rose to 7.9 per cent of GDP in 2010 (Eurostat); the centre-right-led coalition, in office since 2007, pursued quite a lax fiscal policy, though after its convincing re-election in October 2011, it announced ambitious plans to deal with the deficit.

Slovenia was the only country in CEE that succeeded in establishing well-functioning commitment-based centralised fiscal institutions. The long-standing tripartite structures were able to carry along employers and trade unions in achieving wage moderation, much as in Germany and Austria (Dyson 2007). The country became the first among the CEECs to join the Euro Area, in 2007.

The second cluster of CEECs included states that did not establish stable centralised fiscal institutions – the Czech Republic, Slovakia and Romania. In these countries, in the normal course of events the weak powers of the prime minister and the finance minister meant that they were generally not able to impose fiscal discipline on their ministerial colleagues. Even these states, however, demonstrated a capacity to develop relatively effective centralised arrangements when faced with serious fiscal challenges, as in Czechoslovakia/Czech Republic in the transition from a centrally planned to a capitalist market economy in the early 1990s, or in Slovakia in 1998–2006, when the ruling centre-right coalition was preparing the country for membership of the Euro Area (Slovakia achieved this in 2009) (Dyson 2007), though this centralisation tended to be quite 'shallow', i.e., based on party-political and personalist resources, rather than on executive institutions.

While there were significant variations among the CEECs with regard to the stability of centralised fiscal institutions, in overall terms those states achieved quite a high level of fiscal discipline, at least compared with the southern European countries. This could be explained partly by the CEECs' relatively recent experience with a systematic, indeed a revolutionary, economic transformation, from a centrally planned to a capitalist market economy. In terms of magnitude, complexity and economic sacrifices, this transformation far exceeded the challenges posed by the post-2007 financial crisis or those associated with gaining entry into the Euro Area. A fundamental part of this transformation was the acceptance of the 'sound money and finance' paradigm (for an outline of this paradigm, see Dyson 2000, 2002, 21–3), by the vast majority of policy-makers and a significant, if varied, majority of the public. The entrenchment of the 'culture of stability' across the CEECs meant that even in states in which relatively decentralised institutions were a matter of course in normal times, such as the Czech Republic and Romania, the fact that all the mainstream political parties accepted the ultimate need for fiscal discipline, meant that in crisis situations, when the deficit threatened to get out of control, effective measures could be taken to bring it down.

Political parties and the European Union

As discussed in the previous sections, the main factor determining the ability of the CEECs to respond effectively to the two key challenges of coordinating EU policy and achieving fiscal discipline was the coordination capacity of their executives. Political parties, could, however, play a critical role in determining the policy objectives for which the executive institutions were used, in both of these areas: fiscal policy has been discussed above; in the coordination of EU policy, political parties could use executive institutions either to reinforce the integrationist impetus within the Union or to try to rein it back; in this context, the rise of Euroscepticism in the CEECs could become a serious source of concern.

In overall terms, the impact of the EU on the policy programmes of political parties in the CEECs was limited, much as in the old member states (Haughton 2009). Most parties in the CEECs, in keeping with public opinion, were generally in favour of their country's membership of the EU, although some parties voiced Eurosceptic sentiments. Liberal centre-left parties, which dominated the left part of the political spectrum in most of the CEECs, were almost uniformly Europhile, as were the liberal centre-right parties, with the exception of the Civic Democratic Party in the Czech Republic and the Freedom and Solidarity Party in Slovakia, which were critical of the EU from a neo-liberal perspective (the latter party held up the approval of the expansion of the European Financial Stability Facility (EFSF), and brought down the government, in October 2011)). Nationalist and authoritarian parties, both on the right and on the left, tended to be more sceptical towards the EU, as in Poland, Hungary and Bulgaria, though their positions were often tempered by entry into government and by a pragmatic appreciation of the benefits of EU funds (Haughton 2009).

Party positions in the CEECs were thus broadly supportive of the role that these states played within the Union, that of relatively passive 'good citizens'. However, that role could become unsustainable in the future (see Conclusion), and the impact of the Union on issues of core concern to voters and political parties in the CEECs, such as spending and taxation, could increase dramatically, and thus force parties to define their positions towards the EU much more sharply than hitherto.

Conclusion

The analysis in this chapter demonstrates that the CEECs were relatively effective in dealing with the two fundamental challenges of coordinating EU policy and achieving fiscal discipline. The key factor that enabled these states to act as 'good citizens' of the Union in these two areas was the relatively high coordination capacity of their national executives, which had been shaped primarily by experience of post-communist transition. In line with the hypothesis that centralised executives have greater success in the coordination of EU policy than decentralised executives, the chapter found that countries such as Poland, Hungary and Slovenia, which had succeeded in establishing reasonably stable centralised institutions after 1989, were relatively effective both in projecting their national interests at the EU level and (somewhat less so) in managing the work of the Union as a whole as rotating presidents. By contrast, states such as the Czech Republic, Latvia, Lithuania, Bulgaria and Romania, which did not establish centralised institutions on a long-term basis, found it more difficult to project their national positions in Brussels and to run the affairs of the Union (though even these countries tried to increase the coordination capacity of their executives, when faced with major challenges, such as serving as presidents of the Council of Ministers). However, nearly all the CEECs proved themselves to be 'good citizens' of the Union in relation to transposition – in this area, their record compared well with that of many of the pre-2004 member states, from southern Europe and elsewhere – mainly because the institutions dedicated to this task, and the culture associated with them, which had been created before accession, survived into the membership period.

The analysis in the chapter indicates that there was little evidence of post-accession 'backsliding' on the part of the CEECs, as predicted by the conditionality model that has dominated the literature in this field. The concerns that the new CEE members would slow down and disrupt the functioning of Union institutions and add to the disintegrationist tendencies within the Union, were largely not realised. The Union might have been exacerbating its adversarial rather than its consensual characteristics (see Chapter 1 by Hayward in this volume), especially in the context of the post-2007 crisis, but it was usually not the CEECs that were the 'problem cases' or the triggers of dissent. The CEECs acted more as policy-takers rather than policy-makers within the Union and did not play an important role in the shaping of Union institutions. But within the limited remit that they had set themselves, they performed reasonably effectively. Poland was a notable exception to the strategy of passive 'good citizenship'. This was due to a number of factors, including the size of the country and its 'weight' in the Union, the presence of relatively strong Eurosceptic parties, and its aspirations for regional leadership. There were, however, significant constraints on the role that Poland played within the Union, most notably, its structural dependence on Germany.

A similar conclusion can be reached in relation to the achievement of fiscal discipline. The chapter found strong support for the theoretical prediction that centralised executive institutions are likely to produce lower fiscal deficits than decentralised institutions. The countries with the most stable centralised institutions were Estonia, Latvia, Lithuania and Bulgaria – their currency boards were effectively placed beyond party-political competition. Not surprisingly, these countries showed an impressive level of fiscal discipline, even in the face of the post-2007 crisis. By contrast, in all the other CEECs, fiscal policy was still subject to party-political competition. Nevertheless, among those states, the ones with relatively stable centralised institutions – Poland, Hungary and Slovenia – were in a better position to achieve fiscal discipline than those that had not succeeded in establishing centralised institutions on a long-term basis, such as the Czech Republic, Slovakia and Romania.

In spite of these substantial differences, the primacy of the 'sound money and finance' paradigm, which had been entrenched across the post-communist countries as part of the transition to market economy, was not fundamentally challenged in any CEE state. This meant that, in overall terms, the CEECs were able to maintain fiscal discipline relatively well, or at least better than most of the southern European states. The term 'islands of stability' is somewhat over-optimistic in relation to the CEECs; it does, however, convey the fact that these states were able to keep their houses in reasonable order in fiscal terms and were unlikely to become a source of serious problems for the rest of the Union (with some limited exceptions, such as Hungary). This form of solidarity, however, had distinct limitations. Until the European Council in December 2011, most of the CEECs were cautious about undertaking commitments towards the Euro Area. This caution could be motivated by concerns about providing assistance to less fiscally responsible members of the Euro Area, which were often considerably richer than the CEECs in terms of GDP per capita. Even in a country that was already a member of the Euro Area, such as Slovakia, there was strong resistance to providing support through the expansion of the EFSF, though the measure was eventually approved by the Slovak parliament in October 2011. The concerns of the CEECs tended, however, to focus mostly on the temporal management of their Euro Area entry, and in particular, on the need to preserve some room for manoeuvre to operate fiscal policies that promote industrial development, encourage real economic convergence and support social inclusion (Dyson 2007). Their concerns generally did not centre on normative issues. They recognised that they were structurally dependent on the Euro Area, and that their economic prosperity was contingent on achieving a high level of integration into the Euro Area systems of industrial production (Bohle and Greskovits 2007; Dyson 2007). This meant that unlike the UK or some of the Nordic states, their only viable long-term economic strategy was entry into the Euro Area.

The role of passive 'good citizens' of the Union was one that the CEECs were generally happy to play, and one that they played relatively effectively, until late 2011. However, this role might not be sustainable in the longer term, either because the EU might be unable to contain the spread of the crisis and the disintegrationist tendencies associated with it, or the Union might move, in response to the crisis, towards move intensive forms of integration, such as a fiscal union. At the December 2011 European Council, the members of the Euro Area, while not creating a full fiscal union, appeared to take a major step forward, through the establishment of a fiscal compact, though a number of important questions remained open. It was notable that all the CEECs, with the exception of the Czech Republic, including six states that were not members of the Euro Area, have signed the compact. The signing of the compact could mark a turning point in the progression of all the CEECs (bar the Czech Republic) towards the Euro Area, initially in terms of binding fiscal commitments and eventually in the form of full membership. This could mean that that the CEECs would transcend the limited type of solidarity that they had been practising since becoming members of the Union, and move towards a deeper and more wide-ranging form of solidarity, within a more tightly integrated economic and political union.

Acknowledgements

This chapter is based on the findings of a research project on 'The National Coordination of EU Policy in the New Member States', led by the author and Hussein Kassim. Other researchers included Agnes Batory, Danica Fink-Hafner, Jiri Kabele, Juhan Lepassaar, Klaudijus Maniokas, Artur Nowak-Far, Ivo Rollis and Ramūnas Vilpišauskas.

Bibliography

Bohle, D. and B. Greskovits (2007) 'Neoliberalism, Embedded Neoliberalism and Neocorporatism: Towards Transnational Capitalism in Central-Eastern Europe', *West European Politics*, 30:3, 443–66.

Brusis, M. (2002) 'Between EU Requirements, Competitive Politics, and National Traditions: Re-creating Regions in the Accession Countries of Central and Eastern Europe', *Governance*, 15:4, 531–559.

Brusis, M. and V. Dimitrov (2001) 'Executive Configuration and Fiscal Performance in Post-Communist Central and Eastern Europe', *Journal of European Public Policy*, 8:6, 888–910.

Dimitrov, V. (2006a) 'EMU and Fiscal Policy in East Central Europe' in K. Dyson (ed) *Enlarging the Euro Area: External Empowerment and Domestic Transformation in East Central Europe* (Oxford: Oxford University Press), 261–278.

Dimitrov, V. (2006b) 'From Laggard to Pace-Setter: Bulgaria's Road to EMU', in K. Dyson (ed) *Enlarging the Euro Area: External Empowerment and Domestic Transformation in East Central Europe* (Oxford: Oxford University Press), 145–159.

Dimitrov, V., K. H. Goetz and H. Wollmann (2006) *Governing after Communism: Institutions and Policymaking* (Lanham, MD: Rowman & Littlefield).

Dimitrov, V. and H. Kassim, forthcoming. 'The National Coordination of EU Policy in the New Member States: A Comparative Perspective', in V. Dimitrov and H. Kassim (eds) *The National Coordination of EU Policy in the New Member States*, Special Issue of *Public Administration*.

Dunleavy, P. and R. A. Rhodes (1990) 'Core Executive Studies in Britain', *Public Administration*, 68, 3–28.

Dyson, K. (2000) *The Politics of the Euro-Zone: Stability or Breakdown?* (Oxford: Oxford University Press).

Dyson, K. (2002) 'Introduction: EMU as Integration, Europeanization, and Convergence', in K. Dyson (ed) *European States and the Euro: Europeanization, Variation, and Convergence* (Oxford: Oxford University Press), pp. 1–27.

Dyson, K. (2007) 'Euro Area Entry in East-Central Europe: Paradoxical Europeanisation and Clustered Convergence', *West European Politics*, 30:3, 417–442.

Elgie, R. (2011) 'Core Executive Studies Two Decades on', *Public Administration*, 89:1, 64–77.

Epstein R. A. and U. Sedelmeier (2008) 'Beyond Conditionality: International Institutions in Postcommunist Europe after Enlargement', *Journal of European Public Policy*, 15:6, 795–805.

Falkner, G. and O. Treib (2008) 'Three Worlds of Compliance or Four? The EU-15 Compared to New Member States', *Journal of Common Market Studies*, 46:2, 293–313.

Goetz, K.H. (2006) 'Territory, Temporality and Clustered Europeanization'. *IHS Working Paper Political Science Series*, No. 109 (Vienna: Institute for Advanced Studies).

Grabbe, H. (2003) 'Europeanization Goes East: Power and Uncertainty in the EU Accession Process', in K. Featherstone and C. Radaelli (eds), *The Politics of Europeanization* (Oxford: Oxford University Press), pp. 303–27.

Hallerberg, M. (2004) *Domestic Budgets in a United Europe: Fiscal Governance from the End of Bretton Woods to EMU* (Ithaca: Cornell University Press).

Haughton, T. (2009) 'Driver, Conductor or Fellow Passenger? EU Membership and Party Politics in Central and Eastern Europe', *Journal of Communist Studies and Transition Politics*, 25:4, 413–26.

Hughes, J., G. Sasse and C. Gordon (2004a) 'Conditionality and Compliance in the EU's Eastward Enlargement: Regional Policy and the Reform of Sub-national Governance', *Journal of Common Market Studies*, 42:3, 523–551.

Hughes, J., G. Sasse and C. Gordon (2004b) *Europeanization and Regionalization in the EU's Enlargement to Central and Eastern Europe: The Myth of Conditionality* (Basingstoke: Palgrave).

Kabele, J. (forthcoming). 'The Coordination of EU Policy in the Czech Republic: Continuity and Change after Accession', article submitted to *Public Administration*, as part of the Special Issue on *The National Coordination of EU Policy in the New Member States*, edited by V. Dimitrov and H. Kassim.

Kassim, H. (2001) 'Representing the United Kingdom in Brussels: The Fine Art of Positive Co-ordination', in H. Kassim, A. Menon, B. G. Peters and V. Wright (eds), *The National Co-ordination of EU Policy: The European Level* (Oxford: Oxford University Press), 47–76.

Kassim, H. (2003) 'Meeting the Demands of EU Membership: The Europeanization of National Administrative Systems', in K. Featherstone and C. M. Radaelli (eds), *The Politics of Europeanization* (Oxford: Oxford University Press).

Kassim, H. and G. Peters (2001) 'Conclusion: Co-ordinating National Action in Brussels – A Comparative Perspective', in H. Kassim, A. Menon, G. Peters, and V. Wright (eds), *The National Co-ordination of EU Policy: The European Level* (Oxford: Oxford University Press), pp. 297–342.

Kassim, H., B. G. Peters and V. Wright (2000) 'Introduction', in H. Kassim, B. G. Peters and V. Wright (eds), *The National Co-ordination of EU Policy: The Domestic Level* (Oxford: Oxford University Press).

Rhodes, R. A. W., and P. Dunleavy (eds) (1995) *Prime Minister, Cabinet, and Core Executive* (Basingstoke: Macmillan).

Schimmelfennig, F. and U. Sedelmeier (2004) 'Governance by Conditionality: EU Rule Transfer to the Candidate Countries of Central and Eastern Europe', *Journal of European Public Policy*, 11: 4, 661–79.

Schimmelfennig, F. and U. Sedelmeier (2005a) 'Conclusions: The Impact of the EU on the Accession Countries', in F. Schimmelfennig and U. Sedelmeier (eds) *The Europeanization of Central and Eastern Europe* (Ithaca, NY: Cornell University Press), 210–28.

Schimmelfennig, F. and U. Sedelmeier (2005b) 'Introduction: Conceptualizing the Europeanization of Central and Eastern Europe', in F. Schimmelfennig and U. Sedelmeier (eds) *The Europeanization of Central and Eastern Europe* (Ithaca, NY: Cornell University Press), pp. 1–28.

Schimmelfennig, F., S. Engert and K. Heiko (2005) 'The Impact of EU Political Conditionality', in F. Schimmelfennig and U. Sedelmeier (eds) *The Europeanization of Central and Eastern Europe* (Ithaca, NY: Cornell University Press), pp. 29–50.

Sepos, A. (2004) 'The National Coordination of EU Policy: Organisational Efficiency and European Outcomes', *Journal of European Integration*, 27:2, 169–90.

Steunenberg, B. and D. Toshkov (2009) 'Comparing Transposition in the 27 Member States of the EU: The Impact of Discretion and Legal Fit', *Journal of European Public Policy*, 16:7, 951–70.

Weller, P. and H. Bakvis (1997) 'The Hollow Crown: Coherence and Capacity in Central Government', in P. Weller, H. Bakvis and R. A. Rhodes (eds) *The Hollow Crown: Countervailing Trends in Core Executives* (Basingstoke: Macmillan).

Wright, V. (1996) 'The National Co-ordination of European Policy-Making: Negotiating the Quagmire', in J. Richardson (ed.) *European Union: Power and Policy-Making* (London: Routledge).

Zubek, R. (2008) *Core Executive and Europeanization in Central Europe* (Basingstoke: Palgrave Macmillan).

Zubek, R. (2011) 'Core Executives and Coordination of EU Law Transposition: Evidence from New Member States', *Public Administration*, 89:2, 433–450.

Conclusion: European Disunion: Between Sovereignty and Solidarity

Rüdiger K.W. Wurzel and Jack Hayward

The Euro crisis catapulted the European Union (EU) into its most serious political crisis since its inception, leaving it simultaneously torn between opposing demands for more sovereignty and solidarity. In order to save the Euro and ultimately the European integration project itself, the EU and its core policy actors oscillated between partial disintegration, which prepared for the possible exit from the Eurozone of one or several highly indebted member states, and deeper integration in the form of a fiscal union that was agreed in principle in December 2012 by all 27 member states with the exception of Britain.

While the EU has been 'staring into the abyss' (*The Economist* 12 November 2011), there was an abundance of short-lived economic rescue plans and contradictory short-sighted political advice. At one end of the political spectrum, Eurosceptics demanded the break-up of the Union or at least the repatriation of major EU competences in the false hope of reaching a promised land of independent sovereign states, which would successfully fend for themselves to achieve economic, social and environmental sustainability, despite the constraints of increased interdependence and globalisation (see Chapter 1). At the other extreme, a small and dwindling group of federalists argued that the crisis necessitated a move towards full economic and political union. Diametrically opposed proposals were also put forward by economists. Ordoliberals, who dominate German economic thinking, insisted on strict austerity measures to reduce budget deficits and engender long overdue structural reforms in the countries of the fiscal 'sinners' without endangering the economic growth and low inflation of the successful fiscal 'saints' (Chapter 12). Other economists countered this argument by suggesting that the European Central Bank (ECB) should be allowed to issue Eurobonds and act as a lender of last resort in order to collectivise the national budget deficits in the expectation that this would buy the fiscal sinners sufficient economic breathing space for overdue long term structural reforms.

Disunion between intergovernmentalists/Eurosceptics and federalists/Europhiles is not a new phenomenon. It has long accompanied the fits and starts of European integration. What was new and took mainstream political elites by surprise was the fact that populist nationalist and extremist right-wing parties with anti-EU views were able to gain significant electoral support even in some of the hitherto strongly pro-European countries such as Finland and The Netherlands (see Chapters 4 and 17). Their electoral success came on the heels of public rejections of the draft EU Constitution in referendums in France and The Netherlands in 2005. It facilitated recognition by excessively insulated European political elites that the traditional humdrum crisis response mechanisms failed to offer appropriate medium to long term solutions in a rapidly deepening economic and political crisis. These mechanisms had resulted in arcane *ad hoc* compromises negotiated behind closed doors that only superficially papered over underlying disunion between member states and EU institutions (vertical disunion) and between and within core EU institutional actors (horizontal disunion). The permissive consensus between governing political elites and the member states' publics on European integration issues was being tested beyond breaking point by speculators in the unregulated global financial markets and anti-European populist and right-wing extremist parties, which were keen to see the break-up of the Euro and the unravelling of the European integration project.

Although it would be as premature to pronounce 'the end of European integration' (Taylor 2008) in the midst of the Euro crisis as it was to declare 'the end of history' (Fukuyama 1989) in the middle of the transformation of the post-Cold War global political system, there clearly is a need to acknowledge the danger that the EU 'lurches from consensus through compromise to dissensus through disunion' (Introduction).

The lack of a genuine EU demos, civil society and party system has contributed towards the fragility of the European integration project in the face of the Euro crisis (Chapters 2–4). This is not to downplay the consistently high public support, which exists in most member states for some EU projects (Chapter 2) and policies such as environmental policy (Chapter 14). However, the EU's enfeebled democratic legitimacy has left its pro-integrationist political elites and institutional would-be leaders (Chapters 5–10) relatively insulated from the member states' publics and civil society actors. In response to the rejection of the draft European Constitution in the French and Dutch referendums, the Commission launched its so-called *Plan D for Democracy, Dialogue and Debate* (CEC 2005). However, Commission initiatives to bring about greater public participation in EU policy-making failed to enthuse stakeholders and NGOs who still operate within a largely disunited European civil society (Chapter 3). Unions and environmental NGOs in particular have tried, although largely in vain, to act as countervailing societal forces by demanding greater European solidarity as an antidote for increased European Disunion in EU social and environmental policies. However, the EU's skeletal social and labour market policies and much more comprehensive environmental policy contain few explicit references to European solidarity (see Chapters 13 and 14).

Union and disunion

The 1957 Rome Treaty stipulated the goal of 'an ever closer union', significantly dropped from the 2009 Lisbon Treaty. The 'European union' has remained 'an ill-defined terminus' (Dinan 2000: 225). However, the absence of a clear definition in its founding treaties was not accidental but part of an integration strategy which sought to evade disunion by avoiding specification of the exact meaning of 'ever closer union'. While it is useful to conceptualise cooperation, integration and union 'as a ladder' (Dyson and Sepos 2010b: 4) it leaves open the exact demarcation between the different rungs of the ladder. Also, the higher up one goes, the more precarious balance becomes, especially with the additional weight carried as represented by the increased number of member states following the various accession rounds.

European disunion is an even more controversial concept for which, however, strong empirical evidence has been uncovered in the chapters of this book. European disunion covers a wide analytical spectrum that ranges from relatively minor dissent about European integration (weak disunion) to the reversal of integration (strong disunion) (Chapter 12). In its weakest form, European disunion includes relatively minor disagreements, which can be papered over with vague compromises enshrined in complex package deals. In its strongest form, European disunion implies fundamental dissent that leads to the exit of one or several of its member states or even the complete break-up of the EU. There are many different 'shades of disunion' in between its weakest and strongest forms.

Collective action problems can lead to joint decision traps (Scharpf 1999) and cause European disunion including the absence or reversal of union. Differentiated integration can overcome collective action problems (Dyson and Sepos 2010b: 9). However, differentiated integration, which has increased significantly since the 1993 Maastricht Treaty (Dyson and Sepos 2010a; Héritier et al. 2001), does not necessarily lead to union but can also trigger disunion. Moreover, there comes a point when an overly differentiated union ceases to be a union because it either disintegrates gradually or breaks up suddenly.

Different EU policies have exhibited varied degrees of 'union' and 'disunion' over time. Economic and Monetary Union (EMU) formerly showed a high degree of union and a strong commitment to deeper integration when it was set up. However, it developed into Economic and Monetary Disunion during the Euro crisis when highly indebted member states were threatened with expulsion unless they applied stringent austerity measures to reduce their unsustainable budget deficits and responded by using the exit threat in the hope that this would increase their bargaining power because of the dangers posed by such a step to the entire Eurozone (Chapter 12).

The EU's common foreign and defence policy never came close to the degree of union temporarily reached by EMU, because of member states' sovereignty obsession, different histories and irreconcilable national foreign policy interests (Chapter 11). As a result of its Nazi past, Germany has suffered from a 'leadership avoidance reflex' (Paterson 1996) on EU foreign and defence policy issues. Largely necessitated by financial constraints, France and Britain hesitantly launched joint EU defence initiatives, which were only infrequently joined by all member states. Inadequate institutional capacities and the absence of a 'heroic' policy style – military action requires rapid decision-making and troop deployment – has also strongly constrained the EU's feeble attempts towards union in defence policy.

The EU's social and labour market policies are largely devoid of union because different European social models – ranging from relatively comprehensive Scandinavian to rudimentary Anglo-Saxon and southern European welfare states – turned out to be incompatible with the vision for a common social policy model that was advocated by only a small number of EU actors (Chapter 13). While some member states (e.g. Sweden) worked hard to protect national welfare state provisions, others (e.g. Britain) opted-out of minimal EU social policy and labour market protection provisions or even tried to encourage a race to the bottom while justifying it with reference to increased global economic competition.

In contrast EU environmental policy often facilitated a race to the top in which environmental leader states and environmentally concerned EU institutions (such as the European Parliament) were able to set the pace or at least determine the general direction in this policy area. This is not to deny serious incidents of disunity in EU environmental policy. However, especially when considering the absence of explicit environmental policy treaty provisions until the 1987 Single European Act, it is surprising how quickly the common environmental policy matured and developed into one of the EU's most popular policies, leading some politicians and academics to propose a formal environmental union in order to reinvigorate the stalled European integration project (Chapter 14).

Without resorting to package deals, side payments and vague compromises, it becomes almost impossible for the EU to overcome fundamental differences leading to disunion because its institutional structure was deliberately designed to produce a 'leaderless Europe' (Hayward 2008). Moreover, the Council, Commission and European Parliament are all internally structured along functional lines to avoid grand bargains where the winner takes all. Such a functional set up facilitates complex compromises but discourages clear leadership (Chapters 5–7). Instead of a single Council of Ministers there is a 'hydra-headed conglomerate of…functional Councils' (Pinder 1991: 25). At least for high-politics issues the European Council has increasingly tried to assert its leadership on what in effect are Councils of Ministers that have little to do with the legal fiction of a single Council (Chapter 5). However, disunion in the European Council has risen while the Franco-German duumvirate leadership capability has decreased in an enlarged EU (Chapter 16). Despite its internal fragmentation into functional Directorate Generals (DGs), often holding conflicting views on specific policy proposals, the Commissions has achieved a surprisingly high level of policy activity and output (Chapter 6).

The European Court of Justice and ECB are not organised along functional lines (Chapters 8 and 9). Dissenting opinions from judges and ECB officials are not published in order to avoid overt disunion along member state lines. However, within the ECB, the degree of disunion reached such a level that leaks to the press and resignations became a way of making public the views of the mainly German ordoliberal dissenters to the central bank's crisis containment measures. The

European Parliament's powers have increased significantly since the 1987 Single European Act (Chapter 7). However, its influence on EU decisions to resolve the Euro crisis was minimal. It was the national parliaments in the member states of the fiscal 'saints' and the German Bundestag in particular, which exerted a considerably higher degree of influence on the European Financial Stability Facility (EFSF). Neither the Lisbon Treaty nor the Euro crisis have reduced the level of disunity that has often characterised the relationship between the European Parliament and national parliaments (Chapters 7 and 16).

Sovereignty and solidarity

Both sovereignty and solidarity are contested but interacting political concepts. Sovereignty has traditionally been associated with states' legal and territorial independence. However, increased interdependence and European integration in particular have posed serious challenges to the monopoly of (member) states as the definers of territory and their capacity to manage spatial economies under the constraints of globalisation and a single European market that allows for the free movement of people, goods, services and capital (Chapter 10).

The ECJ established the sovereignty of Community over national law in a series of court cases. However, several national constitutional courts only very reluctantly accepted the supremacy of EU law attaching conditions under which this should be the case (Chapter 8). The British sovereignty of parliament doctrine helps to explain the relatively high degree of friction and disunion between the UK government and the EU (Chapters 8 and 16). However, the degree of disunion between the EU and the UK varies considerably among its nations, with Wales and Scotland in particular showing a significantly higher propensity to support European integration than in England where levels of support for the EU are much lower (Taylor 2008: 51–2). Despite these parliamentary and nation-state peculiarities, the UK has generally had a good EU treaty rules and secondary laws implementation record although there have been some exceptions (Chapters 14 and 16).

Solidarity is an even more highly contested concept. It 'means different things to different people (and governments)' (Myrdal and Rhinard 2010: 1). The European Commission has nevertheless argued that '[s]olidarity is part of how European society works and how Europe engages with the rest of the world' (CEC 2008: 412 as cited in Ross and Borgmann-Prebil 2010: 1). Following the establishment of a European Union Solidarity Fund (Council 2002) for major national disasters, the Commission launched several initiatives to foster greater solidarity (e.g. CEC 2005a and b). The Lisbon Treaty made solidarity a quasi-constitutional principle by enshrining a solidarity clause in Article 222. The new solidarity clause has been 'conceived as a treaty-based method of improving EU cooperation on a range of complex threats' (Myrdal and Rhinard 2010: 1) although its practical relevance for humdrum day-to-day EU policy-making is very limited. There are also more than another dozen provisions in the Lisbon Treaty which also mention solidarity.

The Nordic, southern and Central and East European member states have perceived the relationship between solidarity and sovereignty largely in terms of trade off (Chapters 17, 18 and 19). However, while the Nordic countries have insisted on greater sovereignty in order to be able to practice a higher degree of 'domestic solidarity' (relatively generous domestic welfare state provisions), the southern as well as the Central and East European states have supported a higher degree of integration in exchange for greater solidarity from the EU, notably through structural funds.

The 'increased invocation of solidarity appears to reflect a "crisis" mentality' (Ross and Borgmann-Prebil 2010: 2). It is not by chance that '[t]he word "solidarity" hangs heavily in the air as Europe struggles with a debt crisis' (Myrdal and Rhinard 2010: 1). Eurobarometer surveys have shown that solidarity ranks high amongst the values which are seen by citizens as best representing the EU (Eurobarometer various years).

The political economy of European disunion

The tell-tale evidence that the EU as a set of organisations has triumphed over its purpose of integrating an enlarging community of member states has accumulated over the more than half century of its existence. It became an end in itself. Its elite actors, intergovernmentally in the main, gave priority to achieving agreement at the cost of policy expedition and effectiveness, as has been documented in case after decision-making case. However, in a crisis-ridden, rapidly changing economic context, can the propensity to give priority to confidential compromises and continuity over the capacity to innovate persist? Incrementally doing more of what was being done will no longer suffice, so heroic leadership is called for but its emergence has proved elusive (Hayward 2008). External pressures have upset the assumption of an inbuilt impetus to integration by confronting the EU with inordinate demands upon solidarity that its governments and peoples are unwilling to satisfy because the cost of self-sacrifices are regarded as unbearable. Muddling through ceases to be an option. The evasion of fundamental issues of principle about with whom one is willing to be fraternal and at what cost becomes dereliction of political duty.

Jürgen Habermas has bluntly posed the predicament of seeking to establish the capacity for rapid decision by a quasi-federal 'economic government' whilst not short-circuiting the approval of national parliaments of the member states. When output legitimacy has collapsed, input legitimacy by democratic procedures becomes indispensable. Yet what is being challenged is the budget-making authority that has been the historic function of parliaments. Whether performed at the level of the EU or the Eurozone, 'intergovernmental domination by the European Council ... would allow the transfer of market imperatives to national budgets without any democratic legitimacy. To do so, opaque compromises without juridical formality will have to be imposed with the threat of sanctions and pressures on national parliaments stripped of their power' amounting to 'a post-democratic domination' in practice by heads of government (Habermas 2011a; see also Habermas 2011b). EU leaders know that they lack the popular support for their harsh economic decisions. The dysmmetry of power between the deregulated market forces and the political leaders who presided over a debt mountain caused by reckless bank lending to individuals, businesses and governments incapable or unwilling to meet their obligations leaves them at the mercy of international financial speculation.

The speculators know that the EU/Eurozone and national governments lack a credible medium term strategy for economic growth because they are unable to decide and to implement one. Unlike China, India and Brazil, which have done so, facilitated by their catch-up growth opportunities, they cannot resolutely deal with the onset of a global economic crisis. Some member governments, notably Germany and the Nordic countries, have already undertaken painful labour market and welfare state reforms nationally to prevent precipitate industrial decline. Others, such as semi-insolvent Greece and Italy, significantly turned to financial Eurocrats to take the decisions that their political leaders proved incapable of adopting and enforcing. Similarly, the Eurozone governments left it to the non-democratic ECB to fulfil the financial solidarity function on which they were incapable of agreeing quickly enough to be effective. The European Parliament was an impotent bystander, calling upon the European Commission to act, resulting in ineffectual exhortation. Faced with grossly inegalitarian cuts to public services and employment, citizens vociferously protested at the austerity inflicted upon them without consultation much less consent.

The almost universal outrage aroused by the Greek Prime Minister Papandreou's proposal to hold a referendum is eloquent testimony to the deliberate exclusion of the people from a process over which the elites themselves have lost control (see Habermas 2011b).

This pinpoints the tension between democracy and solidarity in member states and the lack of both at the EU and Eurozone level. As resentment against a reluctant German financial hegemony, implying a German Europe more than a European Germany, overshadows gratitude for disproportionate assistance to countries in need, the EU is threatened with fragmentation within and between the ins and outs of the Eurozone. Some would like to make the crisis a stepping stone to economic federalism, via a Minister of Finance, but this presupposes agreement about conceding some sovereignty in return for more solidarity. Others see it as an opportunity to repatriate power from the EU, reducing solidarity in the name of retrieving sovereignty, however illusory this might be in an interdependent world. This has not discouraged Prime Minister Cameron from offering unsolicited advice from the self-excluded sidelines, prompting an overwrought President Sarkozy to intersperse his frenetic attempt to keep up with Chancellor Merkel by telling Cameron to shut up.

As the EU becomes identified as a nightmare rather than a dream of increasing opulence, the incentives to disunion are likely to increase in the panic induced by the unaccountable credit rating agencies pronouncing impending sentence of degradation. Ironically, it is their pressure that has provided much of the impetus to greater EU political and economic integration in the form of a fiscal union, as member states desperately seek to avoid being picked off one at a time. Collective constraint, dictated by a virtuous Germany that had put its economy in order, to avoid the negative solidarity of contagion, has become the unattractive face of unity. The *Bundestag* (thanks to the German Constitutional Court which strengthened parliament's budgetary powers also vis-à-vis German financial contributions to European rescue funds) has taken over some of the *Bundesbank's* role as arbiter of EU public policy.

Avoiding the EU being wounded in its Achilles' heel and becoming a spectacular Greek tragedy, because the fate of even one of its smallest members can prove its solidarity with the others, has revived interest in incrementalist federalist integration. However, the issue is whether this is only possible between the few that are able and willing to engage in fleeing forwards from financial disaster and those that do not. So, this option is a source of disunion between the 17 eurozone states. The

Portuguese President of the EU Commission has tried desperately to prevent the Franco-German duo from sidelining the states that cannot fulfil their exigencies at the cost of splitting the EU. 'The euro area must not be treated as an "opt out" from the European Union. The challenge is how to further deepen euro area integration without creating divisions with those member states that are not part of it' (Barroso 2011).

The polarising predicament is that these objectives are irreconcilable. The interventionist imposition of disciplines to remedy the inability to enact the necessary budgetary reforms and implement them by states already in the eurozone or seeking to join it is both humiliating and yet impossible to enforce on sovereign states. Remote control austerity packages redolent of pre-modern medical blood letting kill or cure treatment, is socially unjust, economically ineffective and politically unacceptable by liberal democracies. (Patients sometimes die of the treatment to cure them rather than their ailment.)

In the bust years which followed the debt-fuelled economic boom of the late 1990s and early 2000s, the (primarily German) ordoliberal hawks of sound money and low inflation recovered their voice (Chapters 5, 12 and 15). Some prominent ordoliberal representatives resigned from influential ECB positions or refused to take up such a position to be able to speak out more freely in public against any attempts to weaken what they perceived as harsh but necessary remedies (Chapter 9). In the negotiations which brought about a fragile political compromise agreement on EU fiscal union amongst 26 member states, Britain opted for unsplendid isolation (Chapter 16). Chancellor Merkel resolutely defended the core principles of German ordoliberalism by remaining steadfast in her opposition to the adoption of Eurobonds and making the ECB a lender of last resort thus risking deep rifts within the Franco-German duumvirate (Chapters 9, 12 and 15). She therefore ignored a 12-point plan entitled 'The euro area must not founder on the narrow-mindedness of the German government', which had been jointly written and signed by a prominent member of the German Economic Expert Council and the leadership of the opposition Social Democrats and Greens. The 12-point plan, which was published shortly before the decisive European Council meeting on 16–17 December 2011, argued that 'solidity is needed as urgently as solidarity' while demanding a 'genuine political union with a common financial and fiscal policy and common development goals for the economic, social and cultural development of the currency area' (Bündnis 90/Die Grünen 2012).

Calls for greater solidarity failed to prevent the replacement of elected politicians with technocrats in the Greek and Italian governments in

2011 and the rising of tensions between the centre, which is economically dominated by Germany, and its southern periphery (Chapter 18). Entrusting the thankless task of implementing austerity measures to technocrats because they are more trusted than politicians is highly problematic in sovereign democracies (see also Habermas 2011b). So the choice for the eurozone is between two emerging coalitions: an integrating hard core of the virtuous insiders plus and more likely minus a few members and a peripheral outsider rump of the unfit and the unwilling, minus and more likely plus a few members. This variable speed, reverse gear Europe would consist of the core that accept the stringent implications of fiscal solidarity, leaving the other sovereignties to fend for themselves in unsplendid isolation.

The EU has reached another momentous moment of truth. Its member states and the market imperatives that they espoused are discredited so that political and economic problems become ever more intractable. A confederal Europe is having to choose between advancing in a solidarist-integrationist direction or retreating in a disorderly sovereignist-disunionist direction. The presumption has been that as the Commission's first President, Walter Hallstein, evoked with his often quoted bicycle metaphor, only when the EU is moving forward will it continue to exist, despite the cacophony of clashing national interests resistant to coordination much less authorative integration. When this is achieved, it is by national elites among whom euroscepticism has made lesser inroads than among their peoples, who are even less inclined towards solidarity as the EU has enlarged to more impecunious and untrusted members.

Protectionism will be resorted to if there is insufficient capacity to reverse a decline into recession and mass unemployment, involving a restriction of the scope of EU solidarity and a reliance upon state sovereignty, which would endanger the single European market. A constraint on global market forces that might be secured by a reassertion of regulatory political control on the EU level would require abandoning the neo-liberal defeatism that has prevailed since the 1980s, posing problems to those, such as the UK, that is both sovereignist and anti-protectionist. As for the integrationists, they will have to choose on which side of the euro coin – the national or European one – they place their hopes, if it spins out of control.

The creation of a European currency without a sovereign political authority to manage it has left it to ECB with its limited remit and especially the financial market to mismanage it. In the first decade of the euro's existence, the interest rates of sovereign debt strongly converged, irrespective of differential risk, in the cases of both Germany and Greece as well as others. Since the euro crisis, they have drastically diverged in a similarly unjustifiable way, because the deregulated financial markets are inclined to both excessive optimism and pessimism. The consequences have been the imposition of such extreme austerity policies that they push even solvent states into bankruptcy and debt default, with damaging social and draconian human consequences that discredit the EU by association with disaster. The conspicuous failure of self-regulation by financial markets and the ECB's inability to act as a lender of last resort, based on a non-market evaluation of the requirements of crisis corrective actions, pinpoints the problem of substituting solidarity for an everyone-for-themselves fragmentation without an effective political authority. The self-correcting role of prices in the market for goods has not operated efficiently in financial markets, so public action has to correct the panic reactions that ensue (Orléan 2009, 2011). This is especially difficult in the disunited EU institutional context.

In the power struggle between bond markets and national governments, the latter have been at the mercy of the former since the 1980s deregulation process. The movements of indignant protest are a popular attempt to pressure governments to reassert control over the financial markets rather than abandon their citizens to the mercy of profiteers. The consequence has been impoverishing austerity resulting from an unequal struggle. The EU's equivocations are a byproduct of the tug of war between enfeebled democracy and aggressive plutocracy for domination. The EU lacks an effective political authority to regulate the financial markets and the European Union has failed to impose a financial transaction tax, which President Sarkozy proposed in the run-up to the French elections in 2012, and thereby protect citizens from the vicissitudes caused by the speculative gyrations of unaccountable speculators.

By dissuading the Greek Prime Minister in 2011 from holding a referendum on the draconian conditions imposed by the Franco-Saxon duo in return for the bailout offered, they denied him the recourse of the Icelandic government (outside the EU) to referendums in March 2009 and April 2010 that led to popular rejection of creditor country demands without resulting in the threatened calamitous consequences. Some parliamentary democracies such as Ireland, Italy, Portugal and Spain (as well as Iceland) have managed to impose substantial sacrifices, legitimised by elections that have changed the government in office, even though the policies have changed little. So, the bond markets have imposed their preferences upon and through the working of the democratic process. They have done so at the cost of disrespect towards sovereign states, discredited and impotently subservient. Handing the repellent decisions to unelected technocrats, e.g. in Italy, is meant to surmount the Luxembourg Prime Minister and head of the Eurogroup, Jean-Claude Juncker's quip: 'We all know what to do but we don't know how to get re-elected once we have done it.'

The EU's democratic leaders do not have enough followers.[1] They may know *what* needs to be done about the euro crisis but are unable to agree among themselves *how* to do it and more especially how to persuade their electors of the need to compensate for public and private over-consumption by compulsory saving to reduce public and private debt. European banks and governments, having both imprudently lent vast sums to each other, are treated by the credit rating agencies on behalf of the bond market speculators, as actually or potentially insolvent. As their credibility approaches zero, bankruptcy becomes a pervasive prospect, Greece and Italy seek to depoliticise painful decisions to counteract popular protest and anti-banker revulsion, with the insolvency of Athens being followed with classical historic logic by the financial crisis of Rome.

The EU risks disintegration into a four-speed Europe: (i) The states that are in the eurogroup and can stay in, such as Germany and its followers. (ii) Those that are in the eurogroup but could be forced out, such as Greece, Italy and Portugal. (iii) Those states that are not members but could join, such as Poland and Sweden. (iv) Finally, non-member states that have no intention of joining such as Britain. The 'speeds' respectively are slow, slower, slowest and stop, if not reverse.

The prospects of European Union are unpromising, with the danger of returning to the pleasures and poisons of the past: beggar my neighbour protectionism and competitive devaluation; closing national borders to unwelcome immigrants; subordination to international institutions and extra-European powers. Interdependence has turned sour so there is a reductive temptation to recoil from the demands of solidarity to the illusory sanctuary of independent national sovereignty. This is a forbiding fate we would not wish for the European Union project.

Note

1. Hayward discussed this problem in three earlier volumes he edited: *The Crisis of Representation in Europe* (1995), at the 1993 conference on 'Are European Elites losing touch with their peoples' published as *Elitism, Populism and European Politics* (1996) and *Leaderless Europe* (2008).

Bibliography

Barroso, J. (2011) 'José Manuel Barroso: 'The speed of the European Union can no longer be the speed of the most reluctant member', *The Observer*, 13 November 2011.

Bündnis 90/Die Grünen (2012) The euro must not founder on the narrow-mindedness of the German government. English translation, http://www. gruene-bundestag.de/cms/english/dok/399/399059.the_Euro_area_must_ not_founder_on_the_na.html (accessed 09.1.2012). First published in German in Süddeutsche Zeitung on 8 December 2012, http://www.sueddeutsche.de /politik/punkte-gegen-merkels-krisenstrategie-spd-und-gruene-attackieren-die-kanzlerin-1.1229829.

CEC (2005a) *The Commission's Contribution to the Period of Reflection and Beyond: Plan D for Democracy, Dialogue and Debate*, 13 October 2005 (Brussels: Commission of the European Communities).

CEC (2005b) *Strategic Objectives 2005–2009. Europe 2010: A Partnership for European Renewal. Prosperity, Solidarity and Security. COM(2005) 12 final, 26.1.2005* (Brussels: Commission of the European Communities).

CEC (2008) *Renewed Social Agenda: Opportunities, Access and Solidarity in the 21st Century Europe. COM(2008) 412 final, 2.7.2008* (Brussels: Commission of the European Communities).

Council (2002) Council Regulation (EC) No 2012/2002 of 11 November 2002 Establishing the European Union Solidarity Fund, *Official Journal L* 311/3–8, 14.11.2002.

Dinan, D. (2000) *Encyclopedia of the European Union* (Basingstoke: Palgrave/ Macmillan).

Dyson, K. and Sepos, A. (eds) (2010a) *Which Europe? The Politics of Differentiated Integration* (Basingstoke: Palgrave Macmillan).

Dyson, K. and A. Sepos (2010b) Differentiation as Design Principle and as Tool in the Political Management of European Integration' in K. Dyson and A. Sepos (eds) *Which Europe? The Politics of Differential Integration* (Basingstoke: Palgrave Macmillan), pp. 3–23.

The Economist (2011), 'Staring into the Abyss. Special Report. Europe and Its Currency', 12 November.

Eurobarometer (various years) Public Opinion in the European Union. (Brussels: European Commission), http://ec.europa.eu/public_opinion/index_En.htm (accessed 9 January 2012).

Fukuyama, F. (1989) 'The End of History', *The National Interest*, 16, 3–18.

Habermas, J. (2011a) 'Rendons Europe plus démocratique. Penser la Crise de l'Union Européenne', *Le Monde*, 26 October 2011, article based on a lecture delivered subsequently in Paris and published in full in the journal *Cités*, January 2011.

Habermas, J. (2011b) 'Rettet die Würde der Demokratie', *Frankfurter Allgemeine Zeitung*, 4 November 2011.

Hayward, J. (ed.) (1995) *The Crisis of Representation in Europe* (London: Frank Cass).

Hayward, J. (ed.) (1996) *Elitism, Populism and European Politics* (Oxford: Oxford University Press).

Hayward, J. (ed.) (2008) *Leaderless Europe* (Oxford: Oxford University Press).

Héritier, A., D. Kerwer, C. Knill, D. Lehmkuhl, M. Teutsch and A.-C. Douillet (eds) (2011) *Differential Europe. The European Union Impact on National Policymaking* (London: Rowand & Littlefield).

Myrdal, S. and M. Rhinard (2010) *The European Union's Solidarity Clause: Empty Letter or Effective Tool?* (Stockholm: Swedish Institute of International Affairs).

Orléan, A. (2009), *De l'euphorie à la panique: penser la crise financier* (Paris: Edition de la Rue d'Ulm).

Orléan, A. (2011), 'Il faut définanciariser l'économie', *Le Monde* 6 December 2011.

Paterson, W. (1996) 'Beyond Semi-Sovereignty: The New Germany in the New Europe', *German Politics*, 5:2, 167–84.

Pinder, J (1991) *European Community. The Building of a Union* (Oxford: Oxford University Press).

Ross, M. and Y. Borgmann-Prebil (eds) (2010) *Promoting Solidarity in the European Union* (Oxford: Oxford University Press).

Taylor, P. (2008) *The End of European Integration* (London: Routledge).

Scharpf, F. (1999) *Governing in Europe. Effective and Democratic?* (Oxford: Oxford University Press).

Index

Adenauer, Konrad 69, 241
Anglo-American 190, 193, 246
Ashton, Baroness Catherine 170–1,
178 fn4, 179, 240
Austerity 142, 180, 182, 183, 184,
209, 249, 284, 292, 295, 305, 314,
317, 323, 324, 325
Austria 21, 25, 26, 54, 76, 105, 142,
158, 189, 192, 209, 210, 215, 224,
226, 244, 306

Baltic states 158, 190, 193, 208
banks, banking system 12, 131–44,
181–99, 206, 207, 212, 248, 278,
290, 292, 293, 305, 318, 321, 326
Bank of England 118, 121, 136, 149,
154, 258, 287, 319
Bank of Italy, Banca d'Italia
134, 136
banking crises 139, 183, 194, 197
German Bundesbank 131, 132,
133, 134, 139, 140, 141, 143, 144,
186, 188, 196, 198, 237, 243, 246,
247, 322
Barroso, José Manuel 18, 107, 171,
240, 323
Belgium 6, 19, 20, 25, 26, 29, 69, 76,
79, 127, 147, 149, 156, 174, 209,
210, 215
Berlusconi, Silvio 173, 284, 294
Blair, Tony 108, 125, 260
bond markets 108, 131, 140–3, 182,
184, 186,193, 194, 195, 196, 198,
246, 248, 291, 292, 293, 325, 326
Brandt, Willy 70
Brazil 12, 242, 321
Britain/UK 3, 11, 67, 74, 103, 119,
168, 174, 179, 198, 203, 216, 222,
224, 227, 240, 252–66, 276, 314,
317, 323, 326
Bank of England *see under* banks
Conservative government 241,
252, 253, 255, 256

Conservative–Liberal
government 122, 125, 261
House of Commons 102, 103,
104, 106, 113, 253, 254, 256,
263, 264; European Scrutiny
Committee 104, 263
House of Lords 106, 109, 116,
126, 127, 263; European Union
Committee 264; Law Lords/
Supreme Court 116, 121,
127, 128
Human Rights Act (HRA) 126, 127,
128, 129
Labour government 254, 255, 256,
257, 258, 259,260, 261
political parties; Conservative,
Tories 240, 250, 262; Labour 217,
252, 253, 254, 255; Liberal 207,
253, 261
Brown, Gordon 138, 256, 260
Brussels 6, 8, 9, 10, 38, 39, 40, 41, 52,
59, 71, 72, 74, 79, 102, 154, 155,
249, 262, 263, 300, 308
Bulgaria 201, 286, 302, 303, 305,
307, 308
burden sharing agreement (*see also*
effort sharing agreement)
181, 184, 194, 217, 225, 226, 231,
293, 294

Cameron, David 103, 128, 248, 253,
259, 261, 264, 265, 322
Central and Eastern Europe 20, 57,
151, 152, 153, 155, 159, 193, 206,
207, 210, 226, 227, 230, 264, 286,
298–313, 320
Central and Eastern European
enlargement 7, 74, 153, 154, 190,
226, 231, 235, 240, 241, 286
centralised institutions 302, 303,
304, 306, 308, 309
Charter of Fundamental Rights 34,
124, 125–6, 127, 129, 200

China 12, 225,242, 321
Chirac, Jacques 135, 174, 239, 241
citizens, citizenship 10, 12, 17–31,
  33, 34, 35, 40, 41, 42, 44 fn1, 44
  fn2, 45 fn4, 45 fn8, 77, 95, 102,
  107, 108, 110, 121, 135, 157, 158,
  195, 202, 206, 215, 216, 223, 267,
  276, 298, 320, 321, 325
  citizen's initiative 42, 101
  good citizens 298, 299, 300, 303,
    307, 308, 310
  identity 18, 21, 23
Clinton, Bill 225
Clinton-Davis, Stanley 228
Cold War 268, 270, 271, 273, 274, 275
  post-Cold War 176, 315
comitology 43, 85, 87, 88, 92
Common Agricultural Policy
  (CAP) 187, 241, 280, 286
  national agricultural policies 268,
    276, 280
Common Foreign and Security Policy
  (CFSP) 165–80, 317
  European External Action Service
    (EEAS) 170, 171
  foreign EU environmental
    policy 217
  High Representative for Foreign
    Policy 77, 78, 170, 171, 172, 220
Common Security and Defence
  Policy (CSDP) 165, 169, 170, 173,
  175, 177, 178 fn2
  European Defence Agency
    (EDA) 172
Commonwealth 256, 257, 258
communism, communist 130 fn2,
  277, 301, 302
  communist parties 19
  non-communist states 268
  post-communist party/
    post-communism 48, 54, 57,
    236, 237, 268, 277, 286, 298, 299,
    301, 302, 308, 309
competition between social
  models 206
Competition Policy 83, 149, 182,
  183, 187, 206, 279, 280
  competitiveness/international
    competition 159, 205, 290, 318
  DG competition 154

conditionality 192, 212, 244, 299, 304
conditionality model 300, 303, 308
confederalism, confederation 5, 6,
  8, 10, 38, 66, 67, 68, 69, 70, 79,
  151, 324
Conference of Community
  and European Affairs Committee
  (COSAC) 104, 106, 107, 111, 263
consensus 3, 5, 8, 9, 10, 13, 49, 71,
  72, 74, 75, 132, 155, 167, 168, 169,
  170, 171, 172, 173, 175, 176, 177,
  178, 184, 193, 194, 218, 221, 238,
  273, 274, 277, 280
  permissive consensus 2, 49, 102,
    294, 315
constitutional convention,
  constitutional treaty 6, 9, 10, 34,
  37, 38, 72, 99, 107, 117, 155, 157,
  260, 269
coordination 8, 68, 71,72, 74, 76, 77,
  100, 102, 134,136, 138, 139, 183,
  187, 188, 191,201, 204, 205, 210,
  211, 236, 298, 299, 300, 301, 302,
  303, 307, 308, 324
  open method of co-ordination
    (OMC) 200, 201, 204, 205
COREPER 10, 55, 74, 262
Council of Europe 125, 129, 152, 169,
  170, 174, 255
Council of Ministers, Councils
  of Ministers 3, 7, 8, 35, 36, 41,
  55, 57, 65–81, 82, 83, 85, 87, 88,
  89, 90, 91, 92, 93, 94, 95, 99, 102,
  104, 105, 107, 109, 110, 112, 125,
  150, 156, 158, 170, 171, 172, 175,
  189, 221, 223, 226, 228, 229, 230,
  243, 261, 263, 280 fn3, 281 fn5,
  298, 300, 303, 304, 308, 318
ECOFIN 78, 134, 138, 194
credit notation agencies 79
credit rating 182, 184, 322, 326
  credit rating agencies 322, 326
Cyprus 25, 26, 158, 215, 286
Czech Republic 21, 25, 26, 125, 189,
  190, 192, 194, 208, 210, 286, 302,
  303, 306, 307, 308, 309, 310

Delors, Jacques 132, 202, 223, 237,
  240, 243
Delors Report 132, 186, 191

democracy 7, 28, 32, 33, 34, 35,
36, 41, 42, 43, 44, 75, 106, 107,
118, 129, 130 fn2, 280, 301, 316,
322, 325
democratic deficit 32, 41, 52, 56,
73, 100, 101, 107, 112
party democracy 49
demos 17, 23, 25, 27, 29,284, 315
Denmark 6, 19, 24, 25, 26, 48, 54, 56,
101, 102, 105, 111, 188, 189, 190,
192, 210, 217, 224, 226, 267, 268,
269, 270, 271, 272, 273, 274, 275,
276, 277, 278, 304
Danish EAC 102, 105, 109
dissensus 9, 13, 75, 165, 166, 167, 169,
170, 173, 176, 177, 178, 315
constraining dissensus 294
disunion 1–4, 5, 13, 21, 23, 32, 33,
40–1, 43, 44, 79, 181–2, 185,
188–97, 198, 215, 217–18, 219–20,
226, 229–30, 280, 283, 314, 315,
316, 317, 318, 319, 320–4

Economic and Monetary
Union (EMU) 108, 131, 132, 133,
135, 136, 137, 182, 184, 185, 186,
187, 188, 189, 194, 195, 196, 197,
215, 219, 267, 269, 271, 272, 275,
276, 277, 278, 279, 280 fn4, 293,
304, 317
Economic and Social Committee
42, 44 fn2
effort sharing agreement (*see also*
burden sharing agreement) 181,
184, 197, 225, 231
elections
European elections 17, 19, 21–3, 41,
42, 50, 51, 56, 57, 58, 60, 100, 253
national elections 19, 22, 28, 29,
50, 53, 100, 212, 271, 275, 284,
305, 325
elites 2, 7, 10, 12, 23, 29, 30, 49, 75,
159, 185, 186, 190, 195, 211, 291,
294, 315, 322, 324
enlargement 5, 7, 11, 72, 154, 173,
193, 202, 235, 243, 264, 265, 277,
284, 285, 304
Central and Eastern European
enlargement 7, 74, 153, 154, 190,
226, 231, 235, 240, 241, 286

Mediterranean/Southern European
enlargement 284, 295, 299
Scandinavian enlargement 285
environmental policy 1, 3, 36, 38, 39,
215–32, 314, 315, 316, 318
climate change 1, 171, 176, 216,
219, 220, 224, 225, 229, 231
emissions trading scheme 119, 225
Environmental Action
Programme 222
environmental advocacy
coalition 227, 229
environmental leader states
226, 227
environmental NGOs 224, 227,
230, 316
Environmental Council 223, 228,
229, 315
Kyoto protocol 216, 225
nuclear power 220, 227, 231 fn1
Erhard, Ludwig 196
Estonia 25, 26, 103, 168, 209,
210, 215, 286, 303, 304, 305,
308, 309
Euro, Area/Zone 1, 2, 60, 78, 79, 131,
132, 133, 134, 137, 138, 140, 142,
143, 144, 181, 182, 183, 185, 187,
188, 189, 190, 191, 192, 193, 194,
195, 197, 198, 203, 206, 207, 211,
212, 235, 242, 243, 244, 245, 247,
249, 250, 253, 260, 261, 267, 276,
277, 284, 289, 290, 291, 292, 293,
294, 295, 296 fn1, 296 fn4, 305,
306, 309, 310, 314, 315, 317, 321,
322, 323, 324
Euro crisis 2, 78, 100, 103, 195,
238, 239, 240, 241, 242, 243, 244,
245, 247, 249, 283, 284, 298, 314,
315, 317, 319, 325, 326
Euro Plus Pact 181, 194, 212
Euro insiders 189
Euro outsiders 181, 198, 203
Eurobonds 108, 184, 193, 196, 248,
249, 293, 314, 323
Euro group 78, 134, 326
European affairs committees
(EACs) 101, 102, 103, 104, 105,
106, 109, 112, 113
European Atomic Community
(Euratom) 220, 227

European Banking Authority
79, 139
European Central Bank (ECB) 72, 78,
131, 131–45, 182, 183, 186, 187,
188, 193, 195, 198, 246, 248, 278,
290, 292, 294, 314, 318, 321, 323,
324, 325
Governing Council 133, 135,
141, 143
European System of Central Banks
(ESCB) 134, 138
European System Risk Board
(ESRB) 139
lender of last resort 132, 141, 144,
181, 183, 192, 196, 246, 293,
314–15, 323, 325
and national central banks 131–45,
189, 195, 246, 305, 318
president; Draghi, Mario 143;
Duisenberg, Wim 135, 137, 138;
Trichet, Jean-Claude 78, 134,
135, 141, 246, 283
European Coal and Steel Community
(ECSC) 42, 48, 69, 220, 255
European Commission 3, 7, 8, 10,
24, 25, 26, 33, 34, 35, 36, 37, 38,
39, 40, 42, 50, 57, 58, 59, 69, 70,
72, 73, 79, 82–98, 101, 104, 107,
108, 109, 110, 111, 112, 113, 125,
153, 154, 156, 160 fn1, 169, 170,
171, 172, 183, 187, 188, 189, 191,
195, 196, 215, 218, 221, 223, 224,
227, 228, 229, 230, 236, 240, 241,
257, 261, 262, 263, 264, 279, 281
fn6, 284, 293, 294, 302, 316, 318,
319–20, 321, 323, 324
COMDOCS 91, 92
Commissioners 10, 38, 85–6, 90,
91, 94, 170, 215, 223, 228, 229,
230, 261, 262, 263, 284
Governance White Paper 33, 34,
36, 40
Plan D 34, 107, 316
seconded national experts
(SNEs) 86–7
European Convention on Human
Rights 122–3, 126
European Council 3, 6, 8, 9, 10, 34,
36, 51, 57, 65–81, 110, 182, 194,

221, 229, 230, 240, 287, 309,310,
318, 321, 323
president 8, 28, 72, 77, 79, 170, 221
European Court of Human
Rights (ECHR) 115, 124, 126–7,
128, 129
European Court of Justice (ECJ) 8, 10,
69, 72, 76, 82, 88, 111, 115–16,
117, 118, 119–20, 122, 123, 124,
125, 126, 127, 128, 129, 154, 155,
169, 200, 205, 222, 223, 224, 230,
318, 319
European Economic Area 267, 276
European Economic Community
(EEC), Community 6, 38, 43, 66,
68, 69, 70, 102, 115, 116, 117, 118,
120, 122, 123, 124, 126, 129, 153,
173, 184, 202, 220, 222, 237, 252,
254, 268, 269, 271, 274, 280 fn1,
280 fn2, 285, 286, 319, 320
European Environmental
Bureau (EEB) 38, 39
European Financial Stability Facility
(EFSF) 142, 143, 181, 193, 195,
196, 206, 291, 292, 307, 309, 319
European identity 17–31, 60, 72, 195,
236, 237,293
European Parliament (EP)3, 8, 10–11,
17, 19, 21–3, 26, 33, 35–6, 41,
48–62,69, 72, 73, 79, 83, 89, 90,
91, 92, 94, 99, 100, 101, 104,
106–10, 112, 113, 125, 215, 216,
221, 224, 227, 229, 230, 231 fn2,
253, 263, 264, 318–19, 321, 322
Conference of Community and
European Affairs Committees
(COSAC) 104, 106–7, 111, 263
Deparliamentarisation 99, 112
European Parliament elections
see under elections
European Social Fund 153, 206, 285
European Social Model 10, 193, 201,
202, 206, 211, 268, 317
European Stability Mechanism
(ESM) 181, 193, 194, 196,
244, 248
European Structural Fund 2,
153–4, 155, 190, 201, 219, 226,
285, 286, 320

Europeanisation 10, 11, 48, 52–3,
    59, 278, 299
Euroscepticism 21, 23, 24, 26,
    160, 267, 269–73, 279, 294, 299,
    307, 324
Eurozone *see* Euro, Area/Zone
Eurozone crisis *see under* Euro,
    Area/Zone
ever closer union 1, 5, 7, 184, 185,
    186, 187, 213, 217, 219, 220, 256,
    299, 316
Exchange Rate Mechanism
    (ERM) 186, 187, 188, 189, 197

federalism, federation 5, 6,
    8, 10, 11, 28, 58, 60, 67, 69,
    70, 78, 83, 88–9, 100, 109,
    133, 135, 148, 150, 151, 155,
    159, 188, 194, 196, 231 fn2,
    236, 246, 255, 277, 314, 315,
    321, 322, 324
financial markets 58, 68, 137, 138,
    142, 183, 184, 194, 198, 203, 245,
    290, 291, 305, 315, 325
Finland 19, 24, 25, 26, 29, 103, 175,
    189, 195, 208, 209, 215, 224, 226,
    227, 244, 267, 269–71, 272, 273,
    274–5, 277, 315
fiscal policy 108, 132, 143, 188, 301,
    304–6, 307, 309, 323
    fiscal compact 310
    fiscal discipline 191, 285, 298, 301,
    304, 305, 306–7, 309
    fiscal union 181, 183, 192, 196,
    198, 295, 310, 314, 322, 323
Fischer, Joschka 108, 238
flexicurity 212
Fouchet Plan 68–9
France 10, 11, 19, 20, 21, 25, 26,
    29, 51, 67, 70, 74, 75, 76, 90, 93,
    105, 118, 119, 130 fn3, 135, 147,
    154–5, 157, 168, 174, 175, 194,
    195, 203, 207, 209, 210, 221, 222,
    227, 230, 236, 237, 239–50, 260,
    292, 294, 315, 317
    AAA rating 249
    Conseil Constitutionnel 118
    Conseil d'Etat 90, 118
    and economic government 11, 67

Franco-German relationship 3,
    27, 69, 70, 185, 188, 194, 197,
    198, 230, 235–51, 264, 292,
    318, 323, 375

Georgia 168, 169
    Georgian crisis 171
Germany 11, 19, 20, 21, 25, 26, 29,
    56, 58, 67, 68, 70, 74, 75, 76, 79,
    90, 93, 103, 105, 108, 109, 118,
    123, 139, 142, 147, 148, 149, 156,
    168, 174, 182, 185, 186, 189,
    191–2, 193, 194, 196, 197, 203,
    208, 210, 212, 215, 217, 221, 223,
    224, 226, 228, 230, 235–51, 287,
    292, 293, 304, 305, 308, 317, 321,
    322, 324, 325, 326
    Bundesbank 131, 132, 133, 134,
    139, 140, 141, 143, 144, 186, 188,
    196, 198, 237, 243, 246, 247, 322
    Bundestag 319, 322
    Economic Expert Council
    249, 323
    Federal Constitutional Court
    (BVerfG) 11, 66, 118, 121, 322
    German Constitution 123, 124
    German Ordoliberalism *see under*
    Ordoliberalism
Giscard d'Estaing, Valéry 6, 69, 70–1,
    78, 245
globalisation 2, 242, 314, 319
Greece 25, 26, 27, 76, 127, 143, 174,
    189, 191, 192, 193, 194, 195, 206,
    207, 209, 211, 226, 279, 283, 285,
    288, 289, 290, 291, 292, 294, 295,
    296 fn2, 299, 321, 325, 326
    Greek debt 140–1, 142, 212
Greenland 6, 280 fn2
Greenpeace 39, 40

Hallstein, Walter 240, 324
Heath, Edward 70, 253, 256,
    258, 259
Héritier, Adrienne 9, 43, 82, 88, 92,
    224, 226, 227, 317
High politics (*see also* low politics) 76,
    165, 166, 167, 178, 229, 318
Hoffmann, Stanley 67, 165, 166, 167,
    175, 178 fn3

Hollande, François 249
Hungary 19, 25, 26, 29, 189, 190, 193, 194, 207, 208, 209, 210, 286, 302, 303, 305, 307, 308, 309

Iceland 96 fn1, 267, 280 fn2, 280 fn3, 325
identity *see under* European identity and National identity
implementation 6, 8, 9, 59, 72, 74, 76, 83, 87, 153, 155, 188, 218, 223, 224, 225, 227, 230, 245, 279, 285, 294, 304, 319
India 12, 242, 321
inflation 131, 132, 133, 134, 138, 140, 141, 142, 143, 148, 184, 186, 189, 203, 245, 287, 288, 289, 290, 292, 293, 314, 323
interdependence 2, 7, 11, 12, 53, 59, 66, 70, 165, 267, 314, 319, 326
interest groups 34, 37, 39, 96
intergovernmentalism 146, 172, 218
International Monetary Fund (IMF) 138, 206, 207, 208, 244, 248, 292, 294
Iraq 127, 128, 168, 238, 239, 241, 260
Ireland 20, 25, 26, 76, 102, 117, 143, 147, 156, 158, 191, 192, 193, 203, 206, 207, 209, 226, 227, 248, 276, 283, 285, 286, 291, 292, 325
Northern Ireland 20, 156, 158, 258
Italy 11, 25, 26, 29, 76, 102, 111, 130 fn2, 134, 141, 147, 148, 149, 152, 156, 158, 173, 189, 191, 193, 203, 206, 207, 209, 210, 283, 284, 285, 287, 288, 289, 290, 291–2, 295, 321, 325, 326
Bank of Italy *see under* banks

joint decision trap 218, 219, 317

Keynesianism
spatial Keynesianism 148, 149, 153
Kinnock, Neil 84, 260, 262
Kohl, Helmut 60, 96, 133, 169, 237, 238, 239, 241, 243
Kosovo 158, 159, 174

Latvia 25, 26, 168, 208, 210, 286, 303, 304, 305, 308, 309
leaders, leadership 1, 3, 4, 8, 9, 11, 12, 27, 29–30, 59, 60, 70, 71, 72, 77, 78, 88, 133, 134, 169, 170, 171, 172, 185, 189, 194, 196, 197, 212, 217, 227, 235, 236, 239, 240, 243, 244, 250, 253, 256, 259, 260, 265, 278, 284, 291, 308, 315–16, 317, 318, 320, 321, 323, 326
administrative leadership 89, 93–4
Franco-German leadership 194, 237–9, 240, 241
party leadership 49, 50, 51, 52, 53, 54, 55, 56
legitimacy 5, 10, 23, 24, 39, 44, 49, 53, 92, 106, 108, 113, 131, 135, 136, 182, 194, 223, 235, 236, 238, 241, 299
democratic 1, 3, 32, 33–7, 40, 41–3, 58–9, 100, 183, 190, 195, 315, 321
input/output 9, 101, 321
Libya 173, 240
Lisbon process 187, 189
Lisbon Treaty *see* treaties
Lithuania 25, 26, 111, 168, 209, 210, 286, 303, 304, 305, 308, 309
Low politics (*see also* High politics) 76, 218, 229
Luxembourg 25, 26, 111, 209, 210, 215, 217, 229, 326
Luxembourg compromise 58, 75

Macmillan, Harold 252, 255, 256
Majone, Giandomenico 6, 7, 100
Major, John 104, 224, 253, 254, 256, 259, 261
Malta 25, 26, 173, 216, 286
Meana, Ripa di 223, 224, 231 fn3
Mediterranean states 151, 193, 194, 283–97
Clubmed 190, 192
Integrated Mediterranean Programmes 285
Merkel, Angela 143, 194, 212, 230, 238, 239, 240, 241, 242, 244, 246, 247, 248, 249, 294, 322, 323

Miliband
    Miliband, David 216, 217
    Miliband, Ed 217
Mitterrand, François 60, 73, 169, 237,
    241, 243
Monnet, Jean 67, 69, 70, 82,
    166, 256
Monti, Mario 284

national identity 11–31, 147, 236,
    237, 264, 272, 274
national minorities 151, 157, 158
national parliaments 3, 24, 26, 43,
    48–62, 66, 75, 83, 99–114, 116,
    118, 120, 121, 122, 129, 257, 258,
    259, 260, 261, 262, 263, 269, 271,
    273, 274–5, 279, 280 fn2, 309,
    310, 319, 321, 325
    parliamentary sovereignty 119,
    121, 129, 257, 319
nationalism 151, 152, 157
neo-functionalism 148, 187, 218
Netherlands 10, 25, 26, 29, 69, 75,
    76, 111, 130 fn2, 189, 195, 209,
    210, 215, 221, 224, 226, 227, 244,
    261, 315
networks 8, 41, 84, 87, 88, 134,
    159, 189
NGOs 33, 36, 37, 39, 40, 41, 224, 227,
    230, 316
Nordic, Scandinavian 3, 75, 76, 103,
    113, 176, 190, 191, 203, 267–82,
    285, 298, 299, 310, 317, 320, 321
North Atlantic Treaty Organisation
    (NATO) 152, 174, 175, 237, 273
Northern European states 212

optimum currency area (OCA)
    191, 192
Ordoliberalism 186, 246, 314,
    318, 323
Organisation for Security and
    Co-operation in Europe
    (OSCE) 158

Papandreou, George 284, 322
parliament *see under* European
    Parliament and National
    Parliaments

participation 22, 34, 40, 42, 50–2,
    88, 106, 134, 153, 175, 206, 221,
    236, 255, 259, 267, 268, 269, 270,
    272, 273, 276, 277, 278, 279, 280,
    289, 316
parties 2, 48–63, 102, 103, 109, 149,
    157, 195, 227, 247, 252, 253, 254,
    255, 257, 270, 271, 272, 273, 274,
    275, 276, 278, 280, 301, 302, 305,
    306, 307
    European parties 3, 19, 23,
    41, 48–63; European People's
    Party (EPP) 48, 57, 60, 100, 111;
    Party of European Socialists
    (PES) 48, 57; S&D Group of the
    Progressive Alliance of
    Socialists & Democrats 100
    Eurosceptic parties 19, 49, 52,
    54, 56, 59, 273, 274, 275, 276,
    278, 308
    extremist parties 2, 29, 54, 315
    national parties 48–63
periphery 103, 148, 243, 283, 286,
    287, 294, 324
Pöhl, Karl Otto 186
Pompidou, Georges 70, 196,
    197, 256
populism, populist 2, 10, 54,
    183, 190, 195, 270, 271, 273, 315,
    326
Portugal 25, 26, 29, 76, 143, 189, 191,
    192, 193, 206, 207, 209, 210, 215,
    226, 283, 284, 285, 286, 288, 289,
    290, 291, 294, 299, 325, 326
protectionism 11, 324, 326

QMV (qualified majority voting) 85,
    86, 99, 105, 111, 189, 225, 226

referendum 6, 7, 10, 42, 54, 58, 59,
    70, 103, 122, 222, 227, 253, 254,
    255, 259, 260, 261, 267, 268, 269,
    270, 272, 273, 274, 275, 276, 277,
    279, 280 fn2, 284, 322, 325
    Dutch 34, 315, 316
    French 22, 34, 239, 240, 315, 316
regions, regionalism 3, 40, 85, 101,
    146–61, 173, 237, 267, 272, 285,
    286, 287, 296 fn1, 299, 308

regions, regionalism – *continued*
  Cohesion Fund 285, 287
  cohesion policy 154, 159, 284,
    285, 286
  Committee of the Regions
    (CoR) 155
  Conference of the Assemblies
    of Legislative Regions
    (CALRE) 155
  Europe of the Regions 151,
    153, 156
  European Regional Development
    Fund (ERDF) 153, 285
Romania 111, 193, 208, 209, 216,
  286, 303, 306, 308, 309
Rompuy, Herman van 79,
  178 fn5, 240
Russia, Soviet Russia, USSR 79, 147,
  168, 169, 242, 274

Sarkozy, Nicolas 103, 168, 169, 171,
  194, 197, 241, 242, 248, 249, 250,
  294, 322, 325
Scharpf, Fritz 17, 202, 218, 317
Schengen 27, 267, 276, 277, 280 fn3
Schiller, Karl 186
Schmidt, Helmut 70, 78, 238, 245
Schmitter, Philippe 5, 6, 72
Schröder, Gerhard 238, 239, 241
side payments 7, 73, 219, 226, 241,
  242, 243, 318
single currency *see under* Euro
Single European Act (SEA) *see under*
  treaties
Single European Market, common
  market 2, 122, 218, 268, 272,
  319, 324
Slovakia 25, 26, 158, 192, 194, 209,
  210, 286, 306, 307, 309
Slovenia 25, 26, 103, 209, 210, 286,
  303, 305, 308, 309
social pacts 204, 209, 210
Socrates, José 284
solidarity 1, 2, 3, 4, 6, 10, 11–13,
  18, 27, 29, 32, 33–7, 44,
  44–5 fn2, 45 fn4, 49, 59, 60,
  66, 67, 79, 80, 84, 96, 100, 101,
  108, 112, 113, 115, 125, 129,
  130, 147, 165, 168, 181–2, 183–4,

    189–90, 193, 197, 200,
    201–6, 211–13, 216, 217, 219,
    220, 221, 225, 225–6, 230–1,
    258, 264, 268, 273, 274, 275, 279,
    280, 284–7, 291–5, 298, 309, 310,
    314, 316, 319–20, 321, 322, 323,
    324, 325, 326
  European Union Solidarity
    Fund 319
Southern European states,
  Southern Europe 3, 140,
    153, 212, 217, 224, 225,
    226, 247, 283–97, 303, 306,
    308, 309, 317
sovereignty 1, 2, 3, 4, 9, 10, 11, 13,
  17–18, 27, 43, 49, 59, 60, 65,
  65–6, 67, 68, 78, 79, 79–80, 82,
  84, 85, 86, 88–9, 96, 101, 104,
  113, 115–22, 129–30, 130 fn2,
  146–7, 151, 158, 159, 165, 177–8,
  182, 183, 184, 190, 193, 195, 196,
  197, 200, 203, 204, 211, 212–13,
  224, 233, 247, 255, 257, 258, 264,
  268, 272, 273, 274, 275, 280,
  284, 287–95, 298, 299, 314, 317,
  319–20, 322, 324, 326
  parliamentary sovereignty 66,
    108–9, 119, 121, 129, 257
  sovereign debt crisis 66, 76, 132,
    140, 141, 144, 206, 207, 211, 247,
    291, 293
Spain 21, 25, 26, 76, 130 fn2, 147,
  148, 149, 157, 174, 189, 191, 192,
  193, 206, 207, 209, 210, 224, 226,
  283, 285, 286, 287, 288, 289, 290,
  291, 299, 325
  Basque Country 152, 157
spill-back 182, 219
Stability and Growth Pact (SGP)
  79, 133, 186, 188, 189, 206, 241,
  245, 289
  Excessive Deficit Procedure 186,
    189, 289
Stark, Jürgen 131, 139, 140, 141, 142,
  143, 246
Structural Funds 2, 153, 154, 155,
  201, 219, 226, 286, 287, 320
  European Regional Development
    Fund 153, 285

subsidiarity 101, 107, 110, 111, 112,
125, 155, 263
supranational 48, 49, 51, 52, 55, 58,
68, 69, 72, 85, 108, 139, 148, 201,
218, 221, 225, 236, 240, 241, 255,
258, 276, 288, 295
Sweden 24, 25, 26, 29, 111, 175, 189,
224, 226, 227, 267, 269, 270, 271,
273, 274, 275, 276, 277, 278, 280
fn4, 317, 326

Thatcher, Margaret 73, 104, 169,
252, 253, 254, 256, 259
transposition 11, 76, 99, 223, 299,
300, 301, 302, 303, 304, 308
treaties 18, 37, 44, 54, 68, 69,
72, 99, 104, 116, 117, 118,
119, 122, 132, 136, 137, 155,
172, 190, 196, 197, 219, 222,
227, 245, 248, 259, 261, 265,
276, 279, 287, 318, 319
Amsterdam Treaty 107, 269
Constitutional Treaty (2005) 6, 18,
34, 117, 260
Lisbon Treaty 6, 8, 9, 12, 42, 58, 68,
77–80, 100, 101, 110–12, 117, 125,
126, 130 fn1, 141, 154, 155, 157,
170, 172, 178 fn1, 181, 211, 219,
220, 238, 239, 242, 256, 261, 263,
269, 316, 319, 320
Maastricht 10, 49, 107, 121,
124, 132, 137, 138, 144, 155,
156, 185, 187, 222, 223, 240,
253, 254, 259, 260, 268, 269, 276,
280 fn1, 317
Nice Treaty 269

Rome 82, 116, 184, 188, 190,
191, 192, 201, 217, 219, 220,
221, 255, 316
Single European Act (SEA) 48, 52,
53, 58, 222, 236, 259, 275, 276,
318, 319

unemployment 7, 133, 202, 205,
209, 210, 290, 324
unions, trade unions 5, 38, 44 fn2,
201, 204–5, 208, 209, 210, 281
fn7, 305, 316
ETUC 38, 204, 207, 208, 209
United Nations 91, 127, 220, 263
Security Council (UNSC) 124, 127
United States, America 58, 70, 89, 90,
135, 142, 176, 197, 225, 255, 257,
258, 296 fn4
Americanisation 140

Visegrad states 190, 193, 194, 208

Weber, Axel 131, 139, 140, 142,
143, 246
Weidmann, Jens 131, 141, 143,
196, 246
welfare state 12, 147, 190, 193, 194,
202, 203, 210, 271, 272, 273, 278,
280, 317, 320, 321
Werner Report 186, 188, 191, 196
Wilson, Harold 70, 256, 259
World Bank 39, 206, 207
World Trade Organisation (WTO) 91
Wright, Vincent 7, 8, 74, 300

Zapatero, José 284